★ **NATIONAL PERFORMANCES** ★

NATIONAL PERFORMANCES

The Politics of Class, Race, and Space in Puerto Rican Chicago

ANA Y. RAMOS-ZAYAS

THE UNIVERSITY OF CHICAGO PRESS
CHICAGO AND LONDON

ANA Y. RAMOS-ZAYAS is assistant professor of anthropology and
Puerto Rican and Hispanic Caribbean studies at Rutgers University.

The University of Chicago Press, Chicago 60637
The University of Chicago Press, Ltd., London
© 2003 by The University of Chicago
All rights reserved. Published 2003
Printed in the United States of America

12 11 10 09 08 07 06 05 04 03   1 2 3 4 5

ISBN: 0-226-70358-4 (cloth)
ISBN: 0-226-70359-2 (paper)

Library of Congress Cataloging-in-Publication Data

Ramos-Zayas, Ana Y.
    National performances : the politics of class, race, and space in Puerto
Rican Chicago / Ana Y. Ramos-Zayas.
        p. cm.
    Includes bibliographical references and index.
    ISBN 0-226-70358-4 (alk. paper) — ISBN 0-226-70359-2 (pbk. : alk. paper)
        1. Puerto Ricans—Illinois—Chicago—Social conditions.   2. Puerto
Ricans—Illinois—Chicago—Politics and government.   3. Puerto Ricans—
Illinois—Chicago—Ethnic identity.   4. Chicago (Ill.)—Social conditions.
5. Chicago (Ill.)—Politics and government—1951–   6. Chicago (Ill.)—
Ethnic relations.   I. Title.

F548.9.P85 R36 2003
305.868'7295077311—dc21
                                                        2002154906

★ CONTENTS ★

★ PREFACE ★

And I was there to be a scholar, there to be an anthropologist. Not there to be a
person, a woman. Not there to care that I was Puerto Rican. . . . Not there to
cry. Certainly not there to cry.

—Rosario Morales, "Concepts of Pollution"

The kindergarten I attended in Puerto Rico in the mid-1970s was close to
the Island's main international airport. Whenever my five-year-old classmates and I would see a plane flying over our school during recess, one kid
or another would say, "There goes my daddy!" and we would all stop whatever we were doing to wave good-bye to the plane. We would do this often,
substituting other family members or even some of our absent classmates
for "daddy" on occasion. Of course, it was impossible to know whether the
family member or classmate in question was in the particular plane we were
waving at, or even if a family member or absent classmate had boarded a
plane on that precise day at all. And yet it was not difficult for any of us to believe that the plane transported someone we knew or a relative of one of our
friends. I still remember when my best friend in kindergarten, Candy, told
me that she would not be returning to school the following semester because she and her mom would be moving to New York. Her parents were trying, in Candy's words, to "salvar su relación" [save their relationship].

Waving good-bye at the airplanes while claiming to have a friend or relative departing was more than child's play. The game reflected the fact that in
Puerto Rico everyone, even in my kindergarten class, had intimate knowledge of the process of starting a new life *allá afuera,* or out there, which back
then generally meant New York City. We rarely learned about life *allá afuera*
through the local news or our school's curriculum; rather, we learned about
it through anecdotes of classmates who would be leaving during the academic year and the ones who came back, perhaps knowing more English
than we did or exerting their claim to fame for having ridden the New York

City subways, unquestionably a status symbol in most kindergartners' view.

An exception to this elephant-in-the-middle-of-the-living-room syndrome that was Puerto Rican migration in Island politics and media happened in the mid-1980s. I remember that I was watching television at a high school friend's house in the town of Carolina when we heard that some Puerto Rican natives of Chicago were being accused of "anti-American terrorist activity." At that time my only connection to Chicago was through a cousin of mine who was staying with some friends in Humboldt Park while receiving medical treatment at a hospital in Cook County. And yet for many Puerto Ricans on the Island, the incidents surrounding these militant Chicago natives suddenly placed the residents of the Windy City in a Puerto Rican diasporic landscape previously dominated by New York.

It was not until about a decade later, after I had boarded one of those planes Puerto Rican children wave at and had been living in various Northeastern cities, including New York, that I decided to revisit my personal and political interest in Puerto Rican Chicago. By then I had met various Puerto Rican natives of Chicago and transplants to Chicago, with whom I had been active in various community projects involving Latino youth in New Haven and Boston. These friends from Chicago were used to hearing comments about the nationalist character of their city in the Puerto Rican imaginary, and they would always ask me why I thought this was. Questions emerging from these conversations lingered in my mind throughout graduate school, and when I headed to the Midwest in the mid-1990s, I intended to expand the long-neglected scholarship on Puerto Rican migration to Chicago, but I did not have a clear thematic agenda.

One of the greatest challenges posed by this project from its inception was that of representing an urban community that by most standards was highly politicized and had a keen characterization of itself in historical, global, and imaginative terms. The difficulty was twofold. On the one hand, I wanted to remain faithful to the multiple and never transparent self-portraits that Puerto Ricans in Chicago had of their community as unique and exceedingly nationalistic. On the other hand, I needed to understand these self-portraits in light of broader anthropological views of nationalism and identity politics and even investigate the ways in which Chicago "nationalism" was or was not about nationalism in the first place. Deconstructing the motivations, agendas, and limitations behind popular views of Puerto Rican nationalism became even more complicated when I tried to consolidate negative and positive images of nationalism in general. Nationalism is often negatively construed as a homogenizing and oppressive tool of the nation-state, but most of the Puerto Ricans with whom I talked had a positive view of nationalism as a loosely scripted and staged mode of identity production, activist rhetoric, and cultural performance in Chicago. Even more challenging was the attempt to recognize when barrio residents had participated in the production and reproduction of narratives and when narratives belonged to a small intellectual elite. I wanted never to fall into dichotomizing barrio residents as "nationalists" and "non-nationalists," or "antinationalists." Such reductionist rubrics would fail to capture the complexity of Puerto Rican life in Humboldt Park. Nevertheless, I accepted those labels when the interviewees themselves used them to describe themselves or each other.

The question of the representativeness of the people whose voices appear throughout this volume is very valid. It is not unique to my work, but is raised in relation to most, if not all, contemporary urban ethnography. The fact that this ethnography explores themes that have been the source of heated conflict for decades in scholarship on Puerto Rican politics and identity in the United States and Puerto Rico exacerbates concerns about representativeness and authorial partisanship. I hope that readers who have visited or resided in Chicago, and particularly Humboldt Park, will find that this ethnography addresses the question of why this community sees history and stages Puerto Rican nationalism as it does. The community residents who have read portions of this manuscript have felt that it is a faithful, though perhaps condensed, representation of their everyday lives, and they have often mentioned that other Puerto Rican areas in the United States were not like those in Chicago. For people unfamiliar with Chicago, the descriptions of nationalism here may appear overdrawn, inordinately subjective, or even partisan. This is a pertinent concern. Thus, I emphasize that the people I interviewed possess a range of relationships to the space racialized as Puerto Rican Chicago. They are not only activists, but also "ordinary" people who live the reality of the urban development around them. The process of scripting, staging, and performing Puerto Rican nationalism is not the exclusive domain of a highly politicized few, but a process in which most residents of Puerto Rican Chicago participate to a greater or lesser degree.

It is critical to emphasize from the start that the interrogation of Puerto Rican nationalism in this ethnography should not be framed within the parameters of overly deterministic debates around Puerto Rico's party politics or the so-called status issue. The performance of Puerto Rican nationalism in Chicago is in no way a tribute to commonwealth, independence, or statehood partisanship. Not everybody in Chicago agrees on politics. The fragmentation is incredible. The people expressing nationalist views are not necessarily affiliated with any given political party on the Island. While divisions along political party lines appear almost inevitable in dogmatic academic circles—whether on the Island or in the United States—I hope this project further contributes to the growing scholarly canon dedicated to de-centering party politics and the "status issue" as the dominant paradigm through which Puerto Rican nationalism and the constructions of the Puerto Rican "nation" are theorized. Rather than resurrecting the rigid discourses that unfortunately characterized examinations of Puerto Rican nationalism in the 1970s and before, I aim to reassert the importance of understanding nationalism not as an Island-bound phenomenon, but as the source of creative performances intimately intertwined with the formation of anticolonial racial politics and diasporic identities among Puerto Ricans living in the United States.

Chicago politics, which involves complex relationships among ward officials and Mayor Daley's machine, forever underlies Puerto Rican life and nationalist production. With the symbolic marking of urban space in the Humboldt Park area with two steel Puerto Rican flags, nationalist imagery took center stage in the mainstream media. An accomplishment for a select group of nationalist activists, the imagery also may be evidence of the Daley machine's perfunctory attempts to address the needs of the most marginal areas of the city without making any clear commitment to upsetting hegemonic power arrangements. Neither electoral politics in Chicago nor the "status issue" in Puerto Rico can be seen as determining factors in the performance of Puerto Rican nationalism in Chicago. The scriptedness of popular narratives inspired by Puerto Rican history, the critical stage that activists occupy and that barrio residents and the media judge as a participant audience, and the development of a citizenship identity in light of the politics of race and migration in the United States constitute a nationalism that, while always firmly grounded in a political economic context, activates imagination and creativity.

Intimate interpersonal relationships, political passion, and scholarly interest account for the physiological reaction I still experience when I travel through the various familiar spaces of Puerto Rican Chicago. Claiming scientific objectivity is perfunctory. I can only attest to the integrity and humility that guided my field research and ethnographic writing.

A project that has spanned almost a decade would not have been possible without the generous financial support of several institutions to which I am highly indebted. The field research and writing of this ethnography, which began as a doctoral dissertation, were funded by a Mellon Fellowship administered through Columbia University's Department of Anthropology (1991–92); a Danforth Compton Fellowship (1992–96); a Spencer Foundation Fellowship and a New England Board of Higher Education fellowship (1996–97); and a Harvard University postdoctoral fellowship (1998–2000). I am particularly grateful to the Harvard Children's Initiative for providing not only funding and office space, but also a group of committed scholars with whom to share my work and engage in enriching dialogue during my time in Cambridge.

An earlier version of chapter 3 appeared as "Nationalist Ideologies, Neighborhood-Based Activism, and Educational Spaces in Puerto Rican Chicago," *Harvard Educational Review*, 68, no. 2 (summer 1998): 164–92 (copyright © by the President and Fellows of Harvard College; all rights reserved). I thank the publisher for permission to adapt this material.

I am profoundly indebted to a group of dedicated colleagues, mentors, and friends who read portions of the book and provided thoughtful suggestions and encouragement along the way. I am particularly grateful for the insights and comments of Amílcar Barreto, Pedro Cabán, Aixa Cintrón, Marion Cohen, Tony De Jesús, Eileen de los Reyes, Ana Cristina de Souza, Linda Green, Roger Lancaster, Peter McLaren, Suzanne Oboler, José Raúl Perales, Pamela Perry, Gus Puleo, Sean Reardon, Bonnie Urciuoli, Ingrid Vargas, and Kay B. Warren. The late Miñi Seijo-Bruno, the best high school history teacher anybody could ask for, and Jill Cutler, a writing tutor at Yale University, instilled in me a sense of academic possibility from very early on as they challenged me to always think critically and to write as clearly as possible.

I want to express particular appreciation to my colleagues and friends Nicholas De Genova and Carlos Vargas-Ramos, whose help with the census data and consistent support I enjoyed throughout the development of this project. I also appreciate the thoughtful comments and questions of Arcadio Díaz-Quiñones and Félix Matos-Rodríguez. Despite their busy schedules at Princeton and the Center for Puerto Rican Studies, respectively, Arcadio and Felo offered feedback at the Puerto Rican Studies Association meeting at the University of Massachusetts Amherst, which helped improve an earlier version of this manuscript. At the American Anthropological Association meeting in San Francisco I was fortunate to discuss some of the themes that are elaborated in this book with Arlene Torres, whose work and commitment to students I continue to appreciate. Ever since I read her work for the first time, Ana Celia Zentella has been a constant inspiration both academically and personally. I was fortunate to share with her candid discussions about our work when she visited Rutgers as a guest speaker of the Global

Futures Fellows Symposium in March 2002. Likewise, ever since I conducted research among Dominican women in Puerto Rico, Jorge Duany has been an important source of academic inspiration and intellectual insight. I appreciate Jorge's comments on portions of this book that I presented as a paper at the "None of the Above" Conference at Rutgers in 2001.

The women of the "Chicago group"—Marixa Alicea, Nilda Flores-González, Irma Olmedo, Gina Pérez, Mérida Rúa, and Maura Toro-Morn—understand the uniqueness of Chicago and have generously shared their research experience and scholarly insight with me. Special thanks are due to Mérida for her consistent support and friendship and to the Rúa family for welcoming me into their home. Frances Aparicio of the Latino Studies Program at the University of Illinois at Chicago sponsored a panel on Chicago-based research and did so "in the community," and Gina Pérez and Xavier Totti produced a *Centro Journal* issue dedicated to Puerto Rican Chicago. My genuine appreciation goes to all of them.

I must single out Katherine S. Newman, mentor extraordinaire, who provided encouragement and guidance from the time this project was presented as a dissertation proposal through the very last stages of the book's publication. First at Columbia and then at Harvard, Kathy's complete dedication to her students, her accessibility, and her ability to see each student's scholarly interest for its greater social relevance has shaped my relationship with my own graduate and undergraduate students. To this day I do not know of many tenured Ivy League professors who are as actively on call and willing to help students—particularly students from underrepresented backgrounds who are utterly unfamiliar with the politics of academia—as Kathy is.

David Brent, anthropology editor at the University of Chicago Press, believed in this project from the very beginning and secured reviewers whose suggestions greatly improved the manuscript. David and his wonderful assistants, Amy Collins and Elizabeth Branch Dyson, as well as production editor Christine Schwab and copyeditor Meg Cox, provided the sustained encouragement and rigorous editorial feedback of the stellar professionals they are. Liz Cosgrove, my book designer, went beyond the call of duty to make the book beautiful.

In 2000 I joined the faculty of the departments of Anthropology and Puerto Rican and Hispanic Caribbean Studies at Rutgers University. I thank the faculty and administrative staff of both departments, especially Asela Laguna-Díaz and Louisa Schein, as well as Larry La Fountain-Stokes, Monica Licourt, Luis Martínez-Fernández, Yolanda Martínez-San Miguel, Ben Sifuentes, Carmen Whalen, and the women of the Center for Latino Arts and

Culture. They have taken time from their extremely hectic schedules to guide me through the complicated bureaucracy that is Rutgers. The students I have encountered at Rutgers are any professor's dream: they embody a rare combination of academic curiosity, personal determination, and critical theoretical engagement colored by their individual experiences as first-generation college students of all nationalities and class backgrounds. My colleagues and students provide a wonderful balance to my research interests and scholarship.

Book writing tends to be an isolating experience, so I am grateful to a group of great friends whom I consider my extended family for making sure I got healthy doses of interruptions, entertainment, and opportunities to have fun. My friend and *hermanito del alma* Oscar Blanco-Franco introduced me to the great art of independent filmmaking, as well as providing numerous dinner invitations and dog-sitting services for Mafalda. My good friend Magali Sánchez and her son, Javier, are not only part of my extended family, but also immediate testament to the personal struggles and tenacity of Dominican migrants in Puerto Rico. They continue to keep me amazed and grounded. Clara Castro-Ponce cultivated our friendship through frequent long-distance conversations and venting sessions, as well as belly-aching laughing sprees. The Cintrón-Burch family, and in particular my goddaughter, Ino, allowed me to continuously reevaluate life priorities and to recognize how much one can learn from a toddler. I am also grateful to Frank Cruz for planning energizing vacation getaways, inviting me to brunch in various New York City diners, and keeping me company during the printing of the final draft of this book. Additionally, Frank redesigned my census-tract maps and made them reader-friendly.

My family is the reason I do what I do, even when they continuously ask me to clarify what it is that I actually do. My mother, Ana Hilda Zayas, and father, Vicente Suárez, are my inspiration, my sustenance, and the best parents anyone could ever ask for. Mami retired after thirty years of working as a public servant in Puerto Rico at the time this book went into copyediting. The enormous financial and personal sacrifices of her thirty years of work, some of them while being a single mother, allowed me to have the luxury of a career as self-indulgent as academia is. I am also very thankful to my aunt, Yolanda, who has been like a second mother to me. Her genuine passion for helping others continues to serve as a guiding principle in my life. My uncle, Tío Mano, has also been a consistent presence in my life for which I am grateful. My grandfather Francisco Zayas was the first person I ever interviewed—for a high school Puerto Rican history project when I did not even suspect that this was what I would be doing for a living later on. My *abuelo* instilled in me the value of education even though his amazing intelligence did not come from formal schooling, but from life, growing up in the sugar-cane town of Juana Díaz, Puerto Rico, and migrating to a working-class area of Santurce later on. He passed away during my first year of graduate school, but in my heart he never left.

Finally, I want to thank the people whose voices appear throughout this book for their time and patience, and more important, for their life lessons and drive and for asking the tough questions. Following the ethnographic protocol of anonymity, I cannot mention them by name, but I am sure they know who they are, and they will probably recognize themselves in the fol-lowing pages. These individuals gave relevance to the above quote by Rosario Morales. I was supposed to go to Chicago to be an anthropologist, but they made sure I learned to become the kind of person, woman, and Puerto Rican I did not know I wanted to become—even if that involved cry-ing once in a while. I hope I have not disappointed them.

★ INTRODUCTION ★

"Los nacionalistas son los únicos que se preocupan por los suyos. Si hay una comunidad aquí, es por ellos" [The nationalists are the only ones who care for their own people. If there's a community here, it's because of them], commented Alma Juncos,[1] an outgoing and energetic parent volunteer I met in the corridors of a high school in the Puerto Rican barrio of Chicago. Alma was one of the many Puerto Ricans who professed Chicago to be the "Mecca of Puerto Rican nationalism." On the basis of Alma's characterization of the nationalists, one would never imagine them to be the same people who were implicated in front-page scandals and deemed "terrorists." In the summer of 1995 the Chicago mainstream media and City of Chicago authorities accused the Puerto Rican nationalists of influencing the local school council at a largely Puerto Rican public high school to spend funds on activities aimed at indoctrinating students into radical "anti-American" politics that, one newspaper claimed, deserved FBI investigation. Hence a group of activists considered to be Puerto Rican nationalists—and the barrio residents, parents, and youth who supported them—were transformed into dangerous anti-Americans, indeed terrorists, and a threat to the Windy City.

Why would a Latino barrio in the contemporary United States otherwise described as pathological and apathetic and excluded from mainstream public discourse occupy center stage in accusations of terrorism and anti-Americanism? Moreover, how did a relatively small Puerto Rican community in the Midwest develop such a radical sense of itself, its position in various historical narratives, and its role in the production of a diasporic

Puerto Rican nationalism? How did images of terrorism—particularly after the incidents of September 11, 2001—organize the daily lives of residents in an urban community of a major metropolitan center? These are some of the questions at the center of this book.

As I will discuss throughout this volume, the staff of and participants in programs with clear separatist or "pro-Independence" agendas for Puerto Rico are considered nationalists by barrio adults and youth, Latino professionals, and the mainstream media. I refer to these people as "nationalist *activists*" because as the most visible or obvious sponsors of a Puerto Rican political nationalism, they are but one group of many involved in the process of performing the Puerto Rican nation in Chicago.

A colleague asked me, "But what about the average Puerto Rican in Chicago?" My colleague was referring to barrio residents who are more concerned with addressing daily family problems, providing for their households, solving arguments with neighbors, and dealing with other issues seemingly removed from a more evident nationalist agenda. My response is that this entire book is about precisely those people. Barrio adults and youth have an unusual level of everyday involvement in projects organized around a Puerto Rican nationalism. In the Chicago Puerto Rican community, and I suspect in other U.S. Puerto Rican communities as well, residents are never irrevocably marginalized from their immediate ideological surroundings. Rather, they are active participants, at various levels and often with contradictory stances, embroiled in political and private spheres that are impossible to untangle.

In this volume I use the term *nationalist* not as an exclusive designator of an activist contingency, but in reference to an identity frequently deployed by Puerto Ricans living in the largely Latino neighborhoods of Humboldt Park, West Town, and Logan Square in their roles as parents, youth, and neighbors, and articulated from an array of social locations. The discussion that results from this book should not revolve around the question of how ordinary or representative nationalist activists in Chicago and Chicago diasporic nationalisms are. Rather, the case of Puerto Ricans in Chicago is notable because of the way nationalist symbols were deployed in the service of multiple ideological and material agendas. Most important, these self-conscious nationalist performances did not subsume all other forms of social differentiation, but accentuated proclivities along lines of class, race, gender, and spatial politics in localized, everyday life. In short, nationalism provided the preferred vocabulary to discuss, challenge, and constantly reconfigure views of class, race, space, gendered identities, and migration histories in Puerto Rican Chicago.

The frequent references to nationalists and the elaborate nationalist narratives among barrio adults and youth, activists, and various city and state institutions in Chicago guide my exploration of the complex terrain of nationalism in diasporic communities. The lives of Alma and other residents of Puerto Rican Chicago contributed critical pieces to the construction, transformation, and everyday practice of nationalism and transnationalism in the ideological and political economic context of the United States. The Puerto Ricans whose voices appear in this volume are poor and working-class people of the barrio who ardently believed, albeit not without contest, in the tenets of meritocracy and upward mobility embodied in the American dream. Yet they perceived themselves to be empowered to claim these rights as U.S. citizens by constructing a popular nationalism that raised multivalent contradictions about the nation, national identity, and civil rights. These voices of barrio residents appear in dialogue with those of the mainstream media, elected political officials, grassroots activists, sectors of the Christian Right, and the Latino professional elite.

I explore the possibilities and limitations of creative constructions of the nation—or more concretely, the creation of a "barrio-nation"—in which nationalism and strategic essentialism are not distant and intractable enemies, but integral aspects of social life. In particular I examine social actors' everyday motivation to construct and recast official idioms of the nation and the historical accounts of Puerto Rican nationalism and separatism from the United States in their pursuit of highly unofficial, localized, and even personal goals. I am interested in how these actions—which in the case of Puerto Rican nationalism are so often in direct contradiction to foundational U.S. ideologies—sustain a range of national, class, racial, and spatial identities. This line of inquiry points to the use of cultural forms as cover for social action in a process that reveals the remarkable similarity in the ways state ideologies and the rhetoric of everyday social life make claims and promote goals.

Activists and barrio residents deployed the idea of the "nation"—particularly the "Puerto Rican nation"—as a means to delineate an urban space in which an "authentic" Puerto-Ricanness was performed and distinguished from the Puerto Rican identities associated with conservative religious factions, a professional Latino elite, and a group of upper-middle-class Chicago suburbanites "from the Island." The Puerto Rican nation, along with the boundaries and symbols that official national idioms entail, was in dialectical relation with constructions of a Puerto Rican barrio, which was considered to be in danger of disappearing as a result of gentrification and urban displacement. The idioms of Puerto Rican nationalism provided activists and residents with the everyday narratives to question the presence of other Latinos, African Americans, and whites in the Puerto Rican barrio-nation. Similarly the separatist Puerto Rican nationalism deployed by the most radical nationalist activists created a critical leverage with which to exert claims over the neighborhood public schools and other institutions, to condemn negative media representations, and to question the political agendas of elected city officials and professionals.

Some scholars of nationalism on the Island claim that culture rather than politics has become the terrain of contestation and that nationalism as a political force has lost popular support and is as oppressive an ideology as colonialism itself (Pabón 1995; Negrón-Muntaner and Grosfóguel 1997). In Chicago the history of the barrio is grounded on the actual or mythologized presence of militant political nationalist groups dating back to Puerto Rico's separatist movement of the 1950s. In the 1970s and 1980s underground militant groups that originated in Chicago engaged in civil rights campaigns, tending to the needs of the poor and dedicating themselves to the release of a group of Puerto Ricans incarcerated for engaging in armed paramilitary activity against the United States in pursuit of their goal of Puerto Rican independence. Puerto Rican nationalism in Chicago has followed a considerably different route from that of nationalism in Puerto Rico. In Chicago, Puerto Rican nationalism has become the instrumental political and cultural ideology formulated in community-building efforts among barrio activists and residents.

PERFORMING THE NATION IN PUERTO RICAN CHICAGO

National Performances: The Politics of Class, Race, and Space in Puerto Rican Chicago examines the political economic, historical, and ideological context in which nationalism becomes everyday social practice to address issues of racial discrimination, residential displacement, educational inadequacy, material scarcity, factionalism in ward electoral politics, and power inequalities. Nationalism as everyday social practice serves purposes that far transcend official nation-state discourses and separatist ideologies to reconfigure spatial, racial, and class identities at a more intricate and intimate political level. Three main areas of inquiry encapsulate the substantive goals of this book.

First, I consider how the cornerstones of the dominant society—in this case, the United States—intervene in the formation of nationalisms among subaltern minorities, themselves members of diasporic national communities. I consider the ethnographic case of Puerto Ricans in Chicago to examine how a diasporic nationalist project has fared under the racialization processes and ideological gambits of the United States. I focus on the relationship between foundational U.S. ideologies, "multicultural" politics, and racialization practices on the one hand, and Puerto Rican nation-building and popular nationalist strategies on the other. To accomplish this I delve into the dialectics of the hegemonic power of a colonial state—on both material and ideological grounds—to impose categories of identity on racialized colonial residents and on the everyday ways in which people resist, deflect, or deploy these social and political taxonomies.

Second, I consider the social processes that formulate a Puerto Rican diasporic nationalism, which, unlike Island-based nationalism, conflates cultural and separatist elements as it becomes popular, performative, and inseparable from urban histories and political economy. This line of inquiry leads to considerations of the role of public and alternative educational programs, media representation, and community-building efforts in reconfiguring understandings of the "Puerto Rican nation." In particular I examine a discourse of internal differentiation that foregrounds class identities among Puerto Ricans in the spaces marked as "the barrio" and "the suburbs," which are equivalent to distinctions between U.S.-born Puerto Ricans and "Islanders" born and raised in Puerto Rico, respectively. Moreover, the creation of a grassroots historiography—a rapidly proliferating body of autobiographical writings produced by area youth—that denounces mythologized views of Puerto Rico as a paradisiacal ancestral homeland, and the deployment of cultural-authenticity discourses by Puerto Ricans from the Island and from the Mainland who share various Chicago locations become critical aspects of this analysis.

Third, I examine how nationalist narratives, projects, and iconography, which most literature on nationalism considers to be attempts to mute divisions within the nation on behalf of a homogenizing and state-imposed national identity, have the opposite effect in Puerto Rican Chicago: they are actually responsible for generating spaces of contention and denunciations of internal subordination along race, class, and gender lines, as well as intensifying discussions of cultural "purity" and "authenticity," between "nationals" on the Island and "migrants" in the diaspora. This paradigmatic finding channels the progression of the book into an exploration of critical areas of contention underlying the constructions of diasporic nationalism and a consideration of how nationalism becomes inherently performative and frequently scripted, while generally spanning multiple stages and surprising a wide array of audiences. Central to my main thesis is the racialization of internal boundaries among Puerto Ricans as staged, scripted, and inscribed in the controversial image of Pedro Albizu Campos, a quintessential Puerto Rican nationalist icon. The ambiguous understanding of the racial and class identities of Albizu Campos as a mulatto and upwardly mobile Puerto Rican man serves as proxy to barrio-wide discussions of the nationalist leader's separatist ideologies in the context of Chicago's urban politics of class, race, and space.

Finally, these embodied and iconographic constructions of separatist nationalist ideologies serve as a road map for Puerto Rican unemployed, underemployed, and working-poor people and white-collar professionals who are navigating official constructions of "Latinidad" in relation to Mexicans, Central Americans, African Americans, and whites. The deployment of a citizenship identity in which Puerto Ricans emphasize a U.S. citizenship in opposition to an "illegal immigrant" Other—their Central American and Mexican neighbors—is particularly revealing. I examine the politics of citizenship and the construction of a "citizenship identity" in the formation of a performative nationalism in the Puerto Rican diaspora as an indispensable characteristic in the interaction between Puerto Ricans and other Latino, black, and white residents populating the space historically marked as "Puerto Rican Chicago."

In the conclusion I revisit my characterization of Puerto Rican nationalism as performative and inseparable from the politics of class, race, and space. In competing mainstream media and Puerto Rican–produced representations of the barrio-nation as a source of both cultural pride and anti-American terrorism, Puerto Ricans in Chicago—U.S. citizens—are racialized as *un-American* Americans. The case of Puerto Ricans in Chicago illustrates the processes by which community activism, colonialist and subaltern relations, and distinctions between nationals and diasporic populations alternatively create, inscribe, and decenter the nation by addressing internal fragmentation in the context of shifting class positions, racial identities, and urban spaces. Like other racialized populations, Puerto Ricans in Chicago have strategically chosen the terrain of the nation and nationalism as an "imagined community" (Anderson 1983) within which state-generated juridical and administrative definitions of citizenship and ideological definitions of Americanness are reconfigured, contested, or embraced. Invocations of the Puerto Rican nation as a site of struggle and contestation are not only part of a politics of identity, but also a denunciation of inequality around citizenship rights and a plethora of social concerns that ultimately point to the conflictual and colonialist transnational politics in which the United States and Puerto Rico have been implicated for over a century.

The case of Puerto Rican Chicago serves as the basis for the formulation of a theoretical framework that contributes to the literature on nationalism

in diasporic communities by considering the influence of colonial hegemonic mythologies—the American dream and multiculturalist discourses
in the case of the United States—on constructions of nationhood among
racialized colonial minorities. Puerto Rican nationalism in Chicago reveals
the centrality of what Herzfeld calls "cultural intimacy," the recognition of
those aspects of cultural identity that are considered cause for external em-
barrassment, ridicule, or even charges of backwardness and antimodernity,
but which nevertheless provide insiders with their assurance of common so-
ciality. Nationalist activists and barrio residents, as well as Latino elected
officials, religious leaders, and other professionals, are familiar with the
bases of power that may at one moment allow the disenfranchised a degree
of creative irreverence and at the next moment reinforce the effectiveness of
intimidation, oppression, and marginalization (see Herzfeld 1997, 3). My
investigation of Puerto Rican nationalism in Chicago is situated at various
critical theoretical junctures. These junctures straddle the social constructions of cultural and political Puerto Rican nationalism on the Island and in
the diaspora, the deployment of the American dream as the myth of origin
of U.S. nationalism and white supremacy, and an epistemology grounded in
a political economic paradigm.

THE RACE, CLASS, AND SPACE OF PUERTO RICAN
NATIONALISM IN CHICAGO

Nationalism in Chicago provides discursive spaces and everyday social practices for the articulation of stratification and inequality as it connects these
conditions to the history of Puerto Rican migrants in the United States and
on the Island. The factions of actors involved in the everyday social life of the
area marked as Puerto Rican Chicago deploy official idioms of the Puerto Rican nation and of U.S. nation-state ideology—often in complex opposition
to one another—to advance a variety of interests and to negotiate multiple
personal relations. The performance of nationalism in Puerto Rican Chicago serves as a community-building strategy to foreground the hidden
transcript of a racialized and classed population, a transcript deeply hidden
under multiple layers of American dreaming, creating a discursive space
where nationalist narratives and iconography question the fluidity of class. I
deliberately emphasize the aspect of performance to illuminate the existence of various rehearsals—strategies that are tried and then rejected or
embraced—in the constructions of "the nation" in diasporic communities,
while understanding that these rehearsals are taking place on the public
stage, in front of an audience, with a well-crafted but never static script. The

nation in Puerto Rican Chicago is a performance in progress; not a final product, but a relational and constantly reconfigured exposé of the politics of race, class, and space in a community otherwise represented as apathetic, pathological, and crime-ridden.

Nationalist narratives contest the various ways in which the American dream obfuscates understandings of U.S. domestic poverty and social welfare policy. The denial that a capitalist economy produces impoverished classes, the artificial moral distinctions between the deserving and undeserving poor, and the history of how state involvement in social welfare both produces and ameliorates power are implicit in the deployment of Puerto Rican nationalism in Chicago. Once constructed, nationalism provides an ideological template upon which various contingencies enact power, create alliances, produce culture, and engender notions of authenticity. Nationalism also serves as a rhetorical modality to criminalize the most radical forms of nationalist activism by rendering it "anti-American" and "terrorist." Chicago's mainstream media represented the Puerto Rican neighborhood of Humboldt Park as a bastion of anti-American terrorists. These public representations emphasized the idea that some Puerto Ricans (e.g., grassroots activists, poor residents, youth) were criminal nationalists, while others (e.g., members of the Christian Right, conservative ward aldermen, actors in the corporate sector) were responsible "American citizens."

By gaining control over the community's educational institutions, promoting community building, and resurrecting nationalist symbols of a militant past to historicize cultural identities, nationalist activists and barrio residents aimed to deflect the prejudicial and assimilationist effects that the dominant culture has on racialized colonial Others in the United States. By claiming territorial sovereignty through the resurrection and transformation of separatist nationalist narratives and iconography, and engaging these discourses in urban community-building efforts among the barrio poor, Puerto Rican nationalism in Chicago conflated anti-colonial politics and porous transnational identities. Class remained the hidden transcript of the localized politics of identity, which alternatively glorified and criminalized nationalism, depending on different interpretations of history and the political economic agendas being advanced. It became the implicated subtext in the ideological divisions between the barrio's popular classes and upwardly mobile suburban Puerto Ricans, as well as being intrinsic to a citizenship identity Puerto Ricans constructed in contradistinction to immigrant groups in the city.

Even though Puerto Rican nationalism articulates internal differences in mobility patterns among Latinos, the hegemonic power on which class identities and racialization processes are premised endure. The hegemonic operations of the American dream and its white supremacist construction of the American nation as a meritocracy sustain the idea that those who fail are deficient on cultural or racial grounds. The performance of a Puerto Rican nationalism in Chicago and its strategies of political mobilization, ideological subversion, and grassroots historicizing raised critical consciousness among neighborhood adults and youth by promoting historical awareness and documenting their condition as racialized, colonial subjects. While one would think that such a critical stance would engender despair and resentment toward the dominant culture, the opposite appears to be true: this increased historical knowledge and raised consciousness encouraged the poor and working classes to destigmatize Puerto-Ricanness and, in some instances, facilitate the very upward mobility that was too often beyond the grasp of Puerto Ricans living in Chicago's Humboldt Park.

My exploration of nationalist performances in Puerto Rican Chicago views diasporic nationalism as embroiled in the operations of a colonial ideological construct whose tenets—success, equality, upward mobility, and meritocracy—are so ambiguous, mythified, and elastic that they have the power to endure in the face of oppositional modes of identity politics and community formation in an ironic process of incorporation that perpetuates existing hierarchical orders. As the boundaries around a previously segregated Puerto Rican neighborhood were blurred by so-called urban renewal processes and the arrival of a growing number of Mexican, Central American, African American, and white residents, official symbols and narratives of the Puerto Rican nation were strategically deployed to symbolically reappropriate physical and political urban spaces. Chicago's adjacent neighborhoods of Humboldt Park, Logan Square, and West Town, in this sense, became marked as Puerto Rican even as Puerto Ricans made up a declining proportion of the neighborhood population.

A NOTE ON THEORY

The theoretical framework of this research emerges partly out of discontent with the current literature on nations, nationalism, and national identities influenced by both postmodernism and traditional Marxism, and with the failure of contemporary anthropology to build an adequate tension between explorations of "culture" and of the phenomenon of state power. Nations are lived not only through the discursive practices of everyday life elaborated in culture, but also in the dialectical relationship between such discursive and social practices and the political economic contexts and histories embedding them. Claims to nationhood are generated from within and beyond the boundaries of states, but also in critical conjunction with the power differentials between the self-proclaimed nation and the formal political state.

The U.S. anthropological tradition has elaborated notions of "people without history, of human groups envisioned as clear round billiard balls, lacking their own internal divisions and variations, lacking the messiness of the ubiquitous intercultural interactions, the power dynamics of real history" (Di Leonardo 1998, 290). This tradition has often focused on a decontextualized, infinitely fragmented, and intractable "Puerto Rican culture," as if these fragments emerged independently of a social environment and complex power differentials. Micaela Di Leonardo compellingly denounces "the progressive culturalization of American political discourse" (1998, 334). This culturalization is "a messy amalgam of valuable new intellectual insights about the role of language/discourse, of liberal bad faith, of well-funded conservative politics, and of a weak opposition—'identity politics'—that operates within the pool hall vision bequeathed to it by anthropology and further evacuated of all economic content by postmodernism" (1998, 135–36). It rationalizes power around discourses of difference, thus leading to a heavily anthropologized popular political sphere while rarely relating contemporary politics to definitions of cultural change, as if the tumultuous political shifts of the postwar era had little to do with "American imperialism and Big Power politics" (1998, 334). Yet it is this "Big Power politics" that orchestrates the widening worldwide gap between rich and poor at the core of transnationalism and globalization.

My ethnography is premised on the understanding that "Puerto Rican culture" cannot be divorced from the global processes and local politics that continue to render Puerto Ricans throughout the United States and on the Island the poorest of the poor—the racialized Others of the U.S. nation-state and the scapegoats for the nation's shortcomings. Conditions of persistent inequality and marginality must be taken into account if we are to avoid reductionistic and essentialist culture-of-poverty or "post-work strategy" arguments, by which widespread Rickymania and salsa dancing are paternalistically considered to be sufficient spaces of resistance. My intention here is not to fall into the fruitless polarity Duany notices among Puerto Rican intellectuals on the Island and in the diaspora alike: the local nationalists and Marxists believe that Puerto Ricans should struggle for independence to preserve their cultural identity, and the postmodernists believe that such struggle invariably invokes an essentialist fiction called the nation (Duany 2000).

The nationalism practiced and advocated by an intellectual and political elite is clearly essentializing, not only because of its rigid constructions of who belongs in the nation, but also because of the cultural and material capital interests underlying such constructions. Hence, classical Marxist understandings of Puerto Rican nationalism defend the Spanish language and other icons of the Hispanic heritage as important elements for uniting the Puerto Rican people against U.S. imperialism. However, such rigid constructions of nationalism generally limit membership in the nation to those who create the criteria of inclusion in the first place. Moreover, this "anti-imperialist" approach is ludicrous for assuming that enforcing the Spanish language over English or promoting other arbitrary determinants of cultural "purity" would even nudge U.S. state power or address class, racial, gender, and other forms of social stratification. Conversely, postmodernist arguments that claim that cultural nationalism is a sufficient tool to challenge social inequality and colonial power disregard the power of the state and are equally inadequate to address the extent of the political economic reality that characterizes the lives of most Puerto Ricans on the Island and in the diaspora alike. Only by critically engaging both approaches in tandem can discussions of the nation and, particularly, of social inequality be effectively undertaken along multiple lines.

A NOTE ON METHOD

The arguments presented here unfold ethnographically through the lives and concerns of barrio adults and youth, activists, white-collar workers, and the state-dominated institutions that indirectly mediate their social practices in Chicago. This ethnography is based on seventeen months of fieldwork (April 1994–September 1995) supplemented by several week-long follow-up visits to Chicago's Puerto Rican barrio (in March 1996, August 1997, May 1998, November 1999, and March 2000).

The more structured aspects of the research generated over eight hundred single-spaced pages of field notes; sixty audiotaped and transcribed life-history interviews averaging three hours each and divided almost equally among barrio residents (e.g., students and parents at public and alternative high schools), grassroots activists (from religious groups and two cultural centers), and middle-class professionals (e.g., local and city politicians, workers at not-for-profit organizations and corporations, residents of the suburbs); an additional fifty or so thematic and semistructured interviews, mostly with students, grassroots activists, and my own neighbors; textual analysis of local publications, mainstream newspapers, school yearbooks, personal letters, magazines, and student essays and private journals;

focus groups with area parents and youth; and exhaustive perusal of generously donated personal correspondence and relevant archives of the Chicago Historical Society and local organizations. The interviews were sometimes conducted in Spanish or English, and, more often than not, in Spanglish or code switching.[2] I personally transcribed and translated the interviews.

Lacking a car throughout the time of the fieldwork, I was privileged to be in close contact with barrio residents in a variety of contexts, including generous car rides to the supermarket and hardware store; walks down the streets after nightly meetings and events; tours of college campuses with high school students; meals at the bakery and two local Puerto Rican restaurants; aerobics classes at a local gym; and conversations on the bus and the "El" (the Chicago subway). Living in a rented basement apartment in Humboldt Park that was a five-minute walk from the local high school, grassroots organizations, and the main commercial strip where most community-building projects were being launched facilitated spontaneous visits with students and neighbors. These visits were as personally rewarding as they were valuable research opportunities.

The collaboration with barrio adults and youth and with grassroots activists was perhaps more intense and consistent than the interaction with middle-class professionals living outside the barrio, most of whom I got to know in predominantly institutional contexts and at organized social events. Nevertheless, structured life-history interviews yielded great insights into the professionals' lives. I volunteered at popular educational programs for youth, public high school programs for parents, and not-for-profit agencies. I also participated in neighborhood-wide activities, such as parades, street festivals, political marches, religious services, barrio museum exhibits, and trips outside the city and the state with young people, teachers, and activists.

The profoundly ethnographic quality of this research begs some commentary on the possibilities and perils of ethnography, the anthropologist's craft. The practice of ethnography poses an intractable problem: "It is the singular means of formal social research that enables a production of the textured knowledge of human perspectives and structures of feeling in the present that emerges only through extended engagement in the everyday lives, labors, and struggle of living people; it is simultaneously an inherently objectifying methodology" (De Genova 1999, 1). The politics of ethnography has been extensively examined for its textual strategies of representation and its discursive practices (e.g., Clifford and Marcus 1986). Only by viewing ethnography itself as inherently performative—that is, as an accumulation of communicative acts and the product of social interactions (Urciuoli 1993, 203)—can we adequately take into account the various forms of human connections under the surface of the printed pages.

"We give them their stories!" teased a barrio activist who met with me at an American Anthropological Association meeting held in Chicago in 1999. He was referring to the various research projects that three other women social scientists and I had conducted in the barrio. A second activist laughed with complicity, perfectly aware of the agency and ownership of the ethnographic texts written by these other women and me. Similarly, various barrio residents and activists contributed personal documents—letters, poems, and journals—and wanted to know if I would include them in the manuscript (some of them I did). This resonates with the complaint of one of the high school students in a Latino literature class I was teaching. When I mentioned that it is customary to change the names of the people in the final ethnographic text, the seventeen-year-old woman protested: "But I want my name to be in it [the book]!" Participation and a sense of ownership demand that these communicative acts be grounded in larger contexts of political commitments, power inequalities, emotive bonds, and complex human interactions. These interactions mediate textual boundaries by creating a public platform from which people can deconstruct their own objectification and collaborate in the creation of alternative representations as active agents of social change.

Paulo Freire, who is particularly conscious of the dangers of allowing the focus of research to shift from the meaningful themes to the people themselves and of thereby treating the people as objects of investigation, elaborated the concept of dialogue (see De Genova 1999; Freire 1993). In Freire's understanding of dialogue, ethnography emerges out of a process of interrogating the world through the critically engaged collaboration of people who "are becoming conscious of their own roles in the production and reproduction of their social realities, and the making of their histories" (De Genova 1999, 8). Thus conceptualized, ethnography can legitimately claim to "learn about the people" only when grounded in a collaborative dialogical endeavor to learn about an objective reality so as to denounce and transform it (De Genova 1999; Urciuoli 1993). Fieldwork can be a productive way to explore a localized set of research relations and interpretive activities and becomes hegemonic only when its format generically precludes any discursive spaces for the people who make the project possible (Urciuoli 1993). Establishing commensurability in the enactment of field relations should therefore involve a focus on those who dialogically help to make the text. As De Genova suggests, the dialogical imperative of Freire's pedagogy—the practice of liberation—can serve the ends of a radical decolonization of ethnography as a research practice (1999, 4).

For so-called native anthropologists,[3] these relations become even more profoundly conditioned by personal and political commitments; constantly shifting self-positioning; and, in the case of anthropologists who belong to groups characterized by high levels of material scarcity and marginality, even survivor's guilt. Not even the roles of militant observer (Freire 1993) and organic intellectual (McLaren 1998; cf. Padilla 1947) can shield anthropologists from informants' accusations around the politics of fieldwork. As one of the students in the Latino literature class I taught commented: "We have so many people come here to get their research and then leave. We've seen it over and over again." The comment was not merely a declaration of the thoughts of the seventeen-year-old student who expressed it, nor was it necessarily a personalized accusation of me as the departing teacher; rather, it was a deliberate enactment of her power to engage me in the process of dealing with the inherently limited and temporary nature of my belongingness in their lives. This was their way of not allowing me to forget the very different planes we occupy as we engage in the same ethnographic craft. The aspiration to engage in an egalitarian, dialogical collaboration in the inherently hierarchical "researcher-researched relation" is an irreconcilable tension of professional ethnographic fieldwork (De Genova 1999; Urciuoli 1993). Critical pedagogy, political solidarity, and life-transforming relations constitute the restless triangle at the core of this research.

As feminist epistemology recognizes, who we are guides what we look for and what we find in research. The aspirations of this research project are inseparable from my own social location. As a Puerto Rican woman who was born on the Island and has lived most of her adult life in the Northeastern United States, I was interested in the lives of Chicago-born Puerto Rican youth. A middle-class, light-skinned, Ivy League–educated professional, I was examining class formation, racialization processes, and educational marginality among residents of some of the most impoverished and neglected census tracts in the United States. As a young woman who has lived in a predominantly Dominican area of Puerto Rico, I was also concerned with issues of gender subordination and inter-Latino relations in organizational contexts. Often I was examining these issues among Chicago-based Puerto Rican political activists who considered themselves "muy nacionalistas" and thus at times sustained rigid gender roles as well as often essentialist understandings of Puerto-Ricanness. These social locations offer the limited lenses through which I understand the lives of the people who collaborated in the production of this ethnography.

My initial interest in the lives of grassroots activists and barrio residents in Chicago arose out of long-term political involvement and social commitments both in urban areas of Puerto Rico and among Latino groups in New Haven, Boston, and New York. The conceptualization of this research project reflected and was guided by those prior commitments and concerns, as well as by my sustained interest in how Puerto Ricans create notions of cultural authenticity on the basis of language, place of birth, and other forms of social capital. In this sense, the fieldwork process ended up being an intrinsically political engagement with people who taught me a great deal about my own politics, social vision, and Puerto-Ricanness; and about the centrality of their own *Chicago* Puerto Rican experiences in various configurations of struggle. Engaging the tension between recognizing our presence in our research and avoiding solipsistic absorption in our personal reactions to ethnography is an arduous task that becomes particularly challenging when doing research in a subject matter so close to home. I do not by any means claim to have accomplished this task, even though I maintained a constant engagement with it from the social relations developed through fieldwork to the textualizing of these processes in this ethnography.

AN OVERVIEW OF THIS ETHNOGRAPHY

In the first chapter of this ethnography I examine the theoretical perspectives on Puerto Rican nationalism in contemporary scholarly literature. In chapter 2 I chronicle migration and settlement patterns and relate some of the political stories central to Puerto Rican community formation in Chicago in order to draw connections between those theoretical perspectives and the historical foundation of popular nationalism among barrio activists and other residents. The chapter examines how the institutional maneuvering of Puerto Rican and U.S. government agencies, and the popular construction of Puerto Ricans' arrival in New York as "the Puerto Rican problem," steered Puerto Rican migration away from New York City and toward the Midwest.

In the next three chapters I examine how Puerto Rican nationalism was constructed, contested, and reformulated by nationalist activists (chapter 3); by a political elite, the mainstream media, and barrio residents (chapter 4); and by a contingent of suburbanite Puerto Ricans who were born and raised on the Island (chapter 5). In chapter 3 I focus on grassroots activists,[4] most of them born or raised in the United States, who constituted a working-class intellectual force considered to be "los nacionalistas" by barrio residents and city and state governments. I discuss an alternative education program

premised on a critical pedagogy that promoted nationalism as an oppositional mode of identity formation among the most disenfranchised barrio
youth, as well as the prescriptive gendered nationalism deployed through
activism and constructions of the "New Revolutionary Woman."

In chapter 4 I examine a middle-class Latino elite[5] of city workers and
media personalities and a smaller group of Pentecostal clergy and churchgoers who either sought services from grassroots activists or rejected them
as criminals. While living on the fringes of the barrio or in nearby suburbs,
members of this Puerto Rican and Latino elite were employed by the city
government and not-for-profit agencies and served as liaisons between political and philanthropic institutions and the barrio. I provide a nuanced
analysis of *middle class* not only as reflective of material and educational resources, but also as a term that shapes identity politics and nationalist discourse. The local public high school, the third largest in Chicago, served as a
predominantly Puerto Rican site where the middle-class Puerto Rican and
Latino elite came in contact with the parents, students, neighbors, and
grassroots activists of the barrio. This was also the site where the mainstream Chicago media interjected its definition of Puerto Rican nationalism
by representing radical grassroots activism as anti-American terrorism. The
efforts of activists and parents to include Puerto Rican history and politics in
the public school curriculum were perceived as a challenge to public education's leading role in producing the "U.S. citizen."

In chapter 5 I explore the consolidation of Puerto Rican nationalism as an
expression of localized, barrio-based identity by looking at the symbolic and
political economic processes regulating often conflictual constructions of
the "authentic" among Puerto Ricans from the Island and Puerto Ricans
from the Mainland, now reconstituted as suburbanites and barrio residents,
respectively. In addition to examining the ways in which nationalist performances were related to class identities, in this chapter I consider how a nationalist identity in Chicago was documented through the production of a
barrio literature. An ancestral Island-nation was narrated in the autobiographical and fictional works of Chicago writers and in the development of
a grassroots historiography—a popular body of literature used to create,
contest, and redefine the nation. I analyze the consolidation of Puerto Rican
nationalism as a self-monitoring historicization of a colonized identity by
exploring the transformation of a young man's personal journal into a public document incorporated into the creation of that historiography. On the
Island this literary task has traditionally been undertaken by an intellectual
elite; in Chicago as in other diasporic communities it is often the poor and
working class who document nationalism.

In chapter 6 I consider the consolidation of Puerto Rican nationalism as a public representation of a racialized and criminalized identity by looking at the image of the controversial quasi-mythical hero of the nationalist movement in Puerto Rico, Pedro Albizu Campos. I argue that Albizu Campos embodies the concept of "social race," the racial classification system in Latin American and Caribbean countries in which racial categories are class categories. This system provides an alternative to the dichotomized black-white racial taxonomy common in the United States, while also sustaining such a dichotomy. Nationalist performances were involved in the process of understanding "race" in Puerto Rican terms in Chicago.

In chapter 7 I examine nationalism as an everyday discursive tool of the most disenfranchised: the unemployed, underemployed, and working-poor barrio residents being displaced from a rapidly gentrifying area and coming in increasing contact with whites, African Americans, and other Latinos. In this chapter I argue that barrio residents reformulated the popular nationalism that grassroots activists promoted by activating their status as citizens of the United States. This citizenship identity was constructed in opposition to the illegal-migrant characterization of Mexicans, Central Americans, and other Latinos—of all legal statuses—who were increasingly moving into the "Puerto Rican" neighborhood. The Paseo Boricua, or Boricua Promenade, as the commercial strip of Puerto Rican Chicago was popularly called, became analogous to the national territory, the Puerto Rican nation, and is critical to this analysis, as the negotiations involved in the process of creating the promenade suggest ways of creating space through nationalist performances. The concluding chapter considers the everyday political consequences of criminalizing Puerto Rican nationalism in Chicago in light of broader criteria involved in the creation of the "good American citizen."

★ **1** ★

Performing the Nation:
Perspectives on Puerto Rican Nationalism

The process of nation formation, like many other processes of identity formation, emerges at the boundaries of group membership. Nation-building relies both on definitions of a collective self as opposite to an Other and a process of creating a national self (Danforth 1995). Nationalism is distinguished from other forms of identity construction by the modes through which simultaneous processes of rejecting a national Other and creating a national self are fostered, contested, and sustained.

POLITICAL AND CULTURAL NATIONALISMS

Critical to examinations of contemporary Puerto Rican nationalism is the distinction between political and cultural nationalism. Political nationalism sees the nation as a political unit, focuses on citizenship rights, and uses reason as the ethical basis for the community. While appealing to ethnic sentiments, political nationalism ultimately aims to secure a representative, sovereign state. The distinguishing mark of political, or official, nationalism is this attempt to establish a separate state (Eriksen 1993; Gellner 1983). When it addresses the relationship between ethnicity and the state, it focuses on definitions of the nation as a physical location where ethnic boundaries should be coterminous with state boundaries (Gellner 1983). As a modernist concept, the nation is perceived as a centralized political unit that binds its members by legal rights and citizenship. Political nationalist movements may transform themselves from urban-based-elite movements to mass movements by "generating grievances against the existing state among different, competing groups" (Hutchinson 1992, 105).

By contrast, cultural nationalism perceives the state as an accident and regards the state with suspicion because of its overrationality and tendency to impose uniformity on the nation's subcultures. The nation is perceived to have creative and dynamic "personalities," and cultural nationalists turn to history to discover lessons for the future. Education rather than machine politics drives cultural nationalism (Hutchinson 1992). The nation is a cultural unit virtually outside the purview of state control.[1] Rather than focusing on a centralized government, cultural views of nationalism perceive the world in polycentric terms (Hutchinson 1992). Cultural nationalism relies on histories that typically present a set of mythic narratives: tales of migration, original settlement, a golden age of cultural splendor, a fall into a dark age, and a period of regeneration. Some of these histories begin in the present (Smith 1984, 292–93; Hutchinson 1992, 104). Cultural nationalism manifests itself in small-scale grassroots self-help movements led by "encyclopedic myth-making intellectuals" who are "moral innovators" in times of crisis (Hutchinson 1992, 186). These intellectuals are "historians, poets, artists who operate as an educational force, inspiring in a nascent public opinion a sense of loyalty to the national model, which furnished a matrix for later political nationalist movements" (Kohn 1946, 429–30).

The enduring distinctions between the culturalist and political views of nationalism suggest how ideas of what the nation is or should be are grounded in several coexisting and often contradictory ideologies, which Fox (1990) depicts as sets of cultural meanings at the bases of a national culture. While both views often converge in movements of new secular groups subversive of traditional orders, the two are very distinctive conceptions of the nation and find expression in quite different organizations and political mobilization strategies (Hutchinson 1992). Nevertheless, both cultural and political nationalisms are grounded in revolutionary doctrines and organizational movements and can best be understood as inherently dialectical. They are complementary and competing responses, communitarian and state-oriented, often forming in alternation, each eliciting the other (Hutchinson 1992, 111).

In this book I transcend dichotomizing definitions of political and cultural nationalism and examine the coalescence of the political and the cultural in the performance of nationalism in Chicago. In using the idea of a performative nationalism, I aim to remedy the inadequate characterizations of political nationalism as inherently official and cultural nationalism as inherently popular (Radcliffe and Westwood 1996). Performative nationalisms are not invariably cultural; nor are all cultural nationalisms necessarily popular, since they are also deployed by national elites, often at the expense of the popular classes. Similarly, political nationalism is not decidedly limited to the official, since numerous popular anticolonial groups have made demands for an independent nation-state outside the purview of official, status quo, colonial state control. Puerto Rican nationalism in Chicago was both political, in that a significant group of residents and activists had engaged in various militant practices with the aim of turning Puerto Rico into an independent nation-state, and cultural, in that these practices were guided by the barrio's "encyclopedic myth-makers" through grassroots educational projects.

THE POLITICS OF NATIONALISM ON THE ISLAND AND IN CHICAGO

As a stateless nation Puerto Rico poses interesting theoretical challenges to conventional understandings of nationalism. The distinction between "nation" as the people and "state" as the government is critical in understanding nationalism in Puerto Rico. Grounded on this distinction, nationalism on the Island is premised on a conception of the nation as "a self-determined group of people who share a sense of solidarity based on a belief in a common heritage and who claim political rights that may (or may not) include self-determination" (Morris 1995, 12). Political self-determination is not essential to a sense of nationhood; rather, nationalism on the Island is an affirmation of a separate cultural identity from the United States in spite of a dependent political status. In this sense, "questions of citizenship, migration, and identity in Puerto Rico acquire a sense of urgency seldom found in well-established nation-states that do not have to justify their existence or fight for their survival" (Duany 2000, 4).

Explicit discussions about the political status of Puerto Rico vis-à-vis the United States invariably address the politics of electoral parties on the Island. Displaying one of the highest levels of electoral participation of all countries and territories in which voting is not mandatory (Jennings and Rivera 1984), Puerto Rican voters consider electoral politics to be the preferred national sport. Indeed, scholars have argued that Puerto Rico's electoral process can be examined as a ritual in the classical anthropological sense (Ramírez 1973). The electoral plane is one of the most evident public spaces in which political parties appropriate the question of Puerto-Ricanness to advance their position about the juridical status of Puerto Rico. Each of the three main electoral parties—the Popular Democratic Party, the New Progressive Party, and the Puerto Rican Independence Party—bases its platform on the status it advocates for Puerto Rico vis-à-vis the United States: commonwealth, statehood, or independence, respectively.

The pro-commonwealth Popular Democratic Party is the only one of the three main political parties that, for the most part, does not consider Puerto Rico to be a U.S. colony. It views the Island as an *Estado Libre Asociado* [Free Associated State, or commonwealth]. The main objective of the party has been to construct the Puerto Rican nation on symbolic and cultural, rather than political, planes, mostly through the defense of all things Spanish and Taíno Indian, while confining the African contribution to Puerto-Ricanness to the realm of sporadic folkloric activities. The significant Dominican and Cuban populations on the Island are excluded from this project altogether. Under the commonwealth party institutions such as the Institute for Puerto Rican Culture have been created to define and safeguard autochthonous folklore and the arts (Dávila 1997; Díaz-Quiñones 1993; Guerra 1998). The party has constructed an artificial sense of agency in the face of U.S. control not by demanding a resolution to the political status of the Island, but by evoking cultural symbols of the Spanish colonial past and metaphors of rural Puerto Rico as evidence of Puerto Rico's autonomy.

Until a decade or so ago the pro-statehood New Progressive Party was less overtly concerned with the cultural and more interested in securing financial transfers from the United States in the form of welfare benefits. To maintain the increase in electoral support that it has enjoyed for the last thirty or so years, however, the pro-statehood party has also been forced to devise ways to make "Puerto Rican culture"—including the Spanish language—appear compatible with the party's ultimate goal of turning Puerto Rico into the fifty-first U.S. state. The concept of *estadidad jíbara* [folk statehood] has been consistently evoked as evidence that one can be both a supporter of statehood and a defender of Puerto Rican culture and, particularly, of the Spanish language and the Puerto Rican flag and anthem. Nevertheless, the possibility of statehood in these terms has been explicitly rejected by the U.S. Congress, the one body that actually has the power to determine Puerto Rico's political fate (Barreto 2001). Members of the pro-statehood and pro-commonwealth parties constitute close to 95 percent of Puerto Rico's electorate, which in turn accounts for over 80 percent of Puerto Rico's population (Jennings and Rivera 1984).

On the Island the Puerto Rican Independence Party consists of radicalized sectors of the petite bourgeoisie, including independent artisans, university academics, and other liberal professionals who advocate making Puerto Rico an independent nation-state or republic. The Independence Party lacks significant electoral support. The extension of public welfare benefits received as transfer payments from the U.S. federal government has solidified popular support for annexation, and local entrepreneurs reject the pro-independence discourse because they identify their class interests with continued association with the United States (see Barreto 2001; Duany 2000, 4). As Puerto Ricans on the Island become aware of the inability of neighboring Caribbean nation-states to incorporate themselves successfully into global economic processes, political party support is being reconfigured (Grosfóguel 1999). The vast majority of Island Puerto Ricans favor statehood or the status of an "autonomous yet associated state" articulated in the pro-commonwealth party platform; they desire to maintain some kind of economic and political affiliation with the United States even though they do not for the most part want to forgo cultural autonomy and representation.

Discussions of political nationalism in Puerto Rico discursively evoke the arrested development of a nation-state, first under Spain and then under the United States. Under Spain's colonial control, prior to 1898, Puerto Rico's economic privation, immigration policies instituted by the Spanish government to strengthen its hold on the island, and political and military repression curtailed the growth of a broad-based separatist nationalism (Ferrao 1990). Poverty and repression overshadowed concerns over sovereignty as Puerto Rico's landowning *hacendados* sought to obtain from Spain more economic and political autonomy on behalf of their class rather than demanding the country's independence or the creation of a nation-state.

Subsequently U.S. colonization of the Island beginning in 1898 further hindered Puerto Rico's aspirations for political autonomy and sovereignty. The 1917 imposition of U.S. citizenship and of the English language, through the educational system and in all government transactions, became critical tools in the Americanization project of the colonial government during the first four or so decades of U.S. occupation (Barreto 2001; Cabán 1999). Ideologically Americanization defined the United States as the model of civility and progress to which the decidedly inferior Puerto Rican subalterns should aspire. At the structural level Americanization required that Puerto Rico's economy be transformed from an hacienda-based agricultural system to a plantation-export system to service the metropolis. U.S. appointees, most of whom were American rather than Creole, dominated local government until 1947.

Increasing discontent with U.S. colonial domination was tempered by massive economic transfers and legal recognition of workers' right to strike. In this ironic predicament, colonial rulers enhanced the potential for a radicalization of the more marginalized sectors of the Puerto Rican population (cf. Guerra 1998). Some members of the working classes in Puerto Rico attributed improvement in civil rights, such as the creation of workers' unions and raised racial consciousness, to U.S. dominion over the Island.[2]

The early decades of the twentieth century saw an upsurge in interest in national identity on the Island, catalyzed by this intensive Americanization agenda. A landowning Creole elite threatened both by the radicalized popular classes and U.S. colonial domination turned to the Island's Hispanic legacy—particularly, the Spanish language—in response to the Americanization project (Barreto 2001). This led to a noticeable resurgence of Spanish metaphors of nineteenth-century Puerto Rico: the classless "hacienda family," Catholic devotion, the Spanish language, and eventually the consolidation of the white *jíbaro,* or mountain folk as the "authentic Puerto Ricans" (Gelpí 1993; Guerra 1998). Constructed around moral values, close-knit kinship, whiteness, hospitality, and generosity, Hispanicity was deployed in sharp contrast to the morally depraved and barbaric American invaders and in negation of the African and immigrant elements of national identity. More significantly, concerns with national identity became embroiled in struggles over who constituted *el pueblo puertorriqueño.*

The nationalist canon was consolidated by a notable group of intellectuals, writers, and artists known as the Generation of 1930. This group of Island intellectuals, and most notably Antonio S. Pedreira (1934), delineated contemporary discourse on the Puerto Rican nation by formulating ideological cornerstones to define the "real" Puerto Rican (Duany 2000; Flores 1993; Gelpí 1993). In his study of the intellectual tradition behind Puerto Rican nationalism, Duany (2000, 7) outlines the five basic principles of the Puerto-Ricanness defined by the Generation of 1930. First, the Spanish language became an indispensable aspect of Puerto-Ricanness typically viewed in opposition to the corrupting influences of the English language. Second, the Island's territory emerged as the geographic entity containing the nation, and manifestations of Puerto-Ricanness outside of Island borders, including those among Puerto Rican migrants to the Mainland, threatened to contaminate or dissolve the nation. Third, common origin was located on place of birth and residence, which became critical to the definition of who was a "real" Puerto Rican. Fourth, the racial triad was consolidated as a shared myth of origin by which all Puerto Ricans were considered to be a cultural and genetic mix of Spanish, Taíno Indian, and African influences. This shared history also made possible strong resistance to assimilation into U.S. racial structures. Finally, a predetermined set of folkloric symbols—mostly involving images of a pure rural past—were superimposed on images of U.S. urbanism, avoiding unwanted mixing of cultural elements.[3]

In the context of these Island-based intellectual debates aiming to define the Puerto Rican nation, the 1930s through the 1950s saw the height of separatist, anticolonial nationalism on U.S.-dominated Puerto Rico. The emerging Nationalist Party (now almost disappeared), under the leadership of Pedro Albizu Campos, denounced the U.S. colonization of the Island as illegal, called attention to Puerto Rico's colonial status in international forums, foregrounded the flag and anthem as national symbols, and engaged in several episodes of armed struggle against the colonial regime (Rodríguez Fraticelli 1992; Fernández 1994; Tirado 1993). To do this the party and its largely landowning constituency turned to the Spanish colonial legacy as a cultural and ideological tool against U.S. influence. The Nationalist Party's Hispanophile conception of the nation and its petit bourgeois membership, along with its emphasis on national sovereignty that precluded all other local issues including deepening class schisms, limited its popular support, and therefore any potential threat to U.S. rule (Ferrao 1990).

Notwithstanding the Nationalist Party's lack of success in its pursuit of independence from the United States, in rare instances the party did engage issues of economic restructuring; for example, it was involved in the sugar cane workers' strikes of 1934. Such instances expanded the party's popular support and thus posed a significant threat to U.S. domination (Pantojas-García 1990), but they also led to the imposition of the *ley de la mordaza*, the "gag law," on anyone who attempted to disseminate ideas against the Island's colonial government.

The gag law became one of many institutionalized strategies for repressing Puerto Rican nationalism in the late 1940s, foreshadowing the McCarthyism of the 1950s in the United States. This law was critical in containing civil unrest in the period leading up to the consolidation of Puerto Rico as a U.S. commonwealth in 1952 (Ferrao 1990). In particular, the gag law and other repressive strategies provided the basis for the arrest and lengthy imprisonment of nationalists during the revolts and the occupancy of Ponce, Jayuya, and other towns on the Island (Seijo-Bruno 1989). The tension between the Popular Democratic Party, under which commonwealth status was attained and which to this day remains the leading proponent of that political formula, and the nationalists, who sought complete separation from the United States, continued to increase throughout the 1950s. This political turmoil framed the rapid industrialization of Puerto Rico and the massive migration of Puerto Ricans to the United States.

Nationalist armed struggles, mostly masterminded by Pedro Albizu Campos, continued outside the Island's territory and political party lines as unofficial grassroots movements. In 1950 two Puerto Rican nationalists attacked President Truman, and in 1954 Oscar Collazo, Lolita Lebrón, and Rafael Cancel Miranda engaged in a shoot-out at the U.S. Capitol. These radicals have since become icons of Puerto Rico's nationalist movement (Fernández 1994). Various clandestine groups in the United States have discursively and symbolically built upon the legacy of armed struggle by the early Puerto Rican nationalists, and they have been further inspired by the U.S. civil rights protests of the 1960s and 1970s (Oboler 1995). One such group, the Fuerzas Armadas para la Liberación Nacional (FALN), was founded in Chicago's Puerto Rican barrio, where most of its members were born and raised. Such separatist nationalism has lost virtually all followers on the Island, where support for independence rarely surpasses the 4 percent mark in elections.[4]

Nevertheless, decreasing electoral support for independence is not symptomatic of a weakening nationalism on the Island, as some scholars of cultural nationalism have argued (e.g., Dávila 1997; Duany 2000; Negrón-Muntaner and Grosfóguel 1997; Pabón 1995). The Island version of Puerto Rican nationalism is significantly different from that constructed in Chicago. On the Island an intellectual elite—especially college professors, scholars, writers, and musicians—has played a critical role in the construction of a nationalist discourse that, as its critics emphasize, is rooted in rigid and essentialist understandings of Puerto-Ricanness. As constructed by this Island intellectual elite, nationalist thinking and practice have tended to embrace a homogenizing image of collective identity that "silences the multiple voices of the nation, based on class, race, ethnicity, gender, and other differences" (Duany 2000, 7). Most Puerto Rican nationalists in Chicago did not belong to a middle-class elite; rather, they were embroiled in popular grassroots politics in the barrio. Most significant, Puerto Rican nationalism in Chicago actually generated spaces of debate around issues of class, race, gender, and other differences, rather than subordinating these issues.

Several scholars have examined the role intellectual and economic elites have played in the crafting of the political nationalist project, often at the expense of the popular classes or in response to colonial pressures. Guerra (1998) and Barreto (1998) speak particularly eloquently to the conflation of nationalist and class affiliations. In her analysis of the historical transformations of the image of the *jíbaro*, Guerra (1998) convincingly shows how people at the margins—in this case, the country folk turned urban dwellers—have served as sites of production and contestation of national images. The *jíbaro* and Puerto Rico's agrarian past authenticated the elite in the midst of the Americanization process and later during the rapid industrialization of the Island under Operation Bootstraps so that this elite could continue to be nationalist without claiming the nation-state, undergoing economic restructuring, or posing any real threat to colonial control. Members of the elite could exercise their uniqueness as Puerto Ricans in the image of the *jíbaro* while continuing to cooperate with the colonizing process. The *jíbaro* became a passive, loyal, happy-go-lucky figment of the elite imagination who hardly represented the increasingly urbanized and politicized popular classes supposedly inspired by such folk images. Hence, the Creole elite in Puerto Rico sought to identify with the peasant masses while maintaining the basic contours of the colonial relationship first with Spain and later with the United States (Guerra 1998).

Similarly, in his incisive exploration of the role of language among the Québécois and Puerto Rican elite, Barreto (1998) demonstrates how local elites turned to nationalism in response to the linguistic hegemony imposed by the imperial powers and the social threat that such linguistic imposition posed to their socioeconomic status. Implicitly theorizing on the basis of Sánchez's claim that the Spanish language is the "house where the Puerto Rican nationalist personality lives and is itself and respects itself" (1994, 30), Barreto documents how local elites in Puerto Rico and Québec have used the Spanish and French languages to protect their livelihood. The manipulation of various linguistic strategies became critical for securing their wealth, status, or mere subsistence in the context of abrasive colonial domination by the United States and Canada, respectively. Hence, depending on who does the objectifying, conceptualizations of authenticity can not only strengthen distinctions between a colonized margin and a dominant colonial center, but also reinforce social and economic distinctions among members of the same nationality who experience different degrees of marginalization; integration; and access to cultural, symbolic, and economic capital. Nationalism legitimized the maintenance of the Spanish language in the face of the increasing threat posed by English-speaking colonial agents commissioned to occupy the most desirable government jobs in Puerto Rico during the early decades of U.S. occupation of the Island (Barreto 1998). These studies show that while political nationalists in Puerto Rico do try to attain some level of equality vis-à-vis the dominant U.S. society, they do not necessarily aim to eradicate power hierarchies or promote social and economic equality with the most marginalized segments of the Island-nation.

Given the lack of popular support for political nationalism on the Island, diverse examinations of nationalism in Puerto Rico have recognized that the most marginalized segments of the nation advance their interests on the terrain of Puerto Rican culture (Dávila 1997; Duany 2000; Negrón-Muntaner and Grosfóguel 1997). These studies of cultural nationalism have rightfully questioned the emancipatory claims on which political nationalism is premised. In the case of Puerto Rican political nationalism on the Island, many scholars have demonstrated how struggles in which national unity serves as a common denominator generally breed the double marginalization of women (García 1982; Ostolaza-Bey 1987); gays and lesbians (La Fountain-Stokes 1999a, 1999b, 2002; Guzmán 1997); foreign-born immigrants, such as Dominicans and Cubans (Duany 2000); black Puerto Ricans (Rodríguez-Morazzani 1998; González 1987); and return migrants and diasporic populations (Campos and Flores 1979; Zentella 1990).

The cultural nationalist perspective generally looks at nationalism as it is expressed in popular culture and identity politics. Most studies of Puerto Rican cultural nationalism both on the Island and in the United States examine or advocate the exploration of music, jokes, beauty pageants, various deployments of Madonna, Jennifer López, and Ricky Martin, and other forms of popular culture as the locus of nationalist resistance (Quintero Rivera 1991; Flores 2000; Negrón-Muntaner and Grosfóguel 1997). Popular culture has been considered the domain on which nationalism is articulated among the working classes and other marginalized populations on the Island even though in practice popular culture has no inherent association with a particular social class (Radcliffe and Westwood 1996). Theorizing about questions of hybridity and border crossing, some scholars rightly recognize that Puerto Rican nationalism is not inherently opposed to the colonial Other; rather, it selectively embraces, deflects, and modifies certain elements of the United States in an attempt to decenter colonial domination (Duany 2000; Flores 2000).

The commodification of Puerto Rican culture by the sponsorship of U.S. corporations is an example of how "cultural politics [are] the social and political struggles . . . which are waged through culture, where culture is conceived as consisting of elements of symbolic identification" (Dávila 1997, 263). Thus, popular class resistance to Creole elite and colonial domination interrogates theories of cultural imperialism that claim that economic or political integration inevitably breeds a loss of national cultural identification. Popular culture generates a space of contestation between official views of *lo puertorriqueño* [all things Puerto Rican] as promoted by government-sponsored cultural organizations (e.g., Institute for Puerto Rican Culture) and the everyday practices that both subvert and reify these dominant definitions of Puerto Rican culture. In this sense Puerto Rican culture is favored by popular classes, the Creole elite, and even U.S. corporations to advance a variety of interests ranging from the selling of products to the promotion of statehood or independence. Cultural nationalism presumably replaces a political nationalism that failed to address the concerns of subaltern groups on the Island.

The scholarship on Puerto Rican nationalism has implicitly equated the political dimensions of nationalism with a dominant "official" state-generated discourse and with the power of an intellectual elite. Conversely, studies generally view cultural nationalism as the tool of resistance of subaltern or socially marginalized groups that can't find expression for their concerns (sexual minorities, racially oppressed groups, or women, for instance) in official forums. Rather than launching their anticolonial struggles in the realm of separatist political nationalism, marginal groups create national autonomy and produce a marketable culture by divorcing nationalist symbols from their official meanings and redefining these symbols in light of particular identity politics. Because of the tendency for political nationalism to focus exclusively on anticolonial separatist struggles on the Island, thus overriding internal conflict and subaltern interests and marginality, many scholars have viewed the political dimensions of nationalism to be as inherently oppressive as colonialism itself. Often the specific ways in which political and cultural nationalism in Puerto Rico are dialectically related and contextually reconfigured receive less attention.

In response to the admittedly limited classical Marxist emphasis on class distinctions in the formation and consolidation of national culture in Puerto Rico, popular in the 1970s (Quintero Rivera et al. 1979; Ramírez 1973), postmodernist scholars charge that Puerto Rican nationalism is as exclusionary and oppressive as U.S. colonialism (Negrón-Muntaner and Grosfóguel 1997; Pabón 1995). This was not the case in Chicago, where it was precisely Puerto Rican cultural and political—or popular—nationalism that created the spaces to interrogate inequality, discrimination, and other manifestations of social stratification. Rather than attaining consensus by overriding internal fragmentation, these national symbols provided the discursive spaces and social practices to articulate internal boundaries. Ironically, many studies that profess the evils of nationalism and the merits of colonialism are based on the Island's sociopolitical context and implicitly generalized to the diasporic population, silencing the very voices some Island postmodernists claim to recognize.

The proposition that nationalism has the proclivity to aspire to an uncritical preservation of an idealized, often essentialist culture is not a new one (Schiller and Fouron 2001; Klor de Alva 1998). However, the assumption that Puerto Rican nationalism and U.S. colonialism can have equal oppressive power and agency fails to consider the disparity in political economy and historical conditions not only between Puerto Rico and the United States, but also between Puerto Ricans in the diaspora and dominant U.S. society. It is important to recognize that Puerto Ricans have a well-developed visual and literary language that represents their national identity. While emblematic of a national collective consciousness, this visual and literary language is limited in its ability to address the goal of achieving the social change needed to ameliorate the situation of the great majority of Puerto Ricans who lack the basic material resources to lift them above persistent poverty. In Puerto Rico nationalism has failed to accomplish this social change, but in many Puerto Rican diasporic communities, including the one in Chicago, nationalism creates both the spaces to illuminate internal boundaries and the possibility of addressing the basic material and social needs of barrio residents.

LA GUAGUA AEREA, CULTURAL AUTHENTICITY, AND NATIONAL PERFORMANCES

The massive migration of Puerto Ricans to the United States resulted from Operation Bootstraps, the coordinated rapid-industrialization effort launched in the 1940s and 1950s by the U.S. colonial metropolis and the commonwealth government of the Island.[5] The official discourse never explicitly recognized that for the consolidation of Puerto Rico's commonwealth status and its rapid industrialization projects to be successful, the migration of the lower strata was required as a way of "cleaning up" the Island so that Puerto Rico could be showcased around the world as a capitalist model of development in contradistinction to the Soviet model represented by Cuba (Grosfóguel 1997; 1999, 239). Because the Puerto Rican showcase was the Island rather than the migrants, the United States channeled its resources to the Island and disregarded the conditions of severe, concentrated poverty faced by the Puerto Rican migrants living in segregated U.S. barrios.

The Puerto Rican diaspora has few contemporary or historical precedents because few other countries have exported such a large share of their population—more than half a million out of a total of two million people between 1945 and 1965 (Duany 2000, 2). According to Duany's (2000) calculations nearly 44 percent of all Puerto Ricans were living in the United States in 1990, and by 1997 an estimated 3.1 million Puerto Ricans resided in the United States compared to 3.7 million on the Island. The "air bus" (Sánchez 1994), the "Neo-Rican Jetliner" (Jaime Carrero in Flores 1993), the "commuter nation" (Torre, Rodríguez-Vecchini, and Burgos 1994), the "air bridge" (Sandoval-Sánchez 1997), the "vaivén" (Duany 2000), and the "U-Turning Oxcart" (Laviera 1981) are terms used to describe the social phenomenon of back-and-forth migration between Puerto Rico and the United States. This phenomenon is one of the elements that differentiates Puerto Ricans, as U.S. citizens, from other migrants from Latin American and Caribbean countries, whose legal status does not allow easy back-and-forth migration. *La guagua aerea,* or the "air bus," is a metaphor of the process of creating a transnational community among Puerto Ricans. However, the metaphor hides as much as it reveals.

The national imaginary on the Island relies on bouts of amnesia about the large proportion of Puerto Ricans living outside Puerto Rico. Migration is the elephant in the middle of the living room; it evidently exists, but it is notoriously absent from substantive discourses, critical analyses, and historical and political economic contextualizations. The historical discontinuity of the official national history is what Díaz-Quiñones (1993) calls *la memoria rota,* or the broken memory.[6] Like other nation-building processes, the process of national formation in Puerto Rico requires not only a collective construction of a glorified past, or a mythical history that will unite people in a national community, but also historical error and shared amnesia, a collective forgetting (Díaz-Quiñones 1993; Gellner 1994; Danforth 1995; Renan 1990).

In their countries of origin Latin American and Caribbean migrants to the United States have been designated by various terms suggesting their cultural impurity or lack of solidarity with their nations. In Venezuela, the *Tabaratos* are those citizens who migrated to Miami in the midst of the 1970s oil boom. Because the change from *bolívares* to dollars favored them, they found that everything "(es)tá barato" [is cheap]. *Pochos* in Mexico; *gusanos* in Cuba; and, most recently, *dominicayork*[7] and *brazucos* in the Dominican Republic and Brazil, respectively, are terms adopted to emphasize the otherness of the migrants or exiles of a nation. The terms are more than simple labels. They implicate the political contexts, economic motivations, and essentialist notions of authenticity in transnational migratory flows. The terms also suggest the migrants' subsequent "Americanization," and an Americanization as abjection, as well as their evolving relationship with the national territories they left behind.[8]

The production of national subjects sustains hegemonic notions of authenticity, that is, of gradations of cultural purity and the means of distinguishing a "true" national from a "contaminated," and "contaminating," hybrid. The creation of a social space in which to express belongingness and at the same time define those who are Other is the effect and practice of the

social, political, and historical power relations of the nation.[9] The relation
between territory and population is naturalized through the power enacted
in the carving out of a unique, national place from a variety of material envi-
ronments and the conceptualization of that place as incomparable, "a
unique place for the expression of identity" (Williams and Smith 1983; Radcliffe and Westwood 1996, 22). Often migrant communities themselves
view some of their members as more real, more authentic, or closer to the
nation than others (Díaz-Quiñones 1993; Di Leonardo 1984; Pope 1985).
The community members explain this authenticity in terms of how closely a
particular member resembles the popular or media-generated stereotypes
of the community. Cultural authenticity is also determined by mastery of
specific cultural elements (e.g., speaking "proper" Spanish rather than
Spanglish) or according to more objective criteria (e.g., place of birth) that
the community associates with genuineness.

Back-and-forth migration not only subverts the territorial segmentation
between the Island and Puerto Rican communities in the United States, but
also produces and reproduces notions of purity and sameness within the national territory and of difference and impurity outside the territory.[10] The diaspora calls into question conceptions of ethnic, racial, gender, and national
boundaries as defined in the "ancestral homeland." Official nationalist discourse in Puerto Rico generally locates the migrants outside the territorial
and symbolic boundaries of the Puerto Rican nation (Díaz-Quiñones 1993).
Puerto Rican migrants are constructed as truly the Other of the Puerto Rican
nation even though the pro-commonwealth government historically labeled
them as "migrant citizens" (Duany 2000).

Island society, and particularly the intellectual elite, traditionally viewed
the diaspora as an obstacle to the consolidation of a national consciousness.
The construction of a transnational community among Puerto Ricans con-
tends with the categorization of its members into *los de aquí* and *los de allá*
[those from here and those from there]. In the context of complex Island-
Mainland networks, nationalist ideologies reify and essentialize national
identity. These ideologies define national identity not as something situational, constructed, and negotiated, but as something fixed, primordial, and
permanent. Debates around who is a "real Puerto Rican" among Puerto Ricans on the Island and in U.S. Puerto Rican communities have been a
source of division between Puerto Ricans born or raised in the United States
and certain factions of the Island elite.

Some researchers have argued that in Puerto Rico being *nacido y criado*
[born and raised] on the Island is the primary criterion for defining Puerto-
Ricanness, rather than self-identification with Puerto Rico, its language, or

its folklore (Acosta-Belén 1992; Zentella 1990). I argue that migrant Others are excluded not only on the basis of their failure to master the Spanish language or because they were born or raised on the Mainland—especially since the 1980s, when members of the Island elite reentered the migration stream—but also on the basis of conceptualizations of cultural capital. The exclusion, grounded on claims of inauthenticity, becomes a condemnation of the migrants for not conducting themselves in "proper" fashion, as described by an upper-class elite living on the Island or having strong social networks on the Island.[11] The intersection of cultural capital, implicit social knowledge, and notions of authenticity were critical components in the deployment of enduring identities as Islanders and Mainlanders and in the performance of nationalism in Chicago.[12]

The image of migration invariably evokes notions of the so-called Nuyorican, who either has an identity crisis or has assimilated into U.S. culture. Most Puerto Ricans in Chicago reacted to the term *Nuyorican* in one of two ways. First, they pointed out that the term did not apply to them, and second, they defined their status in contrast to the Nuyorican Other precisely by focusing on the class identity and racialization processes that saturate the term on the Island. As Edna Acosta-Belén (1992) explains, *Nuyorican,* or *Neorican*—a hybrid of "New York" and "Puerto Rican," or "new Puerto Rican"—initially had negative connotations, especially as it was used on the Island. At their inception the terms suggested a cultural impurity that the Island elite attributed to uneducated younger generations of Puerto Ricans from "El Bronx," a racialized space. *Nuyorican* was one of the first terms coined to articulate distinctions between Puerto Ricans from the Island and Puerto Ricans from the Mainland.

Nuyorican implies double marginality based on both class and blackness. Not unlike Dominican immigrants on the Island, the Nuyorican is generally portrayed as dark, young, and displaying mannerisms and dress styles that some Puerto Ricans on the Island associate with black youth in the United States. Regardless of age, the Nuyorican is always negatively stereotyped as young: loud, irresponsible, immature, and prone to be disrespectful to the elderly by using the informal form of *you* (*tú* instead of *usted*) to address older people. Age becomes a dimension of stratification that cannot be forgotten. Cultural authenticity is implicitly understood as the power domain of adults; it is the way in which adults articulate their power *as adults* against youth, as well as their power as the bearers of Puerto Rican traditions.

The concept of the Nuyorican also becomes a space to designate some Puerto Rican popular classes as crime-ridden and different from the "good" popular classes that are invested in community-building projects, have good "immigrant values," and defend the nation in the diaspora.[13] Puerto Ricans in Chicago remarked that Island Puerto Ricans indiscriminately refer to them as "the Nuyorican," the embodiment of the migrant Other (Zentella 1990; Díaz-Quiñones 1993; Flores 1993, 2000).

Many scholars who examine Puerto Rican communities in the United States automatically subsume nationalism under either the ethnicity rubric or examine it in light of the history of Puerto Rican militant groups (Torre and Velázquez 1998). Perhaps with the exception of Native Americans, racialized groups in the United States are not assumed to be nations. Thus, nationalism is generally equated with patriotism and loyalty to the United States (Klor de Alva 1998, 67). Even among the most radical factions of internal nationalism in the United States, such as the Black Muslim nationalist movement and its leader Louis Farrakhan, cultural affirmation is generally sought in distinctly American terms. The key words in events like the Million Man March become *diversity* rather than *difference, individuality* rather than *collective struggle*, and *self-help* not *rights* (Aronowitz 1997, 189).

A notable historical analysis of nationalism among working-class Latinos in the United States was undertaken by Jorge Klor de Alva (1998), who questions the validity of nationalism as an organizing tool among Chicanos and Puerto Ricans in the 1970s and 1980s. Klor de Alva centers on Aztlán and Borinquen (the Island of Puerto Rico) as comparable symbolic expressions of Chicano and Puerto Rican nationalism, respectively. He argues that Chicano nationalism tended to undermine economic divisions. By focusing on nationalism instead of class, Chicanos created the most inclusive organizational base possible, converging on the mythical image of Aztlán. This organizational base enabled some Chicanos to claim access to a geographical territory in the Southwest where they gained control of education and channeled political power through electoral participation (Oboler 1995; Browning 1973; Morales 1996). A significant number of these Chicanos were students who experienced a "contradictory location within class relations" (Erik Olin Wright in Barrera 1979) because they were upwardly mobile and occupied various social classes simultaneously. As the radicalized climate of the 1960s and 1970s gave way to the conservatism of the 1980s, Chicano nationalism was deflected in nonpolitical directions and came to be located metaphorically primarily in the mythical geography of Aztlán, the symbolic scene of political battles.

Unlike Chicanos, for whom the political situation in Mexico was not a primary driving force behind cultural nationalism, many Puerto Ricans remained invested in the issue of the political fate of the Island. The plight of the "inner-city" barrios was perceived by some second-generation Puerto Rican migrants as intrinsically grounded in the political status of the Island as a U.S. colony. Others, however, grew increasingly involved in local issues and drew alliances with other militant groups of the time, like the Black Panthers, rather than making the independence of Puerto Rico their main concern (Browning 1973; Morales 1996). As pilgrimages of second- and third-generation Puerto Rican migrants to Borinquen became more common, the Island paradise image narrated by parents and grandparents was difficult to sustain, given the Islanders' rejection of the return migrants. This rejection, the lack of support for independence, and an increasing association with African American communities in the Northeast, where most Puerto Ricans lived in the 1970s, led the second- and third-generation migrants to address issues of inequality at home in the U.S. barrios.

Like the Chicano's Aztlán, Borinquen was transformed from an "Edenic island in the Caribbean to a spiritual state within the heart of Puerto Ricans" (Klor de Alva 1998, 75). Nevertheless, the political independence of the Island continued to receive attention as the nationalist movements remained a banner under which most working-class Puerto Ricans could unite to resist social and racial oppression in the United States. Hence, "pro-Independence mobilization in the United States continued to be a valuable symbolic weapon in the Puerto Rican 'class struggle,' both in the cultural and political planes" (Klor de Alva 1998, 76).

Klor de Alva expands the analysis of Latinos beyond the ethnicity rubric. However, he perceives nationalism exclusively as a tool for political mobilization with little reference to internal group boundaries, interethnic racialization processes, or essentialist deployments of cultural authenticity. Puerto Rican nationalism is partially a result of the limited success of Latinos and blacks in deploying ethnicity for the purpose of forging economic niches as the white ethnics had done. As Aronowitz (1997) has convincingly argued, for white working-class immigrants ethnicity was a mechanism for establishing a unique form of working-class identity—whiteness—and had the specific economic goal of establishing monopolies over particular segments of the blue-collar occupations or industries. In the instances in which Latinos and blacks were able to establish hegemony over some occupations, it was primarily in the service sector and the second- and third-tier construction trades (Aronowitz 1997).

Like other analysts of cultural and political nationalisms, Klor de Alva assumes that class-based alliances necessarily diminish cultural ones; he suggests a smooth transition to ethnic cross-fertilization and harmonious interethnic relations. This argument underplays the impact of internal boundaries along class, race, gender, or even ideological lines, thus contributing to a vision of nationalism as static rather than socially contingent. Because this analysis dichotomizes class and culture, it does not make clear how nationalism can be deployed in everyday practices. Moreover, Klor de Alva does not consider the role of the state in imposing legalized, culturalized, and racialized taxonomies or how these imposed classifications, like "Latino" and "Hispanic," are challenged, deployed, or deflected by marginalized groups (Oboler 1995).

THE "AMERICAN DREAM" AND RACIALIZED COLONIAL SUBJECTS

In this book I fill the gap by exploring the deployment of a U.S. citizenship identity, which paradoxically reinvigorates Puerto Rican nationalism among poor and working-class barrio residents. In Chicago's Puerto Rican barrio, the public perception of physical encroachment, displacement, and gentrification reshaped national identities by inducing a popular nationalism that conflated cultural and political modalities. This conflation led to the display of a Puerto Rican citizenship identity that was not inconsistent with separatist nationalism, but actually served the negotiation of boundaries in relation to other Latinos, African Americans, and whites. On the Island some scholars of cultural nationalism have eloquently argued that citizenship and nationality are disjointed because there is no contradiction between maintaining a Puerto Rican nationality and preserving U.S. citizenship. In Chicago this analysis goes a step further. It is precisely the possibility of identifying as a U.S. citizen that fueled Puerto Rican nationalism and national identity in light of other potential modes of self-identification and in the context of alternative politics of citizenship and "illegality."

Puerto Ricans in Chicago challenged their racialization as black in the U.S. black-white racial polarity and also as Latino by creating an alternative nationalist identity that emphasized cultural and political distinctiveness while securing social autonomy and citizenship rights. They deployed historical narratives and nationalist symbols to reject dominant racialization practices while alternately obliterating and exacerbating internal racial divisions on behalf of Puerto-Ricanness. Unlike on the Island, where mythic imagery of the white *jíbaro* is imposed and contested as the embodiment of national identity, the image of Pedro Albizu Campos, a renowned mulatto nationalist, both darkened Puerto-Ricanness as blackness and differentiated Puerto Rican blackness from African-Americanness in Chicago.

The nationalist identity asserted its claim to citizenship rights through control of neighborhood educational institutions and community-building projects. But the challenge to the racialized colonial situation was co-opted by persistent understandings of meritocracy and social mobility. The combination of the American dream and Puerto Rican nationalism required a vocabulary built around class stratification that separated the poor and working classes from the middle class and upwardly mobile. In these processes of racialization the "Latino middle class" served as cosmic villain, a buffer that ironically preserved the legitimacy of the state. Some upwardly mobile Puerto Ricans embraced the identity of Latino as a mobilizing tool of identity formation, but this middle class was subject to the hegemonic racialization—as Latino or Hispanic—that the American imagined community imposes on those aspiring to higher social status (Oboler 1995). Internal class divisions fragmented the nationalist project as Puerto-Ricanness became simultaneously stigmatized by the state, which imposed the "terrorist" label on nationalist activists; by residents of the Island-nation, who designated barrio residents as culturally inauthentic or as Nuyoricans; and by the local middle-class Puerto Rican elite, who criminalized the barrio as the barrio became a constant reminder of childhood deprivation for those few who had "made it."

Nationalism as a community-building strategy and everyday social practice among the popular classes required that distinctions between Puerto Ricans and other Latino groups be made explicitly. These distinctions included emphasizing the perceived advantages that other Latinos had over Puerto Ricans. Most working-class Puerto Ricans in Chicago focused on Mexicans as a majority and perceived members of other Latino nationalities as "more united" than Puerto Ricans. More significant, they associated Latinidad with a middle-class professional and corporate elite. While the term *elite* applies to very few people, there was a sense among the barrio poor that some Latinos "out there" were "making it." The irony is that a popular nationalism that often supported anticolonial politics was sustained by a constant emphasis on its proponents' binding legal identity as citizens of the colonial power and thus as different from those who were the true Others of the American nation: the *mojados,* or "wetbacks."

The intersection of Puerto Rican nationalism and the social-mobility mythology of the American dream contextualizes the somewhat constraining popular-culture and identity-politics approaches to the Puerto Rican nation, national identities, and nationalist ideologies in the diaspora by foregrounding the history and political economy of U.S.–Puerto Rico colonial relations. This contextualization takes into account the multiple ways in which material conditions and human agency interact and often exert unequal power. One of the main distinctions between living in the United States and living on the Island is the presumed ability to pursue the American dream, which remains the coded reason most U.S.-born Chicago Puerto Ricans gave—albeit not uncritically—for their parents' or grandparents' migration.

My position is influenced by the view that references to culture have to be placed in time, "to see a constant interplay between experience and meaning, in which both experience and meaning are shaped by inequality and domination" (William Rosenberry in Di Leonardo 1998, 56). This approach acknowledges the importance of placing the concerns of marginal populations in the context of larger currents of world history and globalization. This understanding is critical to avoiding a repetition of the pervasive unconcern with the phenomenon of state power that has characterized the United States (see Di Leonardo 1998).

The discourse of the American dream represents the United States as a meritocracy, a society in which a solid work ethic invariably promotes upward mobility, regardless of an individual's background or parentage. I do not assume that people believe these myths or lack the ability to be critical of them. To the contrary. I recognize that these myths are already and always available in discourses of inequality regardless of how critical one is. The American dream is a patriotic myth. Media-generated rags-to-riches tales serve as testimony to the most fundamental foundation of the American nation. Because the myth implicitly constitutes middle-classness as a generic and morally loaded cultural identity representing the triumph of individual virtue over adversity, virtually every hard-working person, regardless of wealth or status, self-identifies as "middle class."

Through transnational migration, technological innovation, and other global processes, the American dream has arguably become the main ideological export of the United States. "American dreaming" is one factor that motivates thousands of Central and South Americans to cross the heavily policed borders and coasts of the United States, often with fatal consequences (Mahler 1995). The American dream mythology does not exist without contest, and its elasticity renders it even more pervasive, powerful, and impossible to demystify.

Many who have lived in poverty for generations, who have seen their parents and grandparents hold exploitative jobs and achieve little, if any, success, are suspicious of the dream. But even these suspicions are interspersed with periods of believing certain aspects of the mythology. "Why go to college if I'm not going to be able to find a good job anyway?" commented Uzi, an amazingly bright and analytical Puerto Rican high school dropout and former gang member. However, this same young man would have no doubt that one of his best childhood friends who had gone to law school

would "make it" because of her "hard work" and "dedication to her education." Similarly the working poor in Harlem would continue to wake up
every day, put on their "Burger Barn" uniforms, spend almost the equivalent
of an hour's pay on public transportation, and beg the managers at their
entry-level burger-flipping jobs for extra work hours (Newman 1999). The
question posed when I conducted interviews as part of Katherine Newman's
research team in the early 1990s, "Do you think that anyone who tries hard
can make it?" received an almost unanimous "Yes" from the Latinos and
African Americans working at "Burger Barn" (Newman 1999).

That the American dream can survive even among people who regard it
with suspicion or deny its validity outright is testimony to the hegemonic
power embodied in the national imagery of the United States as the "land of
opportunity," as well as to the dream's enduring and contradictory ideological elements. The consensual society consistently engages in practices of exclusion while such practices are contrary to its precepts of integration and
equal opportunity (Aronowitz 1997).

The contradiction that arises between this American patriotic myth and
oppositional modes of identity construction—such as that of popular nationalism among "inner-city" Mexicans, blacks, Puerto Ricans, and other
racialized populations—is at the center of this ethnography. Myths and interpretations of the past are invented traditions generated by dominant
groups to represent "the nation" in ways that legitimize the power hierarchies and sustain their dominant group status (Chatterjee 1993; Handler
1988; Hobsbawm and Ranger 1983). Like all national myths, the American
dream captures the construction of a peoplehood and is historically contingent and constituted in the boundaries of group membership (Barth 1969).
Its postulate of meritocracy alternatively sustains and co-opts the separatist
elements of Puerto Rican nationalism in favor of culturalized—or perhaps
anthropologized—identities and conceptions of the nation.

"Becoming American" has historically been a rocky process. The leading
criterion for inclusion has been whiteness as socially constructed by a dominant ethnic elite who migrated from Europe. However, European descent
has not automatically constituted whiteness, as the process by which "the
Irish became white" shows (Ignatiev 1995). Enduring melting pot, salad
bowl, and mosaic metaphors emerged from the assumption that racialized
immigrants would emulate the social assimilation of upwardly mobile ethnic groups of European ancestry. The social assimilation of these European-
ancestry groups, as the metaphors suggest, would eventually lead to cultural
assimilation into an American national identity (Gordon 1964) in which
white ethnic culture would be demoted to the folkloric or symbolic (Gans

1979) and would become an optional identity (Waters 1990). The American dream specifically provides the public guidelines for determining who is a "real American" and, therefore, who can legitimately claim social, political, and civil rights by virtue of being a true citizen of the American nation.

The American dream defines national identity as the outcome of an upward mobility that demotes ethnic identification and promotes whiteness as the common characteristic of what it means to be an American. Race as socially constructed by a dominant elite became the hegemonic means of inclusion and exclusion that often is a substitute for ethnicity in the case of groups of European ancestry.[14] Mixed white ethnics have assumed the national identity as the American people. According to the Americanization litany, individualism and consensus are so pervasive that regardless of what language European immigrants speak, their children will invariably speak English. The Old Country's culture is relegated to folkloric displays on holidays, and it becomes "symbolic ethnicity" for subsequent—and upwardly mobile—generations (Gans 1979). Hence, while immigrants retain their cultural Old World identities (Schiller, Basch, and Blanc-Szanton 1992), they are to shed their political and social alliances with the past (Aronowitz 1997).

The American elite, whose immigrant forebears rode the industrialization wave, have served as an advertisement for the American dream. Being Puerto Rican, Mexican, Asian, or Native-American has been incompatible with being "American"; internal colonial groups have been rendered second-class citizens, and racial categories have been used for their classification (Glazer and Moynihan 1970). *Ethnic* and *migrant* became code words for racialized groups in the 1960s, when people of color demanded their political and civil rights as discriminated racialized minorities (Oboler 1995). These racialized groups were expected to follow the same social and cultural paths to assimilation as European groups (Glazer and Moynihan 1970). In fact, because in the conventional account there cannot be structural job shortages, many whites and racialized Americans alike began to ascribe an individual's—or more commonly, a group's—fate of unemployment and poverty to cultural identity rather than to the end of the industrial age.

References to Puerto Ricans as the "newcomers"—the most recent arrivals in a general migration continuum—have concealed their U.S. citizenship identity and colonial experience by lumping them together with the hyphenated ethnics. This model of ethnic migration has not historicized the unique insertion of Puerto Ricans into the U.S. racial hierarchy because it has not recognized colonialism as a driving force in migration. Puerto Rican nationalism is an alternative to dominant discourses of difference in the United States. It subscribes neither to the ethnic pluralism that defines difference as a transitory stage in the process of assimilation to being American nor to the racial-division discourses that use metaphors of positive diversity (e.g., melting pot, salad bowl, mosaic, tapestry) to confine difference to the narrow range of folkloric forms (Goode 1999).

Theorization of the American dream can help us to assess how the foundational ideologies of the United States intervene in constructions of Puerto Rican nationalism in the diaspora. A central tenet of the American dream is that everyone can participate equally and can always start over. It renders the United States an "open society" in which limits are entirely individual; thus class theory in American society becomes entirely obsolete, and structural inequalities can be explained away by reference to culture (Hochschild 1995; Popper 1951; Wilson 1977). Inequality is an entailment of freedom—that is, market capitalism—and a society with inequality is preferable to a society governed by the principles of central government planning (Aronowitz 1997, 202). While recognizing that some injustices exist in capitalist countries, proponents of the open society thesis disdain claims that market capitalism can be convicted for structural inequality that cannot be resolved with piecemeal reform.

Except for the turmoil at the turn of the century and during the Great Depression of the 1930s, class discourse has never entered public attention in the United States. The appearance of ethnicity has been explained precisely by a discursive movement away from class and toward interest group and association—and, I would add, identity politics—in the post–World War II and contemporary eras (Aronowitz 1992, 1997; hooks 2000). Single-issue movements based on ethnicity, race, and gender, and on identity politics in general, have been able to make substantial gains for a few militant constituencies, in part because their demands have not entailed the question of a zero-sum game (Aronowitz 1997, 203). In this sense, while existing political power has been threatened, economic privilege has not been.

Class exists in the United States, but cannot be talked about because there is no language for it. The "hidden class" is displaced or spoken of with other languages of social difference (Ortner 1992, 1998): race, ethnicity, gender, and in the case of Puerto Rican Chicago, nationalism. The American dream and its supposition of social mobility through hard work is a fallacy for most people living in poverty, regardless of race or ethnicity. Nevertheless, when the mobility paths of early-immigrant European whites are imposed on racialized and colonized subjects, most of whom are concentrated at the very bottom of the capitalist pyramid, persistent poverty and marginality are attributed to cultural deficiency, as evidenced in popular culture-of-poverty and blame-the-victim arguments (e.g., Lewis 1966; cf. Rodríguez-Morazzani 1998).

The foundational mythology of the American dream shapes Puerto Rican popular nationalism in the United States in ways that render these oppositional identities different from those on the Island. Migration, settlement, and community building at the grassroots; interaction with other racialized groups; and the experience of being regarded as culturally "inauthentic" by nationals in the home country create the conditions in which nationalism as a mode of identity construction and agency is produced. The hegemonic operation of the American dream as an enduring foundational myth becomes evident precisely in community-building projects whose political-mobilization capability depends on the integration of even the most separatist Puerto Rican nationalism into the plane of meritocracy and upward mobility dictated by the dominant culture. The very process of migration (of oneself or one's parents) and settlement on the Mainland has caused nationalism to become embroiled in the ideological foundations of the United States. In the next chapter I examine how Puerto Rican migration and settlement in Chicago shape the performance of a popular nationalism in the Windy City.

★ **2** ★

Cold in the Windy City:
Migration, Settlement, and Political Stories
in Puerto Rican Chicago

The bare cement floors of Luz Ojeda's impeccably clean house contrasted sharply with the walls decorated with bright religious ornaments. The pungent smell from the uncollected trash in a dumpster nearby penetrated the small living room where Doña Luz—as her neighbors called her out of respect—and I sat, sticky with the summer humidity, on the plastic-covered couch. As I had many residents of Chicago's Puerto Rican barrio, I had met Doña Luz by chance. She was the grandmother and legal guardian of Marisol, a fifteen-year-old student whose aggressive verbal comebacks, physically violent temper, and tacit disengagement from school posed a tough challenge for even the most experienced and committed teachers at Pedro Albizu Campos High School, the local alternative high school where I was volunteering.

On this particular day Doña Luz had not been feeling well, and the state of her health made her concerned about Marisol's future. "I am the only person raising that kid," Doña Luz started reflectively. Then she added: "She has no one else. Her mother is dead and my son still has a long way to get his life together. I want Marisol to move ahead, to get an education so that she can get a good job, have her own house, you know. Not be like me, already old and still with nothing. That's why I wanted her to go to *la escuelita*"—the alternative high school.

Doña Luz was not unlike most adults in Chicago's barrio, and Marisol was not unlike some barrio youths. Doña Luz had migrated to Chicago as a domestic worker in the 1950s, escaping the poverty of her rural barrio in

Puerto Rico. Ever since she was Marisol's age, Doña Luz had worked—
either full-time as a domestic worker or combining an informal baking
business with public assistance or as an unpaid child care provider for her
son's daughter. Doña Luz had constantly blamed herself and her *falta de
preparación* [lack of schooling], as she referred to her sixth-grade education
and limited knowledge of English, for her inability to buy Marisol new
clothes, move to a better-smelling area, or pay all the hospital bills. Another
thing had remained constant: Doña Luz's perception that in the barrio
where she had lived for over two decades the *nacionalistas,* like the founders
of Marisol's school, were "the only ones who have helped me out." While
those considered *nacionalistas* were a heterogeneous group, most of them
had in common their support for the FALN, a radical group of Puerto Rican
nationalists responsible for the bombing of various military facilities in the
late 1970s. This did not mean that the *nacionalistas* engaged in such militant
actions themselves, but many barrio residents were unconcerned with such
distinctions and grouped all activists—militant or not—under the same nationalist umbrella.

Why would someone living in Doña Luz's conditions credit a nationalist
group of grassroots activists for help in meeting the basic needs of her family? An understanding of the migration histories of Doña Luz and other barrio residents, and of the politicization of the neighborhood will partially
answer this question. In this chapter I examine the historical context of the
neighborhood and its popular narratives of the past, which serve as a foundation for understandings of community, activism, and, ultimately, Puerto
Rican nationalism in Chicago's barrio. My analysis is twofold. First, by examining the political economic processes that fueled Puerto Rican migration to Chicago, as well as the historical events that characterized the
community's coming-of-age, I show that Puerto Rican nationalism is en-
cumbered, contextual, and situational. Yet by exploring the discursive and
performative character of that nationalism, I also show that its dynamic nature and its role as a multivocal strategy were deployed differently by various
factions in Puerto Rican Chicago.

The context of Chicago's urban patterns, the civil rights movements of
the 1960s, and the emergence of political nationalist groups in the 1970s
and 1980s exist in dialectical relationship with the way in which Puerto Rican popular nationalism was articulated in Chicago. Folk tales, gossip, and
metahistories around the conflictual political militancy of the Chicago
Puerto Rican community engendered a dynamic nationalist discourse that
was constantly revitalized as the past became relevant to the production of
identity in the present. In this sense, popular interpretations of the commu-

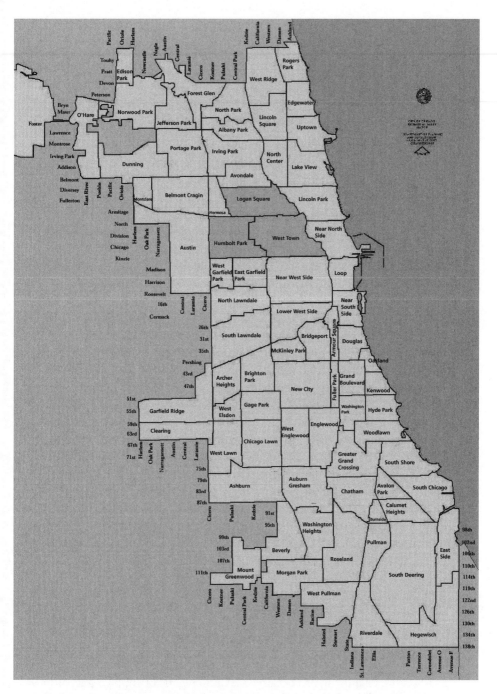

Logan Square, Humboldt Park, and West Town have traditionally been considered Puerto Rican Chicago, although Puerto Ricans have continuously moved to other northwestern urban and suburban areas in and around Chicago. (Courtesy of the Department of Planning and Development, City of Chicago)

nity's past were in themselves endemic to the politics of identity and community building in the present.

Early Puerto Rican migration to Chicago was motivated by an expanding
Midwestern labor market in the 1950s and a series of public and private
efforts to recruit contract and seasonal labor from Puerto Rico.[1] The
Chicago Puerto Rican community where Doña Luz and Marisol lived, as
well as smaller Puerto Rican areas throughout the Midwest, were established at the time of the expanding regional labor market of the 1940s and
1950s.[2] Government and private agencies recruited workers directly from
Puerto Rico and placed them in steel mills and factories in Lorraine, Ohio,
and Gary, Indiana; on farms around Milwaukee, Wisconsin; and in domestic service jobs in Chicago. Unlike laborers recruited from Mexico, the Ba-
hamas, and Jamaica, as U.S. citizens Puerto Rican workers could not be
deported once their contracts expired or even if they abandoned their contracts before completing them. Once they had finished their contract labor,
most of these Puerto Rican workers remained in the Midwest.[3] Doña Luz,
for instance, sought refuge in a facility operated by Chicago's Catholic archdiocese when she could not tolerate her boss's sexual harassment any
longer.[4]

By the late 1950s Puerto Rico was being showcased as the model of the
U.S. program of "industrialization by invitation" otherwise known as Operation Bootstraps.[5] The rapid change that transformed Puerto Rico from an
agrarian into an industrial society was eventually presented to the world as
an alternative to the Soviet strategy embraced by the neighboring island of
Cuba (Grosfóguel 1999). The success of Operation Bootstraps relied on the
transfer of Puerto Rico's "surplus" (i.e., lower class) population to the Mainland so that an instant improvement in the standard of living of the Island's
middle class could be achieved. However, the project offered no provision
for the livelihood of the more than one million Puerto Ricans who migrated
and built barrios in the United States.

While the Puerto Rican government claimed to neither encourage nor
discourage migration, the movement of Puerto Ricans to the United States
was always perceived as an alternative to unemployment and "overpopulation" on the Island.[6] It also became a favorite means of supplying labor to
Mainland industries, particularly during World War II. The Puerto Rican
government became increasingly eager to work with Mainland employers,

and it created agencies such as the Office of the Commonwealth of Puerto Rico to ease the Puerto Rican workers' transition into the new environment (Padilla 1957).

As Puerto Rico changed from a traditional colony to colonial common- wealth of the United States, folkloric expressions became the elite's evi- dence that Puerto Rican culture could coexist with American political control, so it was no longer necessary to launch struggles for political auton- omy. As Arcadio Díaz-Quiñones (1993) suggests, in Puerto Rico the *nation* would come to be defined as a "culture" that did not require a politically in- dependent nation-state. The Spanish language and music and folklore were symbols of nationalism that were not incompatible with political control of the Island by the United States. Because culturalist definitions of na- tionalism could coexist with U.S. domination, the Puerto Rican elite could criticize the emigrants' Spanglish for the sake of maintaining a "pure" na- tionalist culture while condoning U.S. military control of the Island (Díaz- Quiñones 1993, 65).

REHEATING THE MELTING POT

Ironically, while Puerto Ricans on the Island were encouraged to "maintain their culture" in the face of Americanization, the migrants were expected to assimilate into the American mainstream so they could become invisible and further sustain the "success" of the industrialization project (Díaz- Quiñones 1993; Guerra 1998). One of the main assimilation policies of the time was directed at preventing the formation of Puerto Rican colonias on the Mainland. The Puerto Rican community of Chicago, as well as smaller Puerto Rican areas throughout the Midwest, developed partly as a result of these government and private efforts to meet regional labor needs while controlling Puerto Rican population concentrations in the United States. Labor-contract and seasonal migration was even more vigorously directed to the Midwest when New York City's Puerto Rican population tripled. Jobs in that city were quickly disappearing by the late 1950s, and members of the host society feared the newcomers. The so-called Puerto Rican problem in New York City was a primary motivation for redirecting Puerto Rican migra- tion to Chicago, and it became a cautionary tale for agencies responsible for integrating the newcomers into Chicago neighborhoods.[7]

Puerto Rican migration trends have shifted away from the traditional New York City destination to other areas of the United States (Bean 1987), and the proliferation of smaller Puerto Rican communities outside of New York City had been noticed since the late 1940s (Jones 1955; Siegel, Orlans, and Greer 1954; O'Brien 1954; Vivas 1951), when Puerto Ricans began to develop their heterogeneous migration patterns outside of New York City. However, scarce attention has been given to these smaller Puerto Rican communities or even to significantly sized urban Puerto Rican areas outside the Northeast.[8]

The emergence of Puerto Rican colonias, particularly those close to areas desirable to real estate developers, evoked concern, fear, and action on the part of city agencies and local elected officials. The director of the Commonwealth of Puerto Rico office in Chicago, in collaboration with the Welfare Council of Metropolitan Chicago, focused on "urging Puerto Ricans not to settle down with any Spanish-speaking people, but to distribute themselves all over the city in Polish, Italian, Czechoslovak and other areas . . . stressing Puerto Ricans' scattering all over the city and warning against the formation of colonies or residence with the Mexicans."[9] The Welfare Council noticed "the tendency for colonies of Puerto Ricans to grow within the city [and that] unless efforts are made to integrate these groups into the community as a whole, there will be a tendency for them to remain in these groups."[10] The various ethnic identities of the Europeans, while still recognized, were already becoming conflated with Americanness, as is evident in the government's insistence that Puerto Ricans live closer to European groups and away from those racialized as Mexicans.

There were already other Spanish-speaking groups—especially Mexicans—in significant numbers in Chicago at the time when Puerto Ricans arrived, which was not the case in the Northeast, where Puerto Ricans were the group in relation to which other Latinos were racialized (Flores 2000). Integration efforts were attempts at isolating all impoverished ethnoracial groups, rather than at opening channels for social mobility among the racialized newcomers.[11] In many cases Puerto Rican families were placed in Chicago Housing Authority projects, particularly Cabrini-Green and Jane Addams Homes. Government efforts aimed at assimilating Puerto Ricans as soon as possible included relocating recent arrivals in deteriorated areas of lesser real estate value (Martínez 1989; Padilla 1987).

Despite government efforts to prevent Puerto Ricans from forming colonies with Mexicans, Puerto Ricans and Mexicans shared social and physical spaces from the very early stages of Puerto Rican arrival in Chicago. The Chicago archdiocese inadvertently played a critical role in bringing together the two populations, which had traditionally been ardently Catholic and shared the religious and social activities of the parishes. The Puerto Rican newcomers served to increase the power and influence of the Catholic church, which in turn served as a space of social interaction and even networking among Puerto Ricans and Mexicans. Predominantly Mexican nightclubs, like the North Side's Rancho Grande, also served as social mixing places in which Puerto Rican foundry and domestic workers and Mexican *braceros* would meet to eat each other's typical foods and listen to Latin American music (Padilla 1947, 86; Rúa 2000). Mexican organizations, like the Mexican Civic Committee, assisted dissatisfied Puerto Rican foundry workers by suggesting alternative employment options and providing housing among Mexican families (Padilla 1947, 88). Nevertheless, interactions between Mexicans and Puerto Ricans were far from harmonious, and Puerto Ricans were not deliberately trying to move closer to the Mexicans, whom they still saw as less acceptable because of their legal status. The consensual relationships that were common between Mexican men and Puerto Rican women were considered amoral and unstable, and also as an implicit threat to a heavily gendered Puerto-Ricanness. Many of these relationships were seen as legal arrangements rather than romantic liaisons because the Mexican man could benefit from the Puerto Rican woman's citizenship (De Genova and Ramos-Zayas, forthcoming). In the midst of alliances and tensions between Puerto Ricans and Mexicans, U.S. and Puerto Rican government agencies attempted to set Puerto Rican newcomers on the same Americanization path as European migrants, both to prevent them from forming alliances with members of other Spanish-speaking groups and to reduce Puerto Rican visibility in the city.

The vision of white ethnics as the faithful followers of the Americanization path rendered them as capable of drawing Puerto Ricans away from Mexicans, the other Spanish-speaking group in Chicago. This ideological vision points to the shifting racialization process in which white ethnics became the embodiment of American national identity and Mexicans and Puerto Ricans became racialized, undeserving Others. The "unmeltable ethnics," as Novak (1972) referred to the children of European migrants, were not necessarily incompatible with an American nation whose ideological constructs were premised on whiteness. The main problem preventing Puerto Ricans from integrating was perceived to be their culture. Hence, white ethnics would later be nostalgically invented as "the proper urban residents, those who maintain stable neighborhoods that nevertheless have 'character,'" communities upon which visions of gentrification are premised (Di Leonardo 1998). The white ethnic communities were working-class American "enclaves," while Puerto Rican neighborhoods were racialized "ghettos."

Puerto Rican residence in these areas was short-lived, or, as one of the Puerto Ricans with whom I spoke put it: "Esta comunidad va con la mochila al hombro" [This community carries a backpack on the shoulder]. Urban re-

newal projects, gang territoriality, and racial tensions contributed to the location shifts of Puerto Rican colonias throughout the 1950s and 1960s
(Padilla 1987). Many of the people with whom I talked remembered when
certain gentrified areas used to be mostly Puerto Rican. "Look at this now . . .
All these artsy stores and bourgie restaurants were not here before," remarked Luis Guzmán, one of Marisol's teachers, who grew up in what is
now a very trendy and luxurious gay community. In fact, even when Luis and
his sisters were growing up in the 1960s, the Puerto Rican area where he
lived was a short walk from the exclusive Gold Coast. "I remember how I
used to deliver newspapers to these rich people's buildings. . . . I always noticed how even the hallways of those buildings were warmer than any part of
my house in the winter. I was about eight years old," Luis recalled.

IMAGINING COMMUNITY AND NETWORKING WITH KIN IN THE BARRIO

By the 1960s, most Puerto Ricans in Chicago had been displaced to the
Northwest Side of the city. Only two or three train stops from Chicago's
downtown "Loop," the intersection of three adjacent neighborhoods—Logan Square, West Town, and Humboldt Park—served as the point of entry
for recent Puerto Rican migrants from the 1960s onward. While Mexicans
are dispersed all through the city, Puerto Ricans remain heavily concentrated in these three neighborhoods. The convenient location of the Puerto
Rican area allowed easy access to the downtown hotels and restaurants
where Puerto Ricans served as cooks, dishwashers, and domestic servants.
The proliferation of Puerto Rican *colmados* [small grocery stores], barber-
shops, restaurants, and ambulatory *fritoleros* [fritter cooks] pointed to both
the entrepreneurial possibility and the demand for culture-specific goods
and services among the rapidly expanding Puerto Rican population. By the
1970s Puerto Rican migration to Chicago had reached its peak. Ever since
the 1970s the area where Doña Luz and Marisol lived has been called Puerto
Rican Chicago and has boasted the largest Puerto Rican population in the
Midwest, of over 121,000 according to 2000 statistics.

Social and kinship networks replenished the barrio's population and
often redefined gendered spaces, as Puerto Rican women played critical
roles in the migration to Chicago and the development of the kinship networks upon which community-building is premised (Pérez 2000; Toro-
Morn 1995). Migration processes are gendered as notions of ethnic community are constructed on ideas of women as private citizens responsible
for providing spiritual values and moral guidance to their families and
refueling kinship networks. In this sense, Puerto Rican women's power is

derived from the "production of tradition," through which Puerto-Ricanness is granted and guarded (Luna 1993, 10).

An example of these gendered spaces of migration was provided by Alma Juncos, a skilled and determined woman in her mid-forties who worked for Puerto Rico's government social service agency for nearly twenty years. Her life suddenly changed when family commitments drew her to Chicago. Alma explained: "I came to Chicago to take care of my brother. . . . He was sick. I came on the 16th of October . . . 1986. I came to take care of him, and on December 8th he got sick. He died on the 9th . . . of AIDS." At her brother's funeral Alma realized the profound friendships her brother had developed in Chicago. "The funeral was packed. People from his church took care of me and helped me with the funeral arrangements," Alma recalled. One of her brother's friends, a parent volunteer at Clemente High School, recommended Alma for a job at the school. Since then Alma had been a parent volunteer at Clemente, where she monitored the hallways, informally counseled students, and participated in parent workshops. As a single mother of three adolescents, Alma felt disconnected in Puerto Rico. She was attracted to Chicago because "you feel that there really is a community, you know, how it used to be in some towns on the Island."

Stories of migration to the United States invariably implicate ideological constructions of the American dream and the political economy on which such understandings of meritocracy and mobility are deployed. As exemplified by the stories of Doña Luz and other barrio residents, the American dream remains a hegemonic construct involving financial ideas of social mobility through hard work. It was in the context of noticing a disconnection between the dream's promise and its delivery that Puerto Rican militancy and metanarratives of nationalism unfolded in Chicago's barrio in the 1970s and 1980s.

"SHAKING THINGS UP": RIOTS, THE CIVIL RIGHTS MOVEMENT, AND THE YOUNG LORDS

Until the 1960s ethnicity was regarded as a cultural identity inextricable from the Americanization process. Responding to the perceived success of the Black Power and other civil rights movements of the late 1960s, the politics of white ethnicity displaced the politics of class during the 1970s, when social scientists and the general public declared the "unmeltable ethnicity" of whites (e.g., Novak 1972). At the same time the appearance of race discourse among blacks and Latinos signaled the emergence of a new subaltern middle class for which militant politics had become too confrontational for the social system within which it wanted to arise (Aronowitz 1992, 195). With the exception of Chicago and a few smaller cities, the urban political machines once dominated by white ethnic groups admitted a few blacks and Latinos into their confines, though it is increasingly questionable whether these minority contingencies have actually consolidated power. In Chicago the blatant domination of political positions by white ethnics—and particularly the Irish-Americans represented by the Daley dynasty—further fueled the militancy of the civil rights era.

Many migrants and second-generation Puerto Ricans in Chicago came of age in the 1960s and 1970s, a time of rapid social transformation and militancy. The increased consciousness of the time enhanced collective awareness of the plethora of socioeconomic problems affecting Puerto Ricans in Chicago and on the Island. The lack of service workers who spoke Spanish and respected sociocultural differences, high infant mortality rates and incidence of preventable diseases, increasing unemployment due to industrial restructuring, police brutality, inadequate educational opportunities, and high incidence of fires induced by white supremacists to drive residents out of the area were just a few of the issues the emerging Puerto Rican community faced (Padilla 1947; Padilla 1987; Maldonado 1979).

The community's frustration erupted during the summer of 1966. Right after the first Puerto Rican Day parade in Humboldt Park, Division Street became the site of the first Puerto Rican riots in the history of the United States (Padilla 1987). The disturbances, which lasted three days and nights, began when a white police officer shot and wounded a twenty-year-old Puerto Rican man, Aracelis Cruz. Allegedly, this young man was a gang member and suspected to be armed. The crowd's anger was fueled when the police unleashed trained dogs and a Puerto Rican bystander was bitten (Unger 1966). The riots were a barrio-based reflection of Chicago's militancy during the 1960s. The city was the focus of national attention during the summer of 1966, when it was the scene of open-housing marches, black and white riots, the Chicago Freedom Movement, and the summit meeting between Martin Luther King Jr. and then-mayor Richard J. Daley (Anderson and Pickering 1986). However, the Puerto Rican community was in its formative stages at the time of the riots, and particularly because of this, and given the political opportunities brought about by civil rights protests, the disturbances shaped the barrio's destiny in significant ways. The mainstream media superficially categorized Puerto Ricans as either "good citizens" or "anti-American." This tendency is exemplified by an article titled "The Puerto Rican Who Didn't Riot" (Unger 1966).

Regardless of whether most barrio residents approved of, participated in, or condemned the riots, Humboldt Park became associated with Puerto Ricans and disturbance in the mass media (Padilla 1987).[12] Because the riots coincided with the "War on Poverty," several community action programs (CAPs) were instituted in the community to quench more radical manifestations of militancy (Padilla 1987). Many of these programs were staffed by Puerto Ricans, thus temporarily addressing the insensitivity and language problems that had characterized social service agencies until then. From the civic hometown clubs to the Caballeros de San Juan Society, Puerto Rican post-riot organizations created new social service channels in the neighborhood, as well as serving as vehicles for occupational mobility among second-generation Puerto Ricans.[13] These organizations were less invested in maintaining a sociopolitical connection to the Island and preserving folkloric festivities than in establishing a liberal political base and thereby stimulating electoral participation, gaining access to state and federal funding, and creating white-collar employment in the not-for-profit sector.

In addition to the government-sponsored social programs of the time, grassroots groups also emerged. These grassroots groups embodied various levels of militancy, which led to intensive monitoring of Puerto Rican activists by the FBI, the CIA, and Defense Department surveillance units (Anderson and Pickering 1986; Padilla 1987). Like members of the black militant and other sectors of the New Left (Anderson and Pickering 1986; Evans 1979), many Puerto Rican activists in Chicago have suffered the surveillance and harassment of these agencies from the 1970s through the present (see Padilla 1987; Fernández 1994). Personal files were opened to record Puerto Rican barrio residents' activism and "communist tendencies" in the most meticulous ways (see Padilla 1987, 171–73). The Young Lords organization, perhaps the most nationally renowned embodiment of Puerto Rican political militancy in the United States, was one such grassroots effort that emerged in Chicago.[14]

Street gang–turned–Puerto Rican youth organization, the Young Lords consisted of second-generation Chicago Puerto Ricans who took notice of the Black Panthers and tailored a similar community social agenda to the needs of Puerto Ricans in the neighborhood (Morales 1996). The Young Lords' accomplishments—developing day care programs, demanding low-cost housing, and challenging urban renewal efforts that continued to displace Puerto Ricans—are numerous and well documented (e.g., Browning 1973; Morales 1996), and beyond the scope of this book. What is relevant to an understanding of the performance of Puerto Rican nationalism in Chicago is the role the Young Lords and other grassroots organizations played in restructuring social and kinship networks within the Puerto Rican

community. In particular, the Young Lords are illustrative of intergenerational distance between migrants and U.S.-born Puerto Ricans, and they
transformed articulations of Puerto-Ricanness in the sociopolitical context
of the United States.

Not only did the second-generation youth harbor no intention of returning to Puerto Rico, but they actively claimed citizenship rights in the context
of their home base, Chicago. Parental fears that sons and daughters will be
corrupted by the lesser moral standards of the receiving society have been
common to migrant groups (Levitt 2001), and the fact that most second-
generation Puerto Ricans came of age during a period of particularly heated
militancy and rapid social transformation exacerbated intergenerational
tensions. Kinship networks were redefined along political lines, and variations in political stands—in relation to both Chicago ward politics and
Puerto Rico's political status vis-à-vis the United States—often determined
personal associations and social networks.

In his study of political participation among Puerto Ricans in Chicago,
Isidro Lucas (1984) traces barrio militancy to the emergence of the Young
Lords. As Lucas explains, the Young Lords organization had disappeared by
the mid-1970s, "but not before it had major impact on Puerto Rican politics
in Chicago. The militancy that characterized the Young Lords has remained
among Chicago Puerto Ricans as far as the issue of the status of Puerto Rico
is concerned" (1984, 105–6). Likewise, Suzanne Oboler discusses the mythical character of militant Puerto Rican and Chicano leaders in the 1960s and
1970s:

> Much like the Chicano Movement's adoption of Aztlán, [Puerto Rican
> working-class youth] reimagined the history of their community in
> largely mythical and poetic terms and increasingly adopted a strong
> cultural nationalist rationale in their actions. . . . Unlike "Aztlán," the
> reality of the existence of Puerto Rico was never in question, for as
> Jorge Klor de Alva rightly reminds us, Puerto Rico "is an island where
> all national questions are reduced to *the* national question: is Puerto
> Rico a nation?" (1995, 57)

The politicized identity of these second-generation Puerto Ricans resurrected quasi-mythical Puerto Rican nationalist and patriotic symbols from
controversial eras in Puerto Rico's history: Pedro Albizu Campos, the Five
Nationalists, and the Nationalist militancy of the 1930s, 1940s, and 1950s.[15]
These symbols of patriotism, sacrifice, and struggle continue to serve as ideological referents for contemporary Puerto Rican nationalism, grassroots
activism, and educational programs in the barrio. Although there is a poetic,

quasi-mythical component to the narratives, nationalist history and icons are also referents for concrete neighborhood conflict and complex notions of community building. The ideological motivation for barrio activism comes from historical understandings of particularly conflictual aspects of U.S.–Puerto Rico history, and the pragmatic manifestations of these ideologies unfold locally and contextually in struggles for adequate social services, housing, and education.

FUERZAS ARMADAS PARA LA LIBERACIÓN NACIONAL

The early 1980s found the Chicago Puerto Rican community at the center of political controversy in the United States and Puerto Rico. The self-denominated Fuerzas Armadas para la Liberación Nacional [Armed Forces for National Liberation] (FALN), a clandestine group advocating political independence for Puerto Rico, admitted responsibility for a series of bombings at U.S. military facilities.[16] Fifteen of the most visible members of the group, most of them Chicago barrio residents, were eventually caught and given lengthy sentences in the mid-1980s on charges of "seditious conspiracy to overthrow the U.S. government." In 1999 President Clinton offered clemency to thirteen of the prisoners in return for their renunciation of violence. Eleven of them accepted the offer.[17]

When the FALN members were arrested in the early 1980s, Miñi Seijo-Bruno, a renowned historian of the Nationalist movement in Puerto Rico who was then a journalist for a left-wing newspaper of the intellectual elite in Puerto Rico,[18] traveled from Puerto Rico to Chicago to interview the prisoners' families. "We were curious to see who were these 'compañeros' in struggle who were risking their lives for a country they 'did not know,'" the journalist explains (Seijo-Bruno 1981).

Seijo-Bruno continues: "Chained and hand-cuffed [the prisoners] were taken in front of the federal judge Thomas R. McMillan and that was where we realized that those 'compañeros,' although born many of them in the United States and never having lived in the Island, were full-blooded Puerto Ricans. . . . 'They all have the plantain stain' we told ourselves." Seijo-Bruno's report is interesting both in content and tone because she implicates the nationalism of Puerto Ricans in the United States as evidence of their authenticity as Puerto Ricans at a time when Puerto Ricans born in the United States were considered less real by the Island's intellectual, pro-independence elite. As Seijo-Bruno suggests, these "compañeros" born and raised in the United States gained authenticity as "real Puerto Ricans" in the eyes of Islanders by virtue of the enormous sacrifices they underwent as members of a Puerto Rican liberation movement. Most of the prisoners were in their early twenties at the time of their arrest, and the pictures that accompany Miñi Seijo-Bruno's article portray their very young faces (Seijo-Bruno 1981).

At a time when most Puerto Ricans on the Island did not consider those in the United States to be "real Puerto Ricans" and U.S. institutions were pressuring Puerto Ricans on the Mainland to assimilate, these eleven men and women became emblematic of the liberation of Puerto Rico and the diasporic identity of Puerto Ricans. Most telling is the title of Seijo-Bruno's article: "Los once prisioneros de guerra 'Son pobres y puertorriqueños'" [The eleven prisoners of war 'They are poor and Puerto Rican'] (Seijo-Bruno 1981). Although in Puerto Rico most of the contemporary leaders of pro-independence movements are commonly believed to belong to an intellectual and social elite, the Chicago youngsters of the FALN were raised in poor and working-class families in an impoverished barrio.[19] As Guerra argues in her analysis of folkloric politics, "the only true Puerto Ricans were poor, guardians of honesty, decency, and simplicity against the incursions of . . . their colonizers. To be Puerto Rican for the popular classes was first to be oppressed and second to be actively engaged in a community-wide struggle to cope with the experience of oppression" (1998, 161). Nevertheless, in Puerto Rico debates over political nationalism are often associated with the university intellectual elite (Quintero Rivera et al. 1979; Díaz-Quiñones 1993), as are Albizu Campos and other icons of separatist nationalism (Ferrao 1990).

The parents of the political prisoners whom Seijo-Bruno interviewed—and whom I had the opportunity to interview ten years later during my time in Chicago—talked extensively about the discrimination they experienced in the United States and their pride in maintaining *la puertorriqueñidad*. Yet none of them were aware of the extent of their sons' and daughters' political involvement. In fact, most of the parents did not share their children's views or talk to their sons and daughters about Puerto Rican politics; this further suggests that the performance of nationalism in the United States is mostly a second-generation political formation. A political prisoner's stepfather said: "I don't know if he got those ideas from his own studying. He'd read history books. But I never thought he could be involved in something like that, never in my life." The parents emphasized that their children had never given them any problems.[20]

Comments of parents I interviewed include: "He didn't even smoke!" "He was always in my house studying," "He's asked me to take care of his grandmother. He's very close to his grandmother, to his family." One mother mentioned that her son held two jobs so he could pay his way at Loyola University. The political visions that motivated the prisoners' ideologies were forged by a combination of self-initiated learning of Puerto Rican history, particularly the history of the Puerto Rican nationalism of the 1950s, and active participation in the cultural life and activism of the Chicago Puerto Rican barrio. Hence, the parents described their sons and daughters both as family-oriented and responsible young adults and as avid students of Puerto Rican history, an interest to which some of them attributed their children's militant activity. Puerto-Ricanness was experienced as something learned not only in daily social practice, but also by actively reading official history and engaging public intellectual traditions. Learning about critical Puerto Rican history was presented in contradistinction to being a U.S. citizen because it necessarily required examining U.S. colonialism and imperialism from a perspective that questioned the nation-state's core ideological foundations. As reflected in Seijo-Bruno's interviews, some parents were trying to reconcile the contradictory visions put forth by the media: called both terrorists and patriots, the members of the FALN received mixed exposure, as did their arrest. The parents all emphasized the didactic nature of their sons' and daughters' effort to forge identities as true Puerto Rican nationals, emphasizing the power of Puerto Rican history in the political socialization of young people.[21]

The social accomplishments of the FALN members prior to their incarceration had little direct relationship to traditional Puerto Rican nationalism and much to do with a more general political mobilization and racial consciousness, but the philosophical premises on which nationalist activism in Chicago is grounded can be interpreted in light of official 1950s idioms of Puerto Rican liberation and anticolonial resistance.[22] This is illustrated in a personal letter that was written by an incarcerated FALN member to his niece, a teacher at the local public high school where I met many parent volunteers. Like many unpublished barrio documents, the letter focuses on the emotive aspects of "la revolución." A barrio activist who was part of the FALN and was later one of the two who declined President Clinton's 1999 conditional offer of clemency, he writes:

> Don Juan [Juan Antonio Corretjer, journalist, poet, and a leader of the nationalist movement in 1950s Puerto Rico] told us that life was all struggle. He died struggling to teach us, by example, that if we wanted to live, we had to struggle. Doña Consuelo [Consuelo Lee Tapia Corretjer; Don Juan's wife] told us to fight cynicism. Cynicism is not fought

with hate. . . . Ché [Ernesto Guevara] taught us that what has to moti-
vate the revolutionary is love. When a man is killed and, facing the
pain of death and the assassins' cowardice, he responds with a smile,
that teaches us what revolutionary love is. (personal letter, April 16,
1995; author's translation from its original Spanish)

History becomes a source of identity insofar as what supposedly happened in the past has direct bearing on the current state of affairs (Friedman
1994). Metaphorically, if not ideologically, a militant Latin American revolutionary past (e.g., Ché) is perceived as directly related to the struggle of
Puerto Rican FALN members (e.g., Juan Antonio and Consuelo Lee Corretjer). Communities marginalized from official historical narratives reinsert
themselves as historical agents and part of a global continuum with the past.

In U.S. Puerto Rican barrios, nationalism is not only an intellectual ideology, but also the concrete means to forge alliances and advance agendas at
multiple levels—from religious doctrine to usage of education funding to
the safeguarding of urban space from gentrification. As Sánchez comments, "to be a nationalist on the island involves a secret prestige, but to be
a nationalist in New York involves public hostility" (1994, 15, author's translation). Being a nationalist in the U.S. Puerto Rican community of Chicago
was also perceived as the ultimate proof of cultural authenticity, in particular
when others challenged one's nationalist identity on the basis of such criteria as place of birth and mastery of the Spanish language. Popular nationalism and cultural authenticity were not only deployed in the realm of the
folkloric, but also became the discourse through which class stratification
and racialization processes were produced in a U.S. ideological context that
commonly denied that class matters or that class and race intersect in complex ways (hooks 2000).

CHICAGO POLITICS AND THE MAKING OF A PUERTO RICAN MIDDLE-CLASS ELITE

The rise of the race discourses of the civil rights movement corresponds to
the disaggregation of the consensual basis of nationality in the emergence
of social inequality as a visible feature of American economic and political
life, as well as to the emergence of a middle class among groups that
have historically been excluded from professional segments of the salariat
(Aronowitz 1997, 198). A minority, yet a numerically significant proportion, of African Americans and Puerto Ricans became the new class of

managers, politicians, and staff of not-for-profit agencies whose main assignment was to run the decimated "inner-city" welfare, education, housing, and criminal justice systems. The urban uprisings, antiwar demonstrations, and civil rights and feminist marches of the 1960s and 1970s could perhaps best be contained not by widespread police and paramilitary repression, but by promotion of the series of racially based systemic efforts reflected in the panoply of government antipoverty and antidiscrimination legislation (Aronowitz 1992, 1997; Padilla 1987).

Given that radical social change has never been on the U.S. political agenda because it opposes the most fundamental precepts of the country's political and ideological life, social movements have aimed instead for piecemeal reform. A critical consequence of this reformist agenda in Puerto Rican Chicago has involved the consolidation of a small but significant middle-class contingent since the 1980s. The victory of Mayor Harold Washington's multiethnic Rainbow Coalition surprised the Chicago political establishment, as the African American candidate attained the highest Latino and black voter turnouts in the history of the city in his 1983 electoral victory (González 1989). Democratic and Republican Party officials alike had relied on middle-class Latinos as their intermediaries to gain legitimacy in the eyes of the most marginalized Mexican and Puerto Rican constituents, regardless of whether such intermediaries had any insight into the needs of their disenfranchised communities. During Washington's mayoralty Chicago underwent a ward restructuring that resulted from lawsuits by organizations claiming discrimination in the way that the fifty aldermanic wards were structured. Seven new Latino and African American wards were formed, and special aldermanic elections were held. Out of this legal battle emerged a small but significant Latino and black political elite, including Luis Gutiérrez, who is currently one of three Puerto Rican representatives in the U.S. Congress. Harold Washington's reform coalition succeeded in deploying a working-class identity that allowed the political integration—albeit temporary and fleeting—of the otherwise balkanized Puerto Rican, Mexican, and African American communities in Chicago.

After Harold Washington's sudden death in the late 1980s, the reform coalition crumbled as insurmountable class-based differences between middle-class African American and Latino politicians and working-class voters resurfaced (González 1989). These politicians abandoned the reform coalition lines, seduced by positions in the Democratic Party ranks. As González explains, "class issues were at the forefront of the struggle. Everyone realized that those forces trying to reverse the gains of the Washington administration

were from the wealthier Black communities" (1989, 53). Perhaps the greatest consequence of Harold Washington's political efforts is the emergence
of Puerto Rican political officers at the ward and congregational district levels who still act as spokespeople for their respective electoral constituencies.

Harold Washington's coalition included members of the Chicago chapter
of the Puerto Rican Socialist Party (PSP). Luis Gutiérrez, who would become
ward alderman under Washington, belonged to the PSP and was able to secure government funds for the PSP-sponsored cultural center and for party-
sponsored social services and ESL and GED programs. Nevertheless, the
PSP was not able to build enduring coalitions with other local Puerto Rican
organizations, mostly because it was regarded with suspicion both by nationalist activists who perceived the PSP-identified cultural center as an instrument of mainstream electoral politics and by members of the religious
right—and its sizable Cuban exile membership—who considered the center's socialism as too close to communism. Furthermore, barrio residents
who did not receive the center's services felt too distant from the abstract political ideologies the PSP endorsed.

Manuel Burgos, a former member of the PSP who had remained at the
margins of barrio politics since that era, echoed the perception of various local activists regarding the relation between the PSP and a Puerto Rican nationalist constituency:

> In the mid-80s is when the issue with the nationalists starts and it
> brings about serious breakups [between socialists and nationalists]. It
> became a matter of [the Nationalists saying] "Ah, no. You guys don't
> have enough balls to fight like we do." And my position is that "No,
> you were stupid because look what happened. You're in jail and the
> system, the machinery will continue." I always feel that one has to
> have a strategy. That's the difference between the dogmatics [of the
> FALN] and the nondogmatics [of the PSP]. The dogmatics are cold-
> blooded on how they go about things. . . . I admire Gutiérrez. He used
> to be a PSP leader. He had the background. He was able to notice that
> "if I want to make changes, I have to infiltrate the system."

Manuel explained the main divisions in the community as divisions between activists who were socialists and those who were nationalists. Though
both contingents undertook community-building projects—which served
as sites to attract ideological followers—the relationship between the two
groups was very tense. This tension among groups otherwise homogenized
as "leftist" developed into a one-upmanship, a constant assessment and re-
assessment of community commitment, militancy, and radicalism. The so-

cialists were Puerto Rico–born activists affiliated with party politics in Puerto Rico, whereas the nationalists were U.S.-born barrio residents who rejected electoral politics both in Chicago and in Puerto Rico. As time went on the distinction between the two groups narrowed, and the socialists who moved into the echelons of Chicago electoral politics successfully sought the support of the nationalist grass roots.

The emergence of a middle class among traditionally marginalized populations and the piecemeal approach characteristic of U.S. political life did enable certain minority individuals to attain social mobility, but did not invariably involve radical transformation for the broader base of Puerto Ricans, Mexicans, and African Americans living in poverty. Elected officials, like Congressman Luis Gutiérrez and Alderman Billy Ocasio, played mostly symbolic roles among the Puerto Rican barrio poor—evidence that "hard work and working legally get you far." These elected officials continued to face a Chicago political machinery that had limited their ability to consolidate radical social change. It had become the de facto task of the grassroots activists who navigated the margins of electoral politics to deploy official nationalist idioms in ways that engaged the poor employed and unemployed people of the barrio. These activists drew strategic connections between ideological and historical understandings of Puerto Rican nationalism and the protection of urban boundaries, as well as between the creation of critical pedagogic educational spaces and the public schools' role in the construction of the nation-state citizen.

THE POLITICS OF RUMOR: "THEY WERE ONE OF US"

Puerto Rican radical nationalist politics in Chicago illustrates the ways in which the microdiscourses of gossip and rumor constitute a conspiracy of sorts among popular classes, of "nonelites mobilizing their power *as nonelites*" (Lancaster 1988, 146). James Scott identifies this form of resistance as the "third reel of subordinate group politics," which is a "politics of disguise and anonymity that takes place in public view but is designed to have a double meaning or to shield the identity of the actors" (1985, 23). In this sense, a dynamic historical transcript renegotiates the connections between knowledge of the past and political economic conditions of the present. This renegotiation is accomplished through a subtext that, while public, can only be deployed by those familiar with the codes, those who have the necessary implicit social knowledge.

One of the most illustrative narratives suggesting the implicit social knowledge of militant nationalist politics in Chicago was articulated by Doña Luz during one of my afternoon visits:

I wanted Marisol to go to *la escuelita* because my own sons went there, and I'm always grateful for that opportunity. I remember how I used to cook for school activities back then [in the 1970s and 1980s]. But it's not the same . . . since Alejandrina [Torres; one of the prisoners] has been gone. It's not the same. She used to come here all the time, helped my sons. She helped us so much. . . . She helped everyone so much.

Doña Luz saw Alejandrina as a savior of sorts, similar to the saints whose pictures hang on the walls of her home. Alejandrina was a sacred mediator for the poor. Principles of community and humanitarian commitment to barrio residents were central to Doña Luz's reverent image of a woman who was still imprisoned at the time of our conversation.

Barrio narratives around the political performance of nationalism, particularly narratives related to the FALN members, abounded. These narratives, folktales, bits of gossip, mythologies, and collective representations were at the center of both mobilization and factionalism in the barrio. As Roger Lancaster argues, "once told, these tales are nothing; recited a thousand times, they become folklore, myth . . . [and] ultimately pass into mnemonic devices of class consciousness, the guideposts and blueprints of future praxis" (1988, 133). Rarely did a day go by in Humboldt Park when reference to the era of the FALN was not made in community forums, casual conversation, local publications, or artistic expressions. The microdiscourses of gossip, rumor, and murmuring stood in relation to a "public display in the revolutionary state in exactly the same manner that they would function on a smaller scale in a traditional neighborhood setting typified by leveling and envy. They knock down and level differences in the interest of a status quo" (Lancaster 1988, 145).

Barrio nationalists perceived mobility as elusive, regardless of their hard work or even academic preparation. They recognized a grim political economy, which they tended to attribute to an internal colonialism analogous to U.S. domination of Puerto Rico, and the FALN prisoners embodied that recognition. Juan Cruz, the youngest pastor of a Methodist church, explained the prisoners' impact on the life, philosophy, and gospel of the church as he narrated an instance of FBI intervention at the church and possibly at its elder pastor's house:

About 95 percent of the people who come to this church are Puerto Ricans. From here. From *el barrio*. All are from here from the barrio. They arrive to the church knowing that it has this stand. This is the only church that has a ministry to support the political prisoners. In the period when El Viejo [affectionate name for Rev. Rodríguez, which means "the old one"] was pastor, the FBI came various times and broke into the church. I even think they broke into the reverend's house. . . . In this whole process of persecutions, the church purified itself. That is, all those who were not willing to suffer that left. Those who stayed were the ones who kept up the church.

Narratives of FBI involvement in the barrio destroyed distinctions between the nationalists as anti-American and even "terrorist" on the one hand, and law-abiding Puerto Ricans who were "good American citizens" on the other. That dichotomy was hardly reflective of the complexity of Puerto Rican nationalism in Chicago. Rather, seemingly clear-cut distinctions between nationalists and antinationalists were actually complex webs created in the processes of class identity formation and racialization and often positioned in relation to an imagined Island-nation.

Like Doña Luz, Hilda Ayala emphasized the prisoners' familiarity, the sense that "they were one of us." Hilda commented that the prisoners were well-known and respected community members. Even when implicit social knowledge hinted at these individuals' political involvement, the information was handled as gossip. Hilda echoed the sentiment of many barrio residents as she described the FALN members' neighborhood involvement:

The people who were caught, they were arrested because they come from families well-known among us. That young woman, one of the political prisoners, she was my daughters' teacher. They are people from the community. They are well-known. Carmen Valentín was a teacher at Clemente, so you can imagine. For instance, Alejandrina Torres was Reverend Torres's wife. Well-known people. But the things they dared to do were so big, radical. They were caught. And one knew [what was going on] because I always knew, for instance, Torres, since she was my daughters' teacher and we had many friendships with the police. They would tell us "So-and-So belongs to this and this." They didn't tell us for any particular reason. They know I've always respected each person's political ideology.

Hilda remembered two of the prisoners euphemistically as a high school teacher and a reverend's wife and pointed to their mainstream qualities, rather than recalling them as the terrorists depicted in media accounts.

Similarly, Doña Luz's recollection of Alejandrina was based on tales of everyday camaraderie; she shielded Alejandrina's revolutionary militancy under the identity of a compassionate neighbor who helped her, provided

for her sons, and served as a liaison to schooling and mainstream achievement. This was a partly sanitized, ambiguous, and coded version of the hidden transcript that is always present in the public discourse of subordinate
groups (Scott 1988).

At another level, however, barrio residents built a popular memory and
reproduced hidden transcripts of resistance by validating Alejandrina's and
the other FALN members' acts of open rebellion despite the fact that they
were ultimately imprisoned for these acts. As barrio resident Javier Molina
recalled:

> I knew Ricardo from before ... since 1976. We had been friends.
> When he was arrested, his girlfriend back then contacted me, and I
> started visiting him in prison. When I started visiting him in prison,
> the FBI started following me. They used to go to the Puerto Rican store
> on the corner asking for me. The owner, a really good man, would tell
> me "They came here looking for you. I didn't say anything." ... So
> Ricky was my friend before [going to jail].

The FBI persecution and the local mobilization around the amnesty campaigns to release the FALN members bound the nationalist activists and
some barrio residents thereafter. Because prior to their incarceration the
prisoners had participated in grassroots programs tending to the Puerto Rican poor, many barrio residents and activists associated grassroots activism
with militant nationalism.

As these barrio residents demonstrated, marginalized populations often
include criminalized figures within their visions of community. Those who
are considered criminals by the elite, or in the case of Chicago, by the mainstream media, are not necessarily held culpable; rather, they are "Robin
Hood types" in popular eyes (Guerra 1998).

At the peak of FALN activity and FBI persecution, when most group
members were still underground, neighbors appeared divided. The imposing presence of the images and narratives of the FALN in the community
was precisely a result of consistent contestation and selective opposition
among an ideologically heterogeneous barrio population. Despite a persistent tradition of militancy, opposition to the FALN and to their nationalist
supporters was also part of the political landscape of Chicago's barrio. In
fact, the FALN members and nationalist activists in general could be glorified because of the tension arising from their criminalization. "Signs of
'FALN Welcomed Here' appeared on people's houses and cars," commented Lola Rivera, a Puerto Rican woman in her early thirties who was a
teacher at the local high school. It was their criminalization, both by domi-

The not-for-profit Humboldt Park Infant Mortality Rate Initiative (HIMRI) was investigated by the FBI in 1995 for alleged involvement with nationalist groups in Humboldt Park and was eventually closed down. (Courtesy of Leticia Espinosa)

nant society and by marginalized populations, that secured the nationalist activists' self-conceptualization as oppositional and even martyrlike.

The narratives that alternately criminalized and heroized Puerto Rican popular nationalism in Chicago also provided the historical basis for contemporary political processes in the barrio, including Chicago's infamous ward politics (Lucas 1980; González 1989). FALN members were heroes to some and outlaws to others, and their images colored political conflict. For instance, in an election for ward alderman, a flyer entitled "Cut Crime in the 1st Ward" was published and distributed in Humboldt Park. The flyer read: "Roberto Caldero tells 1st ward residents to cooperate with police to reduce crime. But Mr. Caldero, himself, refused to cooperate with police investigating the F.A.L.N. terrorist Bombings in Chicago. As a result, Mr. Caldero was jailed for six months in a federal prison for refusing to cooperate with the F.B.I. . . . Vote No to Caldero . . . F.A.L.N. Terrorist Bomb Thrower." At a Logan Square beauty salon Puerto Rican owner and beautician Ada Dávila was discussing the flyer and commenting on the increasing involvement of Puerto Rican elected officials in the prisoners amnesty campaign. Rather than perceiving Puerto Rican ward politicians' support of the FALN members as evidence of the neutralization of nationalist militant discourse—away from an underground current onto a dominant discursive plane—Ada explained that Chicago Puerto Rican politicians were all nationalists: "You see, Gutiérrez and Billy Ocasio are nationalists. They are with the FALN." While the FALN properly included the small fragment on the left that advocated armed struggle, other sectors of the left and even left-center in Chicago were subsumed under the nationalist label.

Because nationalism was inseparable from various community-building projects, spaces of support and contention became even more amorphous. "I don't agree with their politics, but I see they do so much for the community," commented the mother of a high school student, echoing the perception of many other barrio residents. In this sense, popular nationalism existed not only in spite of but because of barrio residents' selective or outright opposition to the most politicized factions of grassroots activists.

Rafael Otero was one of the many barrio residents who at first glance appeared to support the FBI's efforts to dissolve separatist nationalist groups. "They are terrorists. They give all Puerto Ricans a bad name," Rafael remarked not only in reference to the FALN past, but also to contemporary nationalist activism in Chicago. Rafael pointed to various organizations that, like the FALN, were influenced by political movements of the Puerto Rican left. One of the organizations Rafael mentioned as evidence of anti-U.S. politics was the socialist cultural center, which offered ESL classes and occasional folkloric festivals, and whose members were influenced by the now almost-disappeared Puerto Rican Socialist Party. Any activist involved in politics perceived as anti-American—that is, that ideologically challenge the economic values and mores of the United States—was included under the nationalist rubric in barrio popular imagination.

"I am pro-statehood. Everybody knows that. I'm the representative of the statehood campaign here in Chicago," Rafael immediately told me early on the a Saturday morning when I met him at his furniture store. Later, when I was interviewing him in April 1995, Rafael did not hesitate to express his opinion about the FALN prisoners:

CUT CRIME IN THE
1st Ward
300%

Vote No on these 1st Ward
Aldermanic Candidates

Vote No ➤ Hendrix

Tom Hendrix was tried and convicted of the crime of "Conspiracy to Solicit Murder for Hire" Mr. Hendrix served four years in a federal prison for his crime. His excuse, "I was hooked on cocaine".

Vote No ➤ Caldero

Roberto Caldero tells 1st ward residents to cooperate with police to reduce crime. But Mr. Caldero, himself, refused to cooperate with police investigating the F.A.L.N. terrorist Bombings in Chicago. As a result, Mr. Caldero was jailed for six months in a federal prison for refusing to cooperate with the F.B.I.

F.A.L.N.
Terrorist
Bomb Thrower

Vote No ➤ Almeida

Victoria Almeida, the airbrushed carpetbagging Mob Mistress from Lake Shore Drive is "an indictment waiting to happen." She is the hand-picked succesor of the crime bosses of the old first ward. Almeida's sponsors are Fred Roti, Pat Marcy and John D'Arco. They are all in jail for corruption, bribery and extortion.

This flyer, by an anonymous author, circulated in Humboldt Park during a mid-1990s campaign to elect the alderman for the first ward, which includes Humboldt Park. The mocking of three of the candidates suggests the various ways in which popular anti-FALN discourse portrays the FALN's activities as equivalent to other forms of organized crime and positions them in opposition to mainstream electoral politics. (Author's collection)

Ana Yolanda: Here in Chicago I've heard a lot about political prisoners.

Rafael: No. They don't call them political prisoners. You're not clear on that. They call them prisoners of war. Those have been the ones who have placed bombs, killing innocent people, who have nothing to do with the issue of Puerto Rico. But those are not politicians, they are for war. They have placed bombs, killed people, robbed banks.

Ana Yolanda: Why do you think they are so renowned here?

Rafael: Well, because Chicago is the mecca of the *nacionalistas*.

Ana Yolanda: Why do you think that is?

Rafael: I don't have a powerful reason, but I think that *nacionalista* and *independentista* leaders found a haven here in this area for that movement. In New York, even in the Puerto Rican *colonia* there, it's not this easy to have these movements. Because the Puerto Ricans, most Puerto Ricans are faithful to the American nation, like I am. When they see something suspicious, they report it to the justice system.

More forcefully than most of the people with whom I spoke, Rafael immediately accentuated the fact that the FALN prisoners rejected political means in favor of violent ones to attain their goals. Most significantly, these activists and these politics were particular to Chicago; even the New York Puerto Rican colonia was faithful to the American nation. Rafael's support for the American nation and his belief in the U.S. justice system seemed somewhat tempered by a comment he made after the interview. He mentioned that once an FBI agent had offered him protection from the nationalists and that he had declined. "I don't need protection from them. We are all neighbors here. We have mutual respect for each other." Rafael's relationship with the nationalists seemed to be rooted in strong neighborhood ties that even mainstream institutions such as the FBI could not supersede.

Similarly, Frank Rivera, a Puerto Rican man in his early thirties who worked at the West Town chapter of a well-established Puerto Rican not-for-profit organization, commented on the role of separatist Puerto Rican nationalism on the public representation of Puerto-Ricanness in the United States. Frank's parents had always made the conscious decision "to stay out of the barrio." His work at the not-for-profit organization had brought Frank into contact with Puerto Rican Chicago. When discussing barrio politics, Frank immediately focused on the militant nationalist factions:

I was upset, because that was a terrorist act. They were trouble. That's what we were labeled, as people who caused trouble. They appeared on national TV. Maybe it was in the '80s, I thought it was. They were apprehended by the Fed, because they were trying to commit murder. I think it was out in the East Coast. The memories are fading, but I remember the faces. Because that's what made me really angry. When I knew that they were Puerto Ricans, I really focused on them. I felt like "I can't believe they did that." That makes it worse for all [Puerto Ricans] to try to interact with people in this country.

Ideas of the nation and nationalism in Chicago's barrio were produced not only despite the tension among various shades of militancy, but precisely as a consequence of the ambiguity about what being a nationalist involves. At a West Town gym Puerto Rican aerobics instructor Lisa Marrero told a neighbor and me how she disliked Congressman Gutiérrez, whom she associated with "those people who placed bombs." Lisa commented: "I went to Northeastern [Illinois University] with him. He was friends with all those people who placed bombs and are in jail. I went to school with them. Those people are trouble." The people I interviewed tended to be hesitant when admitting support for the FALN or even other leftist groups, but the interviewees who opposed those groups as anti-American were very vocal. At the time she spoke with me Lisa barely knew me. I was just someone who had taken a few step-aerobics classes at her gym. A few months later, in March 1995, Lisa told me how her parents had repeated stories to her in which they expressed their dislike of the nationalist activists and their politics.

Perhaps one would not expect to discover such militant activity and hype about repression in an impoverished ethnoracial barrio in the United States. Terms like *political prisoners, prisoners of war, national liberation movement,* and *FBI raid* may appear odd in the context of a contemporary U.S. urban neighborhood. However, for people who actively promoted social and educational reform and made claims about cultural authenticity in Puerto Rican Chicago, these were everyday concepts. Alberto Hernández, a talented and mature seventeen-year-old barrio resident whose mother and uncle were nationalist activists, openly rejected the militant aspect of Puerto Rican nationalism in Chicago. After an incident in which a teacher at an alternative high school became an informant for the FBI, Alberto commented: "First fearing that the FBI would take away my father when I was a kid, and now this Pedro [a cultural center infiltrator] issue. . . . You never know who to trust. I can't wait till I can get out of here and out of these politics!" (personal communication, November 10, 1996).

Barrio residents were well-aware of the community's experience with FBI infiltration and surveillance. Rafael Otero, the antinationalist who had rejected FBI protection from the nationalists, remarked, "I respect them [the nationalists] and they respect me. We can work together, but I still think that they support people who are terrorists." He explained that the people who had been criminalized as terrorists were actually a very complex and heterogeneous group. Many interviewees qualified positive remarks about the FALN supporters at a local cultural center (chapter 3) with statements such as: "I don't agree with what they did but . . ."; "they risked too much . . ."; "I never asked whether [a particular activist] was a member of that group [the FALN]. It was a secret that everybody knew." The tacit knowledge and the implicit narratives surrounding nationalist discourse become a gossip of complicity and a collective memory that is kept outside the purview of official discourse and Americanness.[23]

The impact of the civil rights movement and "War on Poverty" programs contributed to the emergence of a small Puerto Rican professional elite that remained connected to the barrio through their employment in not-for-profit agencies. However, the vast majority of Puerto Ricans, like Doña Luz, did not benefit from the short-lived government efforts. By the late 1970s and the 1980s, the reduction in the number of semiskilled and unskilled jobs, the source of livelihood for most barrio residents, shattered the little progress Chicago's Puerto Rican residents had experienced. As factories closed down and hiring for service-sector jobs became more competitive, Puerto Ricans experienced high unemployment and underemployment and increasing poverty, which have continued to the present. The history of Puerto Rican migration and settlement in Chicago is built on the specific residential segregation and real estate structure of the city at the time when the community came of age, the 1960s and 1970s.

Chicago has one of the largest and most diverse Latino populations in the United States. Representing 65 percent of all Latinos, Mexicans are the largest of the twelve Latino nationality groups that have a significant presence (with more than one thousand persons) in the city. According to the 2000 census, Puerto Ricans are the second largest Latino group, with over 130,400 people (15 percent of Latinos) in Cook County, which includes the city of Chicago and its adjacent neighborhoods. Residents of all Latino nationalities combined make up over 25 percent of the city's total population.[24]

In a city that is notorious for its racial segregation, a Puerto Rican nationalist discourse that draws from Puerto Rico's history has served as a vocabulary to articulate social conditions and agendas. Nationalist activists have incorporated the military traditions of Puerto Rico's nationalist party of the

1950s and the U.S. civil rights militancy of the 1960s and 1970s. While Doña Luz remembered Alejandrina, an FALN member, as a confidante and social helper, her granddaughter Marisol saw her alternative high school and the activists affiliated with the Puerto Rican Cultural Center as the leading Puerto Rican nationalists in the barrio.

★ **3** ★

Los nacionalistas: Popular Education, Community Activism, and Gender Ideologies

One cannot pass by the Puerto Rican Cultural Center without noticing the building. The bright colors of Puerto Rican revolutionary flags and quotes of "Viva Puerto Rico Libre," "Freedom to Puerto Rican POWs," "MLN," and "No to Colonialism" on murals on the building's walls are in sharp contrast with the underutilized gray factories and small walk-up houses surrounding the multiservice center. The faces of several men and women—the FALN prisoners who cofounded the center—appear on colorful poster boards hung from the walls of the building.

Inside one encounters more quotes, images, and poems with revolutionary themes that decorate the three-story building's interior. The atmosphere of the cultural center is one of constant motion: people of all ages walking up and down the stairs, answering phones, calling out to each other. The purposefulness combined with the sense that everybody knows each other well evokes the need to be doing something or working on something at all times, as if a sign hangs from the entrance door stating "No lounging allowed beyond this point." Most workers at the cultural center spend long evenings and most weekends in this building—planning activities, printing out flyers, designing projects, writing grants, cleaning and repairing, even doing overnight security shifts to make sure the center is always attended.[1]

The school that Doña Luz's sons and her granddaughter Marisol attended is located on the second floor of the cultural center. The Pedro Albizu Campos High School (PACHS)—or *la escuelita,* as it is known among barrio residents—was created in the 1970s by a group of eleven Puerto Rican students and teachers who had been expelled or fired from the local public high school. As cultural center activists and younger-generation students proudly narrate, the founders were expelled after organizing several strikes demanding bilingual education and Puerto Rican history classes for the predominantly Puerto Rican student body and for refusing to salute the U.S. flag, a pro-independence act of political defiance. Some of these people were members of the FALN. When their petitions for educational reform went unheard, the eleven leaders and other community activists rented the basement of an area Presbyterian church and held Puerto Rican history and Spanish classes there. After the cultural center's building, formerly a Walgreens photo laboratory, was rehabilitated by some of the same students and community activists in 1976, the high school moved to its location on the second floor.

"These kids have had lots of discouraging experiences with schools in general, racist teachers, being put down a lot. . . . Some others just come here because they want a school that teaches Puerto Rican history and culture," commented Amarilis Martínez, who taught women's studies, did individual counseling, and was in charge of most administrative work at the high school. "If even one, just one, student stops coming to the school,

Images of FALN members appear on the façade of the Centro Cultural, formerly a Walgreen's photo lab. The Pedro Albizu Campos High School occupied the second floor of the building, which also housed a day care center, an adult education program, a library, and an HIV/AIDS counseling area. In 2002, the Cultural Center and High School relocated to Division Street, in the Paseo Boricua area. (Author's photo)

drops out, we have all failed," Luis Guzmán, the PACHS director, once said in a faculty meeting when teachers' frustration with a particular student had escalated.

A tall, slim Puerto Rican man in his late thirties, Guzmán looks more like a high school student than the school's director, and his youthful demeanor has more to do with his energetic personality than with his physical appearance. Luis could not sit still. "I don't see myself as having a job," he commented. "This is my life, actually, what I do at the school." Luis had been director of PACHS since the early 1980s, when he was appointed to the position after a year of teaching at the school and about three years of volunteering at the cultural center. "Mondays are the worst days because we haven't seen students in two days and a lot happens in their lives, especially over weekends," explained Luis on a day when he learned that a student had been arrested for writing gang signs on a wall and his mother did not speak enough English to get him out of detention.

Students' recollections about the role of PACHS in their lives were poignant. Isis, a senior attending the Family Learning Center, a cultural center program for teen mothers and older students, remembered how "the teachers took food, clothes, everything to us, when our house burnt down. We had lost everything. People from here helped us a lot." Whenever attendance dropped below eighty-five percent, teachers committed themselves to making sure that the missing students showed up to school, even if that involved giving students wake-up calls, giving them rides to school, or literally dragging them out of bed.

A wooden sign at the entrance of the high school that reads "Dr. Pedro Albizu Campos High School, Excellence in Teaching Award, 1986," evokes one of the many narratives of oppositional heroism common to the school. The sign is souvenir of an incident frequently remembered at the cultural center and in the community as part of "the struggle": the time when an academic excellence award was rescinded because of the high school's political history.

Sitting informally with students on the floor of high school's main area, Amarilis Martínez explained how in the mid-1980s the Council for American Private Education and the U.S. Department of Education selected Albizu Campos High School as one of the exemplary schools of the year. Shortly after the school was notified that it had been selected for the award, a local TV newscast ran a three-day series interspersing shots of the high school with images of the trials of FALN members, suggesting that the school was a poor choice for the award because of its controversial politics. When the series aired, the award was temporarily withheld, and a second team of observers from the award-granting institutions was sent to assess whether the high school deserved the award.

The Council for American Private Education and the U.S. Department of Education decided to reinstate PACHS as an exemplary school, only to rescind the award once again just five hours prior to the high school's graduation ceremony, where the award was to be celebrated. "Eventually, after having it taken back the second time, they said they did want to give it to us. That's when we said we didn't want it anymore," commented Mike Rivera, a charismatic and insightful seventeen-year-old, with evident pride that the school had the last word.

Believing that they did deserve an award for educational excellence, PACHS teachers and students inscribed their own plaque and placed it at the entrance to the high school. "They attack our politics but don't notice the good things we do in the community," commented Juan Medina, another cultural center activist, who approached the group of PACHS teachers and students as they discussed the incident.

The PACHS staff and students then told one of the most repeated stories about the center's history: the time when the FBI raided the center while its founders were being apprehended. As an interviewee recalled, "In 1983 the FBI raided the building. They caused a lot of damage. We thought we'd have to close down, but the community helped out in rebuilding the place. In the first day alone, we collected $3,000 through fundraising. Eventually, we raised $15,000 among the people of West Town." The school and the cultural center had been listed as sites to be searched for terrorist activity, and long thereafter that description colored the community's perception of the center. It was not until the cultural center became a consistent participant in neighborhood projects, particularly in formal and informal pedagogical spaces like the local school council at the public high school, that it overcame its aura of mystery and detachment from the community.

The Excellence in Teaching Award incident and the FBI raid, remembered whenever cultural center staff had just been attacked in the media, served as metahistories. They were heroic narratives that illustrated "the significance of terms like *struggle, resistance,* and the *sacrifices* of standing by one's beliefs," as a PACHS teacher commented. These narratives and the numerous public demonstrations on behalf of the FALN prisoners and against educational budget cuts and media misrepresentations of barrio Puerto Ricans created unique pedagogical spaces for PACHS students. PACHS and the cultural center were leading examples of how nationalism was performed and continuously rearticulated in the context of popular education programs.

In this chapter I examine the forging of the nationalist activist, as well as the problematic constructions of gender and racial difference in the context of a popular education program in Humboldt Park. While the popular education program promoted a militant separatist nationalism constructed in opposition to U.S. imperial notions of Americanization and the American dream, this oppositional pedagogy actually led students onto the very mainstream mobility roads historically denied to them by the public educational system.

THE TEACHER-ACTIVISTS: THE CREATION OF A NATIONALIST

When Humboldt Park, West Town, and Logan Square residents spoke of nationalists, they generally meant barrio activists who based their community projects on ideas of Puerto Rican independence from the United States and were supporters of the FALN. Who exactly belonged in this group varied depending on the issue at hand, but consistent supporters of the PACHS and the cultural center were invariably considered nationalists.

Grassroots activists in the Chicago Puerto Rican barrio hesitated to embrace a nationalist label, not because they did not believe the label applied to them, but because they were aware of the negative connotations the term *nationalism* had in contemporary literature and the media (Warren 1995). While nationalist movements have been examined in light of state fragmentation, collapse, and repression, internal group dynamics have been overlooked, and only recently have anticolonial studies provided new models for understanding nationalism (Chatterjee 1993). The grassroots nationalist groups in Puerto Rican Chicago illustrate how culture is consumed through activism, how social relations mediate involvement, and how identities relevant to youth involvement are juggled or foregrounded.

Approximately fifty or sixty staff and twice as many regular project participants constituted the consistent members of the cultural center. Like most cultural center participants, PACHS teachers were second-generation Puerto Ricans born in Chicago or brought to the Midwest as children; some were the sons and daughters of early steel mill workers. They had strong ties to Chicago's Puerto Rican barrio, where they had grown up, still lived, and had long-standing social and kinship networks. Most cultural center members and the barrio residents and youth who participated in the center's projects lived the daily torments of poverty, which served as an unfortunate common bond among them. However, many nationalists in Chicago—as is the case among most nationalist groups around the world—belong to an elite. This is not an economic elite, but an intellectual one; many nationalist activists are college graduates, while most of the people who seek their help are not.

Many cultural center participants taught, moderated extracurricular clubs, or belonged to the local school council at the area public high school, thus reformulating the PACHS educational philosophy in the public educational setting of Clemente High School. "Live and Help to Live," the words of revolutionary writer Consuelo Lee Corretjer, are painted on the wall of both schools. This involvement was the main source of friction between Latino professionals and barrio residents, including parents and students. A nuanced analysis of this deliberately ambiguous factionalism and the malleability of nationalism and class identities is the subject of chapter 4. Here it is relevant to mention that the state and the mainstream media generally aimed to insulate the public school from the nationalism that characterized barrio activism.

"Nothing ever gets done in Chicago unless José López is consulted first," a Puerto Rican friend in New York who had worked in Chicago for two years had assured me. Throughout the course of my fieldwork I realized that my friend had not exaggerated about José's almost mystical presence. "You *have* to interview José López," most barrio adults and youth emphatically advised as soon as I explained my interest in Puerto Rican Chicago. Many added in a more cautioning, and at times reverential, tone that "José López's brother is of the FALN, a political prisoner" or "José López himself has been in prison because he wouldn't testify in front of the grand jury." A staff member at one of the not-for-profit agencies where I volunteered warned me: "You need to be careful who you interview. It wouldn't be a good idea to interview José López because he'll brainwash you and have you become an Albizuista [follower of Albizu's teachings]."

Meeting José López was a rite of passage for people who wanted to be involved in neighborhood development and popular education projects in the barrio. The executive director of the Puerto Rican Cultural Center, José also taught Puerto Rican history at various community colleges in the area. Some speculated that José's presence had to do with his intelligence and preparation and his well-formulated "visions of community." Others attributed it to personal qualities like charisma, hard work, and a dynamism that many compared to that of world-class leaders or dictators. Most people agreed that José López knew the community very well. In fact, a local newspaper described him as "the patriarch of Humboldt Park."[2] While José was often condemned by the media as a quintessential radical nationalist, he was also the person reporters went to when they needed background for a story.

By the time I finally met José López, a few weeks into my fieldwork, the

narratives around him had acquired mythical proportions. Whatever expectations I had had of what José López looked like crumbled the second I saw
him. Most barrio residents commented on this too. When they met José,
they expected to see, as one informant put it, "this rugged, mean-looking
person, a revolutionary. A tough or mysterious-looking person who eats
children for breakfast." Instead, José was a clean-cut, short and pudgy light-
skinned Puerto Rican man in his late forties who usually wore white
guayabera shirts and black pants. His easy, familiar manner evoked parental
respect, but not unconditional obedience or fear. Nonetheless, it was easy to
feel as though you were in the spotlight upon meeting José; as if he were
checking you out to decide whether to put you on the "possibly O.K." or the
"not trustworthy" list. Someone like José would be considered a "gate-
keeper" in professional anthropological jargon because he had critical access to numerous formal and informal social networks, was recognized as
an influential member of the local community, and was knowledgeable of
implicit cultural codes (Hobbs and May 1993).

From the first time I met José López, at a bakery where he worked part-
time, he elaborated on his vision of community, academia, and activism.
"That's what community building is about," he explained, "building Puerto
Rican spaces. Do you know how many people come by here? The alderman,
senators, congressmen, people working in the community all meet here at
the bakery. Projects come out of meetings that take place here. . . . Why do
you want to do a Ph.D.? Too many anthropologists get Ph.D.'s, but how
many do you think have an actual chance of seeing a community being
built?" Everyday social projects in the community were directed toward
marking the neighborhood as "Puerto Rican" and constructing physical and
ideological boundaries that rendered the barrio a surrogate nation whose
borders were coterminous with Puerto-Ricanness. José understood his work
as a nationalist activist in contradistinction to that of the truly powerful
mainstream politicians—ward aldermen, congressmen, senators—who
came to the barrio's bakery. Although José criticized academia and his statement implied a lack of social relevance in academic endeavors, my initial
contact with him was the first of many informal conversations in which he
would give me ideas about whom to interview and how to proceed with my
research, as well as about trying to reshape the ethnographic project. A few
years after the end of my fieldwork, José took a part-time teaching position at
the University of Illinois at Chicago.

When he introduced me to Puerto Rican congressman Luis Gutiérrez a
few weeks after our first meeting, José showed pride in the fact that I was a
young Puerto Rican working toward a Ph.D. But José's critical stand toward

academia's self-absorption became explicit when he contended, "We give Ph.D.'s the topics of their work."

The nationalist activists are intellectuals, which, according to Katherine Verdery's definition, include "anyone whose social practice involves claims to knowledge or to the creation and maintenance of cultural values and whose claim is at least partly acknowledge by others" (Verdery 1991, 16). Chicago nationalist activists share aspects of the John Hutchinson's "moral innovators" and "encyclopedic myth-makers" (1992), Peter McLaren's organic or committed intellectuals (1998), and Kay Warren's native or public intellectuals (1998), who are particularly responsible for consolidating local histories. However, the class affiliations of intellectuals like José López are not easily explained as elite and university based, as has generally been the case on the Island.

José's family migrated from San Sebastián, Puerto Rico, in the late 1950s. "My father came first, to work in the steel mills. Later he sent for my mother, my sisters, my brother, and me." Like his siblings José lived in the barrio and attended the local public school. "I was one of those kids who escaped the ghetto yoke," José said in reference to his educational experience after high school. Together with other community activists, José founded Pedro Albizu Campos High School and the Puerto Rican Cultural Center. After graduating from high school, José attended Loyola University and upon graduation started a Ph.D. program in history at the University of Chicago. "José was interested in the Irish nationalist movement and Pedro Albizu Campos," explained a PACHS teacher. On several occasions José commented that Albizu Campos had been influenced by the Irish nationalist movement while studying at Harvard. José did not finish his graduate program because he "became involved in politics and community work," the pastor of a barrio church explained to me as he urged me to finish school. José became the executive secretary of the Movimiento para la Liberación Nacional (MLN), which, as he explained, "emerged in the mid-1970s after the Young Lords [and was] the second expansion of the Puerto Rican pro-independence movement in the United States."[3] Many cultural center activists were part of the MLN, and they emphasized that unlike the FALN, the MLN did not engage in or advocate any form of violence. By the late 1970s José López's brother Oscar and other Chicago barrio residents had admitted their affiliation to the FALN.

Perhaps the main feature that distinguished Puerto Rican nationalist activists from other barrio residents and community workers was their social relationships with and commitment to the FALN political prisoners. They were relatives, friends, children, parents, and former romantic partners of the prisoners, and they participated in the fifteen-year-long amnesty campaign to liberate them.[4] When José and other barrio activists focused on supporting the FALN members in the 1980s, they were intensifying an amnesty campaign that had started back in the early 1970s on behalf of five Puerto Rican nationalists from the Island who had been arrested in the 1950s. At a cultural center general meeting José said that "seeing those five nationalists free was the most significant moment of my life . . . as it will be when I see the other political prisoners free."

When most of the FALN prisoners were granted the highly contested and publicized presidential clemency in 1999, José López's brother was one of the few prisoners who was not considered for release. Nevertheless, the fact that José López was well-known among barrio residents, many of whom valued José's community commitment, placed him at the same leadership level as Tito Morales of Hardy-Fanta's study of Boston's South End and Serrano of Rogler's study of Puerto Ricans in New Haven. Hardy-Fanta describes Tito Morales as a Puerto Rican man who has "an almost mythical reputation as a great organizer. . . . Most Latinos who have been in Boston for a while know his name, and he is still, despite his age, a presence to be recognized in the South End" (1993, 65). Rather than downplaying or altogether avoiding pervasive divisions regarding the political status of Puerto Rico—as many other political bosses do for the sake of preventing factionalism—José's leadership was inseparable from his pro-independence visions of Puerto Rico's politics. José's knowledge of an unofficial history of Puerto Rican Chicago, acquired firsthand through personal contact with participants in controversial politics, often caused him to be designated a producer of cultural representations for reporters and scholars researching Puerto Rican issues in Chicago. The nationalist activists had been largely responsible for designing the spaces in which nationalism was constructed and staged and defining what being a nationalist involved. Popular education programs, understanding and imagining Puerto Rican culture in strategically essentialist ways, exalted the didactic character of Puerto-Ricanness by deploying it and all things Puerto Rican as narratives that could be taught, promoted, passed on, constructed, and deconstructed.

The Puerto Rican nationalist activists in Chicago also saw their roles in popular education programs as inherently grounded in the politics of race, segregation, and a totalizing colonialism that has equated Puerto-Ricanness with poverty, inequality, inadequate public schooling, and marginalization. Nationalism was not only a means of expressing cultural pride or emphasizing political visions of Puerto Rico's "independence." Rather, nationalism became a vocabulary to articulate stratification, insisting on citizenship rights and understanding internal colonialism and U.S. colonialist presence in Puerto Rico while promoting creative and dynamic performances of the Puerto Rican nation.

Puerto Rican nationalist activists become moral innovators or public intellectuals engaged in processes of resistance education and critical pedagogy as revolutionary praxis (McLaren 1998). Moreover, resistance education becomes a performative nationalism. It redirects the pedagogical process along Freirian lines, not only by focusing on specific educational content, but also by emphasizing the relationality of learning and participation in the context of community building and even nation building. The pedagogical process is oppositional in that it aims to escape the duality in which "to be is to be like, and to be like is to be like the oppressor" (Freire 1998, 33; Carey-Webb 1998, 135–37). It was in pedagogical spaces like the Pedro Albizu Campos alternative high school where the views of cultural and political nationalism became more evidently complementary, often forming in alternation, each eliciting the other. These nationalist activists were not significantly different from other barrio residents in terms of economic capital, although some distinctions in social and cultural capital were generated in the popular educational programs these activists created. Nationalism as a learned process of identity politics became simultaneously a denunciation of political economic inequality (as understood in specific historical contexts) and a vocabulary that served to articulate class differences while still preserving hegemonic ideas of meritocracy, social mobility, and the land of opportunity.

YOUTH, NATIONALISM, AND PUERTO RICAN HISTORY
AS OPPOSITIONAL EDUCATION

Most PACHS students lived below the poverty level in the barrio sections hardest hit by gang warfare, drugs, unemployment, and a plethora of severe social problems. Their families received some form of government assistance, primarily AFDC and Social Security, even though a strong anti-welfare peer pressure prevailed among the students. Although the School's 1994–1995 annual tuition was just five hundred dollars, only 20 percent of the students were able to pay it in full. Most students participated in the school's fundraising activities or work-study program or held an after-school job to be able to pay the school's tuition. Nevertheless, no student was turned down or expelled for being unable to pay, despite the school's precarious financial situation.

There is a strong tendency among scholars attracted to postmodernism and poststructuralist perspectives to neglect structural changes in the political economy of the United States in "late capitalism." These perspectives have attempted to separate culture from politics and economics, thus contributing to anthropology's general avoidance of poverty issues in the United States. Anthropology is equated with "writing ethnography," while the series of activities leading to that end product are ignored. Most significant, the incursion into ethnography as unencumbered textual analysis overlooks the historical and social reality that "while possibly socially apprehended and historically contingent, can be checked, challenged, debated, and reconsidered" (Di Leonardo 1998, 74).

I am not suggesting that the sphere of culture be demoted to an unproblematic by-product of capital accumulation. Rather, I argue that the micropolitics of race, ethnicity, gender, and sexual identity formation should be situated within a theoretical framework that, while acknowledging agency, redresses structural forces and historical processes in social differentiation. These debates become critical to my argument that oppositional pedagogical spaces, like PACHS and other cultural center popular education programs, contribute to a performative Puerto Rican nationalism in Chicago. Crafted as an anticolonial denunciation of U.S.-dominant racial hierarchies and pronounced from a militant—and mythified—nationalist stance, this type of oppositional education contributes important insights to the literature on academic achievement among minority youth.

As Nilda Flores-González (1999) has argued in her ethnographic study of high-achieving Puerto Rican students at a Chicago public high school, most students do not necessarily associate academic success with ethnic assimilation. Rather, Puerto Rican high-achieving students do not see a dissonance between harboring multiple cultural positionings simultaneously, and it is precisely the navigation between multiple sociocultural locations that accounts for their malleable constructions of authenticity, white culture, and "success." "Acting white," just like "being Puerto Rican," is a complex process that is dynamic and context-specific, rather than prescribed.

Often the historical and philosophical premises upon which U.S. public education is based remain hidden under discourses that implicitly or explicitly place blame on the culture of the students and parents, the school, or the neighborhood (e.g., Ogbu 1985; Gándara 1995; Horowitz 1983; Jankowski 1991). *Culture,* coded as sociopolitically unencumbered identity, values, and attitudes, becomes the catch-all term to explain low-academic performance. Those blamed are invariably classed, gendered, and racialized according to dominant social order; yet the power dynamics that configure these margin-

alization processes remain hidden under the notion that schools are egalitarian institutions that level opportunities. Hence the belief that if the
school successfully creates a culture that values a raceless middle-classness
or praises academic success, students will not be as likely to drop out, join
gangs, act out, or misbehave.

The concept of critical pedagogy fills important gaps in the literature on
the anthropology of education because it considers students' critical appraisal of historical and socioeconomic conditions to be an asset to—in fact,
an essential element in—genuine educational engagement among the
most at-risk students. Drawing from Paulo Freire's educational philoso-
phies, academics in the United States (Giroux 1983; McLaren 1995, 1997,
1998) have examined critical pedagogy as an educational philosophy that
encourages students to analyze power relations by situating themselves in
the context of a totalizing neocapitalist, postcolonial framework. The pedagogical processes at work in barrio popular education programs have to be
deconstructed if one is to understand the various ways in which a performative nationalism becomes a strategy to advance grassroots activism in Puerto
Rican Chicago. Student-lived community experiences generate awareness
of Puerto Rican militant history in the barrio and on the Island (in contrast
to the more passive or media-generated views of the community as pathological) while demystifying the American dream and validating the potential
role of students as sociopolitical transgressors.

David Hernández, a bright and energetic student who had been kicked
out of several schools before coming to PACHS, spontaneously outlined the
main philosophical principles of the alternative high school:

Albizu Campos is a school where the students want an education,
without the gang violence, without racism; a place where you can find
out about your background. This is good because if you don't know
where you come from, then you don't know where you're headed. My
first impressions of this school were many, but what stood out the
most was the different types of murals about people who had committed their lives and their hearts to give us, the next generation, the opportunities that they did not have. This school has changed me in
many different ways. This school taught me to be me, and not what
other people want me to be. This school helped me look at my community and say, "I can make a difference." I can be anything that I
want to be, only if I put my mind to it, only if I want it. This school
taught me about something that I'd never been taught before, and I realized that I needed to learn about my culture. I learned about how

hard it was to come from the island of Puerto Rico or from Mexico and find a well-paying job to maintain a home, and to support children, in the land of opportunities, so to speak.

David's commentary about students wanting an education without gang violence showed his awareness of mainstream representations of area youth as gangbangers. Ironically, David was one of the students who consistently played up a gang identity by wearing colors forbidden by school rules or jokingly telling teachers that there were certain areas of the neighborhood where he couldn't go. When I asked my class to go to the public library branch on Division Street, David winked and told me that he couldn't go into that area, suggesting that it belong to a rival gang. When he realized I was looking at his implication of being in a gang as an excuse for not doing the assignment at the library, we both laughed in recognition of what David was unsuccessfully trying to do: play up a gang identity that he believed people presumed of most area youth and turning this identity around for his own benefit.

Perhaps what predominated in David's understanding of the PACHS philosophy was the insistence on origins, as reflected in the emphasis on learning about one's heritage and connection with previous generations of nationalist activists. The people in the murals of the school, the FALN prisoners, became emblematic of commitment and sacrifice; they were ancestral heroes of sorts. Most significant, culture became something that was not only learned, but learned in school, not necessarily at home. For David, learning about his culture as a "half-Mexican, half-Puerto Rican" young man involved understanding the hardships that Mexican and Puerto Rican migrants faced in the United States and questioning the country's foundational mythologies. David's statement was also important because it suggested that while PACHS promoted an openly Puerto Rican nationalist vision of injustice and inequality, it also created spaces in which a Latinidad could be deployed. In this case, David's recognition of similarities between the hardships experienced by Mexicans and Puerto Ricans in the United States suggested the possibility for such Latinidad to emerge (De Genova and Ramos-Zayas, forthcoming).

As understood in a majority of mainstream and even alternative educational contexts, multicultural education involves folkloric displays and depoliticized celebrations of cultural pride, rather than any real opportunity for uncovering controversial historical and political configurations of power and privilege. In the case of Spanish-speaking groups, Latinidad enters the mainstream as something trendy. Ricky Martin becomes emblematic of all

things Latino, and the specific history that conditions U.S. imperialist influence over Latin American and Caribbean countries disappears from the multicultural educational curriculum. Like schools that sponsor a multicultural
curriculum, PACHS emphasized students "learning about their own culture," but by embedding the curriculum in discourses of U.S. colonialism
and community gentrification, and by problematizing depoliticized panethnic identifications, the school was dialectically intertwined with a nationalism that was not only instructive but also corporeal and performative.

The community building encouraged by PACHS relied on the role of
praxis, critical reflection on what one's involvement means in a broader sociohistorical context, rather than on service delivery or volunteerism, the
trendy "service learning" that is devoid of reflection. Scholars examine critical pedagogy as an educational process "fundamentally concerned with the
centrality of politics and power in our understanding of how schools work,
[including] work centering on the political economy of schooling, the state
and education, the representation of texts, and the construction of student
subjectivity" (McLaren 1998, 103). Some practitioners point to the logistical
difficulties of developing a critical pedagogical classroom, while meeting

A group of students from PACHS march in downtown Chicago to protest FALN members'
incarceration and lengthy sentences. Most of the fifteen FALN prisoners were granted
presidential clemency in 1999, about four years after this student demonstration in Chicago
took place. (Author's photo)

Board of Education expectations. "At the level of classroom life, critical pedagogy is often seen as synonymous with whole language instruction and
adult literacy programs" (McLaren 1998, 45) and must often be relegated to
these contexts.

PACHS emphasized that this pedagogy is not circumscribed by the classroom, but involves redefining epistemological claims through the interpretation of cultural codes and political power dynamics and through critical
engagement with racialization processes. PACHS youth perceived schooling as a conglomerate of interconnected activities that encourage community
building, sociohistorical awareness, and enhanced cultural nationalism.
Some of the school's events, like the Boricua Festival, el Desfile del Pueblo,
the Three Kings Celebration, and the Pedro Albizu Campos Puerto Rican
Week, took place once a year, while others, like Vida SIDA peer counseling
and workshops, were ongoing throughout the school year. These provided
an immediate setting for understanding esoteric concepts of struggle. Students associated pedagogical spaces like PACHS with an enhanced sense of
Puerto-Ricanness, of cultural authenticity, through the forging of an ideological identity grounded in knowledge of controversial elements of Puerto
Rican history and literature and increased neighborhood involvement.
Moreover, raising consciousness about the issues that affect Puerto Ricans
in depressed areas in light of broader political narratives of inequality actually expanded students' analytical framework for understanding the realities
of other groups, like Mexicans. While rarely leading to enduring alliances
among Latinos of different nationalities, this consciousness raising allowed
some instances of celebratory unity between Puerto Ricans and Mexicans,
two groups that otherwise experience great tensions in Chicago (De Genova
and Ramos-Zayas, forthcoming).

For many second- and third-generation Chicago Puerto Ricans, knowledge of Puerto Rican history, politics, and literature was associated with being a "real Puerto Rican," as was listening to "gangsta rap" and wearing the
Puerto Rican flag on t-shirts, caps, and pendants. Often it was precisely elements of popular culture that provided the narratives to articulate the ideas
of cultural authenticity and within-group boundaries associated with political nationalism. Edwin Cruz, a sixteen-year-old student at PACHS, illustrated this extrapolation of authenticity ideals from the gangsta rap youth
culture:

> There are a lot of rappers that rap about living in the streets and how
> they had it tough. The people that live there think that he is going

through the same things they are. In reality that rapper never even lived in the ghetto. A perfect example of this is Dr. Dre. He raps about how he lived on the streets of Campton, and how it was rough for him to survive. The bad part about this is that Dr. Dre never even hung around the streets of Campton until after he started rapping. It's a shame that these rappers have to teach the younger generation this mentality [about committing crimes and being degrading to women] that they have never even lived.

Dr. Dre is an outsider who fabricates a marketable and even exoticized image of the stigmatized Campton neighborhood that suits the rapper's own commercial interests and artistic image. The rapper's legitimacy is drawn from artificial claims about his affiliation with Campton. Edwin Cruz critically analyzed racialization by problematizing understandings of boundaries, belongingness, and cultural authenticity. He criticized Dr. Dre's portrait of a neighborhood to which the rapper does not belong, just as he expressed disdain for the mainstream media's representation of Puerto Rican Chicago. "Those people don't even live here. They don't see the efforts and the positive in our community. They come in to criticize and then go on to live in their big houses in the suburbs and drive their big cars," Edwin commented after returning from a demonstration in front of the *Chicago Sun-Times* building.

Barrio youth analyzed elements of this popular culture through critical frameworks generated by a performative nationalism. In Edwin's case notions of cultural authenticity common to nationalist narratives in Puerto Rican Chicago were the analytical prism through which Dr. Dre's rap was interpreted. Popular culture was in this sense constructed in the realm of social practice and everyday life, which served as the ground on which transformation between imposed orders and resistances were played out (Hall 1990). Edwin articulated popular culture as a critical reflection that necessarily existed in relation to cultural hierarchies in which that culture was placed in a subordinate position.[5]

Among Puerto Rican youth terms like *the movement, the struggle,* and *the prisoners,* frequently pronounced by the nationalist staff at the school, embodied the barrio's political past. These concepts were valued and even admired, but were often perceived as dated and rigid, not representative of the life the youth hoped to emulate. These students continuously negotiated historical and mythologized notions of nationalism and the newness of global popular youth culture (e.g., hip hop, MTV, and so on). Hence, while supported at some levels, nationalist elements were eclectically embraced by barrio youth. Elena Cintrón, a vivacious and mature seventeen-year-old, explained:

> One of the biggest struggles in and out of unity is the release of the prisoners of war, POWs. Activities like Paseo Boricua, Fiesta Boricua, Puerto Rican Parade were also planned in and out of [PACHS]. As I graduate from my *escuelita* I will proceed with my education, by attending Northeastern [Illinois] University and study for my social work degree. I chose social work because as a Puerto Rican woman I want to help my Latino community for a successful life.

The FALN prisoners were a symbol of struggle, and at some level an example of community commitment. However, Elena's commitments were much more mainstream.

The type of nationalist pedagogical experience so heavily criticized in the media for its militancy appeared to be in direct opposition to what Latino professionals advocated for students at the local public high school and to the production of the "good American citizen" in the public school system. Ironically, it was precisely this militant pedagogy that promoted traditional mobility roads among the most marginalized Latino youth. At the same time most public high school students fell through the wide cracks of an educational system that had consistently failed to address their immediate and long-term needs. Even though mainstream literature on education would lead one to think that nationalist pedagogy leads to despair and resentment, the opposite appears to be true. Like most of her classmates Elena spent long hours worrying about college applications, filling out financial aid forms, and valuing academic credentials as her ticket to becoming a professional.

This type of education and the performative nationalism of PACHS creates an ironic predicament. When articulated at multiple institutional and political levels and not just as individual behavior, this politicized education leads the most "at-risk" barrio youth closer to mainstream mobility roads: students finish high school, abandon gangs, and pursue lawful employment (Ramos-Zayas 1998). This form of pedagogy is not necessarily a panacea for structural inequalities, any more than the educational program of U.S. public schools has been for Latino and African American youths. Nor does it necessarily produce other outcomes such as college graduation, pursuit of high-paid employment, and mobility into the middle class. Rather, a politicized understanding of power, inequality, and historical processes engendered by this type of educational praxis actually involves the most disengaged students in a process of critical consciousness that can serve as catalyst for entry into more mainstream mobility routes. PACHS applied this critical consciousness to controversial aspects of popular culture—the way Edwin did when he saw through Dr. Dre's authenticity claims. When students learned to think critically about the political world, they also thought critically about their social world and questioned, for example, gang ethics. Teachers would not have induced such critical thinking without validating students' everyday experiences and struggles, despair and resentment.

Public schools fail to provide non-middle-class students with the opportunity to learn those codes of power—the mannerisms, modes of speech, style of dress, and networking opportunities that are viewed as "middle class" and "appropriate"—because they work under the assumption that the codes are already internalized. It is by denying access to these codes that schools exclude certain students and perpetuate social and economic stratification (Bourdieu 1977a; Delpit 1995; Lamont and Lareau 1988). To provide such training as an explicit agenda would essentially blow the schools' ideological cover, thereby undermining the myth of meritocracy upon which the entire school system and the U.S. class system rest (Stanton-Salazar 1997).

Nationalism as performed by activists and students in Chicago recognized the fallacy of meritocracy underlying the U.S. public education system. Alternative pedagogical spaces like PACHS and other projects of the Puerto Rican Cultural Center challenged the notion that education inherently provides leverage for social equality. These pedagogical spaces served a dual political mission. Not only did they challenge dominant notions of merit, poverty, privilege, and mobility, but they also crafted critical discourses to explain this inequality as a direct consequence of U.S. colonialism in Puerto Rico and internal colonialism of Puerto Ricans in the United States. Students interpreted their negative experiences in mainstream educational settings in the broader sociohistorical context of the inequalities inherent in the U.S. public school system. This was then discursively analyzed and validated through the rhetoric of Puerto Rican nationalism deployed by the teacher-activists.

An examination of alternative educational spaces like PACHS expands and challenges commonly held views of high school student retention. Clemente High School has historically experienced attrition rates approaching 80 percent (Ad-Hoc Committee for Clemente Community Hearings 1998, 5). One hundred percent of the students in the PACHS class of 1995 graduated. Although these two schools are not perfectly comparable— Clemente High School has over 2,400 students, while PACHS has about seventy-five—students at both schools share similar backgrounds. For ex-

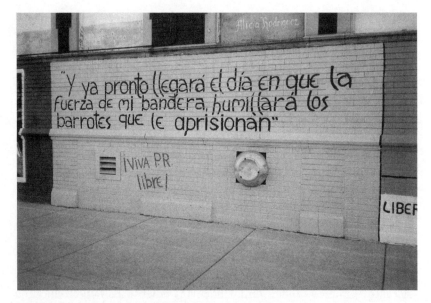

One of the murals painted on the walls of the Puerto Rican Cultural Center read "And soon the day will come when the strength of my flag will humiliate the bars that imprison it. . . . Long live a free Puerto Rico!" (Author's photo)

ample, they live in some of the areas of highest of infant mortality and AIDS infection rates in the country, their parents are often jobless or under-employed, and so on. In fact, PACHS students are often worse off than Clemente students, since the students get to PACHS as a last-resort school after having been expelled from Clemente and other area public schools.

Nationalist activists promoted an oppositional education that was grounded in an understanding of the political economy and colonialist history of Puerto Ricans in the United States and on the Island. These educational spaces forged a nationalism that involved second-generation youth in the creation of dynamic notions of "nation" and of "community" as surrogate nation. PACHS students demonstrated their critical perceptions of the American dream, inequality, the dominant racial order, and privilege, and their perceptions were not only validated by the adults at the high school, but were in tandem with the very nature of the nationalist project. Youth culture was not undermined by or easily displaced to the margins of the nationalist projects. Instead, nationalists were forced to contend with the rhetorical idioms through which younger generations launched their critique of the U.S. system: rap culture, use of Spanglish, perception of essentialist cultural symbols (e.g., traditional rural imagery of the *jíbaro*) as "tacky," for instance.

GENDERED NATIONALISM, RACIALIZATION, AND THE UNITY
FOR SOCIAL ANALYSIS CLASS

The image of the Puerto Rican woman as an exclusive bearer of traditions, grounded in patriarchal images of motherhood and sexuality, is susceptible to colonial transformation of this image into a sign of the inherently oppressive, *machista* nature of the entire Puerto Rican cultural tradition.[6] Chicago nationalist activists aimed to challenge this colonial strategy by presenting women as an amalgam of traditional and revolutionary imagery. Conflictual deployment of traditional gender norms, such as various understandings about motherhood, became evident among male activists at the cultural center during Amarilis Martínez's pregnancy.

Amarilis, a Puerto Rican teacher in her late twenties, was one of the most active teachers at PACHS. Her enormous time commitment and unconditional dedication earned Amarilis entrance into the highest level of political involvement in the inner nationalist circles. This meant that she was expected to show even more commitment to the center's political causes, to attend regular meetings and academic sessions conducted by the center's executive director, to be available to house guests at short notice, and so on. When she became pregnant and gave birth to her second child, her need to limit her involvement caused sudden tensions between Amarilis and some of the other activists, including other women, like Lola Rivera, a highly-esteemed teacher at Clemente High School and a volunteer at the cultural center. "She has become too maternal," Lola and PACHS director Luis Guzmán repeatedly commented. "Breast feeding the baby in public is a way of perpetuating traditionally female stereotypes," another male activist claimed.

The activists' discomfort with traditionally female roles, even when these roles have conventionally been considered elements of authentic Puerto-Ricanness they aimed to promote through community-building projects, describes an unofficial political work of emotion, where "feeling rules" served to sustain the ideological and practical bases of institutionalized nationalism. As Arlie Hochschild argues, "one can defy an ideological stance by inappropriate affect and by refusing to perform the emotion management necessary to feel what, according to the official frame, it would seem fitting to feel" (1979, 567). Local activists' supposedly progressive gender ideology, which rendered traditionally female roles oppressive, served to sustain a political work that paradoxically required the participants to be full-time activists. The irony of Lola's comment became most evident a few weeks later when Lola, Luis, and I went to dinner at a local restaurant.

Lola, an energetic and assertive Puerto Rican woman in her mid-thirties, was an avid advocate for the release of the FALN prisoners. A devoted and engaging educator, she had been recognized as "superior teacher of the year" at Clemente High School, where she had worked for some years. Lola graduated from PACHS and for the previous several years had been teaching on and off at the alternative high school as well. Lola claimed to be single by choice and emphatically condemned marriage as an oppressive institution. "Lola is a ball of fire," people commented of her. "She doesn't let any man take advantage of her." Lola did not walk into a room, but stormed into it. Her strong character and often abrupt manner appeared at odds with the romantic poetry she had written and published in the cultural center's *Editorial Coquí*. She had read many of her poems at political and artistic events in the community. One of the alternative high school teachers showed me Lola's book of poetry, which is accommodated under the gender section of the PACHS book room. In it Lola's revolutionary poems are interspersed with the romantic ones.

Some of these romantic poems are directed toward a fellow nationalist activist whom Lola dated even though he had just separated from another *compañera*. Although the male activist who inspired these poems took pride in being the source of Lola's affection and erratically continued to pursue Lola, he often would admit that he needed to stay away from her because he did not want her to fall in love with him. Her romantic poetry surprised most people: they perceived Lola as someone who "doesn't take shit from anybody," yet she wrote poems of unrequited love to a *compañera*'s former husband. Lola was perceived—and projected herself—as the revolutionary woman who had broken loose from stereotypically female roles; she did not want marriage or children, but chose the struggle for freedom, however loosely defined such visions were.

Nationalist opposition was consolidated in the image of the New Revolutionary Woman as the Puerto Rican ideal of femininity, which provides an alternative to polarized images of "the mother" (of Chatterjee's "inner domain") versus "the revolutionary" (of the public domain). While many females are noted for their participation in political struggle, thus legitimizing struggle as a terrain of women's emancipation, "revolutionary" Puerto Rican women—like Lolita Lebrón, the revolutionary woman par excellence—are present only on the public stage of anticolonialist politics. For instance, Lolita Lebrón's womanness is separated from her participation in anticolonial politics and filtered into the political scene only insofar as it is sexualized as the fantasy of male revolutionaries: the beautifully manicured Lolita Lebrón wearing four-inch heels and a fitted dress during her anticolonial attack on the U.S. Congress. This illustrates the nationalist emphasis on the degree to which and the manner in which women and men challenge colonialism and gender the nation. No matter what the changes in the external condition of women are, they must not lose their feminine virtues.

The New Revolutionary Woman serves two complementary purposes. It is a position from which to consider the historical U.S. colonial control of Puerto Rican women's bodies—for example, in the population-control measures of the 1970s—and from which to challenge the idea that the colonial government's supposedly more liberal views on gender and race are needed to redeem Puerto Rican women and civilize Puerto Rican culture. Nationalist processes orchestrate social reform by claiming to empower women while countering colonial power's focus on oppressive antimodern traditions and its blaming of "Puerto Rican culture" for the presence of such traditions. These processes juxtapose tradition and an image of the new woman as militarily and sexually powerful.

Hence, the contestation around the "woman question" in nationalist discourse has to do with the specific conditions of women within a specific set of social relationships and dynamics of subordination. This contestation is framed by a machismo that has historically been attributed to colonized minorities—a tradition of attribution that was itself produced by the colonialist discourse. This discourse assumed the complete submission of all Puerto Rican women to the dictates of the figure of the mother and emphasized that the way to redeem women from this traditional image was through heavy-handed population-control programs, including the infamous *operación*—the sterilization of thousands of Puerto Rican women without their full understanding or consent (Ramírez de Arellano and Scheipp 1983)—and using Puerto Rican women as guinea pigs for untested birth control pills in the 1970s (García 1982). The U.S. emphasis on civilizing reproduction and sexual practices, both discursively and in action, was critical in demarcating the Puerto Rican nationalist opposition to colonial rule.

Puerto Rican nationalist activists condemn machismo, which is often explained as a by-product of Puerto Rican colonial experience. In practice, however, women are expected to see machismo as a sort of prolonged illness, constantly treated but without real hope for a cure. Author Ana Lydia Vega (1989) cleverly describes this form of neomachismo as being "endowed of a good conscience" that is "bullet-proof." Vega criticizes the painful gender struggles that develop in the context of committed social work, successful community building, and passionate political beliefs.

Tensions between Puerto Rican male teachers and two white female teachers at a youth education program escalated when the male teachers decided that the young male participants would not attend an International Women's Day march unless they marched side by side with the female students. The International Women's Day leaders wanted all the men to walk behind the women, the two white female teachers explained. A male teacher commented, "Our guys are too oppressed by colonialism as it is to also have them stand behind . . . and have white women in front." The white female teachers at the program argued that the march was a one-day women's solidarity demonstration that had already been set up by other organizations, so all men should show their support by walking in back. When a Puerto Rican male teacher joked that "the women cannot use our bus to go to the march, because we're taking the boys to play basketball," tensions peaked.[7] The hierarchy of subordination and oppression—so clearly determined in the colonized-colonizer dichotomy—is unsustainable when gender becomes a category of subjugation and is constructed in opposition to Puerto-Ricanness, which aims to erase gender on behalf of national unity.

Among Puerto Rican nationalist activists in Chicago, restructuring gender ideologies to correspond to the boundaries of the "nation" required better control of the embodiment of the nation and continuous emotion management based on reshaped feeling rules. Hochschild's model of emotion management defines "feeling rules" as "the side of ideology that deals with emotion and feeling. Emotion management is the type of work it takes to cope with feeling rules" (1979, 551).[8] As Hochschild argues, "rules for managing feelings are implicit in any ideological stance; they are the 'bottomside' of ideology" (566). When an individual changes an ideological stance, the rules dictating the cognitive and emotive reactions to the new situation change as well (567).[9]

As Lillian Guerra argues about views of women in the formation of a national identity in Puerto Rico: "Women were viewed as essentially good and bad. Their sexuality made them dangerous, their maternity positive to the community as a whole" (1998, 249). The construction of the nation through popular nationalist discourse in Chicago deliberately subverted such conceptualization of the female body by deflecting traditional female roles perceived as characteristic of the imagined Island-nation. Instead, popular nationalism in Chicago claimed a higher moral ground in its conflation of women and the nation, in which traditional female roles—particularly motherhood—were deliberately subordinated to roles that masculinize the feminine, particularly by idealizing women's sexual prowess. Two processes dominated the articulation of the nation and the body as spaces of resistance. First, traditional female roles were perceived as threatening to the nation and to a nationalism rooted in community building and radicalization.

Second, the imagery of the New Revolutionary Woman, conflating sexual prowess and anticolonial militancy, became the idealized representation of the national female body.

The image of the New Revolutionary Woman, as the sexualized muse of male fantasies, has inspired Puerto Rican popular folklore in Puerto Rico and the United States.[10] The nation is textualized through metaphors of the body that are part of the discourse that has organized, unified, and legitimated various forms of social organization, and the language of the body continues to have a particular importance for the way the nation is understood (Carey-Webb 1998; Radcliffe and Westwood 1996). These metaphors inscribe the female body in the nation and use the body as a strategic space of resistance to militant nationalist discourse. In this sense, conflating the personal and national history in prose and musical lyrics locates and historicizes the inscription of identity. This idealized Puerto Rican revolutionary woman has been described in poetry as well.[11] Identity becomes "textual rather than bodily, something that is constructed out of patterns of discourse, something that must 'be read,' interpreted, something which, like the space within the borders of colonial administration, can be reinscribed" (Carey-Webb 1998, 164). The female body also becomes metaphor of the imagined community of the nation; it is rendered emblematic of the social practices that sustain and reinvent national traditions (Di Leonardo 1984; Hobsbawm and Ranger 1983) and integral to the reproduction of intracommunal hierarchies (Guerra 1998).

The contradictions and double standards in these "revolutionary" gender ideologies surface often. For instance, Lola Rivera often professed not to want to have children. "One's breasts get saggy and men stop liking you. . . . You know how the first thing men notice when you're having sex is saggy breasts," Lola commented in a conversation with another barrio activist and me. "But, if you always say you couldn't care less about what men think of you, how come you're basing your decision [not to have kids] on pleasing men?" I responded. "Well, men don't like to have sex with women with saggy breasts." Lola's reply shows her effort to embrace general attitudes toward motherhood that are consonant with rigid understandings of nation and community. Lola relinquishes aspects of womanhood that her male revolutionary counterparts reject, while continuing to try to please these men sexually. However, she also feels the freedom to express anger and aggression.

Gilda Zwerman (1994, 1995) interviewed fourteen women associated with post–New Left insurgent organizations in the United States. Five of her interviewees are Puerto Rican women, members of the FALN and founders of the cultural center. Examining the lure armed struggle had for these women, Zwerman speculates[12] that it allowed them to cover up aspects of their socialization that made them more vulnerable as women. The New Revolutionary Woman is in some ways the reverse of the traditional woman who was showcased in U.S. anthropology (e.g., Lewis 1965) and the dominant media (e.g., *West Side Story*) as hyperfeminine, matronly, passive, and subjected to brutal subordination to men. It is precisely this degenerate condition of woman that nationalism claims to reform, and it is through these contrasts that the New Revolutionary Woman of nationalist ideology is accorded superior status both to the colonial woman Other and to the traditional woman. Hence, the central ideological strength of the nationalist resolution of the woman question is that the attainment by their own effort of a superior national culture is the mark of women's acquired emancipation (Chatterjee 1993, 127). The dichotomy of the traditional woman and the new woman, while enabling the production of a nationalist discourse that is different from that of colonialism, still sustains false essentialisms and legitimates subordination, precisely by problematizing stereotypical gender norms.

Nationalism has typically considered women as the bearers of tradition and as more traditional than men. They are, in this sense, the more authentic of the authentic.[13] Claribel Irizarry has worked in various programs at the cultural center. In a conversation with Cecile Tono, a Costa Rican part-time teacher at PACHS, Claribel's perception of Puerto-Ricanness as a limited commodity became evident. She was describing a Native American sweat ceremony:

> Unlike my husband, who's white and doesn't have a strong sense of identity based on community, I couldn't help feeling alienated as an outsider to the whole ceremony. . . . I can be solidarious with them [Native Americans], but I can't say I belong or am a part of it. I felt I was intruding, even though I was invited. Look, my husband is white. And I love my husband. He loves anything that's Puerto Rican. We go to Puerto Rico and my family loves him because he pays attention to the smallest little detail of what they tell him or show him . . . and because he's white. But in a way I resent his detached curiosity. It's detached because he cannot be Puerto Rican as much as he may want to. I feel he uses my culture to satisfy his curiosity, his need for community. Through me he feels that he can sort of share in this identity I'm barely starting to reclaim for myself. I resent that. Now that I have a few potatoes, I'm not sure I'm ready to give one out to him. That's

what it would mean for him to try to join in the Puerto Rican parts of my life with me.

Claribel explicitly connected culture with community (or the lack thereof, in case of whites, like her husband). Also, while Claribel herself perceived Puerto-Ricanness as something that needs to be learned, she resented it when non–Puerto Ricans attempted to get involved in this learning process, implying a certain exoticization.

Puerto-Ricanness is commodified and bounded in the same fashion as Native-Americanness is. By contrast, whiteness becomes cultureless, naturalized, and unencumbered. When culture is equated with community, rigid standards of authenticity are deployed by the community-building nationalist projects that create an alternative form of Puerto-Ricanness that navigates the spaces between white and black. Puerto-Ricanness is racialized as a process of political identity formation that has to be deliberately learned. In later conversations Claribel related the Puerto-Ricanness she was raised with to her involvement with PACHS and the cultural center, her knowledge of Puerto Rican militant politics and history, and her growing interest in ethnic autobiographies by Puerto Rican authors, such as Piri Thomas (see Thomas 1967). At a more general level Claribel's ideas of cultural authenticity are emblematic of the progressive culturalization of American political discourse. By focusing on identity politics as a "political stance based on essentializing notions of membership in particular, cross-class social categories (racial and ethnic, gender, sexual orientation), identity politics fails to acknowledge historical change, intragroup economic difference, and a larger progressive vision" (Di Leonardo 1998, 136).

Ideas about gender and racial formation processes are often performed in the context of all-Puerto Rican spaces, like the "Unity" class at the alternative high school. Examining the Unity for Social Analysis class at PACHS is critical for understanding nationalist involvement in public school settings. This town meeting–style class was one of the most obvious Puerto Rican spaces of critical reflection. The entire student body of about sixty students and the five Puerto Rican teachers would sit in a circle in the basement cafeteria. This was a class period, a time designated for the Puerto Ricans in the school to talk about issues affecting the school and the neighborhood, to resolve conflicts, and to plan activities. White Americans, even those who had been teaching at PACHS for years, did not attend Unity unless invited in advance. During the academic year of my fieldwork none of the white teachers was invited; a Mexican female teacher was invited once.

At the cultural center interventionism was strongly guarded against, and the question of who had a legitimate voice to criticize and initiate action and who did not was largely determined by a person's nationality. The white teachers who had been at the high school the longest understood and even accepted the boundaries they were not supposed to transgress because they were not Puerto Rican. The recent arrivals, however, wrestled with the fact that they were expected to remain at the margin of school and neighborhood issues discussed in all–Puerto Rican spaces like the Unity for Social Analysis class.

While most PACHS activists were Puerto Rican, there were many non–Puerto Ricans who volunteered at the center's projects. Nearly half of the teachers at PACHS, for instance, were white Americans. Caroline Richardson's experience as a white woman at PACHS is illustrative of these conflictual feelings that can arise. An upbeat red-haired woman from Minnesota, Caroline began teaching math and English at PACHS as part of a University of Illinois at Chicago (UIC) internship for prospective educators. She recalled: "The first time that I came to the cultural center was with a group from UIC. José [López, the center's director] talked about the center, the prisoners. A lot of people in the group felt that José had a lot of anger in him. I didn't see that. I saw that he was very passionate about the work he was doing in the community." However, after three years of teaching at the school, Caroline began to notice that regardless of the depth of her friendships with Puerto Rican students, school administrators, and teachers, her commitment and involvement would not reduce her marginality as a white American woman teaching in a Puerto Rican nationalist setting.

Caroline's genuine commitment to the students—"I fell in love with the school. . . . as I continued to meet the students, I just wanted to continue to give more"—made her decision to leave PACHS and Chicago very difficult. During a phone conversation Caroline, now a teacher at a Minnesota charter school, commented: "I miss the school, but I also feel that at the school where I teach now, I am getting involved in aspects of teaching in which I wasn't encouraged to participate before . . . like dealing more with parents, attending all meetings."

The rules of the Unity for Social Analysis class regarding who can and cannot attend beg the inevitable question of what message such a nationalist school sends about racial relations and how well the school prepares students for an increasingly multicultural world. Because we assume that multicultural education should create racial harmony, we rarely address the political history that is the context in which racial identities are created. Unity class was intended as a practical tool for conflict resolution through the creation of a feeling of "we-ness" (as in "we are in this together as Puerto

Ricans"). In this context Puerto-Ricanness gave students access rather than denying them entrance, as is generally the case for Latino youths in mainstream institutions.

Moreover, Unity class was perceived as a space for self-criticism—about oneself and one's community. It was perceived as a place where it was safe to air dirty laundry without the threat that such self-criticism will enhance misrepresentation. Finally, Unity class aimed to create a performance of nationalism that would be applicable to other groups. Non–Puerto Rican students (about 5 percent of PACHS students were Mexican, Dominican, or Central American) attended Unity and were encouraged to learn about their own nationalities. They were urged to search into the struggles undergone by the populations with whom they identified and to consider how these struggles related to colonialism, imperialism, and inequality. Nevertheless, PACHS, and particularly the Unity class, exhibited a chauvinism common to most nationalist movements.

The historical context of barrio politics was evoked in the discourse and deployed as a performative nationalist pedagogy as students positioned themselves as "historical transgressors" in their own right. In this sense, "knowledge is not only contemplative but practical sensuous activity, and through such activity human beings can navigate between fatalism and romantic idealism in order to create history with a purpose" (McLaren 1998, 103). These were politics of bodily and affective investment that were grounded in theoretical and relational knowledge and provided students with a language of social analysis, cultural critique, and social activism (McLaren 1997; Kincheloe and Steinberg 1997).

PACHS students knew their school was controversial because of its politics. As PACHS student Mike Rivera mentioned jokingly: "My grandmother thinks they teach us how to make bombs here!" They encountered these images of radicalism and terrorism in press conferences and newspaper headlines. Most students appreciated the role of community building in addressing some of their immediate social needs. However, in the long term these younger Puerto Ricans hoped to pursue mainstream mobility roads—for example, attaining a higher level of education—to relieve their material condition and enable themselves to move out of the area where most cultural center community development was taking place and where the surrogate nation was being constructed. These seemingly contradictory objectives were articulated, transformed, and contested by means of the relational and theoretical ways in which nationalism was performed through a politicized pedagogy.

Nevertheless, at the root of the politicized pedagogical process was the notion of giving back, which was also promoted by PACHS and the cultural center. As Diana Soltero, an upbeat seventeen-year-old PACHS student, powerfully conveyed:

> I came [to PACHS] with very little knowledge about my people, my community, and my history. But I came out with enough to give people a good argument and to know what I am talking about. I chose to pursue my college education and major in Criminal Justice. I would like to come back someday and help my people, and of course my *escuelita*. In the four years that I have been here, we have struggled as a family to keep this school open, and we have luckily succeeded. If I had a wish, I would wish that the students, teachers, and staff would never have to struggle again.

The PACHS pedagogy helped students to understand social obstacles, and while they were critical of the American dream, the students hoped for the social mobility to which they had learned to feel entitled.

The politicized youth culture was grounded in awareness of alternative, militant Puerto Rican history; autobiographical ethnic literature; and positioning of self in a global sociohistorical context—key PACHS philosophical components. In practice these philosophical components promoted resilience among disenfranchised youth and permeated other community forums in which the cultural center's activists were involved, such as the local school council at the area public high school. By becoming acquainted with political protest neighborhood politics and by developing a critical appraisal of socioeconomic opportunity structures—an oppositional educational experience—students gained new insights into their own predicaments, and a unique sense of possibility was generated. And because the school and its students were so involved in community projects, they contributed to the creation of informal critical-pedagogy settings beyond the high school's walls.

The involvement of youth in popular nationalist settings like PACHS was what drove the most disenfranchised barrio residents, including students' parents, peers, and relatives, into this type of critical pedagogy. The performative nationalism unfolded in dialectical relation to a Puerto Rican popular education in Chicago's barrio. Nationalism in these educational spaces was performative because it did not exist in an isolated school context, but was sustained, co-opted, and modified by the political economy of the barrio and by national hegemonic ideas that rendered public schools (such as Clemente High School, examined in chapter 4) the main institutions for the creation of the U.S. citizen and subject.

★ **4** ★

Los profesionales: Public Education,
Class Identities, and the Mainstream Media

Those people come from the outside
to talk about our school.
Looking at the negative,
but never at the positive.
We dedicate this song
to our listening audience:
Don't believe what those people say.
Moving a step forward, never a step back,
studying and working,
our image starts changing.

> —"Echando pa'lante," a song by Son del Barrio,
> a youth salsa band from Clemente High School;
> author's translation from its original Spanish

Son del Barrio, which can be translated as either "The Barrio's Beat" or
"They are from the barrio," was a group of about twenty Puerto Rican adolescents who played salsa music and ballads in Spanish and English. In
1994 the band recorded a popular CD and designated the royalties for college scholarships for Clemente High School graduates. The band served as
the opening act for Willie Colón and other prominent salsa musicians and
played at numerous neighborhood functions in Chicago and other cities.
The main organizer and moderator of the band was a nationalist activist
who taught at Clemente High School, where the band members went to
school. Conservative politicians and Board of Education administrators attacked the salsa band because its moderator and other high school volun-

teers were considered nationalists. Eventually dismantled, Son del Barrio
was challenged as evidence of misuse of funding at the public school.

As some activists commented, Clemente High School is an important
Puerto Rican space. Like so many schools in Latino barrios across the
United States, Clemente has been a site of struggles over bilingual and bicultural education. In the 1970s Puerto Rican students staged strikes and
other protests, demanding culturally sensitive teachers and Puerto Rican
history and Spanish classes. Some of the students involved in these early
protests at Clemente High School are renowned activists at grassroots and
not-for-profit organizations in the barrio, including the founders and some
of the staff of Pedro Albizu Campos High School (PACHS). Son del Barrio's
song about the negative stereotypes harbored by "Those people" who talk
badly about the school refers to a group of Latinos whom barrio activists and
residents construct as *los profesionales*: middle-class white-collar workers,
particularly mainstream media reporters and real estate lawyers.[1] The nationalist activists and parent volunteers at Clemente High School condemned
these segments of the professional class for constructing negative journalistic representations of the barrio, for facilitating gentrification in the area,
and for sabotaging grassroots efforts to "Puerto-Ricanize" Clemente High
School. Barrio residents and activists regarded these Latinos as "Americanized" or "assimilated." In turn, the journalists and real estate lawyers, as well
as the most conservative Latino politicians, criticized the most grassroots aspects of Clemente High School reform for their nationalist overtones. These
middle-class professionals assumed that the nationalist activists on the local
school council and among the staff indoctrinated youth and parents with
anti-American views of Puerto-Ricanness.

In this chapter I examine the role of class, the creation of the U.S. citizen,
and the "Great School Legend" in the performance of Puerto Rican nationalism in Chicago. Given the well-recognized role of public education in the
creation of U.S. subjects, I focus on a public high school (see Bigler 1999).
Clemente High School is a space where popular nationalism is dynamically
performed at the intersection of class identity formation, U.S. citizenship
ideologies, and political factionalism. For the achievement of social mobility
no institution plays a more important symbolic role than the educational
system. The U.S. emphasis on public education is one way of addressing
U.S. ideology's general disdain for all indications of social "incivility," such
as strikes, demonstrations, and other forms of in-your-face political protest
that violates the precepts of orderly conflict resolution and consensus. Society remains responsible for assimilating potential or actual dissent into a

A typical 1970s structure, the Clemente High School building is considered a landmark of Puerto Rican Chicago. (Courtesy of Liz Cosgrove)

prescribed public sphere where values remain unchanged as room is made for new groups to join "the American celebration of culture" (Aronowitz 1997, 192). Thus, while a high school diploma may no longer guarantee a job, it has become the premier evidence that informs employers that the candidate is reliable. The credential signifies a student's mobility aspirations. The centrality of education, and particularly of high school education, is evidence that although U.S. citizens differ with one another concerning economic and social policy and form distinct political parties, "on the whole they agree on the underlying free-market, capitalist framework of social arrangements" (Aronowitz 1997, 191). Among other things, this arrangement presupposes the historic success of immigrant groups, which is attributable to a common ground of values and beliefs, largely transmitted through the educational system.

Such understandings of the public school are at odds with the front-page newspaper articles and other mainstream media coverage in Chicago during the summer and fall of 1995, which depicted Clemente High School as a bastion of Puerto Rican anti-Americanness and terrorism.[2] The controversy these criminalized representations of the public high school generated among Latino professionals, grassroots activists, barrio youth and parents, and religious groups illustrates how nationalism becomes an alternative vocabulary that radically different constituencies deploy to talk about internal class stratification: official U.S. nationalist idioms and separatist Puerto Rican nationalism alike are deployed for the everyday social construction of class identities among Puerto Ricans, who are traditionally and homogeneously "underclassed" by dominant society. Although in the economic sense Puerto Ricans do collectively remain at the very bottom of the U.S. class hierarchy, class identities continue to be internally formed, problematized, and renegotiated. Questions of Puerto Rican internal class categories and stratification in Chicago are inseparable from, mediated by, and even hidden under a separatist nationalist idiom and community-building practices.

The "hiddenness of class" in the United States operates at various levels. At the level of public culture or discourse it "means that the discourse is muted and often unavailable, subordinated to virtually every other kind of claim about social success and social failure" (Ortner 1998, 14). The poverty (or "lower-class") pole of the U.S. class scale has been mapped almost exclusively onto race in both sociological and popular literature on the "underclass" and the culture of poverty (Lewis 1966; Wilson 1987; see Moore and Pinderhughes 1993). The consequent conflation of race and class that routinely appears in the media as the "paradigmatic poor" presupposes the existence of aggregate groups that can be subsumed under single-term categories like race and ethnicity (Urciuoli 1993). The conflation of race and class in a nationalist idiom among Puerto Ricans in Chicago also suggests the hegemonic operations underlying notions of meritocracy, disadvantage, and mobility. In this sense the identity can be fluid in private discourse but demarcated by absolute boundaries in discourses authorized by the state (Herzfeld 1991). In the case of the United States, Sherry Ortner argues that "it is precisely in the internalization and naturalization of public discourses about 'identities' that the fusion of class with race and identities happens in American cultural practice" (1998, 14). In the United States class is "spoken through" other languages of social difference—race, ethnicity, and gender (Ortner 1992). Hence, all class in the United States is already racialized and ethnicized, and those racial and ethnic categories are always understood as class categories (Ortner 1992; Urciuoli 1993). An unexamined dimension of this discussion is how the language and social practices of class are not only talked about and displaced onto additional realms of social stratification by others, but also experienced within the group racialized as Puerto Ricans.

THE GREAT SCHOOL LEGEND AND NATIONALISM

Named after the renowned Puerto Rican baseball player, Roberto Clemente High School has the second-largest Latino enrollment in Chicago. The school is located near the heart of the main commercial area of the barrio and in the mid-1990s had a student body that was 53 percent Puerto Rican, 33 percent of other Latino backgrounds, 11 percent African American, 2 percent Asian, and 1 percent white (Cruz 1995; Ad-Hoc Committee for Clemente Community Hearings 1998, 5). Most Puerto Ricans who attended high school in Chicago went to Clemente, which was known as Tulley High School in its white ethnic past. Built in the mid-1970s, the eight-story Clemente building was perceived by barrio residents, activists, and professionals as a neighborhood landmark. "The building was constructed to be riot-proof; that's why it looks like a prison," a PACHS student once commented, acknowledging that the relationship between the public school and the city government has been conflictual from the beginning.

Clemente High School housed satellite programs for several Puerto Rican community agencies, including Aspira's Parents Institute and a Vida SIDA AIDS education clinic. Educational events sponsored by the school, often in collaboration with other barrio institutions, were well attended and were important components of the barrio's artistic and cultural life. These programs, aimed at serving both the student body and neighborhood parents, brought together white-collar workers from not-for-profit organizations, nationalist activists, other barrio adults and youth, and politicians, as well as the media and Latino professionals. Attacks on Clemente High School were perceived by neighborhood residents and activists as attacks on the Puerto Rican community and on the community-building efforts of *la gente pobre* [the poor people].

The racialized social order prevalent in the Unites States makes schools the primary vehicle for achieving upward mobility and for transforming the children of migrants into "good citizens" of the American nation (Bigler 1999; Greer 1972). Popular sentiment has held that the children of newcomers have to abandon their potentially contaminating foreign cultures and languages to participate in the Americanization project being carried out primarily in schools.[3] According to the "Great School Legend," schools provide the leverage for social equality and the achievement of privilege. But the legend applies primarily to the economic mobility of some white ethnics, and even then it is only a legend: white ethnics' economic mobility predated their educational achievement, rather than the other way around

(Bigler 1999). The economic capital of white ethnics in the expanding 1940s economy enabled white ethnic youths to delay entrance into the workforce and to gain the cultural capital that privileges children of the dominant classes in the presumably meritocratic public schools (Bourdieu and Passeron 1971).

The presumably egalitarian public school rewards the knowledge, skills, and cultural literacy of the dominant classes, thus automatically favoring the children of society's dominant groups. Puerto Rican nationalist activists in Chicago created alternative education programs premised on Freirian critical pedagogy in part as a critical response to the egalitarian claims of the public education system and in recognition of the importance of schooling in the construction of nationalist subjects. Likewise, these nationalist activists addressed the sharp contradictions between the practices, beliefs, and values of Puerto Rican nationalism and those of the public schooling that takes place in a system established by a colonializing Americanism. In this sense, "colonial education and national education are historically related and can be seen to perform somewhat similar social functions" (Carey-Webb 1998, 130). Just as modern state-sponsored educational systems are explicit in their mission to eliminate local differences and unify populations, thus ensuring social order and national alliance across racialized populations, anticolonial popular education also attempted to eliminate internal class and racial differences among Puerto Ricans. In the context of these equivalent yet competing tensions over the creation of national subjects, the local public high school in Puerto Rican Chicago served as a site of the production of nationalism, racialization, and class identity.

In the late 1980s citywide educational reform programs gave more autonomy to residents, parents, and activists through the creation of local school councils (LSCs). Clemente's LSC, consisting of barrio parents, students, and activists, was responsible for administering discretionary funds amounting to about $2.5 million a year. Son del Barrio was part of the LSC's initiative to "promote Puerto Rican culture at the local public school," as one of the band members explained. Frequent attacks on the LSC for its use of discretionary funds charged that Son del Barrio and other LSC programs were unnecessary and even anti-American. These claims were centered on two main arguments: first, that state funds were used for inappropriately nationalist projects that lacked any academic validity for the students; and second, that other community agencies, particularly those partisan to nationalist activism, were benefiting from the federal and state funds directed to Clemente High School. These tensions over funding more broadly reflected disagreements over the goals of formal schooling, in particular among youth from poor backgrounds.

It was the institutional manifestations of Puerto Rican nationalism in public spaces like Clemente High School that caused the greatest conflict in Chicago's barrio because such nationalist discourse challenged mainstream understandings of privilege, mobility, equality, and opportunity. Two articles that discredited the moral upbringing of Puerto Rican youth and the politics of local activism appeared in mainstream Chicago newspapers in 1988 (Blanchard 1988) and 1995 (Oclander 1995), respectively. An examination of how barrio residents and activists received these articles illustrates the shifting discursive strategies for political mobilization in the barrio.

THE MAINSTREAM MEDIA, POPULAR INVOLVEMENT, AND THE CREATION OF THE LOCAL SCHOOL COUNCIL

The Clemente LSC was created in response to an article in which three Clemente teachers, two white and one African American, commented on what they viewed as the unresponsiveness and degeneracy of Puerto Rican youth at the high school. The article, titled "Three Teachers Talking," included comments that had little to do with academic achievement and that had racist overtones. For example: "We've got the cross-dressers, we've got the homosexuals, we've got the Pentecostals, we've got the gang kids, . . . and then we've got just the average kid." "It's so funny to see how the girls— we call them Church girls—take off the long dresses and become hot." "They come in pregnant, they've had one. . . . By the junior or senior year, they get pregnant again. Usually by a different boy." "They [parents] don't support college. . . . They don't read." "The community wanted us to service their youth. But the youth that they were sending us were undesirable." "I just don't know if I'd get away with it anyplace else, and I'm just not willing to change my methods of teaching. I'm not used to watching my language. . . . I'm so used to having absolute freedom in the classroom, nobody's looking" (Blanchard 1988).

Virtually all of the activists, parents, and not-for-profit-sector professionals with whom I spoke spontaneously mentioned the response to this article as the genesis of community involvement at Clemente High School. Nationalist activists who had previously been dedicated to the amnesty campaign for FALN members became involved in demonstrations against the racist teachers. Barrio activists, parents, teachers, and students interpreted the attacks on Puerto Rican youth as attacks on the Puerto Rican community as a whole. The attackers were considered Others, since they were not

Puerto Rican. In response to these tensions, Clemente High School against Racist Teachers (CART) was created. The formation of CART was the first effort of grassroots and not-for-profit organizations, parents, and other barrio residents to consolidate a socioeconomically mixed but predominantly Puerto Rican alliance.

The existence of the Clemente against Racist Teachers (CART) made the Clemente High School reform different from reform efforts at other Chicago Public Schools. Javier Molina, a Clemente high school administrator in his forties, explained what other interviewees consistently described. He said that the teachers who were interviewed in the article

> were saying really bad things about our students. They were talking about us Puerto Ricans. That we don't have a sense of history because we don't know our past. They criticized our culture, our parents. It was very, very bad. I went to an activity and everybody was telling me about this article. I got a copy with another teacher and we read it. And we started meeting. The first meeting was in my home to see what we could do. One of the things we did was to respond through community meetings and other things. We were able to get the district office of the Board of Education to remove the teachers from Clemente temporarily. Two of the teachers decided not to return and did nothing. But one of the teachers, the librarian, she decided to come back and sue the Board of Education.

Some workers in the not-for-profit sector believed that the content of the first newspaper article became secondary to the issue of who was legitimately qualified to criticize the Puerto Rican community. As Ricardo Ramírez, a worker at a not-for-profit organization concerned with Latino education issues, summarized:

> That article created a reaction in the community of disgust against those teachers, especially since they were white and one was a black teacher. But as my mother would say, "I can say you're a shameless person [*sin verguenza*], but nobody else can say it." I think that that was what the community did at that given moment. To say "I can be self-critical, but nobody else can criticize me." That created a momentum, when various community organizations came together in an effort to put pressure on the school to try to get those teachers out.

In the 1980s conflict the people who attacked the Puerto Rican youth at Clemente High School were racialized Others, and Puerto-Ricanness was sustained as a nationalist identity vis-à-vis non-Puerto-Ricanness, which is usually hidden in dominant discourses of race and ethnicity. The alliances formed in reaction to the article included unlikely bedfellows: not-for-profit agencies, nationalist activists, Pentecostal and Baptist churches, ward politicians, parents, and students. Every Friday for a year there were demonstrations at the school against the three teachers, but the three went to court and were reinstated. This instance of community solidarity became an important narrative of a politicized Puerto-Ricanness. Not-for-profit educational agencies and nationalist activists like the staff of PACHS jointly developed a grassroots plan to change Clemente High School. CART provided an important community forum for Puerto Rican activists because, as Ricardo Ramírez explains, "the only criteria to participate in CART is to work in the community, to be involved in a community program." In most of the interviews and informal conversations I had during the spring of 1995, seven years after the appearance of the "Three Teachers" article, barrio residents and activists spontaneously mentioned the great impact the article had on the community.

Community members, agencies, parents, and students, who had always perceived themselves as marginalized from the public school, participated in all aspects of condemning the author of the article and the three teachers, while recognizing that the problems at Clemente High School were more profound than those embodied by three prejudiced teachers. A high dropout rate, a curriculum that failed to address the needs and aspiration of "inner-city" students, dated teaching methodology, and the cultural and linguistic marginalization of parents from the school community were a few of the issues raised by barrio residents in Chicago and possibly across the United States.

The foundation of CART coincided with citywide school reform in Chicago (Attinasi 1990). In 1988 the U.S. secretary of education had stated that the Chicago public education system was the worst in the country. The Chicago Board of Education, which had controlled the system up to that point, passed the responsibility of reforming schools to community-based local school councils. The community members and agencies that had created CART were enlisted as official advisors to Clemente's LSC and provided the vision that shaped the reform. When this transfer of control happened, local class dynamics were reconfigured because professionals wanted to lead the reform efforts. They justified their involvement by claiming that the parents, barrio residents who lacked secondary education, were not qualified to tend to the reform. As Ricardo Ramírez argued: "You are giving the responsibility of improving education to people who do not have the preparation. The advantage that we have at Clemente is that we have CART, where we have representatives of community agencies and people who work with those agencies to counsel parents on how to administer the local school council funds." Unlike the other Chicago public schools' LSCs, in which only parents participated, Clemente's LSC included representatives from the community organizations that created CART and Latino professionals serving in an array of roles.

Javier Molina commented:

> The reason why our CART meetings are so important is that there we define our relationship as Puerto Ricans with agencies outside this community or among agencies inside this community. We really understand what each community agency is about. We try to understand the politics of those agencies, what is the goal that keeps us together. . . . From there, we are also trying to develop a Puerto Rican agenda for this community. Nobody knows our youth better than we do.

And Juan Cruz, a pastor at a highly political Baptist church, explained about the creation of the LSC: "That's when members of this community and representatives from various community organizations had to sit down and determine what is going to be done with this space. . . . That's when Jose López and some other activists at the cultural center created a philosophical basis for the development of an academic program named the Four-Point Program, which at that time became our bible."

Two projects encapsulated the LSC's complicated and elaborate visions most clearly: promoting the community's socioeconomic development by encouraging the participation of parents in school-created jobs, and focusing on historical knowledge and community activism to promote cultural pride in students. The reform aimed to have parents participate in their children's education, thus involving disenfranchised barrio residents—particularly the unemployed—in the mainstream environment of the public high school. As a teacher at Clemente told me, by giving jobs to parents "we challenged the welfare mentality, the ideas that we Puerto Ricans like to be on welfare, dependent on the United States' crumbs. . . . By giving jobs to parents, we are building community, creating autonomy."

Alma Juncos was one of the parents involved in the Clemente High School Parents Institute. Alma's fruitless attempt to find employment, worsened by her limited proficiency in English, was a source of great preoccupation for the single mother of two. Alma was urged by the moderator of the Son del Barrio salsa band and a social worker to become a parent volunteer at the newly created Parents Institute. Although the parents who got involved in the program at Clemente were not volunteers in a technical sense, they were not considered full-time, full-benefit employees of the school either. They got paid by the hour and worked only a few hours a day. Alma commented, "I like to work here because I've met many new people. Well-educated people. People who work in different agencies. Any help I may need, an emergency, I can ask them. It's good to relate to people like that." Alma was one of the over three hundred parents who were paid twenty dollars a day to help at the school. Parents provided security during the day and worked alongside teachers and administrators.

The school reform also brought critical pedagogy and historical awareness to the forefront of the academic experience of Latino youth for whom "learning about my culture" became the key to becoming attached to other aspects of school life. This is supported by the argument that "kids will learn when oppression is the lesson" (Levin 1998). The programs to raise sociohistorical awareness among the students included painting murals of Puerto Rican historical figures, recording a CD of music with social messages by the Son del Barrio band, and a trip to Madre Isla, a coffee plantation run by Casa Pueblo in a small mountain town of Puerto Rico.

Many of the critics of the LSC's use of discretionary funds questioned the choice of Casa Pueblo as the site for the students' cultural immersion experience in Puerto Rico. An ecological and pro-independence program that operated from a house near the plaza of the town of Adjuntas, Puerto Rico, Casa Pueblo was viewed as a Puerto Rico–based equivalent of the nationalist cultural center. As I learned from talking to one of its leading organizers on a visit to Adjuntas, Casa Pueblo was started in the early 1980s when a group of people in the town learned about a plan of the Puerto Rican government and U.S. corporations to exploit mineral deposits in Puerto Rico. The militancy of Casa Pueblo around this issue, as well as their open pro-independence stance, earned the project the label of "subversive" in government intelligence records and led to an FBI raid in October of 1994.

The connections between nationalist activism in Puerto Rico and Chicago are noteworthy here because the assumption that Chicago Puerto Rican politics was centered around the Humboldt Park area appeared to be challenged by the existence of less evident "transnational" networks. Although students also did "cultural immersion" trips to Mexico—there are many Mexican students at the high school—the trip to Casa Pueblo was viewed as more exemplary of the nationalist activists' influence on the use of Clemente High School's discretionary funds. Because Casa Pueblo had supported the cultural center's amnesty campaign on behalf of the FALN prisoners and the cultural center's bakery supported Casa Pueblo by selling

Madre Isla coffee at the nationalist-sponsored bakery, the trips to Casa Pueblo were viewed as evidence that inappropriate *independentista* networks were operating at Clemente High School.

Latino professionals' criticism of the LSC's use of funds served as text for media articles circulating in Chicago in the late 1990s, but another important aspect of the professionals' criticism must be noticed too. The Latino professionals whose voices appeared in various newspaper articles and those whom I was able to interview were challenging the LSC's activities in terms of these activities' limited representation of Puerto-Ricanness. The idea that a single representation of Puerto-Ricanness—that of the nationalist activists—was taking center stage over other potential representations of Puerto-Ricanness in Chicago became a less evident subtext of the Latino professionals' and many statehood-supporters' criticism of the Clemente LSC's activities.

During the heated debates around the "Three Teachers" newspaper article, class identity and class differentiation among Puerto Ricans remained hidden under a dominant discourse of racial difference between Puerto Ricans and non–Puerto Ricans. It was the race of the teachers, as non–Puerto Rican Others, that was the locus of barrio-wide debates. That article was significant because it prompted the creation of CART, which was considered "the first Puerto Rican space" by most of the barrio residents and activists with whom I spoke. The two white and one black teacher who had negatively represented Puerto Rican youth and the community in general became racialized by barrio residents who deployed a dominant discourse of ethnicity and race to generate a collective identity as Puerto Rican.

The article marked the first time that politically nationalist activists like those at the Puerto Rican Cultural Center came out of semi-clandestinity and collaborated with local social service organizations. Until then the cultural center had been mostly involved in the trials of and amnesty campaign for the FALN members. A consequence of the integration of these nationalist activists into the social service mainstream was that a Puerto Rican nationalist discourse that initially challenged dominant multicultural discourses was instead deployed to problematize conceptualizations of middle-classness by challenging middle-class teachers' perception of poor people.

THE CONSTRUCTION OF A CLASSED LATINO OTHER

On an overcast spring morning in 1995, seven years after the appearance of the article that prompted the formation of CART, school administrators, teachers, students, parents, elected politicians, community activists, and reporters crowded the spacious lobby area of Clemente High School. A second newspaper article, written by a Latino journalist who had interviewed Puerto Rican professionals, labeled the reform efforts of the LSC and CART as "anti-American terrorism" (Oclander 1995, 1). A general restlessness, anger, and disbelief set the tone as people prepared to confront the media once again. "Reporters always come to this school to talk bad things. . . . They never have anything good to say," a frustrated parent commented, echoing Son del Barrio's lyrics. "Who wrote that article? Nobody interviewed us about it," an activist added. Disagreements over the role of public education in creating good U.S. citizens out of Puerto Rican barrio youth and the political ideologies diffused through the educational process were critical elements of the conflict around Clemente school reform. Parents and other barrio residents perceived the LSC as a grassroots community-building effort, a symbol of resilience and entrepreneurship among barrio parents and youth. Conversely, those critical of the reform at Clemente High School claimed that the LSC was using discretionary funds for inappropriate political events.

Front-page headlines in mainstream newspapers condemned the Clemente LSC for its use of Chapter 1 antipoverty funds. The Puerto Ricans and other Latinos interviewed, most of whom were elected officials and white-collar professionals, argued that the funds should have been used to raise SAT scores and students' grades. These professionals felt that the parameters of schooling had been extended to include nonacademic components that had questionable relevance to students' education and future career paths. Julia Cintrón, a paralegal and law student in her late thirties, commented that she disapproved of the LSC's use of funds to provide legal assistance to students who "got into trouble, drugs, gangs" and to students who had "immigration issues." Although Julia herself had very limited contact with Clemente High School, having attended the school for only two years in the 1970s before transferring to a nearby Catholic school, she felt that Clemente was a critical space for the creation and promotion of images of Puerto-Ricanness in Chicago. Like Julia, other Latino professionals viewed Clemente High School as a space that had become appropriated by a group of grassroots activists and parents who were not sufficiently informed about issues concerning education or able to orient the students to pursue good careers, which they invariably defined as those in the high-paying professions.

The members of the LSC did not understand why the choices they had made over ambiguously defined discretionary funds were so harshly criticized. The council had invested the money in giving parents part-time jobs as teachers aides or hallway patrollers through the Parents Institute, financing students' trips to Puerto Rico and Mexico, opening a legal clinic to advise students and parents on migration-related issues and drug and gang cases, promoting cultural activities at the school, hiring two consultants to develop a multicultural curriculum, and pursuing other projects that the LSC perceived as educational. Confusion and debate over the use of school funds and divergent views of adequate schooling were certainly not exclusive to Clemente High School; they are common to public high schools nationwide. What makes the Clemente High School case distinct is that an explicitly Puerto Rican nationalist discourse was deployed in the articulation of tensions between the barrio residents and activists who supported the LSC's judgment over funding and other Latinos, mostly Latino professionals, who viewed the LSC as incompetent at best.

In the public debate that followed critics scrutinized how barrio residents, students, and activists had used discretionary funds, emphasizing the connection between the LSC and Chicago advocates of Puerto Rico's independence. "Funds earmarked for the education of poor children have dwindled" (Oclander 1995, 1), a *Chicago Sun-Times* article claims. A Chicago alderman is quoted as saying: "That school has become an economic engine for political purposes. It has nothing to do with education." Then the article points out that the two consultants hired to craft the reform "have close links to the Puerto Rican pro-Independence Movement" and that "the funds also were used to established satellites for Clemente at the Pedro Albizu Campos School and Cultural Center—two Chicago pro–Puerto Rican Independence institutions." The article ends by mentioning that "The FBI would not say whether it is investigating the local school council's spending."

While the three teachers quoted in the 1988 article had been African American and white, the few people quoted in the 1995 anti-LSC articles were Puerto Rican or Latinos of other nationalities. When the possibility arose of facing the media as a unified Puerto Rican community, a reconfiguration and rearticulation of Puerto-Ricanness and community in Chicago acquired a decidedly classed and spatial dimension of difference. One of those quoted was a Puerto Rican real estate lawyer who was accused by nationalist activists of "selling the barrio to whites" several times throughout my fieldwork. A local ward alderman who supported the LSC's programs at Clemente and who attended the high school's press conference objected: "Who the hell is [this lawyer quoted here]? [She] has never lived in this community, worked in this community, and certainly doesn't even know this community! Those people are just trying to destroy the efforts of *la gente pobre.*"

Along with other individuals who openly shared a pro-statehood stand for Puerto Rico and questioned the popular education programs launched by the nationalist activists, the few Puerto Ricans quoted in the article were part of a group that barrio residents constructed with disdain as *los profesionales*. One of these professionals was quoted as saying that instead of spending discretionary funds on cultural immersion trips to Puerto Rico and Mexico or hiring educational consultants to develop a multicultural curriculum, the LSC "should be spending the money improving students' basic skills and preparing them for college and their careers."

Juan Carlos Castro, a Chicago-born Puerto Rican engineer in his thirties, agreed with this perspective. "They would probably claim that I'm not part of the community, even though I live in Logan Square and had many friends in Humboldt Park growing up," Juan Carlos commented when I talked with him informally at a Latin nightclub in Logan Square and later in an interview in his office in downtown Chicago. When analyzing the Clemente High School incident, Juan Carlos, a self-proclaimed statehood supporter, explained:

I disagree with the view that some of these people [the members of the Local School Council] have about education. It's influenced by the *independentista* forces in the community. The nationalists are trying to draw young people into their cause, and they feel that their cause is more important than the fact that students need to get good jobs and have a better life for themselves. . . . You see this office? [Juan Carlos's office has large, spacious windows overlooking the Chicago River.] I walk in here every morning and I'm very proud. Because I don't think that to be a real, committed Puerto Rican you have to be poor . . . or be a social worker. In Chicago if you're not poor and [don't] want to have a low-paid job, then you're not Puerto Rican enough. The nationalists want to be social workers, but we need to learn how to make money too. People are not poor because they want to, but because they don't know how to make money the right way, to invest, buy property. My father was teased a lot when I was growing up because he would always wear the same torn-up shoes to work [at the post office]. But you know what he would say? He would say, "You can laugh all you want, but my son goes to Harvard." But to get there, you have to learn things that white kids are learning. You have to write ten-, twenty-page papers when you're *in high school,* not wait till you get to college to realize that everyone knows more than you do because they went to better schools.

Juan Carlos had an important voice in the debate around Clemente High School for various reasons. First, he clearly viewed education as a way to achieve a mobility denied to his own parents' generation. The symbols of status—such as the Harvard credentials and the downtown office—were great sources of pride, not only because of what they meant to his individual well-being, but also because his achievements spoke of his parents' sacrifice, and more generally to the reality of most Puerto Ricans who did not share his financial security. Juan Carlos viewed the goals of the nationalist activists as too limited, since, as he saw it, they were endorsing educational programs that centered on glorifying social service—community involvement or being "a social worker"—while undermining the value of pursuing financial wealth through real estate investment and a high-paying career. Finally, Juan Carlos and other Puerto Rican professionals claimed that they were perceived as "not Puerto Rican enough" precisely because they did not conform to the more common image of Puerto Ricans as poor. Nevertheless, Juan Carlos and other Puerto Rican professionals emphasized not only their present financial solvency, but also their humble beginnings; they were "self-made" successes who had attained the "American dream."

Puerto-Ricanness, an identity that had brought together the community in the case of the offensive white and African American teachers back in the 1980s, did not serve as a unifying theme a decade later. Rather, a critical outcome of the responses to the 1995 newspaper articles was the deployment of complex class identities and solidarities, along with spatially constructed views of authenticity—of who was eligible to evaluate the actions of the LSC. That eligibility depended on each individual's connection to the space considered the real Puerto Rican Chicago: namely, landmarks like Clemente High School and, more generally, the greater Humboldt Park area. "Those people are seeing too much power in this community and they're scared. We're trying to change the image from below, . . . but the efforts of *la gente pobre* are overlooked," claimed a ward alderman considered supporter of the nationalist activists. And yet the alderman also referred to spatial identities that mark Humboldt Park, the ward he represented, and particularly the area of Division Street where Clemente High School is located, as the "most Puerto Rican" area of the larger neighborhoods of Humboldt Park, West Town, and Logan Square. In this sense, Puerto Rican professionals technically living in the community—if one defines the community to include Humboldt Park, West Town, and Logan Square—were excluded from definitions of authenticity when Puerto-Ricanness was spatially inscribed to characterize only Humboldt Park, and more particularly, Humboldt Park's Division Street. The ward alderman claimed to act on behalf of his constituency, consisting largely of the Puerto Rican poor, while relying on the nationalist activists to exercise their classed identity as *la gente pobre* and their spatial identity as Humboldt Park residents in contradistinction to the presumably middle-class, professional residents of the "better" areas of Logan Square.

Self-identifying as poor implies not only the construction of nonagency, but also the political representation of *la gente pobre* as the undeniable embodiment of exploitation and, hence, as those people whose value relies on imponderables, such as honesty, genuineness, goodness, and decency. In the public discourse among ward politicians, nationalist activists, and barrio residents involved at Clemente High School, being poor was simultaneously emblematic of lack of agency and of denunciation of power inequalities.

The debate around the politics of public education points to the development of a Puerto-Ricanness that was internally classed as well as externally "underclassed." These processes cannot be reduced to the formation of a consumer-based class identity because parents and other barrio residents, like Doña Luz, demonstrated their understanding of middle-classness in connection to an education that was considered the route to social status and mobility. More significant, not only did barrio residents and nationalist activists recognize the value of education, but they also wanted the professionals to know that they—the barrio poor—recognized and embodied this value. Pursuing middle-classness involves the important element of being seen by others as middle class (Urciuoli 1993). Status markers facilitate the process by which one is judged on an equal ground with dominant society and resists the unproblematized conflation of "Puerto Rican" and "poor." Barrio residents recognized that when Latino professionals tuned in to indicators associated with poverty (e.g., area of residence, educational level), they generally tuned out the barrio residents' accomplishments as community builders, concerned parents, and "deserving" U.S. citizens. Conversely, Latino professionals did not necessarily view themselves as outsiders to the Puerto Rican community; many of them had deliberately decided to live on the fringes of the barrio, albeit in the gentrified areas. These professionals, while viewed as assimilated and disconnected by nationalist activists and Humboldt Park residents, viewed themselves as having the right to intervene in the welfare of the Puerto Rican community, which they defined as consisting of all of Humboldt Park, West Town, and Logan Square. Nevertheless, the professionals still recognized their problematic stance in relation to residents of the more poverty-stricken areas of the barrio.

While the Puerto Rican population had traditionally occupied parts of Humboldt Park, Logan Square, and West Town, the perimeter of the com-

munity expanded or contracted depending on individual relationships, social networks, and the ideological and political issues at hand. However, *the
barrio* most often referred to the Division Street area marked by the commercial strip known as Paseo Boricua. Whereas Humboldt Park's Puerto-
Ricanness appeared secured in Paseo Boricua with its nationalist symbols
and rhetoric (chapters 6 and 7), the spatialized Puerto-Ricanness of Logan
Square and West Town was destabilized because the residents of these areas
tended to be more mixed along race and class lines.

Popular discourse in Puerto Rican Chicago associated nationalism with
grassroots activism, authenticity, and living in the barrio, and antinational-
ism with professional status, assimilation, and suburban lifestyles. This
association of barrio residents with militancy and of professionals with assimilation was sustained in discourse and reiterated by barrio residents and
workers in the social service sector acting on behalf of the barrio poor. Latino
professionals and barrio activists and residents generally expressed social
distance not in terms of class, but in terms of the political affiliations implicated in competing community-building agendas around education. The
Latino professionals affiliated with the mainstream media, real estate interests, and city politics considered the nationalist activists to be anti-American
terrorists, while grassroots activists framed the conflict as one between *los
profesionales* and *la gente pobre.*

The presence of a conservative evangelical—and particularly Pentecostal—faction of parents and youth at the high school complicated the dichotomized association of the "anti-American nationalists" with the barrio
poor, on the one hand, and the "assimilated professionals" with the suburban lifestyle, on the other. One of the predominant religious sites in Humboldt Park was an Evangelical church located in the middle of Paseo Boricua.
Pastored by a renowned old-guard politician, the church received financial
support from the government to conduct social service programs for the elderly in the area.

When I met Daniel Alvarez, one of the leading pastors of the church, in
the fall of 1994, he had been appointed as a City of Chicago official and had
an office in a large downtown building. Nevertheless, Daniel sustained his
ties to the church and stressed his role of preventing "those nationalists
from increasing their local power." Daniel saw himself and his sizable
barrio-based congregation as antinationalist. Because Daniel and his wife
were very active in Humboldt Park, where they directed a well-established
home for elderly Latinos, they were not easily excluded as not Puerto Rican
enough on the basis of physical disconnection from Humboldt Park or a
lack of community commitment. Indeed, Daniel was instrumental in the ar-

ticulation of Puerto-Ricanness and nationalist views of belongingness the summer of 1994, when a group of nationalist activists circulated the idea that Daniel was not really Puerto Rican even though he was born in Puerto Rico and was active in Humboldt Park's social and religious life. Daniel's "inauthenticity" had to do with his unconditional support of mainstream Chicago politicians and, more important, the fact that Daniel's parents were Cuban exiles in Puerto Rico. Daniel's Cuban-accented Spanish and white racial features, as well as his open criticism of nationalist projects and his affiliation to the Daley administration, accounted for the selective ways in which he was marginalized from the community.

Nevertheless, members of Daniel's congregation were barrio parents and other residents who problematized the idea that all nationalists were poor and working class and that all antinationalists were suburban professionals. Daniel and many of the Evangelical, and particularly Pentecostal, parents and board members of Clemente High School opposed elected officials who openly supported independence for Puerto Rico or who worked closely with nationalist activists. Now and then barrio residents who were members of Daniel's and other front-store evangelical churches in the area used the terms *communist, independentista,* and *nationalist* interchangeably to describe grassroots activism in Humboldt Park.

Violeta Carrasquillo, the mother of three Clemente High School students, was a resident of Humboldt Park whose primary social network consisted of other members of the Pentecostal church she attended. I met Violeta through her daughter Janet, a senior and straight-A student who had been accepted to a college that would require that she live on campus, a six-hour drive from home. Janet was interested in learning about "college life" and "going away to college," but Violeta had been very reluctant throughout the entire process. In particular, Violeta did not want Janet to go with some other students and teachers on a trip to visit colleges, because, she claimed, some of the teachers and students who were going promoted "communist" and "terrorist" ideals. When I asked Violeta what she meant, she contended:

I believe in God and God is my all. Those people don't believe in God. They have artificial gods. Have you seen that mural they have there on North Avenue? They have a Calvary and political images [of Pedro Albizu Campos, Lolita Lebrón, and other nationalists]. I'm a Christian. I cannot accept that paganism. They try to put their cause of nationalism or communism or whatever it is above all else. And they are doing that at Clemente and at every organization in this community, even the local school council. Mariela [the mother of one of Janet's class-

mates] is very involved with them, and the other day she was telling me
to go to some activity they had, because the newspapers were saying
bad things about them. I don't even know what it was. But, what I told
her was: "Those people hate this country, and if they hate the U.S. so
much, why don't they leave and go to Cuba?" . . . I've always told my
daughters to stay away from that. I've raised them in the church. They
are good girls. But these are tough times, and you have to be careful. . . . And instead of helping young people get closer to God, instead
of leading them to the Bible, the only truth there is, what do they do?
They support gangbangers and get them lawyers to get them out of
jail. But they *should* be in jail!

My conversation with Violeta was very telling because she was not dis-
missed as a religious fanatic by other barrio residents as many of the Pentecostal churchgoers were. Rather, she was respected for being an exceptional
mother who had a very close relationship with her daughters, as well as for
being a homeowner and having a steady clerical job and family life, all
viewed as clear symbols of success and stability. Moreover, Violeta had been
invited to Clemente to teach other parents and the students about various
forms of traditional Puerto Rican crocheting and other handcrafts, which
were skills associated with maintaining Puerto Rican traditions. And yet Violeta significantly disagreed with her close friend Mariela about nationalist
activism and the LSC and clearly agreed with the newspaper report that
stated that the LSC had misused discretionary funds by seeking legal assistance for students presumably involved in criminal activity. Likewise, Violeta perceived any criticism of U.S. domestic or foreign policy as an
endorsement of communism, and thus anybody who was anti-American
was evidently procommunism and should "go to Cuba." The comment on
leaving for Cuba resonated with a comment made by Daniel, the pastor of
Violeta's church, when I interviewed him, which suggested that "Cuba" as
proxy for antireligiosity and communism—especially in contradistinction
to religious practice and capitalism in the United States—was a central
tenet of this particular church's liturgy.

Notwithstanding the presence of barrio residents like Violeta who disagreed with the LSC's use of funding and charged that members of the LSC
were influenced by nationalist activists, most nationalist activists and many
barrio residents assumed that there were two clearly defined angles on community activism: that of the poor and working-class nationalist activists and
supporters, on the one hand, and that of the middle-class or affluent anti-
independence contingent, on the other. "That [article] was initiated by those

people again!" fumed a furious José López, the controversial nationalist leader and director of the Puerto Rican Cultural Center. Whenever José mentioned "those people," he never named names, but other activists, not-for-profit workers, and local youth seemed to know whom he meant. When I asked for clarification, he explained that "Those people behind the *Sun-Times* article are the same ones selling [the barrio] to the yuppies. They are against Gutiérrez because he's *independentista* and against anybody who affiliates with us [the cultural center]. They have power."

"Those people," the "assimilated" professionals whose real estate interests conflicted with grassroots community-building projects to mark the area as Puerto Rican, had become the cosmic villains. But designating who is poor and who is middle class constitutes a slippery semantic slope among Puerto Ricans. The terminology has as much to do with social and political tensions involved in the dialectical constructions of classed identities, national loyalties, and social capital within an "underclassed" population as it does with economic capital. After the Clemente leadership's press conference in response to the *Sun-Times* article, barrio residents continued to draw distinctions between *los profesionales* and *la gente pobre* by categorizing the actors involved in the conflict along a nationalist axis. In public spaces barrio residents associated middle-classness and the area professionals who had reacted negatively to the reform with pro-statehood ideologies in Puerto Rico and assimilated suburban lifestyles in the United States.

LOS PROFESIONALES AND THE MIDDLE CLASS

A gregarious and upbeat Puerto Rican barrio resident in her mid-thirties, Elda Aponte had an energetic disposition that was immediately evident. When she was a representative on the Clemente LSC, Elda spent most of her time at the high school and at the main office of a not-for-profit agency. Elda commented that she believed fewer Puerto Ricans were living in the Puerto Rican area than before. When I asked her where she thought those Puerto Ricans had gone, Elda replied:

> I think some have moved to the suburbs. I know people who have moved north. Because . . . when you mention that you live in Humboldt Park, just mentioning the area of Humboldt Park, they already tell you that you're a gangbanger or a drug addict. The people who move out are escaping that fame. Humboldt Park has already been identified as Puerto Rican. By putting up the flags, they already know this neighborhood belongs to us, the Puerto Ricans. Some people have

lived in the community and they have graduated and earned a high position. After they reach that position, where do they have their houses?
In the suburbs. Because they have the money to pay for it and then
they forget about the area.

Like other barrio residents and activists, Elda focused on the nationalist ideologies that characterized the LSC as a predominantly poor and working-
class body. Those who left the area, much like those excluded from the
nationalist imagery, were considered less authentic. Many barrio residents
focused on a dynamic class identity as *la gente pobre* and saw themselves as
authentic for living in an area marked as "Puerto Rico" in the Chicago context. The Latino professionals Elda described considered barrio activists to
be terrorists. Many of these Latino professionals had objected to the campaigns launched in the barrio on behalf of "anti-American" figures of Puerto
Rican history, like the FALN prisoners and Pedro Albizu Campos. Furthermore, this barrio activism was the primary feature in the debates around
Clemente High School, its use of funds, and broader questions of education
and success.

Elda lived on one of the most impoverished blocks of East Humboldt
Park. She was the mother of three adolescent sons who at the time of the interview were flirting with the possibility of joining a gang. When one of her
sons was arrested, Elda sought legal assistance from several Puerto Rican
politicians and lawyers to no avail. "Nobody lent me a hand. . . . I just wanted
information, that's it. I didn't ask them to give me anything more than legal
information . . . to tell me where should I go," Elda recalled with evident
pain. Lack of support from Puerto Rican politicians, coupled with the powerlessness of being unfamiliar with the judicial system and the English language, inspired Elda to write a poem, which I have translated from its
original Spanish:

> *Those of you who are better off*
> *Those of you who have studied*
> *And learned the language of this Land*
> *And who have an opportunity,*
> *Remember those of us who are*
> *Left behind*

The poem, which Elda handed to me after a life-history interview, is part of
the proliferative tradition of autobiographical literary production in the barrio (chapter 5). Her experience of trying to find help for her son also colored
Elda's perception of the Chicago Puerto Rican community. She explained:

The Puerto Rican community here is not united. It's not. I don't know
if it's because of positions, money and all that, but it's not united. It's
not like the Mexican community or the blacks that if something happens to you, your race goes to back you up. The people who don't have
much money are closer. Those get together. Because if you and I have
been raised in the barrio and I see that you need something, you don't
even have to ask me for it. I see that you need it and there I am for you.

The lack of vertical affiliation between the elite and popular classes
erodes the myth of cohesion upon which nationalism is built. A nationalist
discourse served to articulate class identities that were marked not only by
economic distinctions, but also by ideological stands related to Chicago's
ward politics, Puerto Rican politics on the Island, and most significantly, the
political economy of the barrio. In this sense, a nationalist discourse was
used as an alternative vocabulary to articulate internal stratification in the
context of allegedly limitless social possibilities and upward mobility and
professed equality for all. A naturalized class stratification and legitimized
meritocracy, arguably more covert than discussions of race and nationality,
challenges the very core of the Americanization project, more than even anticolonial nationalism ever has.

The antinationalist undertone of the criticism against CART and the
Clemente High School reform, which criminalized nationalist activists as
enemies of the state, legitimized the state's reallocation of funds away from
the school and back to the centralized downtown office. Thus, class did not
remain confined to identity formation processes, but also directly bore on
the everyday lives, community-building projects, and public policy outcomes of the barrio.

Nonetheless, the state remained the invisible actor as Latino professionals became the cosmic villain that was blamed for inequality, denounced for
its capitalist goals, and charged with betrayal. The distinction between two
contingents—the Latino professionals who criticized the LSC and the barrio activists and residents who developed and implemented it—remained in
constant flux and came forth in the Clemente High School conflict. The construction of a vilified classed Other inadvertently protects the state and the
American dream. As nationalism and class are discursively conflated, the
class identities of the interlocutors and their political economic locations are
foregrounded. The middle-class elite and barrio popular classes mutually
created one another as "different" when, or precisely because, they shared
close physical, economic, and social spaces.

While the popular classes tried to articulate class identities, on the margins an amorphous Puerto Rican middle class created an essentialized discourse about anti-American separatist nationalists. "Terrorism" and "anti-Americanism," rather than structural factors, became the vocabulary used by the elite to explain the persistent poverty of barrio residents and activists. Antonio Ortiz, a Puerto Rican banker in his forties, advised, "These kids need to be doing better on the SAT instead of getting involved in those leftist politics. That's the only way they'll be able to get out of there [the barrio]. This is a country of opportunities, but you have to work for them and be well-prepared to make it." Not unlike some of the other upwardly mobile Puerto Ricans I met in Chicago, Antonio was readily able to provide the explanation for his economic success by drawing from well-crafted narratives of his parents' struggles: "My father had the same coat for twenty years. His friends would make fun of him because the coat was so worn down. He never bought anything for himself, because for him the greatest source of pride was that he was able to put his three sons through private school and college. He came here with nothing, straight from the *campo,* working in the factories and later cleaning hospital floors and bathrooms so that we could have a better life." The middle class provides hegemonic success stories and thus cooperates with dominant U.S. nationalism in the project of preserving rags-to-riches folk tales.

Two predominant views of class that operate within the basic Marxist framework are the economic perspective, according to which class factors have primacy in determining people's life chances, and the culturalist perspective, according to which ethnicity and (in the case of the United States) race have primacy. As Ortner explains, "class differences emerge from a logic of capitalist economic rationality, a logic of profit and loss, while racial and ethnic differences emerge from a logic of internally shared identity and externally projected pollution and stigma" (1998, 9). A third view is the discursive perspective, which essentially argues that class is not an objectively defined position in the world, but a culturally and historically constructed identity (Scott 1988; Ortner 1992, 1998). As such, class must be examined within a discursive field of related terms of social identity and social difference (Scott 1988; Ortner 1998, 3).

While class is culturally and materially constructed in particular situations, as are other forms of stratification, the role of political economic forces and colonial history in class stratification carries a particularly significant weight in the context of the United States. The country's national foundation mythology inherently negates the primacy of class and parentage as an impediment to pursuing social mobility. Class comes in racialized and ethnicized packages in the United States, and race and ethnicity are actually "crypto-class positions" (Ortner 1998, 13). The relatively homogeneous lack of economic capital among Puerto Ricans does not preclude the formation of class identities grounded in the deployment of cultural, social, and symbolic capital in the United States.

Among barrio residents, activists, and professionals in Chicago, the formation of class identities and the development of political mobilization around class spanned multiple social locations. These social locations were mediated through a nationalist discourse that positioned Puerto Ricans of different occupations, incomes, and relations to the barrio on different ends of the class spectrum. When a significant segment of the popular classes accused *los profesionales* of siding with the state and criminalizing nationalist activists' educational reform efforts, the class identity of *los profesionales* did not necessarily correspond to precise sociological definitions of the middle class, but was conflated with an antinationalist stand. This class identity was based on the ways in which these professionals attained upward mobility and how such mobility strategies sustained or subverted the barrio community-building projects. In this sense, there was a tacit recognition that there are "different ways of being middle class" (Warren 1998, 180).[4]

Despite the complexity of the term *middle class* as used in popular discourse, and despite multiple affiliations and mobility across occupational lines, there are three general types of professionals in Puerto Rican Chicago: workers in not-for-profit, barrio-based organizations; professionals in the corporate sector; and high-paid state bureaucrats.

WORKERS IN NOT-FOR-PROFIT BARRIO-BASED AGENCIES

Aware of the consolidation of class identities, the Latino professionals whose occupations involve continuously straddling the working-class and middle-class boundaries—specifically, those working in not-for-profit community service agencies—strive for alternative social formations and class identifications. When workers at these agencies "class themselves," they deploy a working-class identity in solidarity with their clients. They themselves grew up as poor or working class and they are proud to narrate their stories of success through their own or their parents' hard work. However, they go to great lengths to avoid association with the bottom of the class spectrum or with welfare dependency.

The not-for-profit agencies tending to barrio needs have traditionally provided an occupational path for upwardly mobile college-educated Puerto Ricans who have been marginalized from mainstream job markets (Padilla 1987). These professionals negotiated class identities that, while valuing notions of giving back and seeking cultural authenticity on the barrio's margins, also open employment options and social mobility networks and generate social and cultural capital. They have developed networks that are very different from yet overlapping with those in which barrio residents are embedded.

These professionals are living testimony to the discourses of bootstrapping, making it, and social mobility through education. They are the poster children of the American dream, not only to the Puerto Rican popular classes, but also to the dominant society. They are the success stories of the land of opportunity. Because of this, their constructions of nationalism are sometimes compromised by their complicitous position as validators of the American nation. To articulate resistance they turn to the identity of *Latino,* neither American nor Puerto Rican, and in their search for what is Puerto Rican, they fabricate cultural nationalist discourses based on their barrio life experiences.

Rafael Otero lived right above his business, a combined travel agency and furniture store in Humboldt Park, and he was involved in the political campaign on behalf of the pro-statehood candidate for governor of Puerto Rico. His clientele was almost exclusively Puerto Rican and, to a lesser extent, Mexican. When asked if he noticed differences among Puerto Ricans in Chicago, Rafael replied:

> Of course, my dear. Of course. That's one of the problems that we have, of Puerto Ricans spread through the suburbs. I could have lived in the suburbs. But for nothing in life would I live in a suburb! I live right here, upstairs, at your service. Because I want to be part of this community. If I live of this community and I am part of it, why do I have to go to the suburbs? No! I want to be part of these Puerto Ricans. When Puerto Ricans need me, they come and knock on my door.

Many of those professionals who move to the suburbs or to the "better areas" of the barrio have extended-family members who live in poverty, and thus they have multiple class identities localized in different ways. Nevertheless, moving to the suburbs (broadly defined as most places outside the barrio), even to working-poor Chicago suburbs, is associated with financial prosperity.[5]

Rafael created his own American dream narrative by expressing his sense that he had options. Yet by virtue of staying in the neighborhood, he focused on the class identity of a "real Puerto Rican"—he was a member of the working class, those who work for the well-being of the community. He said of suburban Puerto Ricans:

They should be part of the solution, not part of the problem. And right now they are being part of the problem. Because if they disperse out there, out of the environment, then they can't be a part of this. There's a lack of loyalty to the Puerto Rican cause. The cause of being Puerto Rican, of being better citizens, providing facilities to other Puerto Ricans. Because the [Puerto Rican] professional has much more skills and more economic power than those of us who are more poor. The Puerto Rican who was able to grow, he should contribute something to this community. He owes it to this community. Because many of those people have studied with scholarships.

Rafael explained that Puerto Ricans moved to the suburbs because of their "insecurity about what they are."

Ironically, Rafael's oldest son did not live in the barrio, but was a banker living in Scotland with his British wife and children. Rafael's evident pride in his son's success, however, did not complicate his view of Puerto Ricans who move out of "the community," as he called the areas of high Puerto Rican concentration in Chicago. Rafael added:

Even though they are educated and all that, they are uncertain. It is like a clown. The clown wears a mask to hide. I think they use a mask. It's not that they feel more American or less American. To some extent, they think that by leaving the area, they are getting farther away from the problem. They don't know that they take the problems along. . . . But how are you going to dirty the water after drinking it? How can you say "I'm Puerto Rican. I advocate for the well-being of the Puerto Ricans" and then move to the suburbs? No. Stay here. If you are really [Puerto Rican] stay here. If they were good professionals, they'd say "Well, what I've learned in college I'm going to apply to improve other Puerto Ricans, so they can improve and move ahead." That is my philosophy.

Most of the Latinos Rafael mentioned did not belong to the class of high-paid corporate executives, but were employed by not-for-profit agencies and state bureaucracies, including the public school system, social service agencies, and government-supported national research centers. Many of these professionals had lower-middle-class or middle-class wages and poor job security because their positions depended on government and private agency funding. They had consolidated social identities that involved the navigation of various cultural and class spaces that, in turn, gave them access to specialized jobs, contracts, and networks.

Most upwardly mobile young people, particularly those who worked in the not-for-profit sector, associated the barrio with cultural authenticity. This authenticity was measured by the degree to which one was a homeboy or homegirl, terms that helped the popular classes to determine whether an upwardly mobile Puerto Rican remained committed to the barrio or was a "sell out." In mixed ethnoracial contexts, professional or upwardly mobile Puerto Ricans could assert a lower-class (homeboy or homegirl) identity as a political statement of solidarity with barrio residents. However, these internal class boundaries were negotiated and coded as nationalist discourses in all–Puerto Rican (or Latino or minority) contexts.

Young, college-educated Puerto Ricans, like Tony Santiago, Tamika Miranda, Brenda Ramírez, and María Echevarría recognized their ability to selectively choose the symbolic elements that were consistent with their professional status and future aspirations. I met Tony, Tamika, Brenda, and María while volunteering part-time at the not-for-profit agency where they worked, and I was able to spend time socializing with them in the early stages of my field work.

An insightful and dynamic Puerto Rican man in his mid-twenties, Tony Santiago taught at a junior high school in West Town and coordinated a program for Latino high school students. Tony's growing-up years were characterized by financial uncertainty. He was born and raised in the barrio, where his father, an entrepreneur at heart, was able to buy a building and set up a *colmado* (grocery store) and a hair salon for Tony's mother. The relative prosperity generated by these family-owned businesses allowed Tony's family to move out of the barrio. Tony lived for about six of his adolescent years in a mixed-income Chicago neighborhood.

But Tony's family's prosperity was short-lived. Increased competition from chain supermarkets forced Tony's father to sell the building and the *colmado,* thus losing his greatest source of income. Tony commented: "My father had bought the building from a Puerto Rican and sold it to an Arab. Now it doesn't cater to Latinos, but to blacks. At that time there weren't places like Jewel or other chain stores, so people really relied on *colmados* to buy their food. It was a really good business." Tony's father thought that if he sold the business and bought a house his financial situation would improve, but the opposite happened. The proliferation of chain stores eventually threw him out of business.[6]

Like other upwardly mobile, college-educated Puerto Ricans working for community organizations, Tony perceived his adaptation to the traditional academic system as "a whitening process." As shown in his connection to his own seventh grade students, Tony aimed to negotiate cultural identity and class mobility in a political economy that deemed upwardly mobile minorities as "culturally inauthentic" (Di Leonardo 1984). Nevertheless, Tony deployed a middle-classness that was not necessarily equivalent to Americanness or whiteness. Rather, he was middle class in his own racialized terms. He explained:

> *Tony*: Okay. I'll put it in the way that my students put it. They see me in two ways: as someone who knows wassup [what's up] because I came from the neighborhood and I used to be involved in a lot of things, like the drugs, gangs, and stuff. So they can't mess up with me in that. Another way in which they mess with me sometimes is [by telling me] "Oh, you're dressing like a preppy" or a yuppie or whatever. I say, "Well . . ." [doesn't deny it]. I talk to them about setting an example and things like that.
>
> *Ana Yolanda*: Why do you think they think of you as preppy or yuppie?
>
> *Tony*: They say that. But at the same time they know that I'm Puerto Rican and proud because of all the things that I'm involved in. The clubs, teaching about Puerto Rican history. So it's a two-way thing. This is what it is: you can make it, but you still . . . you have to give up something to make it. Some crossing. They feel that. I think some of them know that you can still keep parts of yourself. You keep what you wanna keep. Once I took them to my house and they were like, "Wow, it's cultural." Because there were Puerto Rican flags, music. I think they see me in a weird way. They like my car, my jacket. There are certain things that they notice are different from their parents.

In a sense, Puerto Rican cultural commodities become upgraded or eliticized as symbolic capital and acquire a certain cachet. Tony's consumption practices involved the commodification of Puerto Rican culture. Listening and dancing to salsa music, displaying various ornaments and mementos with the Puerto Rican flag, and eating traditionally Puerto Rican foods were viewed as evidence of nationalist consciousness among professionals in the not-for-profit and academic sectors.

National markers were commodified as economic-cum-cultural symbols that, along with other high-culture consumption symbols (e.g., a leather jacket, a European car), were emblematic of an upwardly mobile identity among young barrio professionals and academics. As María Echevarría remarked: "Sure, I have my car that is a nice car [a Saab] and I always have the Puerto Rican flag [hanging from the rearview mirror]. That's the first thing I did when I bought the car. Put up the flag."

María, a college-educated Puerto Rican woman in her late twenties, most specifically separated herself from a sector of the "middle class" that "plays up their barrio Puerto Rican identity while hanging out with white coworkers." María and Brenda Ramírez explained that many upwardly mobile Puerto Ricans, particularly men, "try to hang out with the barrio homies pretending there is no difference between them." While these young women were advocates for the barrio clientele they served in the not-for-profit organization where they worked, they recognized their own privileged position as a sign of deference to those who were still behind. They condemned the use of a "barrio identity" as a political tool, especially by people who had never really "given back" to the neighborhood.

This perspective suggests that there is a "right way," even a morally acceptable way, of being middle class as an upwardly mobile racialized person. The middle class of the not-for-profit sector recognized its academic and occupational formation in mainstream educational institutions, but still sought authenticity by looking to the marginal image of the "homie" and maintaining connections to the barrio. Tony explained:

> When I talk, I can't do it from the poor, coming-out-of-the-community stand anymore. At one time that was me, but I gained position, whether I like it or not. That's why my grandparents came from Puerto Rico to here, so I could gain these positions, you know. . . . When Puerto Ricans reach a certain position it is up to them how they get involved in community politics. It's a conscious choice whether or not they want to. Many don't. Those go into business, banking. The whitewashers. They may still hang out with the boys, but they're more whitewashed. . . . The tough street kid, that's where my heart is.

Puerto-Ricanness, or most commonly, Latinidad, became the cultural capital these professionals evoked into discourse. They argued that they bring into social service jobs specialized knowledge, fluency in the language and culture, and the ability to serve as translators between "their people" and the dominant society.

There were some instances of cross-fertilization between Latinos in not-for-profit agencies and Puerto Rican nationalist activists, particularly because many individuals were active in both camps, and they borrowed ideas from each other for their own projects. Moreover, they negotiated class identities that conflated upward mobility and mainstreaming with barrio social service commitment and giving back. The discursive connection to community building and the perception of the barrio as the site of culturally authentic nationalist identities distinguished the middle-classness deployed by these upwardly mobile youth from that of Puerto Ricans working in the corporate sector.

PROFESSIONALS IN THE CORPORATE SECTOR AND GOVERNMENT

Among the popular classes there is a construction of certain factions of the middle class—particularly the corporate sector—as the cosmic villain. When we deconstruct such projections, we can see that the demonization of the corporate middle class is related to the formation of a nationalist discourse among the popular classes. The performance of nationalism required the vilification of the elite Other who was perceived as a collaborator with the colonial project.

These corporate—and especially real estate—professionals criminalized nationalist discourse. When that discourse was objectified and criminalized in public forums, like meetings about Clemente High School, it was forced to become mainstream to counter accusations of terrorism or anti-Americanism. Hence, barrio activists practiced nationalism as an instrument of civic engagement, mobilization, educational advancement, hard work, and the attainment of other quite mainstream objectives. Nevertheless, government officials considered the presence of the most militant faction of Puerto Rican nationalists in the barrio to be evidence of indoctrination or of barrio residents' opposition to a crucial building block of the U.S. nation-state—the public education system. As grassroots participation was criminalized, educational reform remained controlled by the centralized state, and autonomy was rescinded from the LSC. However, the role of the state remained hidden and was inadvertently naturalized and legitimized by both the middle class and the barrio poor.

The abstract cosmic villain is a powerful metaphor that is critical to the construction of a class identity among a racialized and "underclassed" population. Paradoxically, that vilified identity applied to almost no one except for the handful of Latinos in the corporate world and in high positions in the government bureaucracy who were not significantly more socioeconomically powerful than the barrio activists and residents themselves.

Mike Morales, a Puerto Rican lawyer for an investment banking firm, was particularly vocal about how he felt excluded by the views of Puerto-Ricanness he associated with Humboldt Park and about what he viewed as a nationalist-inflicted Clemente High School. The son of a retired police officer father and a nurse's aide mother, Mike had grown up in a solid working-class section of Logan Square and had attended a Catholic school in the area. When I interviewed Mike, he voluntarily commented on the Clemente High

School "mess," as the media-generated debates were popularly character-ized in the summer of 1995:

> I can't relate to what these nationalists try to do at Clemente. It's as if sending kids to the mountains of Puerto Rico is going to make them more Puerto Rican. . . . I feel very proud of being Puerto Rican, but when I see what's happening at Clemente, I get mad. Because I don't think that being Puerto Rican has to be more important than provid-ing for your family, getting a good education, going on to college. Not that you have to choose one or the other, but I'm just trying to figure out how do I fit in all this.

Because I had known Mike for many years as a personal friend, I knew how involved he had been throughout college and graduate school in efforts to create more access for Latinos, and specifically Puerto Ricans, in higher ed-ucation. While he had never questioned his Puerto-Ricanness when he was in college, once Mike entered the corporate world of Chicago's downtown, he began to question his position in the ongoing community debates about gentrification, cultural authenticity, and community building.

By the time I interviewed Mike in the summer of 1999, he had gotten married and was the father of an energetic toddler. Mike gave me an update about his life since our previous talk and teased me about wanting an auto-graphed copy of whatever book came out of the interview. He explained:

> I still live in Logan Square. I have a better house than my parents, closer to the Boulevard, and now I own a few buildings that I rent. I have learned how to make money, how to secure my children's future. I owe that to my education . . . and my parents' sacrifice and hard work. I will never move to the suburbs, though. I won't do that to my kids. Because I know what happens to the kids of parents who do that. They grow up around white kids, never knowing about being Puerto Rican, feeling insecure. That's why my wife and I plan to stay here in the community.

Like some of the other U.S.-born Puerto Ricans whom I met in Chicago, Mike viewed the Puerto Rican community in expansive terms, as including not only the predominantly Puerto Rican Humboldt Park, but also the more racially and socially mixed areas of West Town and Logan Square. While elected politicians, the media, and even Puerto Rican activists delineated the Puerto Rican community as Paseo Boricua, the commercial section of Divi-sion Street in Humboldt Park and the locus of community development projects, middle-class Puerto Ricans and the Latino elite participated in the production and reproduction of a Puerto-Ricanness that was also spatially constructed, but that encompassed the more integrated areas of the Northwest Side—specifically, Logan Square and West Town.

Moreover, these corporate professionals viewed staying in the community as evidence of a deliberately anti-assimilationist stance and a continuous commitment to acknowledging their working-class backgrounds. Arlene Rivera, a good friend of Mike who attended the same Ivy League school and works as a stockbroker, commented:

> I'm doing very well. I have a nice house in Logan Square. . . . A lot of white people [live in the area], but you can still find your rice and beans and *tostones* [fried plantains], you know. I plan to give my child, if I ever get married and have a child [laughs, doubtful], I plan to give my child all the stuff that I didn't have. Not to spoil them or anything, but I would like my child to go to —— [the same Ivy League school she attended]. . . . But I would not move out of the community to the suburbs. Because if the kid ever thinks he or she is white, I'll be like "What, you think you're white? Let me send you down to Humboldt Park for a few months, so that you get it right about what you are!" [laughs].

The ambiguity of "community" is evidenced by Arlene's characterization of Logan Square as "the community" while she also emphasized that sending her child to Humboldt Park would be a certain way of ensuring that the child would make no mistake about his or her Puerto-Ricanness.

Like other corporate professionals, Arlene viewed Puerto Rican nationalism as a spatially constituted understanding of community commitment. The ways in which this nationalism was deliberately sustained—and even performed—partly because of increasing contact with whites and whiteness became evident in her understanding of buying real estate as an expression of community commitment. Arlene stated:

> Now that I can afford it, I'm investing here, in the community. I've bought two buildings and I'm rehabilitating them. Of course I want to rent it to anybody who would pay me the better rent . . . and sometimes that means white people. Activists in Humboldt Park, they think they are the non-plus-ultra, the most Puerto Rican of the Puerto Ricans. They criticize that whites are moving into the area. And if you are doing well, they feel that you are forgetting where you came from.

They are involved in Clemente and that is good, for the most part . . .
although there is that messy situation now. But they don't see that
maybe this is an improvement for the community, to have landlords
that are Puerto Rican even if it's with white tenants. It had usually
been the other way around. Not that whites are really moving into
Humboldt Park—they are still scared of that area—but Logan Square,
Bucktown, West Town, all that area . . . that's another story.

Arlene is an avid advocate of traditional schooling and repeatedly mentioned the importance of raising standardized test scores at Clemente High
School and of Clemente's Puerto Rican students' entrance into prestigious
schools and high-paid professions. She does not see having these goals as
necessarily incompatible with being an active member of the Chicago
Puerto Rican community.

While barrio residents and activists recognized different middle classes
in practice, a homogenized middle-class Other, or *los profesionales,* frequently
resurfaced in everyday discourse. This classed Puerto Rican or Latino safeguarded an otherwise failed American dream. As evidenced by the Clemente
High School conflict, this segment of the middle class consisted of individuals whose livelihood depended on generating capital from corporate
ventures or who worked as high-ranking government employees. A small,
mixed group of professionals, including real estate agents who reportedly
"sell property in the barrio to gentrifiers"; personal injury lawyers; media
personalities; and high-ranking employees in the Board of Education, the
Chicago Park District, and other bureaucracies, constituted the abstract,
vilified middle class. By virtue of their perceived detachment from the barrio and, in some cases, their criticism of the barrio "from the outside," they
were associated with the state and with dominant institutions like the
media. These Latino professionals, who exerted the power to influence what
is published in mainstream newspapers in which dimensions of self-
determination are promoted or sidelined, operated with their own internal
hierarchies, ideologies of difference, and plural identities.

A year after the end of my fieldwork, the city's Board of Education dismantled the school reform activities that emerged from Clemente's LSC.
The Board of Education claimed that the activists and residents who participated in the LSC were "terrorists" and "advocates of the Independence of
Puerto Rico" (see the front page of the *Chicago Sun-Times,* February 4, 1997).

The nationalist discourse was criminalized as it was manifested in public
spaces like Clemente, as well as through clandestine means, such as an

anonymous newsletter that first appeared on barrio newsstands on the anniversary of Pedro Albizu Campos's birth. The newsletter's content consists of personalistic attacks of openly pro-independence barrio activists and supporters of a certain congressman and an alderman, both Puerto Rican. Every other month a new issue of the newsletter would mysteriously appear. One of the early issues questioned certain activists' sexual orientation and charged that they were carrying on illicit romantic liaisons; described the leading nationalist organization in the barrio as "the Puerto Rican Cult Center"; and suggested that the organization's main mission was to brainwash easily impressionable youth.

Eventually, the publication of the newsletter, which was titled *El Pito* [The whistle], was traced to antinationalist factions including the professionals who attacked the Clemente High School reform. As the Spanish supplement of the *Chicago Tribune* explained: "*El Pito* does not overlook any pro-independence supporters in its attacks. Its favorite victims are the director of the [Puerto Rican] Cultural Center, Jose López; the congressional representative Luis Gutiérrez (D-4); and the 26th ward alderman, Billy Ocasio."[7]

The emergence of *El Pito* provoked nationalist activists to create *El Gran Pitón* [The great whistle] in response. *El Gran Pitón* refers to the authors of *El Pito* as "annexionist traitors" and frames the conflict between barrio activists and the corporate middle class along the axis of identities based on the political status of Puerto Rico, suggesting that the authors of *El Pito* were pro-statehood partisans.[8] Hence, "both newspapers consist of personal and political attacks . . . between the pro-statehood and pro-independence sectors of Chicago Puerto Ricans."[9] Moreover, they pointed to the class and educational distinctions among Puerto Ricans and among Latinos in general.

Unlike professionals in the not-for-profit sector, members of the high-paid corporate segment of the middle class often looked away from the margins or the barrio for cultural authentication while remaining engaged in barrio political disputes, as evidenced by *El Pito*. They did look to the margins for class-identity affirmation, to recognize themselves as *not poor*. Nevertheless, the margins also symbolized the uncertainty of the social mobility promised by the elusive American dream and were a reminder of their own proximity to poverty and scarcity, which they hoped to have buried for good.

The livelihood of this middle class demanded that its members legitimize the state, giving the state evidence of why popular classes were not to be trusted with federal moneys because of their "terrorist" nationalism. The ambiguity of the middle-class identity is a key to how nationalist discourses were rearticulated. The barrio had negative associations for these corporate professionals, yet they still were called upon to represent or speak for those racialized as Puerto Ricans, themselves included. The professionals did not necessarily feel they could be incorporated into the dominant social structures; rather, they emphasized an identification as Latinos.

I challenge the assumption that varying class identities and stratification take place only between differently racialized groups by looking at how these class distinctions are played out in the interactions between various Puerto Rican populations. In all–Puerto Rican spaces nationalism embroiled in racial discourses becomes the main rhetorical strategy to unpack class differences along the axes of community activism, cultural authenticity, and spatial urban politics. Whereas in socially integrated spaces the logic of Puerto Rican nationalism homogenizes hierarchically arranged racial and class groups, in spaces marked as Puerto Rican, nationalism became the main vocabulary for talking about within-group stratification and the political economy in which difference was embedded.

Nationalism in Puerto Rican Chicago did not cover up internal group boundaries; instead, it provided a vocabulary to articulate class stratification among Puerto Ricans, as illustrated by the Clemente High School conflict. Internal class boundaries among Puerto Ricans complicated notions of upward mobility and middle-classness by rendering some expressions of Puerto-Ricanness more culturally authentic than others. In this sense, Puerto Rican nationalism in the diaspora actually served as a means to articulate class-based distinctions in a social context in which class was muted or not generally acknowledged as a major obstacle to individual advancement. Nationalist performances were not only sustained by the debates generated by public education and the media, but also crafted around conceptions of cultural authenticity in reference to the poetics of the homeland. The ways in which the politics of cultural authenticity intersected with nationalism in Chicago were most clearly evident in the readings that U.S.-born Puerto Rican residents of Humboldt Park and an Island-born contingent living in the Chicago suburbs had of each other. A central aspect of the politics of authenticity was the configuration of a grassroots historiography that entered into dialogue with Island-dominant narratives of the inauthenticity of the migrant Other and U.S.-born Puerto Ricans.

★ 5 ★

Cultural Authenticity: The Suburban Islanders, Historiography, and the Island-Nation

Many Puerto Ricans born and raised in Chicago frequently characterized a Puerto Rican elite from the Island living in the Chicago suburbs as lacking a true commitment to the performance of Puerto Rican nationalism. Many barrio residents associated the Chicago suburbs with a corporate professional elite recruited straight from Puerto Rico by U.S. multinational corporations. Contact between Puerto Ricans from the Island and from the Mainland has traditionally occurred when Mainland Puerto Ricans returned to Puerto Rico (Zentella 1990; Vargas-Ramos 2000). Most recently, however, more Puerto Ricans from the Island and the Mainland have met on U.S. ground as more Island Puerto Ricans have migrated in pursuit of academic degrees or higher paying jobs. In Chicago the suburban Islanders have found alternative ways to generate and negotiate nonterritorial forms of being "from the Island" while categorizing barrio residents from the Mainland as a foreign Other. "Mainlanders" and "Islanders"—or *los de aquí* and *los de allá* as translated in Spanish—have remained forceful internal categorizations that in the context of fluid migratory waves have become less and less grounded on geographical location, but have remained ideologically critical in sustaining notions of "the authentic" in Puerto Rican Chicago. I use the designators *Chicago Mainlander* and *Chicago Islander* to emphasize the fact that these transnational identities are locally constituted in reference to Chicago as a racializing space.

The massive and continuous Puerto Rican migration to and from the Island—the *guagua aerea* phenomenon—has undermined conventional definitions of the nation that are based exclusively on territorial, linguistic, and juridical criteria, and renders the Puerto Rican case quite distinct from that of sovereign nation-states (cf. Duany 2000, 5). A Puerto Rican born in the United States continues to be a Mainlander (or some variation of the term, such as *de allá* or *Nuyorican*—who is *de aquí* and who is *de allá* depends on whether the speaker is a Mainlander or an Islander) even after relocating to the Island for good (see Zentella 1990). Similarly, Island-born Puerto Ricans can continue to assert an Islander identity despite having lived most of their adult lives in the United States (LaSalle and Pérez 1997).

While territorial, linguistic, and juridical criteria challenge modernist constructions of the nation, new boundaries—based on implicit social knowledge; strategic essentializing of an American Other; and the possession of various forms of symbolic, social, cultural, and economic capital—generate internal mechanisms of exclusion and boundary-setting among Puerto Ricans from the Island and from the Mainland. In this sense, Puerto Rican identity politics and nationalism respond to the dual nature of globalization, whereby the Otherness of marginalized groups is co-opted, folklorized, or appropriated and new configurations of difference emerge (Hall 1990; Appadurai 1990). In this chapter I examine the intersection of cultural capital, implicit social knowledge, and notions of authenticity in the deployment of enduring identities as Chicago Islanders and Chicago Mainlanders. I explore the production of a grassroots historiography—a collection of autobiographical writings in the barrio—in an effort to deconstruct the ways in which the Island/Mainland polarity is problematized precisely by the formulation of alternative identities that explicitly transcend modernist modalities of the nation. My goal here is not to cast a unique regional Puerto Rican identity as a generic Puerto Rican Mainlander identity, but to illuminate how the identities of Islander and Mainlander are alternatively produced in particular political economic locations and continuously reformulated to convey various relations to dominance, power, and cultural capital.

Among many Puerto Ricans living in the barrio and the suburbs of Chicago, the cultural authenticity of Puerto Rican national subjects was largely understood through three critical, complementary, and contextual racializing discourses concerning national identity. First, authenticity was equated with possessing implicit social knowledge, the unspoken recognition of specific sociocultural codes readable only to those considered "insiders" by that culture, and that social knowledge was context specific. Second, Puerto-Ricanness was necessarily related to processes of strategically essentializing the American Other (and hence, a Puerto Rican self) and whiteness. Finally, "real Puerto-Ricanness" was viewed as a form of cultural capital[1] with social, symbolic, and economic ramifications as it was also inscribed in the body (e.g., in a person's gait and fashion choices), performed, and represented among Puerto Ricans who considered themselves from the Island or from the Mainland.

WHAT DO YOU NEED TO KNOW TO BE PUERTO RICAN?
IMPLICIT SOCIAL KNOWLEDGE AND AUTHENTICITY

Despite the diversity of Puerto Rican *guagua aerea*[2] experiences, the term *migration* often evokes the imagery of the pioneer migrants of the 1940s, 1950s, and 1960s.[3] In the collective imaginary the most pervasive type of migrant is the one who left the Island, escaping poverty, to settle in the New York Puerto Rican barrio; the one whose patriotic love would always be tempting him back to the Island; the one who attempted to attain the American dream as long as it would enable him to buy a parcel of land and return to his beloved Island; and ultimately, the one who died poor and still exiled on the streets of Spanish Harlem. Chicago barrio residents recognized the marginality that the term *migrant* (or even worse, *immigrant*) implies. The emphasis on the difference of the Puerto Rican migrants was almost inextricable from characterizations of this population as poor and starving or living off welfare. Puerto Ricans in the United States, and the action of migrating itself, are embroiled in constantly shifting social planes.

Other migrations have coexisted with the persistent migration of the Island poor. The *guagua aerea* has transported members of the Puerto Rican elite as well: college-bound students to Boston, software engineers from the prestigious Colegio Mayaguez to the San Francisco Bay Area, renowned medical doctors and surgeons to Houston. Working-class Puerto Ricans who lose their government jobs as a consequence of a change in the political party in power also end up boarding *la guagua aerea* to Orlando, where they work in service sector jobs around Disney World. Similarly, marginalized sectors of Puerto Rico's society, from gays and lesbians (Negrón-Muntaner 1994) to divorced and single pregnant women, also experience the back-and-forth trips or self-imposed exile. Individual motivations for migrating, the particular gasoline that fuels *la guagua aerea,* is critical in determining Island or Mainland status. Given this diversity of *guagua aerea* experiences, why does the image of the 1950s endure? This question is key to understanding how Island/Mainland boundaries are sustained despite heterogeneity and massive Puerto Rican migration.

The Island elite folklorizes Puerto Rican migration (Guerra 1998) and defends the project of rapid industrialization by commodifying the experi-

ence in movies like the bittersweet *La guagua aerea* and in the multiple Nuyorican characters interpreted on Island TV shows. Most important, the elite
maintains the right to decide not only which elements of Puerto Rican folklore are authenticated, but also how the representation of these folkloric expressions takes place to ensure one's authenticity. For instance, waving and
wearing the Puerto Rican flag and participating in cultural pride parades
and street festivals were evidence of being a "real Puerto Rican" among barrio residents in Chicago. Ironically, it was precisely such cultural expressions and the preservation of real or symbolic places common to the
performance of a popular nationalism in the Puerto Rican diaspora that
were the main evidence Chicago Islanders used to point to these barrio residents' lack of authenticity.

Many Islanders who had recently moved to Chicago questioned the barrio residents' "exaggerated" displays of Puerto-Ricanness, as evidenced by
the widely publicized cultural festivals and political polemic in the barrio.
Ernesto Villanueva, a thirty-year-old systems analyst for a multinational
computer firm who was recruited by his company directly from the Island,
commented: "I know I am Puerto Rican. I don't have to be talking about it
every second. Puerto Ricans here have to be saying that they are Puerto Rican, displaying flags, all that. I know who I am." Similarly, Nilda Font, a
Puerto Rican woman from the Island who came to Illinois to do a master's
degree in Spanish literature and education, disapprovingly focused on
Mainland Puerto Ricans' idealized perception of Puerto Rico: "They always
paint Puerto Rico as this paradise. They focus on the warm weather, the
palm trees, the mountains. [To them] everything in Puerto Rico is perfect.
But we [Island Puerto Ricans] know that that's not the case." Like other
Chicago Islanders, Nilda pointed to the high crime rate and low-paying
professional jobs in Puerto Rico and depicted Puerto Rico with the cos-
mopolitan images of tall buildings, long highways, shopping malls, and international airports often associated with the metropolitan elite. Chicago
Islanders judged authenticity on the basis of implicit social knowledge of
current practices on the Island. For this Island elite, rural images were evidence that the Mainlanders are "stuck in the past," as a manager at a
telecommunications company from the Island mentioned, and hence that
they were "closer to nature"—the ultimate primitives.

Some barrio activists and residents mentioned that Chicago Islanders'
characterization of Mainland Puerto Ricans was homogenizing and based
on the stereotyped Nuyorican. Most of these barrio residents and activists
rejected the term, believing that it did not apply to them or that it caused
more divisions among Puerto Ricans. Some jokingly suggested terms like

Chicagorican and *Illinoisrican,* then discarded them in favor of a more encompassing Puerto Rican identity. Other scholars have noted that Puerto Ricans in the diaspora remark that Island Puerto Ricans indiscriminately refer to them as "the Nuyorican," the embodiment of the migrant Other (Zentella 1990; Diaz-Quiñones 1993; Flores 1993, 2000). While I never heard Puerto Ricans in Chicago refer to other area residents or themselves as Nuyorican, or even Rican or Spanish (another term frequently used interchangeably with Latino or Hispanic in the Northeast), they did recognize the term as applying to somebody else: namely, Puerto Ricans in New York. Most Puerto Ricans in Chicago reacted to the term *Nuyorican* in two main ways. First, they asserted that the term did not apply to them, and second, they redefined their status as Other away from the term *Nuyorican* by focusing on the class identities and racialization processes that saturate the term on the Island.

Like Nilda and Ernesto, other Chicago Islanders understood common narratives of real or imagined rural landscapes as evidence of the Otherness, the inauthenticity, of diasporic communities. Nuyoricans presumably lack a critical understanding of contemporary life on the Island, and hence, their way of being authentic through folklore is backward or dated, rooted in historical images that do not represent present-day Puerto Rico. The discourse of difference that Chicago Islanders and Chicago Mainlanders evoke ironically involves the very folkloric displays crafted to imagine the Puerto Rican "nation" as a "community" (Anderson 1983) and suggests the performative aspects of Puerto Rican nationalism in Chicago. The implication is that there is a right way of being Puerto Rican: by understanding Puerto Rico in urban, contemporary, and upper-middle-class terms, rather than as a rural landscape or with images equivalent to those of poor urban areas in the United States.

The cultural authenticity associated with being a true Puerto Rican in Chicago's barrio often involved a selectively folklorized vision of rural Puerto Rico and various understandings of the past. These representations and interpretations of the past were demonstrated in public displays of the *jíbaro* (or the Taínos, or Afro–Puerto Ricans) in festivals, in the construction of casitas (small houses resembling the houses of rural Puerto Rican that serve as gathering places for Puerto Rican residents of urban areas), in artistic events, and in ward political campaigns.[4] The Islanders living in the nearby Chicago suburbs perceived these performances of Puerto-Ricanness as indications that the U.S.-born barrio Puerto Ricans were trying too hard. A critical component of this ironic predicament of disjunction between Chicago Islanders' and Chicago Mainlanders' perceptions of the authentic was not always evident in these folkloric performances: some Chicago bar rio residents evoked rural images and narratives as coded interpretations of and concrete referents to the reality of poverty and marginalization their own poor and working-class relatives experienced on the Island, not merely as nostalgia for the rural landscape.

Tony Santiago, a junior high school teacher, visited Puerto Rico for the first time when he was an adolescent and his parents were thinking of moving back to the Island to try to save their marriage:

> We stayed in Ciales with my mother's family. My cousins were already giving us the *gallinas* [chickens], everything that we needed. That was a very powerful experience for me, being there. We went up into the *montaña* [mountain]. We learned Spanish better. I felt they were looking at me like "Wow, over there the U.S." When I went there I did everything. Acted like a *jíbaro*. I jumped in the river, went with my cousins. Played basketball with them. So they accepted me even more. I also gave away a lot of things. My Walkman, my college stuff, *bulto* [book bag], money, whatever. Because I knew they needed it more. I saw their level of poverty.

While reconstructed in the migrant imaginary, Tony's description also had political economic referents to the common material contexts shared by barrio residents and their even more impoverished relatives in towns and barrios on the Island. Second-generation Chicago Mainlanders intertwined their Island relatives' poverty with rural and *jíbaro* images to avoid the perhaps more accurate images of urban dwellers on the Island who are not unlike those in Chicago's barrio. Puerto Rico's urban dwellers remained folklorized as rural *jíbaros* in the imaginary of their U.S. relatives, while the recognition of a shared historical and economic reality of colonialism, poverty, and the marginality of the Puerto Rican poor prevailed.

Conflicting notions of authentic Puerto-Ricanness suggest that folklore may or may not be an adequate expression of nationalism, depending on who is responsible for its performance. Among the Island elite, Puerto Rican folklore is bound to the realm of official cultural events and institutions (cf. Dávila 1997). Being cultured implies neither associating oneself with a repertoire of exclusively modern objects and messages, nor claiming immediate genealogical connections to a rural background. Rather, it involves having the implicit social knowledge of how to incorporate the artistic, literary, and technological advances into traditional matrices of social privilege and symbolic distinction. This is not to say that the Island elite relinquishes popular folkloric traditions in favor of contemporary, modernist knowledge, but that popular traditions are valued according to how official institutions—like the Instituto de Cultura Puertorriqueña, for instance—measure their genuineness (Dávila 1997; García-Canclini 1992). Puerto Rican cultural authenticity is based on understandings of what kind of knowledge is required to be a true Puerto Rican; that is, it depends on the different ways of "converting yourself into what you are" (Bourdieu in García-Canclini 1992, 135) and on knowing the how-to of Puerto-Ricanness.

Among the Puerto Rican nationalist activists, youth, and other barrio residents with whom I worked in Chicago, notions of cultural authenticity were not based only on a putative connection to the Island, Spanish language skills, birth on the Island, or knowledge of "official traditions," although these were often cited as characteristics of "real Puerto Ricans." Rather, in Chicago cultural authenticity involved displays of ethnic identity and natural solidarity (e.g., participation in festivals and grassroots politics, residence in the area marked as Puerto Rican) as racialized subjects in strategic essentialist ways. Involvement in community-based projects and being knowledgeable of Puerto Rican history and politics in the United States relied on being marked as Puerto Rican and deploying this markedness for navigating the social margins.

As LaSalle and Pérez (1997) demonstrate in their autobiographical article, this strategic essentialism often excludes Islanders of elite background. I agree with them that transnational subjects who expose the heterogeneity and inequality of a national constituency destabilize the grounds on which the Puerto Rican "nation" and U.S. citizenship are built, because contradictory images of national selves are sometimes read as confusion about identity. Nevertheless, my findings present a complementary view to LaSalle and Pérez's argument that discourses that pretend to vindicate "native knowledge" through unstrategic forms of essentialism reinforce rather than destabilize the dualisms of inside/outside and authentic/inauthentic (1997, 56). In Chicago, being marked was indeed strategic, particularly when the historical conditions and civil rights discourses associated with that marked identity were evoked for social and civic involvement. Puerto Rican history in U.S. communities became another lens through which to interpret concrete Chicago realities, so knowledge of history—regardless of how mythified or official—was critical to belongingness. In this sense, being a "real Puerto Rican" was based not exclusively on knowing specific aspects of history, but also on mythologizing such history in relation to everyday life in Chicago. Certain forms of essentializing the self were actually ways of culturalizing and bounding the American Other.

STRATEGIC ESSENTIALIZING AND THE AMERICAN OTHER

Though references to culture and to nation appear to embrace community and equality, they provide a model to locate and position individuals and groups hierarchically within society (cf. Virginia Domínguez in LaSalle and Pérez 1997, 64). However, there is a mode of strategic essentializing that draws its references from a history of inequality and oppression and actually recognizes the ways in which essentialism is to be alternately criticized and elicited. Forms of strategic essentializing and Puerto-Ricanness in Chicago were not measured exclusively against a homogeneous American Other, as is frequently the case in Puerto Rico and Latin America, because the United States is not experienced as a monolithic category. Rather, U.S. culture was understood in light of racialized groups—Mexicans, Central Americans, African Americans, whites—sharing various social, political, economic, and urban spaces. Some aspects of Chicago life, particularly those associated with minority groups (e.g., Black Nationalism, popular culture, gender relations) were appropriated and manipulated. The adoption of these alternative U.S. elements enabled Chicago Mainlanders to reject ideas of inauthenticity leveled at them by many Chicago Islanders. This was done while preserving the integrity of anticolonial struggle—for example, being part of the United States without "becoming American"—and while constructing an authentic Puerto-Ricanness that involved multiple processes of self-invention. A component in the negotiation and in Chicago Islander and Chicago Mainlander identities was such a relationship to U.S. culture and implicit social knowledge of Island society.

Essentializing the self strategically involved the construction of American culture and an American Other among both Chicago Islanders and Chicago Mainlanders. The relationship to American culture was ironic because class and racialization processes actually rendered the Chicago Islander elite—bearers of the authenticity badge—as more "assimilated" than Chicago Mainlanders and U.S. Puerto Ricans in general because of their nexus with the U.S. middle class. As Ingrid González, a Puerto Rican from the Island, claimed: "When I was in high school in Puerto Rico, we'd listen to American music, never salsa. We'd listen to rock, pop, you know. But Puerto Ricans here don't understand that." It was this sort of understanding that convinced Ingrid and other Chicago Islanders that they possessed implicit social knowledge.

The distinction between *roquero* and *cocolo* is more ambiguous than suggested by this 1980s characterization of rock and salsa lovers, because listening to a certain refined salsa ("Salsa con clase") is common among the middle class on the Island.[5] Nevertheless, it is critical to listen to the "right kind" of salsa, because salsa music is also racialized and fragmented by class. An upwardly mobile Puerto Rican from Chicago who happened to be a college classmate of mine still remembered how at the Ivy League school we attended it was Mainland Puerto Ricans who used to organize salsa parties. While organizers aimed indirectly or at times deliberately to promote unity between Islanders and Mainlanders along national lines, Puerto Ricans from the Island generally avoided those events in favor of parties with rock or Motown music. Likewise, Chicago Islander discourses of authenticity that invoked the knowledge that in Puerto Rico the upper-middle class listened to rock music were often contested by Chicago Mainlanders, who projected their own ideas of Americanization on the Island-nation. As many Chicago Mainlanders emphasized, their U.S. communities were Puerto-Ricanized and safeguarded and performed nationalism through the creation of grassroots organizations, pride parades, and ethnically oriented businesses. Puerto Rican writers and poets in the United States highlight the great irony of assimilation among Puerto Ricans; that is, Puerto Ricans on the Island claim that Puerto Ricans from the United States are assimilated, while the Islanders are the ones who "eat McDonald's in the American discotheques" (Laviera 1981; author's translation). For many barrio residents, the Island is Americanized, and the fast food chains, suburbanization, and middle-class consumerism on the Island provide evidence of this.

The Chicago barrio became Puerto Rico, the surrogate nation, while the Island remained a fragmented, incomprehensible Other. Barrio activists and residents in Chicago drew upon the intersection of community-building projects, civil rights narratives, and a reimagined nationalist history as modes of strategic essentializing, a way to demand recognition as the culturally authentic Puerto Ricans. The Mainlanders who returned to Puerto Rico and the barrio poor and working classes became the embodiment of cherished Puerto Rican values that had been lost on the Island. The process of revitalization is common in ethnopolitical movements, like those that create community-building programs. The Island invariably remained a geographical referent of cultural authenticity and a driving force in nostalgic narratives and imagery among Puerto Ricans in Chicago. However, discourses of Americanization were reenacted and evoked by barrio activists and residents to describe both elite Puerto Ricans on the Island and Puerto Ricans who were foreign to barrio life, the suburbanites.

Some Chicago barrio activists and residents believed that one of the most significant distinctions among Puerto Ricans was that, ironically, Puerto Ricans in the United States seemed to experience less social mobility than those in Puerto Rico.[6] Adela Díaz, a staff member of a not-for-profit organization who had lived in Chicago for the previous ten years, commented: "My impression is that opportunities here are extremely limited compared to opportunities in Puerto Rico. It doesn't matter how poor the educational system in Puerto Rico is, me and other children from working families were able to attain a higher education. I don't see those possibilities here. The system is structured so that kids don't go to college. Only those who adapt to the system go." Perceptions of Puerto Rico as poor and of poverty as the motivating factor for migration contrast with the fact that a college education is more accessible to Puerto Ricans on the Island, regardless of class, than to those in the United States.

Most barrio residents explained that going back involved a process of self-invention. Carmen and Héctor Colón were contemplating going back to the Island, but they did not have the money to construct a good enough house in Puerto Rico to maintain the distorted image of affluence they had tried to convey to their relatives there. Elena, Carmen and Héctor's daughter, talked about her parents' hesitation to go back:

> My parents have an OK house here. It's nicer on the outside than on the inside. But my father's relatives [in Puerto Rico] are very poor, and my father has created this image around himself, the image of a rich man who has made it in the U.S. So whenever his relatives need money, my father sends it back to protect that image. And when my parents visit [Puerto Rico], they wear nice clothes and bring things for everybody, to pretend that they are really rich. I think that if they went back, the relatives would expect my parents to have a big house and help them out.

Adela, one of Elena's friends and coworkers, elaborated on this idea:

> They [Puerto Ricans in Puerto Rico] get the impression that our conditions are better than theirs. That we are earning a lot of money. A lot of Puerto Ricans from here go back with fantasies in their mind, trying to impress people, saying that they live the great life here. They do this because it justifies that they came here and realized whatever dreams they had. They want to believe they lived the American dream. The problem is that when they go back, their families there are better off than those who are here. In a sense, the Puerto Ricans who go back don't want to see themselves like they failed. The best way is to say that they've made it.

Many Chicago Mainlanders who returned to the Island or visited there constructed an imagined life of affluence, mobility, and wealth to justify their migration to the United States. They conveyed their success to the relatives who stayed in Puerto Rico to prove that they had made it because they had undertaken the challenge of migrating. Yet their limited social mobility in the United States made this difficult to sustain. Nationalist activists in Puerto Rican Chicago believed that the experience of Puerto Rican colonialism was similar for those Puerto Ricans on the Island and the ones living in the United States. They looked around themselves and at their relatives on the Island and did not see a significant difference in mobility paths.

Puerto Rican nationalism in Chicago was performed through immediate social practices and material processes that rendered colonialism a palpable, quotidian phenomenon related to racism, racial tensions, and urban displacement. A failed American dream was lived in the form of social and economic marginalization. This marginalization gave the separatist discourse, and at times separatist actions, of racialized subjects pertinence. Everyday nationalist performances provided the discursive tools to question the American dream myth while preserving it as a hegemonic foundation and giving legitimacy to the migration experience. For Elena's parents migration was justified by the creation of images of success, of having made it, of having achieved the American dream.[7] Because, unlike Latin American immigrants who are not U.S. citizens, Puerto Ricans can travel frequently and relatively inexpensively between the Island and U.S. cities, their attempt to preserve images of mobility, middle-classness, and having made it requires even more effort. Moreover, being from the Island or from the Mainland in Chicago was associated with certain aspects of cultural capital.

THE POLITICS OF AUTHENTICITY: CULTURAL CAPITAL AND NATIONALIST PERFORMANCES

The identities of Chicago Islander and Chicago Mainlander gained relevance insofar as they deviated from or conformed to prescriptive behaviors understood as appropriate at concrete political, socioeconomic, or cultural junctures. They were grounded on critical material realities, such as occupational status, education, and even social networks and fashion and music preferences. Mainlander and Islander subjectivities involved in the deployment of cultural, social, and symbolic capital were only readable by those who possessed that capital. Subjective constructions of the Islander and the Mainlander are severed and conflated in complex ways in diasporic communities. Cultural capital was invoked to distinguish Islanders from Mainlanders in order to preserve a hierarchical differentiation in lieu of a differentiation that is based on actual geographical referents or place of residence. These distinctions became particularly critical at a time when increasingly more Chicago Islanders and Chicago Mainlanders lived on both sides of the water.

A tall light-skinned woman in her early thirties, Ingrid González grew up in Puerto Rico, the daughter of the general manager of a large U.S. corporation on the Island. Ingrid, her Puerto Rico–born Cuban husband, and their two children lived in a middle-class southwestern Chicago suburb. Ingrid emphatically explained that "Puerto Ricans who come here following a job are in a different predicament than those who are from here." She resented that "Americans think that all Puerto Ricans are like the ones who live here. That's why I tell them to go to Puerto Rico and see that that's not true. We don't live in ghettos like here. We're not like them. When they meet Puerto Ricans from the Island, who are professionals, they start to realize that we are not all the same." Most of the distinctions Ingrid made were based on class and on attachment to Puerto Rico, but they were perceived as inherently cultural and as pertaining to all U.S. Puerto Ricans.[8]

When asked about her community involvement, Ingrid replied that "all the Latin Americans we know we've met through [the telecommunications company's] Club de Hispanos. . . . It's a very mixed group, not just Puerto Ricans." She explained, "I never hang out with Puerto Ricans from here. Where I live is more mixed. We see ourselves as Hispanos. Not Puerto Ricans, but Hispanos. I guess this is a loss of identity or something." Like other upwardly mobile, college-educated Puerto Ricans, Ingrid had adopted the *Hispano* label through her husband's work affiliations. This resonates with Suzanne Oboler's (1995) finding that middle-class migrants from Latin America are more ready than members of the working class to integrate into the U.S. system of racial classification. Since Ingrid was married to a man who, though born and raised in Puerto Rico, "considers himself Cuban," the *Hispano* label was useful because it served as common cultural ground between them.

Francisco Ruiz, another Puerto Rican born and raised on the Island, was an electrical engineer who worked for General Electric and lived in the Chicago suburbs. A tall and dark-skinned Puerto Rican man in his early thirties and a graduate of West Point Academy, Francisco had only limited contact with the Chicago barrio. Like Ingrid, Francisco questioned the authenticity of most Chicago Puerto Ricans: "Some Puerto Ricans from here do not even speak Spanish, or if they do, they speak a dialect, Spanglish. They don't speak English well either. They speak Black English, not the English we learn in high school in Puerto Rico or in college."

Even before migrating Ingrid and Francisco had harbored media-enhanced stereotypes of Mainlanders as "uneducated," "loud," "too ethnic," and lacking updated knowledge of life in Puerto Rico. The distinctions that Island professionals like Ingrid and Francisco emphasized between Puerto Ricans from the Island and those from the Mainland were not necessarily based on occupation, since they did not see themselves as similar to U.S.-raised Puerto Rican professionals. Chicago Islander professionals tended to use Islander and Mainlander distinctions to point to differences in attitudes, behaviors, and lifestyles between themselves and their U.S. coethnics. Rendering Mainlanders as Other involved racialization processes that attempted to simplify and transform difference by overvaluing particular bodily differences and imbuing them with lasting social, political, cultural, economic, or even psychological significance. This Chicago Islander elite was aware of the prejudicial attitude toward Puerto Ricans in the United States, and they created alternative Puerto Rican identities that continued to reproduce their dominant status, the one they experienced on the Island on the basis of their social privilege.

Several upwardly mobile Puerto Ricans born and raised in the Chicago barrio commented that the first time they experienced sustained contact with Puerto Ricans from the Island was in college. Tamika Miranda, a Puerto Rican woman in her twenties who was born in New York and raised in Chicago, attributed the distinction in political participation around Latino issues to a distinction in the self-identification of Islanders and Mainlanders. When Tamika was attending an elite four-year college in the northeast, Puerto Ricans from the Island

> had their own social get-togethers. If they participated in political events, it would be events that had to do with the Island, . . . like doing relief brigades for hurricane victims. . . . Stuff like that, they'd participate in. But not in issues around Latinos, race, affirmative action. They would participate in organizations that consisted mostly of Latin American students directly from Latin America, not Latinos. The Latinos from the U.S. would participate in more political organizations. We would make alliances with Chicanos and African Americans. I could tell that I had little in common with Puerto Ricans from the Island, but I thought it was because they all knew each other before they even came here to college. Their families knew each other in Puerto Rico. Some of them went to the same private schools on the Island.

Steven Figueroa, another upwardly mobile Chicago Mainlander, perceived this Islander contingent as an elite that "knew each other from Puerto Rico, even before coming to college here. I remember that I thought it was weird that they had all gone to the same three or four schools on the Island. For a while I thought, *Aren't there any more schools in Puerto Rico? Everyone I meet has gone to the same ones!* And they all lived in Guaynabo [an upper-middle-class suburb of San Juan]. And we'd be like 'What's Guaynabo anyways? A fruit?'"

What was at stake here was that the Chicago Islander and Chicago Mainlander identities were constructed, negotiated, and sustained despite the evident deterritorialization of the Puerto Rican nation, precisely because these internal boundaries were based on symbolic, cultural, social, and even economic capital, as well as on the ways in which nationalism was performed. Elite high schools in Puerto Rico are one of the central spaces in which these identities are grounded, referenced, and marked. For some, higher education is a struggle, while for others it is an expected and legitimate heritage. Privilege is translated into merit and is consecrated by being ignored. Francisco's unproblematic classification of Chicago Mainlanders as inauthentic—based on his perception that Mainlanders speak Black English rather than the standard English he learned in high school—revealed how the weight of cultural heredity is such that it is possible to possess exclusivity without even having to exclude others. In Bourdieu and Passeron's words, "Everything takes place as if the only people excluded are those who excluded themselves" (Bourdieu and Passeron 1971, 27).

Claribel Irizarry, whose childhood and adolescence were characterized by constant back-and-forth migration between Chicago and Arecibo, Puerto Rico, illuminated Island cultural practices that rendered certain Puerto Ricans—namely, those possessing the right symbolic capital and economic background—as more authentic than others:

> When we returned to Puerto Rico [in 1976], we lived in Arecibo again. I wasn't accepted there either. The image that exists of the Puerto Ricans from here was very bad. Also that thing about "now that you're out there you don't know what's going on here. You're American." I've been able to counteract that by maintaining the language, mannerisms, [knowing the] current events that happen there. So that when I drop by there, I can camouflage. They don't see me as something weird. But, back then, when I was a kid, I also had to deal with how I was treated in school. "Ah, you're from out there." And of course everybody thought that "out there" meant New York, you know. I mean, I'd say Chicago, and they'd be like "where's that?" Everything was New York. They'd think that all was the same thing. When I came back to Chicago for the second time [in the late-1970s], I felt that in Chicago I was criticized for speaking Spanish, but nobody's in your

business. You can go out and walk as you please, dress as you please. They're not into the status mentality of "Are your shoes from González Padín [a fancy store in Puerto Rico] or Payless Shoes?" In Puerto Rico there were strong class distinctions, those from the *campos* [rural areas], from the *pueblos* [towns], from the *arrabales* [slums]. The distinctions were based on where you lived and how you'd dress.

Area of residence, fashion style, phenotypical features, and high school affiliation are status symbols deployed by Puerto Ricans from the Island to maintain an identity separate from the barrio in a variety of U.S. contexts. Some upwardly mobile college students from the barrio focus on their ability to camouflage their class background. These negotiations become evident in gendering and racialization processes deployed by these working-class Puerto Ricans. In interactions between Islander and Mainlander actors in the U.S. college environment, identities become rooted in the body—in ways of talking, making things, moving, and walking.

An image that repeatedly surfaced in interviews and casual conversations with Chicago college students was that of the stereotypical Chicago Islander woman whom they had encountered on campus. This woman was invariably described as very fair skinned or fashionably tanned; with shoulder-length, straight black hair worn *paje* style; and having a coy "ñe-ñe-ñe," hyperfeminized and infantilized, voice. The image was very different from that of the more boisterous, street-smart, and explicitly sensualized or sexualized Chicago Mainlander woman. These gendered images created instances in which the idiosyncratic, or personal, combined with the systematic, or social, to serve as the mediating link between the individuals' subjective worlds and the political worlds into which they were born.

Interestingly, cultural readings associated with style, dress, and mannerisms became codes not only for a racialized identity of Chicago Islanders as white, whitewashed, or upper class, but also for questioning Island understandings of masculinity. The term *blanquito,* used by upwardly mobile college students from the barrio to refer to their Chicago Islander classmates, was both a racialized and a gendered term. It implied and called into being the toughness, street-smartness, and masculinity of Chicago-born Puerto Rican men, in contrast to the more Americanized, and hence whitened and feminized, masculinity attributed to Chicago Islander men.[9] As an upwardly mobile college student from West Town commented in reference to his classmates from the town of Ponce, Puerto Rico: "Many of the guys have their cars, nice clothes, but they don't buy that themselves. They can't do that on a work-study salary. Their parents send them money. They are *bien blanquitos.*" The brash masculinity associated with working-classness has been extensively documented in the United States and elsewhere (e.g., Halle 1984; Willis 1977). What is critical here is that the state or appearance particularly of the body becomes the "acquired system of generative schemes" to consecrate privilege among members of the "nation" (Bourdieu 1977b).

Claims to knowledge and authenticity are part and parcel of struggles over the monopoly of power in which those in dominant positions operate essentially defensive strategies designed to perpetuate the status quo by maintaining themselves and the principles on which their dominance is based (cf. Danforth 1995, 83; Bourdieu 1977b). Chicago Islanders maintained their self-conceptualization as dominant even though in the U.S. racial discourse they are considered a minority. Their rejection of subalterity and their self-positioning as dominant served also as means of inclusion and of exclusion of those who are the "true minorities" of the nation; namely, the U.S. barrio poor. This dominant stand was based on the possession or the lack of cultural capital, as defined by dominant norms, that was associated with the Puerto-Ricanness promoted, sustained, and negotiated by an Island elite.

The production of bilingual texts by second-generation Puerto Ricans writers in the United States awakened among some Island intellectuals old concerns about the deterioration and preservation of *puertorriqueñidad*. Yet many nationalist activists in Chicago claimed that U.S. Puerto Ricans were more militant or more willing to express their militancy than Puerto Ricans from the Island. The activists engaged forms of strategic essentializing by which they themselves were the producers of the culture that was being represented and the ones who intervened in decisions about what to represent and how on the basis of given political, economic, and historical contexts. In this sense, strategic essentializing was in tension with cultural hybridity in the process of destabilizing and exposing inequalities among Puerto Ricans in Chicago and simultaneously asserting Puerto Rican nationalism in relation to other Latinos, whites, and blacks. From a strategic essentialist perspective, knowledge of Puerto Rican militant history and the creation of a grassroots historiography in Chicago were understood as subaltern resistance, but this knowledge was not blind to the biases of historical narratives.

GRASSROOTS HISTORIOGRAPHY AND THE PRODUCTION OF "THE AUTHENTIC" IN THE BARRIO NATION

The cultural production of intellectual elites has been cited for shaping hegemonic, popular, and even subaltern approaches to the nation (Bhabha 1990; Chatterjee 1993; Duany 2000). In Chicago, however, the cultural production of the popular classes, particularly the creation of a grassroots historiography generated among the barrio poor, stretched the parameters for the public debate on nationalism.

Grassroots historiography refers to the process by which the personal writings of Chicago Mainlanders were reproduced and interpreted as a collective documentation of the community's intimate politics and history. In Humboldt Park popular education programs were avid promoters of autobiographical writing, not only as an instrument to sharpen reading, writing, and critical thinking skills among participants, but also as part of a community-building agenda for self-representation. Not-for-profit organizations and schools and community colleges with a high proportion of Puerto Rican students—like Northeastern Illinois University, Pedro Albizu Campos High School (PACHS), and even Clemente High School—disseminated these writings through newsletters, magazines, school yearbooks, poetry readings, and theatrical performances.[10] The conceptual position of autobiography as grassroots historiography is presented not only through the content of the work, but also through its staging (Abu-Lughod 1986); its ability to transform a mythified past into a new social movement (Warren 1995); its transcendent understanding of the past as an "ethic workable for the future" (Fischer 1986); and, most significantly, its capacity to use historicity and historicizing in the construction and negotiation of the nation (Chatterjee 1993). When autobiography is available, anthropologists cannot simply view an ethnoracial community as a "people without history," and their subjects cannot be reduced to folkloric images that prevent any critical staging of a counterhegemonic critique.

Puerto Rican nationalist activists in Chicago created spaces in which a grassroots historiography was written, published, distributed, and interpreted, but they were not the sole creators of these documents. The grassroots historiography was created by participants in popular education programs and even independently by barrio residents, rather than by people who were scholars in the more mainstream sense. Despite the postmodernist focus on textualizing social relations and decontextualizing textual documentations, the political economy in which this historiography was forged became a critical foundation for its analysis. The documents presented mythic patterns of migration; of a golden age of political militancy or past affluence on the Island; of periods of settlement, political persecution, and displacement; of multiple placements; and of regeneration and community creation (Smith 1984, 292–93).

Renowned published Puerto Rican and Latino authors have inspired some of the literature produced in the barrio. Popular education programs incorporated published autobiographies and autobiographical fiction to satisfy students' interest in "learning more about ourselves," as a Puerto Rican woman in her early twenties described the process of learning about Puerto Rican culture and about being Puerto Rican. Learning about Puerto-Ricanness was the basic theme used to engage students in school, academic culture, and skill development activities. Like other Puerto Rican and Latino authors of autobiographical works, Piri Thomas was read as a guideline to Puerto-Ricanness. The renowned author of *Down These Mean Streets* (1967), Thomas is a pioneer in contemporary Puerto Rican autobiographical writing in the United States. His acclaimed book is a first-person narrative of his coming-of-age as a black Puerto Rican male growing up in the streets of Spanish Harlem: he succumbed to drugs and criminal activity, spent years in jail, and eventually transformed his life and became one of the leading Puerto Rican writers and poets in the United States. When Melvin Salgado, a teacher at an educational program sponsored by a not-for-profit agency in West Town, was encouraging his new girlfriend, Marta, to learn more about Puerto Rican culture, he led her to *Down These Mean Streets* as a point of departure in her learning process. A young Puerto Rican who grew up in a predominantly white area of upstate New York in the 1960s, Marta had recently started to participate in some barrio cultural activities, to read and discuss Puerto Rican literature and history with Melvin, and to learn Spanish. A Puerto Rican from upstate New York himself, Melvin understood Marta's awakened interest in "learning about herself."[11]

The writings of Wanda Rivera and Danny Cordero, discussed below, illustrate how autobiographical writings became critical elements in the production of a grassroots historiography and the performance of Puerto Rican nationalism in Chicago. Rather than being a mere narration (Bhabha 1990), the construction of Puerto Rican nationalism in Chicago is embedded in the material and imaginative spaces of collective and individual subjects (cf. Radcliffe and Westwood 1996). While Danny presents Puerto-Ricanness as various stages of belongingness, Wanda creates images of Island life that allow her to belong by reshaping notions of cultural authenticity.

Wanda was a talented, assertive, and insightful seventeen-year-old PACHS student and a resident of Humboldt Park. In the school and in the neighborhood Wanda was constantly praised for her poetic ability and maturity. She produced some of her writings for a Latino literature class she was taking at the high school, where she also read books by renowned Latino authors. I met Wanda when I was volunteering at the school during my fieldwork.[12] Like many of the other U.S.-raised Puerto Ricans I met, Wanda interrogated the problematic ways in which nationalism was fueled by the tensions between the populations of Puerto Ricans on the Island and in the diaspora. In her poem "Why," Wanda navigates the physical and ideological spaces between seeing Puerto Rico as an ancestors' homeland and experiencing rejection by that same mythified Island society (see Barradas 1980):

> *Why is it that if I would fight for you,*
> *defend you,*
> *you make me feel unwanted?*
> *I am part of you*
> *and feel proud of being raised by your riches.*
> *Yet, I feel isolated and strange.*
> *I figured you would accept me,*
> *but still you sent me away.*
> *You don't smile the way you used to.*
> *Was it because I had nothing or no one?*
> *Was it because you wanted someone who would return those values to you?*
> *But I have some news for you.*
> *I have a new Puerto Rican heart,*
> *a new Puerto Rico where I can find my own refuge.*
> *Where people value your presence and preserve all your love.*
> *I now live in a place where I can dance my culture.*
> *So please do me a favor,*
> *don't try to hurt me this time.*
> *I think about the times when it could have been so nice.*
> *Instead I'm here asking myself WHY?*

Wanda's poem, inspired by Puerto Rican writer Tato Laviera, was published in the PACHS yearbook.

Having lived in Puerto Rico until she was eleven, Wanda creates her growing-up years with compelling images that allow her to belong to the Island-nation while living in the Chicago barrio. In an autobiographical essay she titled "Having Pride," Wanda writes:

> Born in Guayama, Puerto Rico, in a small town called Pueblo de los Brujos. Everyone knowing everybody's name, walking barefoot, greeting the *dueños* [owners] at the *bodegas* [small grocery stores], *fiándose* [laying away] cigarettes and beer, day and night. Fighting off the mosquito bites on one hand and holding the bingo board in the other. People sit under trees looking for shade instead of darkening their skin. We have people from Cayey planting their hammocks on other

people's *marquesinas* [open garages]. Eating mangos while hearing a child's mother screaming *maldiciones* [curses] while chasing them with a broom.

Wanda's descriptions focus on the social interactions and the imagined quotidian life of the town while recognizing that although the Island may exist discursively as the overlapping of territory, culture, and population, it is also very much grounded in material dimensions that challenge paradisiacal views. One of the first questions Wanda asked me was: "Where in Puerto Rico is your family from?" I told her my family is from Juana Díaz. She continued: "I don't understand people down there anymore. They want to be so American. For them everything in Puerto Rico is bad. The crime, the heat, they complain about the jobs."

An important theme in Wanda's writings is the emphasis on Puerto-Ricanness as at least partially rooted in biology as the symbol of a unifying moral "blood" that all Puerto Ricans share. Since people cannot choose what they naturally are, Wanda assumes that a biologized Puerto-Ricanness guarantees her belongingness in the Puerto Rican nation. By reinforcing a different set of equally essentialist claims, Wanda contests culturalist definitions of belongingness (Handler 1988). Her emphasis on "blood" shifts Puerto-Ricanness away from location and Chicago Islanders' claims that one has to be *nacido y criado* [born and raised] on the Island to be authentic. Wanda writes:

> A Puerto Rican is someone who is not only born on the island, but someone who recognizes the wonderful values we carry. Many don't recognize what a Puerto Rican is for the simple fact that we don't receive as much education about our background because we live in a country where the people are so diverse and our identity is hard to identify. Many prefer being called Americans just because they don't recognize their real heritage. The stereotype that has been used for many decades is that I live in America, I was born here, I went to the war, therefore I am not Puerto Rican. This is something we hear when we ask someone how do they identify themselves. Being Puerto Rican is a natural born gift. It's sharing and loving just like our parents taught us to do. It is something not gained but given. It is something kept for the rest of our lives, cherished by all our brothers and sisters.

Blood and law—in this case the citizenship claims related to serving in the U.S. military—are two of the most powerful symbols expressing the unity of people who share a common identity, whether in the domain of kinship, religion, or nationality (Schneider 1990; Handler 1988; Herzfeld 1991). In autobiographical writings and daily conversations, barrio residents regarded Puerto Rican "blood" as a natural substance, a shared biogenetic material that they often thought constituted a permanent, unalterable aspect of a person's identity. National identity is naturally and biologically given, as it is determined first and foremost by "blood" or "birth" (Danforth 1995). If national identity is a fact of nature, determined by blood or by birth, then to change it is "unnatural," if not impossible. A biologized conception of national identity is expressed both explicitly and in metaphors personifying the national homeland as a parent or a lover (Danforth 1995). Of course, the biologized and culturalized definitions are equally essentialist because in an effort to discount the material reality they fail to consider history, political economy, and internal logics of race and gender.

Like other Latino youth in the U.S. barrios, Wanda felt that reading history and narrating personal stories were inroads into documenting the community's history, which would, in turn, encourage others to identify with her narrative and find their own politicized voice in the process:

> Many don't know they are Puerto Ricans until they pick up a book that talks about us. Many don't know they are Puerto Ricans until they discover what our blood carries. It's hard to say what we are when every time we say who we are they reject us and throw bottles at us. Knowing who and where you come from is being Puerto Rican. Holding that bandera Puertorriqueña that liberates us from this American oppression is being Puerto Rican. Working for a living, fighting for our salary today, tomorrow for ever they will stay the same.

Wanda alludes to the sharp contradictions between the practices, beliefs, and values she attributes to the Puerto Rican community and those of the U.S. school system, which is grounded in an assimilationist ideology. Given these contradictions, many anticolonial writers turn to an examination of their own identity in order to resist colonial domination (Carey-Webb 1998). The autobiographical elements of these writings are not solipsistic exercises, but part of a deliberately politicized project to reevaluate the dominant culture, the homeland, and the problematic reconfigurations of the intersections between home and diaspora.

Barrio residents' interpretations of Danny Cordero's diary were illustrative of the ways in which a grassroots historiography generated spaces for the performance of nationalism in Chicago. After Danny, a bright, handsome, and talented Puerto Rican man in his early twenties committed suicide, his family found the college-ruled notebook that he used as his journal.

One of Danny's college classmates recalled, "When we were on the plane to Puerto Rico together, he saw me writing in my journal that I had begun two days prior to the trip. When I explained why I was writing, he immediately started to write one of his own." The story of Danny's journal illustrates how a private document becomes part of a protected and carefully crafted community historiography.

As a student at Northeastern Illinois University, Danny had expressed interest in writing for the widely distributed Latino student publication, *Qué Ondée Sola*. His journal was eventually published in a memorial issue of the student magazine.[13] Three main themes framed popular interpretations of the manuscript and conversations about Danny's journal: the impact of feeling culturally inauthentic because of having been born and raised in the United States, the development of a political consciousness around colonialism that is based on barrio activism; and the clash between morally driven scripts of masculinity and the material realities of being a young man in the barrio.

Danny was a neighborhood jewel by most people's standards: the great kid brought up in a two-parent, church-going family who always excelled in school and sports; a loving son and brother; a caring boyfriend; a much-cherished community activist; and a popular college student. In a conversation I had with Danny's older brother after Danny's death, Roberto described his brother as a straight-A student who attended one of the best magnet schools in Chicago. "He was on the varsity wrestling team and won many awards for that. At the school where we went, if you were poor and you couldn't wear great clothes, your only hope for being accepted was to be good in sports. Everybody loved Danny for that," Roberto commented.

Because of all of this, Danny's death took those who knew him by surprise. "His girlfriend found him dead. They found a note he'd left and his journal," explained a high school student who had worked with Danny at a barrio health clinic. The note contained Danny's last words:

> It is difficult for me to express what course of events led me to the decision that I can no longer continue dragging myself through this wretched life. . . . I can not begin to fully explain the powerlessness that I have. . . . I wish I could find it within me to change this—but I'm a product of my own unraveling. Nothing has snapped in my brain, I am just missing something. That something is lack of faith. Not only lack of faith in myself, but also in ascribing meaning to life.

The importance of Danny's journal lies not only in its textual content, but also in its contextual interpretation by relatives, barrio activists, and area youth in their creation of a grassroots historiography. As posthumous collaborators with Danny, the editors and interpreters of Danny's journal became instrumental in turning it into a community document. Local activists and barrio youth affiliated with popular education programs examined Danny's journal for possible clues to the frustration behind the young man's action. The document became the way into Danny's cognitive processes, and provided hindsight understanding of experiences common to other community youth. Sketches of the Puerto Rican flag, incomplete sentences, and bold letters screaming "Please Help Me!" covered the pages of the journal and were reprinted in a published version that was distributed through the community.

Danny's personal writings became part of the community's public history when they were published. "Without a doubt, this publication of the journal will serve not only as a memorial to Danny Cordero, but also as an educational tool for all those who read it. And we hope that it will help us become better human beings," the editor's note mentions. When the gift shop at the Pedro Albizu Campos Museum of Puerto Rican History and Culture was named after him, even more people learned who Danny Cordero was, despite his short life. As a young Puerto Rican artist and friend of Danny's explained about the play in which the friend was participating, "*El Caracol* is about a Puerto Rican family's struggle, in the West Town/Humboldt Park area, to survive in urban America. The director of this play dedicated this performance to the memory of Danny Cordero, a Puerto Rican raised in this country who lived to the sounds of *El Caracol*."

Eduardo, a friend of Danny's and one of the editors of his journal, writes: "This journal that Danny began during his trip to Puerto Rico—full of his thoughts, his views of the world, his troubles—we publish in this memorial issue to help us better understand him and ourselves" (Arocho 1995). Danny's self-positioning as a young Puerto Rican man "between two worlds"—not quite from the United States and not quite from Puerto Rico—became one of the main points of analysis for the nationalist activists and barrio youth involved in editing and publishing the journal. As a staff member in a popular education program commented upon reading the journal: "One can see the impact a colonial condition has on our youth, especially the youth that believed mainstream rules, the ones that believe that it's only up to them to meet society's expectations, the ones that attribute their failures to themselves and their successes to the 'Great American Nation.'"

The transformation of this private journal into an element of a grassroots historiography documented the performance of a popular nationalism in

Chicago. The process by which Danny's personal narrative became a public document suggests ways in which nationalism is textualized in the production of a grassroots historiography—especially when autobiographical writings are reinterpreted as testimonial representations of colonialism and racialization processes. Danny's brother and other Puerto Rican students and activists distributed the published version of Danny's journal through various community organizations, high schools, and local colleges. Danny's brother and the editors of the journal emphasize the common trends in Danny's life and the lives of other barrio youth as a cautionary tale. In the introduction to the published journal they commented: "When we can accept Daniel's problems, we can begin productive efforts to help our friends, families, community, and ourselves to find meaning and continue in the struggle to reach our full potential."

Many of Danny's entries are contemplations of the displacement he felt during a visit to his grandmother in Puerto Rico. He had traveled to the Island with a group of students from Northeastern Illinois University, a Chicago college that has ties to the barrio and a strong tradition of Puerto Rican student activism. The most structured sections of the journal were written during the excursion to Puerto Rico:

> 10-12-95
> Today is the first time in 13 years that I have visited my ancestors' homeland. As in everyday of late, I had troubles in relating to people at certain points in the day, but there exists the all encompassing feeling of home. I know that this is where I would be if the steps taken by my grandparents hadn't taken me away from what I truly feel alienated. I want badly to jump right in and act as though I am a true Boricua, but the fact of the matter is that I have to take several steps before this can be achieved. I had a conversation today with my father's mother—my Abuela—for the first time in my life. Not only was this the first conversation with her (at 22-yrs. old), but it's the first time I've ever felt a true contact with my "Puerto-Ricanness" in relation to the island.

The reference to Puerto Rico as the "ancestors' homeland" points to Danny's self-positioning as one removed from a direct connection to the Island yet experiencing an "all encompassing feeling of home." Danny's reflections lead back to the "steps taken by my grandparents," as if a twist of fate had channeled him into a completely different being. Just as telling is that Danny attributes the twist of fate to a decision made by his grandparents, without regard to the structural circumstances that compelled them to migrate. It is in those understood-but-disregarded structural circumstances that we find the political economy of cultural authenticity. To Danny, being a "true Boricua" acquires a normative quality on the Island. It involves performing the subjectivity of an authentic Puerto-Ricanness in a sequence of implied stages presumably leading him closer to that authenticity. In this sense, "the more successful one is in commodifying oneself, the less one is able to reproduce the self that has been commodified" (Di Leonardo 1998, 95).

Danny's trip to Puerto Rico was initiated by a search for his roots, which had been triggered by involvement in Chicago nationalist politics and exposure to new versions of important events in Puerto Rican history. The search for his roots—for his belongingness—was consolidated by a visit to his parents' hometown in Puerto Rico and by his meeting of some of his relatives on the Island for the first time. Hence, in some ways the production of a Puerto Rican nationalism in the United States conflates the construction of a new national identity with the realization of a "true identity" that remains incomplete until a critical point of discovery (cf. Danforth 1995).

A theme that surfaced in barrio residents' interpretations of Danny's journal was the young man's increasing involvement in local political activism around controversial issues, like the amnesty campaign for the FALN members, which awakened his political consciousness and ideological identity. Pablo Suárez, a local high school student who read the journal, commented: "He had such high standards for himself, you know, that Catholic mentality. Going back to Puerto Rico got him thinking about a lot of things related to his involvement here in the community. He was slowly becoming more of an activist, but not really radical." The school trip to Puerto Rico included a seminar related to the Chicago-based amnesty campaign for the imprisoned FALN members. Danny describes one of the activities in which he participated during the visit to Puerto Rico: the political debates around the political status of Puerto Rico in relation to the United States:

10-14-95
The last couple of days I've been experiencing half sleep. . . . Between this ever impending lack of rest and heat, I am finding it difficult to stay attentive. Regardless, just being in the presence of these people—most of whom have dedicated their lives, hearts and minds to the cause—is making me feel at home. I am still at the beginning stages of my identification with who I am, rather, where I am from.

The stages toward authenticity implied in Danny's journal interrogate the "space of the nation" (Radcliffe and Westwood 1996), in which the disjuncture between the national place and national identities is partially consolidated in the imagination and discursive formations of diasporic populations. Nevertheless, the activists who interpreted the journal emphasized that the massive Puerto Rican migration influenced by U.S. colonialist control of Puerto Rico was responsible for the identity issues that migrants and second-generation Puerto Rican youth in the United States have to contend with. In light of these activists' interpretations, other global, transnational processes become secondary to the colonialist relationship between the United States and Puerto Rico. Danny's journal transcends the imaginative or discursive to incite the historical and political economy behind conceptions of the culturally authentic Puerto Rican crafted by the Island elite. Hence, the independence movement that Danny supported was more than an exclusively political project; it became a symbol of spiritual values (e.g., struggle, compromise, sacrifice) perceived as inherently opposed to U.S. materiality. In this sense, it was not necessary for the independence or nationalist movements to press toward concrete economic goals; the function of these separatist movements was to sustain the spiritual, not the material, domain.

Puerto Rican authenticity was associated with a militant margin in the barrio, with an activism that Danny admired but did not pursue—or at least did not pursue at the expense of the American dream that motivated his grandparents' migration. In another journal entry Danny writes:

> I ate breakfast with Eduardo—oatmeal, a banana, coffee. After breakfast we began the first seminar, which involved the political aspects of the prisoners. There are several people present who are related to the Puerto Rican Political Prisoners. The most emotional display I have seen since I have been here was by Rafael Cancel Miranda [one of the Five Nationalists]. . . . His expressions and emotional gestures reflected a lifetime of dedication to a cause that is real. I cannot bring myself to fully agree with the tactics that he and others like him used to get his point across, but I can understand the frustration instilled in those who attempt to fight a system in power. A system that creates laws and only utilizes the ones that it deems necessary at the time.

Danny conceptualizes a nationalism that is grounded in rigid ideas of the authentic, that actually equates home with those devoted to the struggle, most of whom are connected to Chicago's barrio rather than more directly to the Island. This perception provides an interesting contrast to the focus on an Island-based nationalism that excludes migrant Others. Danny's journal sustains the idea that nationalism is one of the most definitive venues for cultural authenticity in Chicago's barrio. Moreover, this popular nationalism contextualizes modes of identity formation—barrio-based rather than suburban, Chicago-based rather than nationwide—and thus problematizes generalized analyses of Puerto Rican identity or, more commonly, Puerto Rican culture.

The literature of the Puerto Rican migrant community serves both as testimony of the deplorable material conditions Puerto Ricans face as a consequence of a history of colonialism and as autobiographical documentation that straddles individual accomplishments and collective consciousness (Acosta-Belén 1992; Flores 1993). Linguistic nationalism on the Island negates the validity of the diasporic literature, which is mostly written in English or Spanglish. This literature lies outside the Island's national heritage (Hernández 1997), and the work of U.S. Puerto Rican writers are excluded from the Island's elementary and high school curricula. Neither Spanish nor English departments at local universities have incorporated these authors as required reading, largely because their writings are hybrid and bilingual (Duany 2000). Mainlander Puerto Rican narratives are simultaneously autobiographical and testimonial in nature.[14] The nationalism promoted by barrio activists in their community-building efforts, as well as the continuous historical references articulated in public neighborhood spaces, leads to an enhanced understanding of the power of recording. In this sense, *testimonio* becomes a mutual legitimation of an individual's perception of a particular social context and of the collective condition of the group for whom the individual intends to speak.

Activists' efforts to document local struggles that became part of the neighborhood's grassroots historiography partially relied on the production of testimonial and autobiographical writings. Danny's document, while a literary production in its own right, was interpreted as testimony of how the material lives of racialized and gendered subjects were shaped by local understandings of colonialism and the unequal economic integration into a global community. While identities are fragmented, this fragmentation is not infinite, but grounded in interwoven historical and political processes that continue to characterize the colonialist relationship between Puerto Rico and the United States.

The activists who distributed the journal explained that Danny's struggles with mainstream society's expectations of self-reliance, social mobility, and individualism clashed with the "colonialized identity of Puerto Rican men." Barrio activists perceived colonialist processes as the power differential that was produced and reproduced in ways that were always entangled in social relations and that retained an intractable and enduring significance. Like racialization processes, the forms and substantive meanings of colonialization were eminently historical, socially contingent, and gendered. The processes by which male and female roles were socially constructed were negotiated primarily in the spiritual domain, where they could be manipulated outside the purview of public criticism or dominant feminist discourses. Not surprisingly, Danny's mainstream definitions of being a responsible, reliable man—which resonate with the role of provider in American-dream parlance—were deployed by barrio activists to further advocate for alternative notions of masculinity restructured around nationalist definitions and reconfigurations of gender norms. Danny illustrated his "unrevolutionary" masculinity in his own journal. In a poem entitled "To Be a Man Is . . ." Danny defined masculinity as follows:

> *To keep your word*
> *to be trusted—respected*
> *to stand up for what you believe*
> *to be physically and mentally strong*
> *to strive beyond your potential*
> *to stand alone*
> *to get up when you fall down*
> *to keep climbing*
> *to take action when necessary*
> *to carefully think out—reason the course of action you will take*
> *to justify your actions and explain your motives*
> *to be open to the world about you*
> *to live your life in happiness*
> *not at the expense of someone else's happiness*
> *. . . is to be a man.*

The journal, including Danny's poem, became everyday evidence to legitimize the nationalists' appraisal of the New Revolutionary Woman. In all its unacknowledged contradictions, the ideal of the New Revolutionary Woman was not only the route to women's emancipation, but also the avenue for Puerto Rican men's (and Danny's) survival.

Just as nationalism selectively embodied the cultural authentic in certain female traditions in ways that preserved postures that subjugated women in the name of national unity, cultural scripts of masculinity were similarly manipulated around the image of the New Revolutionary Woman. This nationalists' version of a "virgin"/"whore" duality—the devoted mother in the sexualized Amazon costume—became the image capable of alleviating Danny's "unrevolutionary" masculinity scripts. As the nationalist interpretation went, had Danny sponsored such nationalist conceptions of gender norms, he would still be alive. Images of the New Revolutionary Woman that were instrumental for the sustenance of nationalist activism in the barrio became validated through grassroots historiographic production.

Danny's journal was published with a cover that Danny himself had designed for a previous issue of the magazine. It suggests Danny's own embodiment of the nation. He explained the cover in that earlier issue of the magazine:

> The muscular bodies represent the struggle and efforts that must be emphasized in maintaining a sense of identity and community within, as well as outside the Island. It is particularly crucial to pass on the importance of organizing together to build the same community in which they were raised. The four role models depicted in the drawing are placed within the silhouette. Arturo Schomberg [*sic*] (left), Julia de Burgos (right)—to represent that role models must be made obvious (to our youth) through education and active participation in the community with "La Isla" [the Island of Puerto Rico] through these role models. The flag is another connection that we brothers and sisters on the mainland have to our parents' homeland. The connection with the roots is the shelter, which nurtures the growth of the spirit and knowledge of the self—represented by the flag draping over the other aspect of the drawing.

Most scholarly work on nationalism has focused on the construction of national identity as a large-scale, top-down, collective phenomenon. Some scholars have recognized that the one of the few means available to national minorities to resist the cultural hegemony of nation-states are jokes, folklore, protests, and other unofficial tools of resistance, including autobiographical writings (cf. Scott 1988; Danforth 1995). These forms of resistance are often overshadowed by powerful hegemonic ideologies. By disseminating Danny's writings and interpreting his words, barrio activists deployed a strategy that resonated with Benedict Anderson's recognition of the use of the printing press in the building of imagined communities (Anderson 1983).

Despite its apparent claim to indigenous authenticity, the anticolonial autobiography is inescapably a hybrid, as it narrates into being a cross-cultural and incipient national subject whose full realization is deferred or postponed to the moment of independence (Carey-Webb 1998), which in Puerto Rico never happened. As Allen Carey-Webb argues, the colonial subject is thus tied to the narratives of anticolonial resistance and national independence that literally call him or her into existence. In postcolonial writing the

narration of personal identity in a collective struggle against an "easily iden-
tifiable foreign enemy is no longer the central theme" (1998, 149). Instead,
the hybridity that is repressed in anticolonial writing comes to the fore, and
national identity itself is recognized as both complicated and fractured. Foreign oppression may be seen to have its counterpart in domestic collaboration and corruption, "domestic oppressions and difference display the
foreign enemy, and 'we the people' become the site of difference, division,
and struggle" (Carey-Webb 1998, 150).

Puerto Rican grassroots historiography "shares with Black poetry the didactic intentions to politicize by demythifying, by stripping away the veil of
'false consciousness' that's thought to maintain the status quo in the Third
World ghetto" (Cruz-Malavé 1988, 48). Hence, simultaneous inclinations,
in every author, in every work of prose, and in every poem, toward demythifying and toward mythification and the construction of a utopia (Barradas
1980) dominate Puerto Rican autobiographical writings. Danny's journal
and Wanda's writings illuminate the construction of national identity as a
short-term biographical process that takes place over the course of the life-
times of specific individuals. Readers of autobiographical and testimonial
writings printed in local publications interpret these narratives in light of
contemporary political conflicts affecting Puerto Rican barrio residents both
at the local barrio level and in the broader relationship to the Island. This literature reflects the "awakening of a national consciousness or the consciousness of nationality" (Flores 1985, 14) and the consciousness of an
emergent class that arises from the validation of popular culture (Acosta-
Belén 1992, 349). Grassroots historiography is considered instrumental in
configurations of nationalism because it incorporates the individual into a
broader political collective and because it emphasizes a glorified historical
past rooted in the ancestral Island, as well as notions of cultural authenticity—for example, in the idea of stages that move one closer to being a "real
Puerto Rican."

The performance of Puerto Rican nationalism in Chicago was partially
shaped by the tensions created by distinctions between Chicago Islanders
and Chicago Mainlanders. These distinctions were grounded in the deployment of contradictory discourses of cultural authenticity, in a different positioning of self against an American Other, and in differences in material and
symbolic capital. Displacement and deterritorialization, rather than simply
leading to more inclusive hybrid identities, sustains unequal claims to the
nation in ways that require the problematization of understandings of
transnational communities that are both diasporic and rooted in the homeland. In relation to the migrant Other, discourses around cultural difference

are superimposed over the reality of poverty and marginality caused by a frequently unacknowledged colonial condition and white supremacy. Puerto Rican nationalism is consolidated as a localized—and in the case of Chicago, barrio-based—yet decentered identity shaped by political economic conditions and notions of authenticity. Notions of the authentic are premised on a subtle appreciation of cultural capital and the reproduction of internal social hierarchies on both the Island and the Mainland. These social hierarchies are decontextually created and contested in cultural terms, as levels of Puerto-Ricanness rather than as differences in resources, status, and privilege. The production and dissemination of a grassroots historiography authored by Chicago Mainlanders questioned elitist discourses of authenticity. In the next chapter I examine how nationalist performances produce and reproduce images of race and class through the revival of controversial symbols and representations of the Puerto Rican nation in the diaspora. The conflict over a statue of nationalist leader Pedro Albizu Campos offers the point of departure for the deconstruction of such nationalist performances.

★ 6 ★

Creating Race: Pedro Albizu Campos, Representation, and Imagination

On the centennial of the birth of Pedro Albizu Campos, a Puerto Rican leader whom nationalists often compare to Ché Guevara or Malcolm X, Puerto Ricans on the Island and in cities throughout the United States celebrated with commemorative art exhibits, lectures, festivals, and other activities. The quintessential leader of the Puerto Rican nationalist movement of the 1950s and the contemporary popular symbol of the nationalist barrio contingent in Chicago, Albizu Campos is also the embodiment of racialization processes in relation to African Americans and internally among Puerto Ricans. In the early 1990s, a conflict erupted in Chicago over whether a statue of Albizu Campos—considered by some a Puerto Rican nationalist hero and by others an anti-American terrorist—should be erected in Humboldt Park. Among the competing discourses were those of the nationalist Baptist pastors and the pro-statehood Pentecostal clergy, who put forth images of "Albizu as Christ" and "Albizu as terrorist," respectively. Albizu Campos became a symbol not only of nationalist production, but also of the alternative ways in which Puerto Rican nationalism is deployed in the production and reproduction of racial difference in reference to blacks, whites, and other Latinos.

THE PEDRO ALBIZU CAMPOS STATUE:
LOCAL FACTIONALISM, RELIGIOUS NARRATIVES

Research on Albizu Campos is extensive, and to contribute substantively to that literature is beyond the scope of this book.[1] The goal here is to deconstruct social practices that evoked the image of Albizu in Humboldt Park and to show how internal racialization among Puerto Ricans was mediated by a political economy that alternatively heroized and criminalized nationalist narratives. The Albizu-as-Christ and Albizu-as-terrorist metaphors were grounded in local factionalism, threats of spatial displacement and gentrification, and U.S. racial taxonomies.

Puerto Rican nationalist activists in Chicago created the Committee for the Celebration of the Dr. Pedro Albizu Campos Centennial, whose goal was to request that the main commercial sector of the barrio be named after the celebrated nationalist. In 1993, a year after the street was renamed, a six-foot-tall, larger-than-life statue of Albizu Campos designed by a Puerto Rican sculptor at the request of nationalist activists was previewed by hundreds of people while, surrounded by Puerto Rican flags, they listened to renowned guest speakers talk about Albizu Campos's historical significance.

Shortly after the statue was unveiled, the Chicago Park District informed the activists that it was not suited for Chicago weather and that it needed to be bronzed. To bronze the statue would cost $35,000. Many activists felt that the Park District was aiming to discourage them from erecting the statue in the park because the presence of the statue stood in the way of the continuing effort to displace Puerto Rican residents from a residential area in which there was increasing real estate interest. The activists continued fundraising activities in the barrio, and in about a year they collected enough money to bronze the statue according to the Park District's stipulation. Activists, barrio youths, and religious leaders remembered standing at traffic lights collecting quarters and selling Albizu posters, T-shirts, and bumper stickers with "I support the Albizu statue" logos. When the newly bronzed statue was ready to be unveiled once again, the first public opposition came from officials at the Park District, who claimed that a statue of an "anti-American terrorist" could not be placed in the park. The deconstruction of these conflicting views of Pedro Albizu Campos enables a better understanding of nationalist performances in which a variety of perspectives toward a mythico-historical image were interwoven in the intimate process that led to the production of flexible representations of Puerto-Ricanness in Chicago.

As accounts of the historical events in which Albizu Campos was involved began to circulate in everyday conversations in Humboldt Park, West Town, and Logan Square, the opponents of the statue recalled that Albizu had been openly critical of U.S. policies toward Puerto Rico and that he had been implicated in various upheavals in which separatists fought U.S. intervention on the Island. Statue opponents referred to these events in ways that

Above: A replica of the controversial statue of Pedro Albizu Campos was initially placed in front of the Pedro Albizu Campos Museum of History and Culture, formerly a Russian Orthodox Church, on California Avenue across from the Humboldt Park green. *Facing page:* The original statue, created by a Puerto Rican sculptor, was housed inside the museum until the museum closed, then later moved to a community garden on Division Street, where it currently stands in front of a little house known as La casita de Don Pedro [Don Pedro's little house]. (*Above,* author's photo; *facing,* courtesy of Liz Cosgrove)

were valuable not for their historical factualness or lack thereof, but for their selective objection to Albizu Campos's anti-U.S. actions. Alberto Morales, a retired police officer in his late fifties, commented:

> Albizu Campos did not like the United States. In fact, he hated it here and declared war on this country. He killed innocent people. And people who believe in Albizu Campos are always criticizing the U.S. They, in a way, don't like the U.S. either and so they can identify with

Albizu Campos. But, what I tell those people is: "If you don't like the U.S., if it's so terrible to live here, why don't you just go back to where you came from? Go back to Puerto Rico." . . . I mean, if you hate it here so much, why endure so much pain by being here?

Alberto was representative of other opponents of the statue in that he viewed Albizu Campos and the celebration of the nationalist leader as incompatible with Puerto Rican life in the United States. In Chicago the question of the legality of Latin American, and particularly Mexican, migrants accounted for heavily political debates about welfare and citizenship. In this context the idea that anyone who did not appreciate the United States should "go back to where they came from" illuminated a subtext of deservingness and civic responsibility.

Supporters of the statue likewise articulated their views of the Albizu Campos image using a rhetoric of civil rights and civic responsibility. However, unlike the opponents of Albizu Campos, Albizu supporters drew on critical aspects of the nationalist's accomplishments to articulate an equivalence between his separatist politics and the social and political autonomy of barrio residents in Humboldt Park. Rafael Arrollo, Alberto Morales's close friend and frequent domino partner, and the owner of a Humboldt Park bodega, was more or less representative of Albizu supporters. Rafael commented:

> People focus on the bad things, without thinking that that was back
> then, when things were done in a different way. But they don't under-
> stand that Albizu Campos stood for what he believed in and was
> driven. He was black and poor, and he was still able to become a lawyer
> and go to Harvard. I don't know if he really killed people. One thing
> that they were saying at an activity where they were talking about Al-
> bizu was that he never got a fair trial and that he was subjected to radi-
> ation in jail.

Rafael, like other Albizu supporters, emphasized his belief that Albizu Campos was unfairly treated by the U.S. legal system. Although Rafael harbored
a more critical stance than Alberto did in relation to how legal justice is dis-
pensed in the United States, he still contextualized Albizu's accomplishments in very mainstream discourses of social mobility and professional
success. These contested views, and the cultural intimacy that related them
to the Albizu Campos image, were important in the performance of nationalism as a strategy for urban development, historical consciousness, and
processes of racial formation in the construction of Humboldt Park as a
Puerto Rican space.

While they were awaiting the Park District's decision, nationalist activists
bought a run-down Russian Orthodox Church building (a remnant of the
neighborhood's white ethnic past), rehabilitated it, and painted its walls and
ceilings. Three months later the building became the Pedro Albizu Campos
Museum of History and Culture. The museum housed the controversial
statue and served as a site for exhibits in which young local artists displayed
their creations. The imposing statue stood on a red carpet in the middle of
the majestic main area of the museum for the five or so years in which the
building was operating. However, running the museum proved more costly
than the activists and residents had anticipated, and a few years after all ap-
peals of the Park District's decision regarding the statue failed, the museum
was closed.

Barrio nationalists then sought funds from a community-garden program to rehabilitate a vacant lot on the commercial strip of Paseo Boricua,
and they placed the statue in the garden. Area youth and activists built a casita, a little house architecturally similar to those in rural Puerto Rico in the
1950s, a practice common in Puerto Rican barrios in many U.S. cities
(Aponte-Parés 1998). This revitalizing process of political articulation and
cultural hybridity is not inevitably a nostalgic escape to the past (cf. Fischer

1986; Flores 2000). Rather, it can be a claim to urban space and self-representation. The Chicago barrio's only casita is called "la casita de Don Pedro." The statue of the nationalist leader stands against a rural landscape in Humboldt Park, surrounded by the revolutionary flags of Puerto Rico and Lares. The casita serves as a meeting place for numerous political rallies and artistic events.

The Pedro Albizu Campos statue incident reached the front page of neighborhood-based and mainstream Chicago newspapers, where the nationalist leader was alternately revered as a Puerto Rican Christ and condemned as a terrorist traitor comparable to Lee Harvey Oswald.[2] For over three years the statue and the leader it commemorates were discussed at numerous town meetings and artistic events and on radio talk shows. Even a student group at the University of Michigan organized discussions about the incident. Whereas the image of Albizu Campos was often neutralized or appeared only in elite academic spaces in Puerto Rico, it became simultaneously the embodiment of popular nationalism and a symbol of cultural and political autonomy in a self-conscious process of marking and creating a Puerto Rican community and alternative representations of Puerto-Ricanness in Chicago. Of particular significance here are the tentative and conflict-ridden ways in which Albizu Campos became a representation of Puerto-Ricanness in Chicago and how an implicit understanding of Puerto-Ricanness was being staged and therefore subjected to the broader gaze of a dominant U.S. national audience. Likewise, Puerto-Ricanness was a consistently configured and reconfigured racial formation that, while specifically related to Chicago as a racially producing urban space, also centered on a diasporic view of nationalism that furthermore implicated Puerto Ricans on the Island.

The erection of a statue of Pedro Albizu Campos in Ponce, Puerto Rico, attracted little attention. Several towns in Puerto Rico celebrated the Albizu Campos centennial by renaming streets and unveiling statues, and these commemorative events faced little opposition and barely made the mainstream news on the Island. The one time when Albizu-as-representation caused considerable controversy in Puerto Rico was when the organizers of the New York Puerto Rican Parade of 2000 decided to dedicate the annual celebration to Albizu Campos, Tito Puente, and opposition to U.S. military intervention in the Island municipality of Vieques. The controversy on the Island around the dedication of the New York parade to Albizu was significantly different in scope, substance, and implications from the controversy around placing an Albizu statue in Humboldt Park. On the Island, the decision was condemned, largely by pro-statehood and some pro-commonwealth politicians who were concerned that the representation would lead

the U.S. government to think that most Puerto Ricans wanted to sever all political ties with the United States. The politicians also emphasized Albizu's
political crimes. Suddenly the U.S. Puerto Ricans who are generally excluded from the national imaginary had become problematic for the statehood and commonwealth projects. The image of Albizu represents Puerto
Ricans as separatist and anti-American. When the representation takes
place in a high-profile event in the United States, such as New York's National Puerto Rican Parade, Island Puerto Ricans are aware of its impact on
U.S. society and government. Island politicians are aware of the media attention U.S. Puerto Ricans can attract and of the electoral power they have,
as a significant ethnic voting bloc, in urban politics (Jennings and Rivera
1984). In Puerto Rico an exhaustive three-week-long debate took place in the
newspapers, primarily among a political and intellectual Island elite, over
whether or not the parade should be dedicated to Albizu.[3]

While nationalists in Chicago used strategic church spaces to create an image of Albizu as Christ, city officials and a faction of the Christian Right rendered an image of Albizu as terrorist. Ironically, it was the Albizu-as-terrorist
image that reified and legitimized the nationalist representation of Albizu's
martyrdom. The use of a religious plane to interpret Pedro Albizu Campos—
whether as terrorist or savior—was also critical in the development of popular educational spaces. Competing interpretations of Albizu Campos's historical significance generated popular debates about him that were located
specifically in the everyday social performance of Puerto Rican nationalism
in the barrio. When the folkloric politics around the image of Pedro Albizu
Campos were represented in the context of a barrio church, Albizu navigated
the ambiguous spaces of nationalist leader and Christian icon.

The controversy around the Albizu statue also nationalized blackness as
a means to extend internal boundaries of racial acceptability among Puerto
Ricans. The conflict circumvented the black-white polarity of the U.S. racial
order by focusing on a blackness that, while selectively conflated with
African-Americanness, was ultimately nationalized as Puerto Rican and
classed as representative of the poor. Discussions of national identity were
alternately deployed toward and away from ideas of racial mixing (*mestizaje*),
racial whitening (*blanqueamiento*), and the racial triad that is considered the
genesis of Puerto Rican national identity. Among Chicago barrio residents
and activists, the image of Pedro Albizu Campos as an upwardly mobile
black Puerto Rican became critical in resistance to the dominant racial order
and in local representations of internal productions of racial difference, as
well as evidence of mainstream achievement by Puerto Ricans.

ALBIZU AS CHRIST; ALBIZU AS TERRORIST: THE CONFLATION
OF POLITICS AND RELIGION

"Who would have told us a year ago that we would have our own Puerto Rican museum! After all the opposition by those people from outside of our community to the Albizu Campos statue, we now have an Albizu Campos museum and are celebrating its first-year anniversary," rejoiced Juan Cruz, a nationalist pastor, in a sermon at the First Congregational Church. The sermon was part of an ecumenical service to celebrate the first anniversary of the Albizu Campos Museum. The congregation cheered as the minister pronounced emphatically that "Jesus and Albizu Campos talked to us about one and the same surrendering to the values of God's kingdom. God gives us the courage to listen and live in our daily life the words of these two prophets." The service "in honor of Pedro Albizu Campos, the Apostle of the Struggle for Puerto Rico's Independence" was well-attended. Barrio residents and community activists filled the old wooden-paneled church located in one of the most depressed areas of the barrio. A church member who spoke after the sermon drew an analogy between "Jeremiah's willingness to die for Christ and Albizu's willingness to die for *la patria*."

The First Congregational Church service juxtaposed Christianity and nationalist elements in a crossing of nationalist religion and religious nationalism that is perhaps equivalent to the intermingling of *Sandinismo* and Christianity that Roger Lancaster (1988) observed in revolutionary Nicaragua. Lancaster noticed that "the narrative myth of Sandinismo so closely corresponds to both textual (biblical) and popular Christianity, that in Managua's non-propertied classes, only a tiny element actually opposes Sandinismo proper. This meshing of political and religious symbolism baptizes political undertakings with a religious charisma that few have any desire to confront directly" (1988, 139). Initially Albizu was Christified, and the image of love, compassion, sacrifice, and redemption was filtered through the evangelical lens of local religious leaders. Local activists drew their alliances among barrio residents who followed "the preexisting hagiology of folk Christianity," which includes the images of Sandino, Ché, and the Cristo Guerrillero noticed in Latin American countries (Lancaster 1988; Guss 1993; Santos Febres 1993a). As Lancaster comments, "In the same manner and with the same attitude that Christ hangs on the cross, suffering for and expiating the sins of mankind, the guerrilla endures his tribulation in the mountains—and to much the same end: each offers hope, liberation, and redemption" (1988, 132). Christ and Albizu dialectically constituted one another as their juxtaposed images encouraged a "surrendering to the values of God's kingdom," the values of revolutionary "valor and sacrifice."[4]

One of the largest murals in Chicago's Puerto Rican barrio depicts a revolutionary Lares Puerto Rican flag serving as background to a very peculiar Calvary: in the center, a black man is crucified in a three-piece suit. The cross reads not "INRI," but "Don Pedro Albizu Campos 1891–1965." On one side of this cross a woman is also crucified, and on her cross is an inscription that says, "Lolita Lebrón Crucificada en Vida" [Lolita Lebrón crucified alive]. On the other side a man is crucified under the inscription "Rafael Cancel Miranda Crucificado en Vida." Lolita Lebrón and Rafael Cancel Miranda are two nationalists who were convicted of political crimes and later granted pardons by President Jimmy Carter.[5] As a barrio resident commented, the mural "is respected even by gang members, . . . who have never written graffiti on it." As Stuart Hall writes, "The past is not only a position from which to speak, but it is also an absolutely necessary resource in what one has to say" (1990, 393).

Peter McLaren (1998) compares the "Chesucristo" or the "Christification of Ché" in middle-class college culture to the image of Malcolm X in visual iconography. Sandison argues that "Ché's message has been overcoded by radical chic consumer culture and must be pried away from the Christ-like

In one of the many murals in Humboldt Park, West Town, and Logan Square that alludes to Pedro Albizu Campos, the revered nationalist is drawn as very dark-skinned rather than mulatto, and he is presented as "El Sembrador," or The Harvester. (Author's photo)

image of the man in the beret that adorns the walls of alternative bookstores and that was once 'sold as de riguer decoration for the campus dorms'" (Sandison 1997, 118). In this stage of transformation Albizu became commercialized as Albizuist imagery appeared on the T-shirts, posters, and Albizu-statue memorabilia that nationalist activists and students in popular education programs sold on street corners. However, the image was not depoliticized through consumerism (McLaren 1998), but exactly the opposite: the sale of the goods with the Albizu logo made the financing of the Albizu statue possible in the first place.

Nationalist activists, like Juan Cruz and his congregation, perceived the fundraising for the statue as an expression of neighborhood autonomy rather than as a preservation of the more evangelical narrative articulated in the sermon. When Pedro Albizu Campos's martyrdom was emphasized, its political mission was not obscured, but magnified. The dialectical relation between Albizu Campos imagery and grassroots development projects to secure affordable housing and promote Puerto Rican business resurrected the militant rhetoric of 1950s Puerto Rican separatism, and participants engaged the debate from a mythico-historical standpoint that was not only relevant, but critical in the contemporary formation of images of Puerto-Ricanness in Chicago.

A view of adequate image-generating processes was articulated by Teresa Pérez, a barrio resident who was proud of having called a radio show in which the Albizu statue issue was being debated. She mentioned that she felt that Albizu Campos was not a hero, but a "terrorist who had supported the Nationalists who engaged in an attempt to assassinate a U.S. president." Drawing a connection between Pedro Albizu Campos and everyday social practices in Chicago, Teresa exclaimed: "We tell our youth not to join gangs and we place a statue of a terrorist in the Park!" Gang-related violence in Humboldt Park was in this instance understood as an expression of the extreme militancy associated with Albizu Campos. The statue itself would presumably become the physical and ideological marker of Humboldt Park, a space commonly racialized as Puerto Rican and therefore commonly associated by Chicagoans with danger, criminality, and pathology. Teresa's comment implied that the creative value of the image of Albizu Campos was not attributable to its historical significance, but to its *representational potential* and its ability to filter everyday discourses of racial formation around social positioning and claims over space.

Ray Acevedo and Mariela Ochoa, two Logan Square residents in their thirties, viewed the conflict between Albizu supporters and opponents as responsible for producing, or at least exacerbating, tensions and dividing what they viewed as an otherwise well-integrated Puerto Rican community. Nevertheless, Mariela and Ray disagreed on what an adequate representation of Puerto-Ricanness in Chicago would be. Ray argued: "Pedro Albizu Campos represents division. He represents controversy. We don't need divisions in our community. Why not erect a monument to the memory of all the Hispanics who have died in combat for this nation?" For Ray, who often expressed his disappointment over how Puerto Ricans are "too dependent on welfare," erecting an image of a Puerto Rican veteran of the U.S. military would be an opportunity to insist that Puerto Ricans have contributed in very explicit ways to the creation of the American nation, that they are law-abiding U.S. citizens dedicated to protecting U.S. nationalism.

Mariela, a worker in the not-for-profit sector, likewise preferred a figure who would represent Puerto Ricans as law-abiding U.S. citizens and contributors to U.S. society and culture. In her view a more adequate representation of Puerto-Ricanness would be the late baseball player Roberto Clemente. Mariela argued that Roberto Clemente—after whom the public high school is named—was a Puerto Rican whom everyone could admire. His was a less conflictual image that would mark Chicago Puerto-Ricanness as a distinctive identity that was nevertheless consistent with the goals of sportsmanship, competitiveness, and civic engagement on which the United States bases its own nationalism.

Precisely by stimulating such heated debates, Pedro Albizu Campos as the embodiment of a separatist Puerto Rican nationalism questioned a presumed national unity rather than uncontestedly favoring it over other forms of identity formation. The image of Albizu Campos contributed to the problematization of racial and class identities among Puerto Ricans. The distinction between barrio outsiders and insiders, as determined by nationalist activists and some barrio residents, was blurred by the cultural intimacy in which all Puerto Rican constituencies recognized the power of the statue and became engaged in the production and interpretation of Albizu Campos's political significance. It was this militant history that was emphasized by those labeled "from the outside" by barrio residents, activists, and youth, like members of Son del Barrio (chapter 5). While nationalism has traditionally been assumed to undermine a group's internal boundaries along various axes, such as class, race, and gender, the performance of nationalism in Chicago actually brought those divisions to the forefront.

Ironically, the criminalization of the Pedro Albizu Campos image by the city government, the media, and a faction of the Latino elite actually legitimized the nationalist activists' power in a manner in which militant discourse or isolated actions alone could not. This criminalization also marginalized the nationalist activists from normative discourse. The image

of Albizu Campos challenged mainstream appropriation by generating conflict not only around whether the nationalist leader and the FALN members
were saviors or terrorists, but also around the representations of Puerto-
Ricanness as a racial formation in the United States. The statue itself was
secondary to the dialogue and popular education spaces it created, and to the
intricate relation between Pedro Albizu Campos and adequate or inadequate representations of Puerto-Ricanness in Chicago. Supporters and opponents of the statue were engaged in the same production, reproduction,
and performance of the nation, and they shared a cultural intimacy that was
implied in their deployment of a common rhetoric of 1950s Puerto Rican
nationalism to interpret everyday political factionalism. Very rarely does a
monument cause as much commotion and debate as did the Pedro Albizu
Campos statue in Chicago. Front-page articles in mainstream newspapers
depicted the statue controversy to the rest of the city. The extensive dialogue
that the statue generated suggests ways in which political socialization and
informal education and everyday social discourse—the incorporation of academic learning into everyday life—are promoted in many poor communities.[6]

ORALITY, REPRESENTATION, AND HISTORICITY

A potluck meal of *arroz con gandules* [rice with chick peas], salad, chicken,
fresh bread, and coffee from a local bakery followed the First Congregational
Church service. About fifty people sat on folding chairs in the basement of
the museum, while others carried their paper plates to the buffet-style food
table. As if guessing my perceptions of the religious service, Irma Burgos,
the mother of a PACHS student in my Latino literature class and one of the
people in charge of cleaning the church building, approached me and explained: "We didn't always know this much about our history, . . . but by now
so many things have happened. The statue [issue] brought more people into
the church. People wanted to learn more about their history." Three years after the Paseo Boricua portion of Division Street was named Pedro Albizu
Campos Street, and two years after the year-long debate over the statue
started, Albizu Campos was still a topic of conversation in Humboldt Park.
The conflict around his image had become not only a debate about the representation of Puerto-Ricanness in Chicago, but also a way of refurbishing
dominant images of the Puerto Rican community as politically involved and
interested in the welfare of younger generations, rather than as apathetic or
irresponsible, as the media often portrayed it.

As William Aponte, a student at Clemente High School and member of
the youth salsa band Son del Barrio, commented: "Those people never knew

how this Albizu Campos issue would backfire on them." A community activist joyfully explained, "*Everybody* talked about it. Most people, who would
have never known who Pedro Albizu Campos was, now know. A popular way
of learning history!" This echoed the comment made by Andrés Maldonado,
a nationalist pastor at a local Protestant church: "The basic idea was not so
much to put up the statue for the sake of putting up the statue, but to create
an *educational* process. That the process of putting the statue over there
would lead people to understand our cultural roots, our history as a people,
the value of the person of Albizu as an example for our youth. That was just
another step in the process of engaging people in a community dialogue."

The popular educational process also included informational meetings
to talk about widespread displacement and gentrification in Humboldt Park,
West Town, and Logan Square. Various community groups emerged to share
real estate information with Puerto Ricans interested in selling or buying
property in these areas. Most interest in "saving *el barrio*" was concentrated
on the commercial strip popularly known as La Division (Division Street) or,
after the urban development process started and a collaboration between the
City and grassroots activists emerged, as Paseo Boricua. Tomás Ocasio, a
barrio resident, activist, and *fritolero* [ambulatory fritter cook], recalled attending one of these meetings, where he first learned that "our property
here has value. That's why so many *blancos* [whites] want to move in here
now." Nevertheless, the main assumption behind the nationalists' urban development projects and the rhetoric of protecting Puerto Rican space in
which they were embedded was that a commercial strip of upgraded buildings and stores would convince people who could afford to move out to stay
in the neighborhood instead. Improving the dilapidated housing on the
streets adjacent to Paseo Boricua, like the house where Doña Luz and
Marisol lived, was of only secondary interest in the initial conversations
about development.

Barrio residents and activists also began articulating a variety of narratives to contextualize the various national symbols that ultimately became
critical components of the ornamentation of Division Street—including the
image of Albizu Campos. These narratives dominated the mainstream media's coverage of the community as the Pedro Albizu Campos statue and the
various stages of the development process became interwoven and it appeared more difficult to disentangle where the transformation of Division
Street ended and where nationalist discourse began. Throughout this
process the media served as a vehicle to convey to Chicago that Humboldt
Park was not to be marginalized any longer, or at least that it would not be ignored. As Juan Cruz, the pastor who gave the sermon at the ecumenical ser-

vice, explained, the great publicity around the Albizu Campos statue had placed Humboldt Park in the mainstream media in a way that was unconventional for a community typically discarded as "underclass" and undeserving:

> All this statue issue was widely publicized in the newspapers. The interesting thing is that this makes the whole Albizu issue public. Suddenly, all those people who have been here for years, who know about Albizu, not because they read about it but because they lived it, came out. What is this? Very few times you'll see in the main Chicago newspapers, on the cover of the *Chicago Tribune* and the third page of the *Sun-Times,* the Albizu statue. So, those people's attempts to repress, to avoid the position of the statue, backfired.

Albizu moved away from being the subject of exclusively religious imagery to become a representation of the barrio, of *la gente pobre,* in the mainstream media. The same population that is pathologized in mainstream media challenged ideas of passivity and conformity as they produced a self-representation as involved political agents in their neighborhood.

When I asked Tony Santiago, a junior high school teacher at a West Town public school, about the Albizu Campos statue, he warned me: "I've talked about it so much by now, that I probably won't be able to do it justice." Tony emphasized the intersection of orality, popular education, and community activism when he continued:

> When I went to see [the unveiling of] the statue inside the museum, that was a very memorable moment in my life. Because everybody was chanting—I felt very Puerto Rican I guess—everybody was chanting, "Se siente, se siente. ¡Albizu está presente!" [Feel it, feel it. Albizu is here!] or something like that, you know. And I felt very proud. It was very touching because it was people who knew what was going on. They were educated. But the majority of these people are not college—even high school—educated. I guess they're just enlightened. They've read. They've spoken. Oral tradition. People know about someone like Albizu because they talked a lot about it. Dialogue. My brother was into it a lot also, so we'd talk about it. The things I've learned the most in my life I've learned on my own.

As Tony narrated, the statue triggered dialogue around historical and local issues even among the most disenfranchised barrio residents. Precisely because of the strong positions barrio residents, nationalist activists, city officials, religious leaders, and the media took in promoting their views of Albizu Campos as either a terrorist or a hero, a vast space for critical pedagogy developed, a space for oppositional educational among the most detached barrio residents. As one resident expressed: "It became a process in which people were talking about it. You'd stand up in a corner and instead of hearing people talking about the seven o'clock soap opera you'd hear 'Hey, what is that about the Albizu Statue?'" Clara Pérez commented: "My sister is a retired librarian. She explained the Albizu Campos issue to me." Clara's comment pointed to the dialogue that was generated by the heated polemic.

PACHS director and teacher Luis Guzmán explained how the statue stimulated an educational dialogue: "People are already used to hearing about Albizu. Albizu has been talked about publicly. It was a conscious task. Flyers. Promotions. As part of the statue process, and even earlier. The educational process around Albizu Campos aimed to have people learn about the [FALN] prisoners and get involved in issues around the prisoners. That's how it started, but the statue issue gave it concreteness." As Clara and Luis suggested, the statue issue initiated a dialogue about the role of militant nationalist leaders both in U.S. politics toward Puerto Rico and in the history of the Chicago barrio; it also gave concreteness to local factionalism. Albizu statue was politicized not only for its subject's historical militancy, but also for the boundaries the statue challenged along class lines and for the racialization process it embodied.

Eduardo Arocho, a Puerto Rican man in his mid-twenties, was born and raised in Chicago. He attended Clemente High School and Northeastern Illinois University, where he was editor of a Latino campus publication. He was also one of my neighbors; we rented different parts of the same house. Eduardo had published poems in local magazines and had read his poetry at several community forums. Eduardo was proud of his most renowned poem (Arocho 1993), which emerged from the Albizu Campos polemic. In the poem Albizu Campos is the bandit or thief, the ultraliberal Robin Hood who lives by his own rules:

> *BUT HISTORY NEVER*
> *VISITED*
> *THE COLORFUL CHILDREN*
> *IN THE DIRT. ERASED.*
> *WAS THEIR FATHER'S NAME*
> *FROM THE UNPALATABLE BOOKS*
> *ON SCHOOL SHELVES*
> *TELEVISION AND NEWSPAPERS*
> *CALLED THEIR FATHER*

CRAZY, COMMUNIST AND TERRORIST
BUT THE CHILDREN
HAVE NEVER SEEN
THE SMILE ON HIS FACE

Albizu becomes a critique of the public education system and of Clemente High School, from which the author graduated, when Albizu's name is "erased . . . from the unpalatable books on school shelves" just as Albizu's mural was erased from the Clemente building's walls. Hence, "history was a new debate camp: it had to construct other places, and engage in a struggle for new significance. . . . 'There is nothing more alive, more present in a society than the relationship it sustains with the images of the past'" (Claude Lefort in Díaz-Quiñones 1993, 66). Most significant in the case of the Albizu statue is that the images of the past showed how "those considered 'criminals' by the elite are not necessarily culpable in popular eyes, according to popular expression" (Guerra 1998, 171).

When the Chicago Park District refused to allow the Pedro Albizu Campos statue to be erected, barrio residents and nationalist activists perceived this criminalization by the state, concealed behind the image of a Latino elite, as similar to the persecution suffered by Puerto Rican nationalists, like members of the FALN and Albizu Campos himself. By condemning the city, State of Illinois officials, and factions of the Latino elite and humanizing, even heroizing, Albizu Campos, the barrio residents became discursively affiliated with society's deviants. Creative expressions like Eduardo's poems served to assert the higher morality of the barrio poor's communal system of dispensing justice. In this sense, criminalization and rebellion were occasionally approved, even heralded, as testament to the popular classes' resistance to the onslaught of the legal incursions into daily life wrought by colonialism and white supremacy.

As Eduardo expresses, "history never visited" until the church ceremony that placed the Albizu Campos prophetic tradition at its center. But history was never considered a clear, unquestionable narrative in Humboldt Park when viewed in reference to events concerning Puerto Rican nationalism, past and present. Many other Puerto Ricans viewed nationalist activists' self-contained community projects as disadvantageous to Puerto Rican integration and acceptance into mainstream U.S. society and thus as advocating, quite self-consciously, alternative representations of Puerto-Ricanness in Chicago. The power of choosing which history was worth producing, reproducing, and transmitting across generations framed the Pedro Albizu Campos statue debate. The statue issue reflects ways in which an "inner-city" Latino community saw history as a narrative grounded in everyday social practices and having concrete political consequences; a discourse that retained contemporaneousness because of its social implications, the political economy behind its symbols, and the educational forums it created.

Current anthropological literature has examined "selective uses of the past" (Chapman, McDonald, and Tonkin 1989). This literature recognizes the acknowledgment or denial of history as a reflection not of the accuracy of memory, but of the relationship to power (Guss 1993). It recognizes that the "debatability of the past" and the normative ways in which this debatability is regulated leads cultures to change (Appadurai 1983). The recovering or reinterpreting of history is perceived as necessarily counterhegemonic (Williams 1977). It is understood in dialectical relation to the production of identity (Friedman 1992) and as an essential element in the formation of national cultures and nationalist thought (Malkki 1990).

The narratives generated by the Albizu statue debate contribute to this anthropological literature by recognizing the role of urban spaces, political factionalism, and popular education in the formation of a racial and class consciousness among Puerto Ricans in Chicago. The act of resurrecting and reinterpreting the past has been associated with the emergence of social movements premised on a cultural nationalism that can endure despite subordination to a dominant Other (Warren 1995; Duany 2000). When the past evoked in the present has been constructed as inherently controversial, spaces are created in which racial and class power dynamics are mediated by an emergent nationalist discourse. As Eduardo's poem mentions:

> *LONELY ARE THE CHILDREN IN THE DIRT.*
> *AS THEY WAIT*
> *HUMBLY IN HUMBOLDT PARK*
> *FOR "EL MAESTRO"*
> *TO STAND WITH THEM*
> *AGAIN IN BRONZE*
> *VAINLESSLY*
> *GIVING*
> *HIS MEEK*
> *AND SUBLIME*
> *SELF*
> *TO ALL*
> *THE COLORFUL CHILDREN*
> *OF BORINQUEN.*

Eduardo describes an Albizu removed from the militant historical figure who becomes a terrorist in the eyes of city officials, the Christian Right, and a Latino elite. Albizu becomes the bronzed image of those who "wait humbly in Humboldt Park." The poet emphasizes the class divisions embodied in the term *humble*: its Spanish equivalent, *humilde,* is another word for *poor.*

In Chicago the production of the Puerto Rican nation and the performance of nationalism was significant partially because it furnished a vocabulary to articulate class consciousness and denounce the politics of race among Puerto Ricans, while inadvertently preserving hegemonic ideas of meritocracy, social mobility, and the American dream. Thus, while the dimensions of class and race did not figure as prominently as the rhetoric of nationalism in Puerto Rican Chicago, it was the nationalist vocabulary that enabled class and internal racialization to be manifested at all. The performance of nationalism and the production of the nation in Chicago involved the strategic propagation of a folkloric politics and popular education initiatives that inadvertently provided a stage on which to explore and rehearse various configurations of racial formations and class consciousness.

History as a metanarrative and interpretive device serves as a source of nationhood and a political discourse for present constructions of nationness (cf. Chatterjee 1993; Malkki 1990). Among subaltern groups "mythico-histories" act as ideologies that denounce present conditions of marginalization by provoking the past into narration, transforming it in the process (Malkki 1990). The resurrection and transformation of narratives of the past becomes a social practice with concrete, everyday consequences. As local artist Manuel Burgos once commented: "There is a mural of Albizu on Calvary, because that was a Puerto Rican response to the riots of the 1960s, a way of telling the city to stop burning down our buildings . . . that we, too, have a history." Making history becomes a way of producing identity and meanings insofar as it conflates interpretations of the past and specific social conditions of the present (Friedman 1994). The importance of determining which aspects of history were resurrected in Chicago's Puerto Rican barrio, how were they reconstituted, and which motifs were advanced in the process illuminates the contestation of nationalism as a class vocabulary, as well as the way in which racial identities are historicized as nationalist discourse.

The history provoked into narration juxtaposed intertextual references to the history of Puerto Rico's separatist nationalist movement of the 1950s and the local barrio militancy embodied in the members of the FALN.[7] Pedro Albizu Campos was a militant, separatist, anti-American freedom fighter, like the FALN prisoners. His image first became prominent in

Humboldt Park at the time when the FALN members were arrested and sentenced. Albizu became the image that could give the FALN actions legitimacy as the group's members were portrayed as a link in a long chain of controversial historical figures who had sacrificed and suffered on behalf of their *patria*'s freedom. In this sense, the FALN members were separated from conventional criminals, and the criminalized images were embraced by poor employed and unemployed people. Albizu supporters and opponents alike became keenly aware of their role in the production and reproduction of historical narratives that would then be incorporated into mainstream representations of Puerto-Ricanness in Chicago. As these intimate nationalist performances unfolded, Albizu Campos's image was strategically deployed not only in relation to its role in Puerto Rico's history, but, more significant, in its usefulness in conveying and altering images of Puerto Rican Chicago in the imagination of its supporters and opponents alike.

The heroic past of militancy redeemed by Chicago's barrio nationalists resembles that of the Mayan intellectuals described by Kay Warren, who "are reviving the heroic imagery of Mayan warriors in an attempt to deal with the passivity they see as one of the scars of Latino racism and its language of inferiority for indigenous populations" (Warren 1995, 135). As Eduardo writes in his poem:

> *AND WITH HIS VAST KNOWLEDGE OF NATURE*
> *AND PROFOUND INTELLIGENCE*
> *HE TAUGHT THEM TO BE BRAVE,*
> *FREE AND INDEPENDENT*
> *AND GROW UP AS MEN AND WOMYN*
> *LIBERATED FROM THE IMPERIAL*
> *UNITED STATES.*

Warren shows that the specific narratives articulated among Mayan intellectuals and transmitted in popular educational material emphasize "images of self-determination and adversity [as] weapons for a population that has been defined by conquest rather than by their own historical agency" (1995, 135). The heroic history aims to overcome a sense of powerlessness in the face of racial prejudice and socioeconomic stratification. Forging narratives of a militant history that highlights an anticolonial past and Puerto Rican resilience enhances a sense of nationhood and cushions deplorable living conditions. Tracing neighborhood political lines back to the FALN and Pedro Albizu Campos in this chronology, barrio residents and activists saw their lives resonate in a broader global context as they sustained a connection to the history of Puerto Rico, from which they, as migrants, had often been excluded.

Nationalist activists' appropriation of Albizu Campos as a hero was filtered through the prism of local events that had shaped the barrio's characterization in mainstream forums in Chicago. As nationalist pastor Andrés Maldonado explained: "Everything [related to Albizu Campos] started as a process to start dealing with the issue of the political prisoners and the prisoners of war. What you'd see back then weren't pictures of Albizu. It was poster boards of Alejandrina, Carmen Valentín, on each corner." Grassroots images of the political prisoners enhanced everyday interpretations of Puerto Rican militant history among nationalist activists and their opponents.

In his study of Sandinista Nicaragua Lancaster examines "the indistinguishability and synchronicity—of religion and politics, tradition and revolution" (1988, 129). In the case of the Albizu statue, the nationalist imagery illuminated forms of social stratification, rather than undermining them in the interest of national unity, as nationalist discourse on the Island generally does (Pabón 1995). In fact, the Albizu imagery foregrounded racialization and class boundaries among Puerto Ricans by straddling the tension between a Christianized view of Albizu, which drew churchgoers to a more active political involvement in the community, and a terrorist characterization that some Latino professionals associated with the FALN.

In the performance of nationalism, the polemic around Pedro Albizu Campos did not suggest that barrio residents sought refuge in glorified images of the past, but rather that they aimed to analyze the values of their own community. In Chicago the racial and class consciousness enhanced by the Albizu Campos polemic was deflected onto nationalist discourse precisely because the hegemonic mythologies of the United States (e.g., the land of opportunity, the American dream) superseded beliefs that class background and parentage influence an individual's life outcomes.

In addition to creating popular forums for interpreting Puerto Rican and barrio history, the Albizu Campos image illuminated internal racialization among Puerto Ricans. As Eduardo describes in another fragment of his poem:

THEN THE COLORFUL CHILDREN
COME OUT TO PLAY
WITH THE MUSIC
CALLED "LA PLENA"
THEY CHANTED HIS NAME:

HURRICANE "PEDRO"
HURRICANE "ALBIZU"
HURRICANE "CAMPOS"
THEIR SPIRITS SOARED
SO HIGH
THAT THEY COALESCED
INTO BEAUTIFUL RAINBOWS.
"EL MAESTRO" SAID
THESE ARE
THE COLORFUL CHILDREN
OF BORINQUEN

The African and Afro-Caribbean referents of the *plena* music decidedly render the "colorful children of Borinquen" unequivocally black. Eduardo's poems and other poems by local artists transcended Afro-Caribbean folklore to become historical narratives and documentation of barrio political conflict and the continuous reconfiguration of racial boundaries among Puerto Ricans.

PEDRO ALBIZU CAMPOS AND THE RACIALIZATION OF INTERNAL BOUNDARIES

Many activists and residents in Chicago's Puerto Rican barrio reinterpreted the nationalist past in the context of everyday tensions over urban spaces and resources by continuously reassessing the politics of race and class in which the activists and residents were embroiled. The public space of Juan Cruz's Protestant church, where the ecumenical ceremony was held, served as popular education site. But in order for this ecumenical setting to serve as a learning site, an equally compelling counternarrative denouncing Albizu's controversial militancy was indispensable. Radio talk shows, the mainstream media, and popular resistance to the more heroic images conveyed by nationalist activists furnished the counternarratives. On the site of Cruz's church the official, state-sponsored narratives of Albizu-as-terrorist were challenged, while a nationalist militancy was legitimized by the Christification of Albizu Campos and, most significant, by the racialization of his image as that of a black Puerto Rican.

The image of Albizu exalted by nationalist activists and some barrio residents in Chicago was not exclusively one of militant politics or armed struggle. Rather, in nationalist narratives Pedro Albizu Campos was Don Pedro, the black Puerto Rican born in the poverty-stricken rural barrio of Tenerías, Puerto Rico, as the illegitimate son of a white Spanish *hacendado* and a black and poor Puerto Rican mother. He was the man who, through hard work and dedication, became the first Puerto Rican to graduate from Harvard and subsequently acted as a civil defender of the poor. Don Pedro was in many ways the Puerto Rican nationalist embodiment of the American dream.

The production of racial difference in the everyday regimentation of Puerto Rican nationalism was situated in the interaction and imagining of blackness between Puerto Ricans and African-Americans in Chicago. Chicago Puerto Ricans participated on the same social plane on which U.S. racism against African Americans is produced. Nevertheless, this racial ideology was continually re-elaborated in a process of re-racialization (De Genova 1999; Omi and Winant 1986). Nationalist activists, for instance, emphasized that they had honored the *real* Albizu Campos by recognizing and representing the nationalist leader's racial identity as a *black* Puerto Rican, rather than the whitened mulatto of official historical accounts. Albizu was darkened by migration. "Albizu was dark," commented José López, "but for a long time people in Puerto Rico wanted to believe he was white." José perceived the efforts of nationalist activists in Chicago to darken Albizu Campos as evidence of Puerto Rican moral superiority and acceptance of racial diversity—as compared to the presumably more racist U.S. racial taxonomy—and also as a denunciation of racial attitudes among a Puerto Rican elite on the Island.

Nationalist activists interpreted the criminalization of Albizu Campos by the state as evidence of racial prejudice on the part of the city's mainstream institutions and a "white" Latino elite. It was precisely this criminalization that prevented Albizu Campos's image from being neutralized or depoliticized. The statue of the nationalist became the symbol of *la gente pobre* not because barrio residents were indiscriminately advocating for the statue, but because people whom barrio residents perceived as outsiders were attacking the statue the most. Because the statue's opponents were those who had access to mainstream forums for public criticism, such as the media, Humboldt Park residents necessarily became advocates of the statue. Nationalist activists emphasized the many efforts that *la gente pobre* undertook to finance the statue. Ironically, the statue denounced oppressive living conditions and racism much more than the nationalist patriot ever did.

In barrio residents' us-and-them narration of the statue incident, *them* was used in reference to a generalized cosmic villain, rather than to any particular group (see chapters 4 and 5). When prompted to identify "them," residents pointed to "the Park District," "other races," or "the anti-*independentistas*." Elda Aponte referred to Albizu not as a nationalist, but as a catalyst of the party-politics fragmentation that characterizes Puerto Rico's society: "The *independentistas* were in favor of the statue. If they had said that they planned to put up a statue of Ferré [former pro-statehood governor of Puerto Rico], the *populares* would have objected to that. It's all about politics! People don't see these leaders as a glory to Puerto Rico unless they are from your own political party." While Puerto Rico's party system provided the facile framework for interpreting the debates around Albizu Campos, the disassociation between the nationalist symbols, Puerto-Ricanness, and party politics in Puerto Rico was noteworthy because in this disassociation—rather than in any alternative overshadowing of social difference on behalf of nationalism—lay the foundation of Puerto Rican nationalist performances in Chicago.

The statue and other imagery of the nationalist leader transcended political party affiliations to serve as a discourse of the historicization of racial difference. As a worker at a Logan Square health clinic commented: "When you stand on a corner with a little Puerto Rican flag, people give you money. People get the money from where they don't have it. And that leads me to believe that no matter whether you are statehooder, *popular,* or pro-independence, Puerto Ricans here are *nacionalistas.* They are, in a sense, more *nacionalista* than the ones in Puerto Rico. Because here the one thing you cannot offend is *la puertorriqueñidad.*" The debate actually disjoined identities formed around the technicalities of the political status of Puerto Rico to localize Albizu Campos as an image of Puerto-Ricanness organically constructed in Chicago. Nationalist activists insisted on interpreting opposition to the statue as evidence of how U.S. mainstream institutions, such as the Park District and the media, and even some members of the Latino political elite viewed the Puerto Rican barrio as pathological and crime-ridden. In this context the racialization of Daniel Alvarez as Cuban and as an outsider takes prominence.

A Latino officer for the Chicago Park District, Daniel Alvarez objected to the statue, maintaining the position that Albizu Campos was an anti-American terrorist. When I interviewed Daniel in his downtown office in the fall of 1994, he emphatically asserted that members of the predominantly Latino church he attended in Logan Square would ask him to take action to prevent the Albizu Campos statue from being placed in the park. Daniel commented:

> They call me and ask me to do something about this. . . . They didn't want to be considered criminals because the statue of a criminal is put in their neighborhood. Because that's what Albizu Campos was. [The members of his church would say] that there was enough violence in the area already. Why bring about more? So when the [other officers of

the Park District] consulted with me about this and told me they were
thinking of putting up this statue, I told them: "How can you do that?
This is who Albizu Campos was." And I would explain.

A white-collar worker for the city government, Daniel was a meaning broker
of sorts. The Park District learned about Albizu-as-terrorist from Daniel.
There was a cultural intimacy between statue supporters and opponents,
who evoked the same historical narrative—the militancy of the 1950s
Puerto Rican nationalist movement—to sustain their position on this local
incident.

More significant is the fact that Daniel was racialized as Cuban by supporters of the Albizu Campos statue. Although Daniel's mother was Puerto
Rican, he became unquestionably Cuban in the eyes of his opponents. A
flyer that was distributed in Humboldt Park in the spring of 1994 describes
Daniel as "The #1 Enemy of the Puerto Rican Community" and outlines
Daniel's ulterior motives for objecting to the statue, including his interests
in Humboldt Park real estate. The flyer asks: "Will a Cuban decide the destiny of the Puerto Rican community?" The widely distributed flyer questions
Daniel's authenticity even though his mother was Puerto Rican and Daniel
grew up on the Island: "A man of Cuban descent has been trying to pass for
Puerto Rican. Occasionally, he even says his mother is Puerto Rican to try to
justify his unwelcome intervention in our community's issues. . . . Nowa-
days he occupies prominent positions in the City [government]. He owns
various expensive properties on California Avenue." During the interview
Daniel was particularly interested in emphasizing that he felt Puerto Rican.
He pointed to what he saw as a great irony: "I was raised in Puerto Rico and
lived there for the first thirty or so years of my life. I went to school there. My
sisters still live there. And yet some of the people who say that I'm Cuban
and deny my Puerto-Ricanness were born here and haven't even been to
Puerto Rico. What makes them more Puerto Rican than me?"

Daniel recognized that in Chicago one's Puerto-Ricanness was rarely secured and uncontested. Puerto-Ricanness in Chicago was not a matter of
natural belongingness, but was subjected to constant scrutiny and was
based on the performance of the nation in ways that centered on the barrio
as a space of racial production. In this sense Puerto-Ricanness was subjected to fluid configurations and reconfigurations along axes of class, race,
space, and numerous social positionings. Daniel was hurt by characterizations circulating in Humboldt Park during the statue debate and by subsequent challenges to his cultural authenticity: "Now, after I've worked for
thirty years in the community . . . with the elderly, with the church . . . now

Daniel Alvare$:
Enemigo Público #1
De la comunidad puertorriqueña

*¿Decidirá un **cubano** el futuro de la comunidad **puertorriqueña**?*

Lea la próxima página para detalles...

This double-sided anonymous flyer was circulated in Humboldt Park in 1993 and 1994, during the conflict surrounding the Pedro Albizu Campos statue. Because Daniel Alvarez, then a commissioner for the Park District, objected to the statue, claiming that Albizu Campos was a terrorist, supporters of the statue singled him out as an enemy of the Puerto Rican community. The flyer also emphasizes the qualities of Albizu Campos that make his image a good choice for a statue, particularly in the section entitled "Despierta, Boricua . . . ¡Defiende lo Tuyo!" (Author's collection)

Despierta, Boricua... ¡Defiende lo Tuyo!

SOHNBOY

No Dejes Que Un **Cubano** Decida Por Tu Futuro

HOY:

Demuestra tu Apoyo por la Estatua Albizu Campos

Piquete: 4:30 P.M.
Frente A Holstein Park
2200 N. Oakley (Esq. Palmer)

Vista Pública: 6:00 P.M.

HECHOS SOBRE LA VIDA DE PEDRO ALBIZU CAMPOS Y LA ESTATUA DE HUMBOLDT PARK

SOBRE ALBIZU CAMPOS:

HECHO: Pedro Albizu Campos, puertorriqueño negro y pobre del Barrio Tenerías de Ponce fue un destacado estudiante quien, en el 1921 se convirtió en el primer puertorriqueño en graduarse de la Universidad de Harvard con títulos en Ingeniería Química, Letras y Filosofía, Ciencias Militares y Derecho. Rechazó varias ofertas de empleo muy lucrativas a nivel diplomático y político y optó por ser abogado defensor del pueblo trabajador en su país.

Se convirtió en Presidente del Partido Nacionalista de Puerto Rico en el 1930, realizando una inmensa labor educativa y propagandística en pro de la independencia de su patria. En el 1934 Albizu dirigió la huelga de los trabajadores agrícolas a petición de éstos. Por sus principios intachables, su verticalidad, y por su ética de no-colaboración con los intereses imperiales y su negativa ante el intento de sobornarlo, se ganó el título de "El Maestro".

Albizu Campos se convirtió en el líder imprescindible de la lucha libertaria del pueblo puertorriqueño en el Siglo XX. Ya para el 1935 se revela un plan de la policía secreta de los EE.UU. en Puerto Rico para asesinarlo.

HECHO: Albizu Campos jamás fue encontrado culpable en relación a, o vinculado a un acto de violencia en Puerto Rico. Albizu Campos fue encarcelado en el 1937 luego de ser acusado dos veces en dos juicios distintos por el mismo "delito" de abogar por la independencia de su patria. En el 1950 es arrestado en su residencia y sentenciado a 80 años por abogar por, y defender la independencia. La ley utilizada para encarcelarlo es la notoria *"Ley de la Mordaza"*, la cual prohíbe que cualquier persona abogue, escriba, o defienda la independencia de Puerto Rico. En otras palabras, era delito pensar en, o ser independentista. Esta ley fue diseñada de acuerdo al Acta Smith de los EE.UU. Albizu no fue encarcelado debido a su envolvimiento en la Revolución de Jayuya de 1950, ni por el ataque a la Casa Blair, entonces residencia del Presidente Harry Truman. Albizu es indultado por Muñoz Marín en el 1953 debido a la presión recibida de países latinoamericanos, quienes sentían

un alto nivel de respeto por éste. Albizu Campos es encarcelado nuevamente en el 1954. En el 1956 sufre una trombosis que lo deja semiparalítico y sin habla. En el 1964, casi al borde de la muerte, es indultado por segunda vez. El 21 de abril de 1965 muere Albizu Campos. Su funeral fue el más atendido en la historia de Puerto Rico.

HECHO: Estudios recientes extensamente documentados demuestran que Albizu fue sometido a una "muerte lenta" por medio de radiación en la cárcel.

HECHO: Durante los últimos tres años (1991-1993) en más de 40 municipios de Puerto Rico se le han dedicado obras públicas, desde escuelas, centros culturales, parques, bibliotecas, calles y avenidas principales, entre otras.

En México, Perú, Venezuela, Argentina y otros lugares se le ha reconocido la obra de Albizu Campos, dedicándole varias obras públicas con su nombre, entre éstas, centros docentes entre otras.

SOBRE LA ESTATUA:

HECHO: La comunidad puertorriqueña de Chicago, mediante múltiples esfuerzos, ha logrado recaudar los $50,000 para cubrir los gastos de la estatua, originalmente creada por el escultor puertorriqueño Ramón Moreno.

HECHO: La estatua fue ofrecida como donación de la comunidad al Distrito de Parques de Chicago para exhibición permanente en el Parque Humboldt.

HECHO: En ningún momento se ha pedido al gobierno, o cualquiera de sus agencias o dependencias que asuman los gastos de dicho monumento.

HECHO: El Comité Pro-Celebración del Centenario de Dr. Pedro Albizu Campos asumirá toda la responsabilidad por el mantenimiento de dicha estatua y velará por los predios donde ésta iría colocada (entrada al Parque Humboldt, esquinas de División "Calle Dr. Pedro Albizu Campos" y Western).

HECHO: El Comité Pro-Celebración del Centenario de Dr. Pedro Albizu Campos ha cumplido con todos los requisitos para la aprobación de la estatua.

HECHO: ¿Quién Se Opone? Ese grupito de personas, dirigidas por el cubano mentiroso Daniel Alvare$ y la persona que aspira a ser candidato a Consejal por el distrito 26: Ray Rubio—que hasta su nombre se ha cambiado, y está dispuesto a cambiar hasta a su patria por un precio.

I'm not Puerto Rican? I was born in Mayaguez, Puerto Rico. My mother is from there. I grew up eating *arroz con gandules*. But noooo, to them I'm Cuban because my father was Cuban." While growing up in Puerto Rico was often seen as unequivocal sign of cultural authenticity, a second-generation Cuban like Daniel Alvarez and Dominican residents of Puerto Rico were excluded from official constructions of the nation (see Duany 2000). These categories of exclusion on the Island were sustained in Chicago. Supporters of the statue attributed the Park District's decision not to place the statue in Humboldt Park to the political power of members of certain Latino nationalities, particularly Cubans. In this sense, re-racialization processes among Latinos rendered Cubans as "closer to white" and Puerto Ricans as "closer to black."

Nevertheless, when other Puerto Ricans—particularly a group of real estate agents, lawyers, and high-ranking politicians—joined Daniel in his opposition to the statue, the nationalist activists and barrio residents created them in decidedly classed terms. These opponents of the statue became the villain camp: they were upper class, disconnected from the poor, and assimilated, according to local activists' and residents' subjectivities. Nationalist activists argued that these cosmic villains enabled the state to criminalize Albizu Campos and the statue-unveiling process. Through these perceptions of the assimilated Latino the state remained safeguarded and legitimized, as the ultimate polemic was expressed as one between an abstract Latino elite and the Puerto Rican barrio poor. The nationalist activists viewed the state's reinterpretation of Albizu-as-criminal as having more to do with racial and class prejudice and preconceptions of the American self as white than with the reality, past or present, of Albizu as a threat to the American nation. Barrio-generated views of Puerto Rican nationalism in Chicago were not attentive to official languages of nation-state formation, but rather served as a lens through which to filter denunciation of everyday inequalities and prejudice. The denunciation was limited, however, by the ways in which nationalism was frequently embedded in discussions of terrorism and anti-Americanism.

Moreover, Albizu became an image configured by the working class to continuously question the authenticity of some factions of the middle class as truly Puerto Rican. By equating "true" Puerto-Ricanness with commitment to the neighborhood, the nationalist activists promoted a politics of space that stipulated that the only right way of belonging to a Puerto Rican elite while maintaining one's cultural authenticity was by expressing solidarity with the barrio poor. Barrio residents and nationalist activists simultaneously homogenized all white-collar Latinos as an elite, a classed Other, and maintained a hierarchy of levels of authenticity to which the elite could aspire on the basis of the nature of their involvement in urban development in the area.

Conversely, members of this white-collar elite claimed different social locations, depending on their connection to the state and to the barrio's grassroots activism. Workers at local non-profits who maintained strong personal and professional connections to the barrio poor alternately looked to the barrio margins for authentication and fragmented the margins by selectively supporting aspects of Albizu that were not inconsistent with dominant U.S. ideology: they focused on Albizu's mainstream accomplishments while condemning his radical militancy. Workers occupying higher positions in the city government and real estate, who constituted a more nationality-diversified Latino group, publicly criminalized the statue as anti-American and representative of terrorism, and they demonized it as counter to dominant social norms. Barrio nationalist activists perceived the criminalization of Albizu Campos as evidence that these members of the corporate sector had real estate interests in the Humboldt Park area. The barrio activists argued that these real estate agents would have a hard time renting or selling property to their white clients if a statue of a Puerto Rican, and particularly of a Puerto Rican separatist, were erected in the park.

By criminalizing Albizu and rendering him anti-American, the opponents of the statue legitimated their mobility on the basis of an identity as law-abiding citizens, while limiting the inclusion of members of the working class to those who fit a discursively constructed ideal type characterized by loyalty to the United States and the American dream. This faction of the elite, and opponents of the statue in general, became the legitimate guardians of the American dream in Chicago by emphasizing the rules that lead to social mobility and by turning Albizu into the embodiment of cautionary tales. This is not to say that the Latino professionals became unproblematically assimilated into a white, middle-class mainstream, but rather that their identities as Puerto Rican or, more commonly, Latino, were often in great tension with the space racialized as the Puerto Rican barrio in Chicago. Precisely because members of a largely professional Latino elite who acted as meaning brokers for the agents of city government criminalized the nationalist activists' project of placing the Albizu statue in the park, the rhetoric around the image of the nationalist leader provided the vocabulary for publicly denouncing mainstream prejudicial attitudes using codes and narratives comprehensible only to the subalterns who experienced such prejudice. The statue created spaces to address intragroup conflict in the public sphere (cf. Scott 1988). The Latino opponents of the statue acted as intermediaries and interpreters—meaning brokers—to the state by explaining publicly Albizu Campos's militant significance and why his statue was an inadequate symbol of Puerto-Ricanness. These urban spaces generated a public history that served as a counterhegemonic discourse and that remained powerful precisely because it was criminalized by the state and by some Latino professionals.

The Albizu Campos image was maintained as oppositional by a polarized interpretation of the nationalist as either Christified patriot or anti-American terrorist. Dominant representations of members of the Puerto Rican popular sector as passive, opportunistic, and "underclass" were incompatible with the iconography of militancy and struggle put forth by grassroots activists and alternately contested and transformed by barrio residents.

ALBIZU AS NATIONALIZED BLACKNESS:
RESISTANCE TO THE DOMINANT RACIAL ORDER

The image of the controversial nationalist leader Pedro Albizu Campos was promoted by nationalist activists not only as a counterrepresentation to dominant views of residents of the U.S. "inner-city" as apathetic, opportunistic, and "underclassed," but also as an element of resistance to the dominant insistence on a black-white racial taxonomy. Albizu was emblematic of resistance not only because of his party politics, which were quite conservative and even reactionary (see Ferrao 1990 and Lopes 1982),[8] but also because of his upward social mobility and blackness.

Declarations of community solidarity among barrio residents and activists involved both an advocacy of regarding racial mixing as the foundation of Puerto Rican national identity in the United States and a denial of racism among Puerto Ricans. Grassroots activists devised a political ideology that created a unified nationalist movement in which the tenets of community-building projects and self-representation were based on ideas of racial mixing. These ideas of racial mixing not only stretched the boundaries of racial acceptability to include all Puerto Ricans, but also allowed Puerto Rican popular nationalism to be performed in contradistinction to the U.S. bipolar racial order.

Nevertheless, the vision of Puerto Rican culture as black gains value in the market of symbolic goods only insofar as it is assumed to be pure and representative of resistance (Guss 1993; Gomes da Cunha 1998). Hence, activists could frown upon rap as co-opted and as an expression of Puerto-Ricanness that is identified with U.S. blacks while celebrating Albizu along the lines of Afro–Puerto Rican pride. Albizu's blackness is, in its essence, Puerto Rican. Circumventing the dominant black-white racial taxonomy involved evoking the racial triad, the Puerto Rican *mestizaje* according to which all Puerto Ricans have some combination of Spanish, African, and Taíno Indian blood. The racial-triad discourse recognized difference on the basis of commonly demarcated historical attributes while avoiding discourses of multiculturalism and diversity. For instance, high school student and barrio resident Wanda Rivera articulates in an autobiographical essay what many second- and third-generation Puerto Rican youth explained as the "genesis of Puerto-Ricanness." "Being Puerto Rican is being mixed with that Taíno, Spanish, African and every other blood god has placed in us. Being Puerto Rican is struggling for your rights and fighting for what belongs to you. Being proud, happy and wealthy with your race is being Puerto Rican. Not complaining about your hair or how dark your skin is, or how brown your eyes are instead of green. This is what being a Puerto Rican is all about." The racial genesis of Puerto-Ricanness focuses on the elements from the Taíno Indian, African, and Spanish heritage that are most closely associated with anticolonial resistance, and popular education programs and nationalist activists insisted on emphasizing the aspects of the triad that were viewed as representing resistance. At PACHS, the alternative high school Wanda attended, it was the African *cimarrón,* the rebellious escaped slave, who became the true representation of Puerto-Ricanness in the diaspora.

Many literary and scholarly works have noted that Puerto Rican migrants, particularly black Puerto Ricans, deliberately exalt certain aspects of Puerto Rican culture in an effort to avoid the dichotomized black-white racial hierarchy in the United States (Thomas 1967). Speaking Spanish, listening to salsa, and displaying or wearing cultural markers like the Puerto Rican flag are common practices that Puerto Rican migrants and U.S.-born Puerto Ricans of subsequent generations have traditionally sought to negotiate their relationship with—or usually away from—African Americans, even while consuming "black culture" in daily life.

While some recent studies on race in Puerto Rico argue that an emergent racial consciousness and black pride are evidenced by the appropriation of rap music and Rastafarianism among urban youth (see Santos Febres 1993a), the ideology of racial mixing tends to undermine other forms of racial consciousness. *Mestizaje* is the conceptualization of the self as the embodiment of racial diversity, while it promotes normative understandings of racial configurations and taxonomies (Torres 1998). In Puerto Rico the myth of racial democracy has frequently co-opted the development of a black consciousness (Whitten and Torres 1992; Torres 1998), often in favor of a *blanqueamiento* [racial whitening], or a preference for "marrying white" to "improve the race." The *mestizaje* promoted by Puerto Rico's national ideology has historically circumvented discussions about race on the Island.[9] Difference and diversity are attributes used to configure other possible unified national wholes.

Many barrio residents agreed with Alma Juncos's perception of Puerto Rico as more class-oriented and less race-oriented than the United States: "In Puerto Rico everybody is Puerto Rican regardless of how dark or light you are. There are differences, but they are socioeconomic differences, not racial ones. Here in Chicago socioeconomic differences are not as big as the ones in Puerto Rico, where you find neighborhoods with $500,000 houses and projects." Although in Puerto Rico a deeply ingrained cultural conditioning has rendered any open reference to racial distinctions taboo, Puerto Rican society exhibits what Lancaster (1992) cleverly describes as "colorism." "Color relations are power relations," Lancaster explains, and the people to whom different color designations are applied experience materially different life opportunities (1992, 223). In Puerto Rico as in other parts of Latin America, people comment on color constantly, even though they are not speaking in terms of separate racial groups. Hence, Alma's implication that in Puerto Rico race is more fluid, relational, and ambiguous was not necessarily a suggestion that any referent to race on the Island is an index or proxy for something else, such as class.

Among barrio residents, community solidarity was partially grounded in a denial of the importance of race or racism among Puerto Ricans, as well as in an emphasis on the racist attitudes and actions of the dominant society. Puerto Rican nationalism challenged U.S. racialization processes by imposing views on race that, rather than directly challenging the U.S. black-white dichotomy (Rodríguez 1990), are more concerned with the reconfiguration of Latin American and Caribbean views on social race and power. Puerto Ricans use racial adjectives in addressing one another, regardless of the race or class of either person involved, to undermine standard racial order. Thus, *rubia* [blonde] can be used to compliment someone for her beauty regardless of whether she is actually blonde or brunette, just as *negro* [black] is a term of endearment applicable to anyone.[10] *Indio* [Indian] is often used as a phenotypic description of someone who has European features, straight hair, and a suntan, but the term also implies physical beauty that is perceived to be especially authentic because it embodies all the elements of the racial triad.

By raising the standard of racial Otherness to one in which a black Puerto Rican like Albizu Campos became emblematic of the Puerto Rican nation in the diaspora, Puerto Rican nationalist activists and barrio residents rearticulated the significance of race and claimed a higher moral ground in relation to dominant society. The racial triad—African, Spanish, and Taíno Indian—constituted a powerful myth of national origin that is evoked as evidence of Puerto Ricans' moral superiority over the "true racists" of the United States. In Chicago that triad was deployed in ways that validated community-building strategies in the barrio.

UNPACKING THE RACIAL TRIAD IN CHICAGO

In Chicago nationalists acknowledged the Taíno legacy and mythology through commercial items and folkloric displays, considering it an integral part of the Puerto Rican "blood." Things Taíno included hand-made crafts, murals, and other artifacts that recognized the racial triad as the national myth of origin. However, the performative vision of the triad focused on its militant aspects. Because Taínos have been constructed as passive, as having always been attacked by the sanguine Caribe warriors of neighboring islands, they were not as effective ideological instruments of political consciousness as the "rebellious Africans," the *cimarrones*.

Perhaps what became most significant among Puerto Ricans in Chicago was the connection between Puerto Rican indigenous roots and Puerto Ricans' relationship with other Latin American or Latino groups for which Indianness was often associated with backwardness, gullibility, marginality, and antimodernism. For the large Mexican and significant Guatemalan populations, as well as for other populations in Latin America, Indians are a tangible and recognized presence, and Africans have been effectively minimized in the national imaginary.

By selectively exalting blackness, Puerto Rican activists accomplished three main goals. First, blackness was associated with the struggle of African American civil rights leaders, many of whom held nationalist views, rather than solely with an ahistorical African heritage or folklore.[11] Second, the activists explicitly recognized that Puerto Rican as a racial identity formation was related to how Puerto Ricans were racialized as black or similar to black by dominant society and other Latinos alike. Finally, Puerto Rican blackness could be negotiated as different from African American blackness. Emphasizing this distinction between "how we see ourselves" and "how a dominant Other sees us" further sustained the performance of a Puerto Rican nationalism in Chicago. The racialization of most Puerto Ricans as proxies for blacks in the bipolar racial system of the United States, the nationalist activists claimed, is another attempt by dominant society to oppress Puerto Ricans as it oppresses African Americans. To some extent, however, Puerto Ricans in Chicago had adopted the dominant black-white polarity: white Puerto Ricans were internally considered less authentic.

"People don't understand that you can have blue eyes and blonde hair and be proud of being Puerto Rican," commented a local artist.

Sectors of the popular classes in Puerto Rico have historically attributed improvement in their living conditions and civil rights—for instance the creation of workers' unions and enactment of labor laws—to the increasing presence of the United States on the Island (Guerra 1998). In contrast, Chicago barrio residents and nationalist activists associated civil rights accomplishments not with mainstream U.S. society, but with the struggles of other oppressed populations, particularly African Americans, in that society. Unlike Islanders, Mainland Puerto Ricans perceived advances in civil rights not as opportunities provided by U.S. colonialism, but as results of resistance to a dominant society reluctant to grant equality along racial or class lines. By focusing on Pedro Albizu Campos in the context of Puerto Rico's nationalist history, racial identification became conflated with the colonial power dynamics it signified.

Barrio activists deployed the term *black* not only to describe how dominant society and other Latinos classify Puerto Ricans, but also as a racial identity that was inherently militant. Among many Puerto Rican barrio residents, black culture as resistance against oppression was redeemed, valorized, and promoted, while kept guarded from efforts to commercialize it. Commercial black culture was considered adulterated culture, which was perceived as the distinct realm of African American popular expression.

While on the Island whiteness is coded as having "more Spanish blood," in the diaspora it is deployed to describe members of dominant U.S. society, *los blancos.* Referring to Americans as *los blancos,* or whites, creates solidarity between the Puerto Rican speaker and listener and generates a space in which Puerto-Ricanness is deployed independently of the skin color of the interlocutors (Ramos-Zayas 2001a, 2001b). On the Island alliances between popular and elite sectors required that a large mulatto popular class evoke a racial discourse that valorized whiteness and thus reinforced dominant racial hierarchies (Guerra 1998, 213). Puerto Ricans in the United States perceived valorizing whiteness as evidence of acceptance of the U.S. classification scheme, while they recognized the impossibility of infiltrating the power conceded to whiteness from the standpoint of racialized subjects.

Resistance entails not only a reconfiguration of the racial ideology of *mestizaje,* but also a recognition that the embodiment of Puerto Rican Creole culture, the *jíbaro,* is a militant black, rather than the passive white peasant of Puerto Rican national imaginary (Torres 1998). For instance, recall how once the Museum of History and Culture was forced to shut down, the Albizu Campos statue was placed in the middle of a community garden in front of a casita (see Aponte-Parés 1998). The casita has a sign that distinguishes it as "la casita de Don Pedro," and Puerto Rican and Lares revolutionary flags adorn its front yard. Albizu's statue militarizes the rural landscape traditionally dominated by the jíbaro. The Humboldt Park "rural landscape" did not absorb and neutralize Albizu Campos because the rural casita is itself a politicized and politicizing space.

This image of the *jíbaro* is significantly different from the images that have historically appeared in Puerto Rico (Guerra 1998; Torres 1998). As the Creole elite on the Island sought to establish a nation in opposition to the Spanish colonial government, the *jíbaro*, portrayed as white, represented the nation (Torres 1998, 294). Puerto Rico's elite insisted on the *jíbaro*'s whiteness because that was the only way in which the *jíbaro* imagery could represent the elite's self-concept as white. The *jíbaro* became the authentic cultural and biological incarnation of the Spanish colonial past at its best, and his passivity rendered him infinitely good and loyal (Guerra 1998, 102).

The fusion of *jíbaro* and *negro* in Puerto Rico alters how race has been essentialized in racial categories in the Puerto Rican cultural imaginary; the union represents a movement toward blackness (Torres 1998, 294–95). The *jíbaro* is no longer just a white-skinned peasant; he is a *jíbaro negro*. In Chicago this movement toward blackness took a step further because it was nationalized; *Puerto Rican* blackness was not to be conflated with *African American* blackness. In this sense Pedro Albizu Campos became the black *jíbaro* and the Puerto Rican nationalist of Chicago's barrio, with its own rural casita and Lares flag.

By shifting away from the ideology of racial mixing, which has traditionally been praised as evidence of racial harmony among Puerto Ricans, nationalist activists created a space for the insertion of class as an indicator of social locations that are analogous to race at some level.[12] In the United States popular constructions of class are stretched by making race, not class, the key component of popular consciousness. While people are categorized by phenotype, ancestry, class, and status, the acceptance of blacks is conditioned by cultural "lightening" (Torres 1998, 296). The assumption is that upward mobility cannot be achieved if a black identity is maintained because there are negative cultural ascriptions associated with blackness.

Chicago nationalist activists fragmented the Albizu Campos image so that the revolutionary nationalist represented a blackness that, by virtue of being that of a Puerto Rican nationalist, allowed the attainment of power as measured by the dominant Other—for example, in the form of upward mobility. Cultural capital and the way in which nationalist history was reinterpreted in light of the racializing processes of the present were evidenced by the fact that Puerto Ricans in Chicago continued to racialize African Americans as lazy and undeserving while vindicating themselves in the nationalist discourse as hardworking and socially committed. Albizu Campos's mobility did not whiten him, but actually darkened him so that Albizu became inclusive of the darkest Puerto Ricans—or rather, particularly representative of these Puerto Ricans. However, the "Africanness" that could potentially unite African Americans and Puerto Ricans as a symbol of social marginality was subverted by Albizu Campos, who was so dark that most Puerto Ricans literally pale by comparison, but so Puerto Rican that African Americans remain excluded.

As performed by barrio activists, popular nationalism reminded members of the Latino elite who opposed the statue of their own continuous marginality in the land of opportunity. The colonial condition elided under discourses of social mobility and equality was evidenced by the persistent poverty of barrio residents. In this sense, and despite a limited degree of social mobility, the class background of the poor was part of the construction of the self for the Puerto Rican middle class. When this elite looked at the margins, it was unable to fabricate myths of a population of good-natured, politically apathetic, and passive barrio Others. To articulate the complex racial and class inequalities in the United States, barrio activists and residents performed a nationalism that was rooted in images of Albizuist militancy, rather than in a harmonious, easily folklorized agrarian past.

Instead of lifting up the white peasant as the champion of national identity, barrio activists lifted up Albizu Campos, who was then jíbarized by the rural casita, "la casita de Don Pedro" in the Humboldt Park community garden. The activists engaged in efforts to Africanize Albizu away from the Hispanophile tradition to which the nationalist leader actually belonged (Ferrao 1990). Albizu was recognized not for his role as an *hacendado,* but as a rural poor person. The production and performance of a Puerto Rican nation thus contributed to class consciousness among the poor and advanced FALN advocacy and community building efforts. As constructed by barrio activists, Albizu became a cautionary tale of how traditional mobility roads in and of themselves are not sufficient for the attainment of the American dream, but how loyalty to the Puerto Rican nation might be.

Albizu statue supporters agreed about specific accomplishments of Pedro Albizu Campos that focused on mainstream visions of success: he overcame the adversities of being black and growing up in an impoverished area of Puerto Rico to become a revered political leader and speaker, and he rejected profitable employment offers to pursue a less lucrative career as an attorney. Above all he was Puerto Rican, and his would be "the first monument to a Puerto Rican in the entire United States and the first monument to a non-white in the City of Chicago."[13] The activists who advocated for having the Albizu statue placed in the park filtered the nationalist image through the evangelical lens of the local Protestant church. Some elected officials, particularly those seeking votes in the wards where the nationalist activists had great influence, supported the statue, while others opposed it. Despite the presence of numerous murals and the street-naming events, the Albizu image had remained relatively neutral prior to the statue conflict, when it became criminalized.

Many barrio residents and activists agreed that the Albizu Campos conflict was "not about the statue," but about *personalismo* and power relations along class and occupational lines.[14] Opposition to the Albizu statue ac-

At the Pedro Albizu Campos Museum of History and Culture, multiple community-wide events, including theatrical performances, poetry readings, history classes, and art exhibits, are held. (Author's photo)

quired concreteness once the focus became real estate interests and the protection of urban spaces in Puerto Rican Chicago. Nationalist activists associated the opponents of the statue not with criticism of Albizu's role in Puerto
Rico's militant history, but with the dreaded gentrification process, the influx of Latin American immigrants and blacks, and the changing political
economy in the barrio.

Luis Guzmán, the director of PACHS, explained the debate in terms of
self-serving real estate and electoral interests: "The statue is not so much the
big issue. The issue is that there are certain people who are worried about
their political fiefdoms. . . . When I talk about fiefdoms, I mean people like
Daniel Alvarez, who is Cuban and left Cuba because he . . . his quote was
'seeing too much red.' He has lots of connections with the people in the Park
District and people in the media." Political and economic leaders were able
to negotiate their closeness to the barrio Other by alternately criminalizing
and neutralizing Albizu Campos. Because Daniel Alvarez owned several
buildings right across from the park where the statue was to be erected, his
opposition to the statue was seen as a reflection of his desire to maintain his
"fiefdom" and of his Cubanness, which was conflated with whiteness, evoking issues of Latinidad.

The statue conflict generated multivalent meanings that involved the
continuous mythification, criminalization, and reinterpretation of Albizu
Campos. The nationalist leader's biography became contested terrain for
the interpretation of the past, which transformed mythico-historical narratives into ideologies for the present. The Albizu image allowed a glimpse
into the meanings of social practices and the actors who had the power to define such meanings, as it embodied the appropriation of public spaces by
traditionally subordinate groups. In these spaces cultural politics are enacted and subaltern identities, demands, and needs are shaped (Alvarez,
Dagnino, and Escobar 1998, 19). Controversial aspects of Puerto Rican nationalist history retain their power and avoid neutralization precisely by deploying conflictual understandings of an inherently debatable history and
engaging in continuous struggles over the social interpretations of that
history.

It is precisely the willful or inadvertent recognition of the past as a tool for
political mobilization and the production of racial difference that rendered
historicity in Puerto Rican Chicago a central project of the performance of
nationalism. Albizu Campos remained conflictual in Chicago because his
statue not only symbolized local autonomy, but also resurrected and transformed a Puerto Rican nationalist history and rhetoric that problematized

dominant racial taxonomies and hegemonic conceptions of equality and social mobility in the United States; it promoted racial reconfigurations once
the city government's actions were read as attacks on Puerto Ricans as
racialized subjects. It is precisely the multiple meanings imbued in the
symbol of Albizu that allowed a variety of experiences, visions, and aspirations to find themselves represented in the imagery. However, despite the
accommodative qualities embodied in Don Pedro and selectively activated
by various parties, the image remained on the margin of law.

For nationalist activists nationalism involved the sort of popular education processes by which debates around the controversial figure of Pedro Albizu Campos became a flashpoint for local issues of autonomy, historical
awareness, and internal boundaries. Once Albizu was resurrected through
local conflict between the city, a Latino government elite, and barrio residents, nationalist activists appropriated the image of militancy to counter
dominant representations of Puerto Ricans as politically passive. Pedro Albizu Campos became a symbol of a people's autonomy to choose their heroes, a marker of limited resources and volatile urban patterns, and the
focus of a politicized youth identity in the barrio.

The Albizu statue embodied a powerful irony: the figure that was Christianized and even commercialized among the barrio poor was centered on
humanitarian and natural views of love, compassion, and redemption until
it was labeled terrorist and anti-American in public debate by some Latino
professionals and city officials. The image of Pedro Albizu Campos was
strategically deployed to assert a *Chicago* Puerto-Ricanness while marking
and influencing the negotiation of internal social boundaries along class,
race, and space among Puerto Ricans. By virtue of the controversy the statue
served as a counterrepresentation because for the first time ever a racialized
community's political ideologies, rather than its social pathology, occupied
the front page of the major Chicago newspapers. The Albizu statue pointed
to the underside of the politics of space in an area that, while continuously
marked as Puerto Rican, was reflective of the increasing Latinization of
Chicago. The deployment of a U.S. citizenship identity allowed Puerto Ricans to be nationalists and to express their nationality in the context of alternative modes of Latino identity formation.

The transnational and transurban displacement of people and subsequent creation of "global cities" (Sassen 1998) had concrete repercussions
for the everyday life of the barrio, as Mexicans, Central Americans, African
Americans, and whites continued to arrive in the area that Puerto Ricans actively tried to nationalize. Identity formation in light of transnational dis-

placement transformed notions of space, territoriality, belongingness, and the objectification of the nation through material bases of authenticity, while still demarcating the existence of a culturally distinct community. In the following chapter I examine the counterintuitive proposition that the performance of Puerto Rican nationalism in Chicago thrived not in spite of, but largely because of, its association with the very U.S. citizenship targeted by separatist nationalist discourse.

★ 7 ★

Creating Space: Barrio-Nation, Urban Landscapes, and Citizenship Identities

The Three Kings Day festivities were starting early in the barrio. Flyers announcing activities for the January 1995 holiday invited everyone to join in the celebration of "Three Wise Men Day," so as not to allude even indirectly to the Latin Kings, one of the gangs fighting for the territory where the celebration would be taking place. Three Wise Men Day was especially significant this year for it was also the day when the first of two fifty-ton, steel Puerto Rican flags would be unveiled on Division Street, marking the main commercial area of the barrio. Nationalist activists proudly commented: "This is the only monument to the Puerto Rican flag in the world. This is the use of nationalism to reclaim space . . . away from gentrifiers." "This is our way of building community," emphasized Vanessa, a bright young woman and one of the many West Town residents involved in the flag-unveiling ceremonies.

Puerto Rican youth and participants in popular education programs in the barrio were involved in planning the activities around the unveiling of the flag on Three Wise Men Day. Students at West Town and Humboldt Park public schools helped produce and design flyers, decorated their yearbook and graduation invitations with Chicago-style Puerto Rican flags, and mobilized their families and neighbors to attend the ceremonies. When the first flag was officially unveiled, activists and barrio adults and youth marched under the red and blue steel arch, with three young men dressed as the wise men and riding horses. Eduardo Arocho, the young man who had earned a reputation for writing poems that chronicled barrio events, recorded the day:

> The *Tres Reyes Magos* ride singing
> *ven ven* little *boricuas*
> look at what we've brought you
> *dos banderas grandes*
> with a star that shines
> four stories high "three sixty five."
> (Arocho 1994)

"The two flags are the Three Wise Men's gift to Humboldt Park," barrio residents commented during the celebration.

The monument to the Puerto Rican flag was emblematic of the increasing tensions between the Puerto Rican residents of Humboldt Park, West Town, and Logan Square and "newcomers," including Mexicans and other non–Puerto Rican Latinos, young white artists, and African American families, themselves displaced from the nearby Cabrini-Green housing project, which was being demolished. Fear of the "disintegration of the Puerto Rican community" had prompted nationalist activists to distribute flyers explaining concepts like gentrification, ethnic cleansing, and urban renewal, and urging Puerto Ricans to "sell to other Puerto Ricans" and "support Puerto

On Three Wise Men Day (renamed from Three Kings Day to avoid reference to the Latin Kings gang), three riders wearing royal costumes rode their horses down Division Street and under the steel Puerto Rican flag as part of a celebration of the unveiling of the monument. (Author's photo)

Rican businesses." These efforts to protect urban boundaries and Puerto Rican culture were attached to racial readings and racialization processes.[1] The steel Puerto Rican flags transcended the media-generated interpretation of them as apolitical folkloric forms to become public manifestations of underlying subordinate-group discourses that are accessible only to those groups (cf. Scott 1985). Puerto Ricans shared an intimate understanding of the conflictual meanings of the flags, whereas the dominant media described the flags in apolitical terms.

Puerto Rican barrio residents deployed their identity as U.S. citizens strategically to exert claims over urban space and perform a Puerto Rican nationalism while negotiating relationships with blacks, whites, and other Latinos living in the neighborhood. The unveiling of the steel Puerto Rican flag was part of the plan to mark the Humboldt Park area as Puerto Rican. The nationalism performed among barrio residents in Chicago emphasized their status as U.S. citizens in contradistinction to Mexicans and Central Americans living in Humboldt Park, whom they indiscriminately considered "illegal" or "less American." Barrio residents also constructed blackness in their interactions with African Americans and also attributed an essentialist "white culture" to the young white artists moving into the easternmost section of West Town.

PASEO BORICUA: PUERTO RICAN FLAGS, PUBLIC DISCOURSES, AND THE LATINIZATION OF HUMBOLDT PARK

Chicago's neighborhood-oriented urban pattern has contributed to the strong associations between cultural groups and specific city areas. Puerto Ricans in Chicago have the highest segregation indices in relation to both whites and African Americans of all Puerto Ricans in the United States (Massey and Bitterman 1985; Massey and Denton 1989). The predominantly Latino neighborhoods throughout the city occupy the interstitial zones between African American neighborhoods and receding white working-class communities (De Genova 1998). The Puerto Rican community has traditionally been coterminous with the area comprising the three adjacent Northwest Side neighborhoods of Humboldt Park, West Town, and Logan Square, and the heart of the Mexican community, especially Pilsen and La Villita [Little Village], is on the Southwest Side. African Americans are largely concentrated in the West and South Sides of the city. The North Side as a whole is far more affluent than other parts of the city, and the majority of its residents are white, but several integrated North Side communities are major points of entry for immigrants from all over the world. Far-north

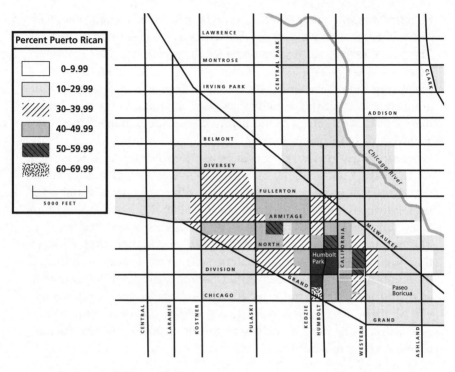

In much of Humboldt Park 40 percent or more of the population was Puerto Rican in 1990. (Courtesy of Liz Cosgrove and Frank Cruz)

Rogers Park in particular has large Mexican and African American populations.

Nationalist activists and some barrio residents explained gentrification in terms of the "invasion" of Puerto Rican space. At its inception, the community-building project of which the steel flags are a part was referred to as *la Islita* [the little Island], suggesting that the barrio was a surrogate Puerto Rico. Business owners, barrio residents, and community activists voiced their concerns about community displacement in town meetings, and with representatives from neighborhood-based organization they composed a Division Street consortium that successfully requested community development funds from the city government.[2] As my next-door neighbor commented, "I remember when Division Street was almost dead. Most businesses closed down, empty buildings. Now it seems to be picking up again." Shortly before our conversation, that neighbor and her family had sold their house to move to Florida. When they sold it to another Puerto Rican family, other neighbors were relieved.[3]

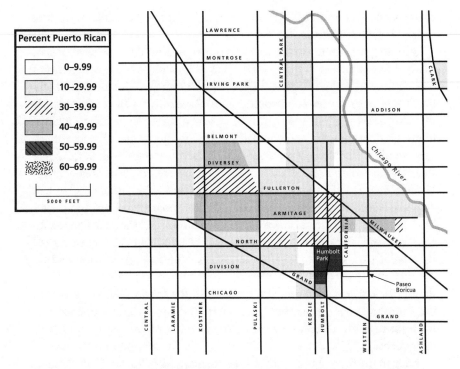

The 2000 census recorded a significant decrease in Puerto Rican concentration in the area historically considered "Puerto Rican Chicago." In only a very small number of census tracts do Puerto Ricans constitute a significant percentage of the population, and on most blocks they share urban space with African Americans, Mexicans, and whites. The maps also show that Puerto Ricans are being displaced from the Paseo Boricua area to neighborhoods farther north and west. (Courtesy of Liz Cosgrove and Frank Cruz)

Adela Santana, a resident of Logan Square and white-collar worker at a not-for-profit organization, commented on the problem of gentrification and its impact on neighborhood institutions: "If we don't do something radical at this moment, like what we're doing with Division Street, we're going to lose this community. In probably ten years Clemente will be a white high school." What remained concealed in Adela's expression of concern was that the incoming student population at Clemente High School was not white, as Adela suggested, but African American; Mexican; Central American; and, most recently, Dominican. Barrio activists had a great deal at stake because the "disappearance of the community" posed a real threat to theirs and others' jobs. It was possible that workers at community-based institutions, vendors who sold their wares from rolling carts, and owners of ethnic-specific businesses would not find a place in the institutions newly located in the barrio—fancy hospitals and proliferating coffee shops that were "not created for Puerto Ricans."[4]

Prior to the unveiling of the Division Street flags on Three Wise Men Day, many Puerto Ricans felt that the area lacked the cultural distinctiveness of other ethnic neighborhoods in the city, like Chicago's Chinatown or La Villita. There have always been some Puerto Ricans living in predominantly Mexican areas (Padilla 1947). In the 1950s anthropologist Elena Padilla, then a graduate student at the University of Chicago, argued that Puerto Ricans would probably become Mexicanized because there was not a stable Puerto Rican colonia (Padilla 1957). Nevertheless, Puerto Rican residents in Humboldt Park, identifying Mexican culture by folkloric markers, almost exclusively located Mexicanness in the neighborhoods of Pilsen and La Villita.[5] By situating cultural markers in specific urban locations, Puerto Ricans not only bound Mexicanness to La Villita, but also emphasized Humboldt Park's Puerto-Ricanness. In this context of production and reproduction of space in which Mexico and Chicago implicated each other, Puerto Ricans also constructed the nation in the barrio—Puerto Rico and the Chicago barrio implicated each other (De Genova and Ramos-Zayas, forthcoming). The effort to perform a Puerto Rican nation was embroiled in this process.

After many meetings of activists, residents, and politicians, an architectural firm designed ten community development projects. The Puerto Rican flag arches were one of the proposed projects and the one area activists and the popular education centers they represented pushed for. Puerto Rican symbols—like Old San Juan *garitas* [Spanish fortress], Taíno Indian hieroglyphics, and Afro-Caribbean *vejigantes* [festival masks and costumes]—were inscribed on steel boards that hang from Spanish-style *faroles* [light poles] along the sidewalks of Paseo Boricua. About a dozen small plazas with cement tables and chairs and iron loveseats also decorate the commercial Puerto Rican section of Division Street, where various Puerto Rican *colmados* [grocery stores] and restaurants, Mexican and Chinese fast food establishments, a Dominican cultural center and sports shop, music stores, a supermarket, and a bakery are found. An HIV/AIDS education clinic directed by nationalist activists and a large Pentecostal church that is considered antinationalist also mark Paseo Boricua.

Buildings and businesses in the area were given financial incentives to rehabilitate their facades, so that eventually the entire area would resemble the Spanish colonial style of the commercial streets of Old San Juan. The development became known as Paseo Boricua [Puerto Rican promenade]. Several not-for-profit Latino organizations, including PACHS and the Puerto

Rican Cultural Center, had plans to relocate to Paseo Boricua at the time of my fieldwork and had actually bought various buildings for this purpose. By 2002 both the cultural center and the alternative high school had moved into these buildings. In the late 1990s a community garden was built, and the controversial statue of Pedro Albizu Campos was erected there.

The multiple meanings of the steel flags as the markers of Paseo Boricua were debated publicly but only understood by those familiar with Puerto Rican history and political codes. Puerto Ricans who were familiar with barrio history and the multiple interpretations evoked by the Puerto Rican flag transformed these debates into political commentaries. This public discourse of a subordinate group was only understandable and meaningful to a group's insiders, even though the polemic publicly developed at a city-wide level.

Dominant society read the flags through the prism of ethnic pride common to European Americans. An article in the *Chicago Tribune* titled "Urban Gateway" suggests that the flag monument "symbolizes the Puerto Rican community's rising spirit of hope and renewal on Division Street. They are Chicago's newest feats of design, engineering and free style popular culture, spanning 56 feet across Division about half a mile apart. Buoyant fancies of the highway, high-tech crocheting in welded metal, civic art, ethnic imagery and proud gateways to a neighborhood hungering for its place in the sun" (Wagner 1995). Other newspaper journalists interpreted the flags as the Puerto Rican community's attempt to "reconcile with mainstream Chicago society," thus suggesting the poor behavior—the bad-boy, or anti-assimilationist, attitude—of Puerto Ricans in Humboldt Park. One article's claim that "the neighborhood yearned for image and identity" suggests that prior to the erection of the flags—which were paid for by Mayor Daley—the Puerto Rican community was just another deindustrialized wasteland in an otherwise majestic city. The flags were described as "an identity outside the U.S." (Wagner 1995), the ultimate insistence on the incompatibility between certain neighborhoods and their residents—the "underclass," the "inner-city," the "ghetto"—and true heartland Americanness, along with the values, mores, and lifestyles implied in such characterizations.

Among Puerto Ricans, however, the flags were not simply ethnic markers, but a monument generating various historical and political narratives, as well as everyday visions of neighborhood life and factionalism. Nationalism in Puerto Rican Chicago insisted on a nationality-based distinctiveness from other Latinos, as well as a popular representation—a self-representation "from below"—that challenged the representations of the dominant U.S. media and society. Ramón López, a Chicago-based artisan, anthropologist, and self-proclaimed *santero* (practitioner of the Afro-Caribbean religion of Santería), was director of a West Town alternative high school for students who had abandoned public school. López eloquently described the meaning the unveiling of two steel flags on Division Street had for the culturally intimate:

> The flag is a monument with multiple meanings. . . . It commemorates the 100th anniversary of the Puerto Rican patriots who fought against Spanish colonialism and declared it the national flag. . . . It also commemorates the nostalgia, the visible symbol of our belonging to a territory that we always remember, always with the hope to return or to visit. . . . It commemorates the tradition of images—the Three Kings Day celebration, *coquís, vejigantes* . . . —that accompanies us in a city that belongs to another climate and whose rented walls we want to paint and ornament with our own footprint. . . . It commemorates the many times when Puerto Ricans filled the streets with the flag during parades and protests. . . . It commemorates all the times that we hung the flag from our necks. . . . It commemorates the blood shed in the history of that Island and in the pavement of this street. (López 1995, 20)

López concluded that "here in Chicago the flag is planted in the most total sense: to reclaim space, to mark a point, to announce that our presence is much more than a transitory passage, that we have made history in Chicago and that we are going to continue making it (López 1995, 21). The flag was not associated exclusively with cultural pride—though its significance as a marker hanging from rearview mirrors, displayed at National Day parades, and emblazoned on T-shirts is not to be undermined.

Libertad Negroni, the director of a grassroots organization that offered ESL and GED classes for barrio residents, remembered the first months after he moved from Boston to Chicago in the 1970s. A self-proclaimed socialist, Libertad explained: "My house's garage was burned down on the same night I put a Puerto Rican flag in front of the house. . . . Just by waving a Puerto Rican flag you could make the FBI lists!" References to how you could get in trouble for waving the Puerto Rican flag in the 1970s were common among Puerto Rican activists. Racial prejudice toward Puerto Ricans was represented as an attack on the Puerto Rican flag and thus contributed to narratives that insist on the popular nationalist historicity of that flag *in Chicago.* The flag monument signifies the oppositional resistance discourses that emerged when the validity of dominant norms was questioned from the perspective of an everyday practice that challenged belief in the de-

The two steel Puerto Rican flags cross Division Street from sidewalk to sidewalk. *Top:* A flag being constructed in the winter of 1995. *Bottom:* A completed flag in the fall of 2002. (*Top,* author's photo; *bottom,* courtesy of Liz Cosgrove)

politicized nature of the "steering mechanisms" of law, bureaucracy, and consumerism (cf. Franco, Yúdice, and Flores 1992).

The reappropriation of the Puerto Rican flag as belonging to Chicago and to Puerto Ricans in Chicago was evidenced in narratives around the material used to build the flags—steel from the same local steel mills where early Puerto Rican migrants had worked under exploitative conditions. One local politician did not miss the poetic justice: "These monuments represent the past of the Puerto Rican presence in this city, since the first Puerto Ricans who arrived here came to work in steel factories."

Rafael Otero, a representative of the pro-statehood party in Chicago and owner of a furniture store in the barrio, pointed to the campaigning behind the flags, as well as to the political implications of the monument. Rafael's comment suggested the role of the monument as both a public display of a depoliticized ethnic pride and a public expression of politicized historical content understood only by those represented by it.

> Los nacionalistas put two Puerto Rican flags on Division Street. I don't know if you have seen them. [I nod.] So, they put that flag over there for the Puerto Ricans. That is disrespectful to this nation [the United States]. Because in Puerto Rico when we raise the Puerto Rican flag, we [also] raise the American flag. So that [to raise just the Puerto Rican flag] is a mocking of the Americans. If they try to turn that area into a center to bring in other cultures, they [members of the other cultures] are going to say, "No, that over there is a Mafia of Puerto Ricans." Knowing the issue, I understand [why they chose Puerto Rican flags] very clearly. That is a protest of the nacionalistas.

Rafael's comments, while not representative of those of other residents, were telling. Reading the flags as incompatible with belongingness in the United States, Rafael recognized the factionalism and heterogeneity of the barrio, which the dominant media overlooked. The history of the Puerto Rican flag was retold in commemorative issues of smaller Latino newspapers dedicated to the Division Street development project and Paseo Boricua.[6]

Given their crocheted architectural style, the Puerto Rican flags on Division Street are markers unique to the Puerto Rican barrio of Chicago. Merchants in the informal economy of Division Street placed their stands on the sidewalks near the flags and sold T-shirts, bumper stickers, and posters with the monument's image. Instead of overriding internal boundaries in the interest of national unity, the flags generated conflict and symbolized internal divisions along race, class, and geographical lines that may or may not have had to do with national identity.

The production of a Puerto Rican urban space involved the maintenance of Puerto Rican markers because of the increasing presence of Mexican *taquerías*, Dominican sports clubs, and Central American households. It was a response to difference-producing encounters and struggles over space in an area commonly racialized as a Latino neighborhood. Interpretations of the Puerto Rican flag were grounded not only in the context of a history of the Puerto Rican homeland, but also in local ways of producing and reproducing racial difference, of promoting discourses of political ideologies, and of performing a popular nationalism in Puerto Rican Chicago.

LATINIDAD, CITIZENSHIP IDENTITY, AND URBAN POLITICS

Because Puerto Rican populations have traditionally located primarily in the Northeast, in that region other Latinos would often find themselves conflated under the Puerto Rican label, given dominant U.S. society's tendency to overlook nationality-based distinctions among Latinos. By contrast, in Chicago, a traditionally Mexican city (De Genova 1998), new expressions of Puerto-Ricanness accentuated and negotiated relations with other Latino populations. Chicago expressions of Puerto-Ricanness included the performance of a popular nationalism that expressed patriotism for the Island as an ancestral homeland and resistance to U.S. domination of Puerto Rico, while also insisting that Puerto Ricans be seen as different from Mexicans because of their U.S. citizenship.

Contemporary debates around Latino identities in the United States have centered on the possibilities and limitations of consolidating a Latinidad— the process of Latino identity formation—as a panethnic political strategy that is deployed situationally (Padilla 1985), a symbol of solidarity among Spanish-speaking groups against prescriptive assimilation in the United States, (Acosta-Belén and Santiago 1998), a "new social movement" (Franco, Yúdice, and Flores 1992), or an ahistorical and often contested label (Oboler 1995). The range of perspectives articulated by these studies shows the complexity of the term *Latino* in light of alternative identifications among people of Latin American and Caribbean descent, as well as in the context of the black-white U.S. racial polarity.[7]

The dynamic ways in which Puerto Rican barrio residents, activists, and middle-class professionals conceptualized Latinidad and Puerto-Ricanness in Chicago illuminates this debate in several ways. First, among the upwardly mobile and middle class, identifying as Latino presented an alternative to the more stigmatized identity of Puerto Rican. For Puerto Ricans, against whom most of the discrimination embedded in the characterization

A group of students from Pedro Albizu Campos and Clemente high schools, as well as barrio residents and politicians, walk under the Puerto Rican flag archway, at the time still under construction. (Author's photo)

of Hispanics is directed, a Latino identity became cultural capital. For the working class and barrio poor, however, Latinidad was simultaneously embraced, modified, and contested through the construction of a U.S.-citizenship identity that ironically *reaffirmed* Puerto Rican nationalism by enforcing distinctions between Puerto Ricans and non–Puerto Rican Latinos in the barrio. This citizenship identity was a social construct rooted in perceived legal, political, and economic access, rather than an accurate referent to superior legal status or even actual access to such rights. It was deployed by some Puerto Ricans not only as a justification for receiving public assistance in the form of welfare, but also as a vehicle for gaining at least partial insertion into U.S. society as citizens who had met their full duties (e.g., by serving in the U.S. military, by working in factories and on farms). The discourse of illegality applied to all Mexicans, even to those who were second- and third-generation Chicanos and therefore U.S. citizens with the same citizenship rights as Puerto Ricans.[8]

These discourses were not only compatible with, but actually sustained and shaped a Puerto Rican popular nationalism that challenged the core assumptions of U.S. citizenship because Puerto Ricans do not hold full citizenship or institutional power, despite their legal status. The emphasis on a

citizenship identity was illustrated by Alma Juncos, a Puerto Rican parent
volunteer at Clemente High School, when she was asked to describe the area
where she lives.

> Where I live some Puerto Ricans and some Mexicans moved in.
> There's a building that is mostly Mexican, Guatemalan. Puerto Ricans
> don't live there. Mexicans live their own lives. They don't help each
> other out, not even among themselves. I think that many of them that
> are jealous of Puerto Ricans. My [Puerto Rican] neighbor told me:
> "The thing with Mexicans is that they know they are wetbacks." And,
> since we are citizens, they hate us because of that. . . . A couple of days
> ago, I was walking with my son in front of the building where the Mex-
> icans live. They wouldn't let us walk by, but then my son said "Look,
> take your car out of the way or I'll call *la Migra* [Immigration]." And the
> Mexicans flew out of there! [Laughs.] There's a lot of undocumented
> people.

Puerto Ricans were aware that in Chicago Mexican migrant workers ful-
fill a need for cheap labor that is more easily exploited because the workers
are in a protracted predicament of legal vulnerability (cf. De Genova 1999).
Claims over one's identity as a U.S. citizen thus became a defense mechanism against association with the migrant reality. When Alma and other
barrio residents had Mexican neighbors, the social space that separated
them seemed to take precedence over the physical space they shared. Alma
knew that some buildings were "Mexican," and that Puerto Ricans "don't
live there." Citizenship not only emphasized a separation from those perceived as undocumented Latinos in the barrio, but also generated greater legitimacy for claims over material and social resources.

Moreover, Puerto Rican political savvy was emphasized in contrast to
Mexican gullibility. The humor in Alma's narrative about invoking *la Migra*
to scare Mexicans off also emphasized that Puerto Ricans have more access
to mainstream institutions—in this case, the INS. It suggests that Mexican
migrants' vulnerability is due not to the Mexican population's "illegal" status, but to their naïveté (De Genova and Ramos-Zayas 2000).

When Puerto Ricans provoked into discourse a citizenship identity and
welfare benefits, they were selectively positioning themselves in the racial
configuration of the United States. Barrio residents responded as victims of
oppression in a discourse engendered by their experience with colonialism
and white supremacy. In Chicago the idea that Puerto Rico as a U.S. territory
is better off than Latin American nation-states was articulated alongside the
recognition that in the United States Puerto Ricans are at the very bottom of

the Latino totem pole. Thus, the Latinidad that stretches the boundaries of racial acceptability for a small Puerto Rican middle class also reinforces the power of whiteness for Puerto Ricans who are grouped together with African Americans through racialized images of welfare dependency. This discourse of difference is not only coupled with claims on compensatory rights grounded in the historical black-white polarization (Goode 1999, 10), but also rearticulated as a narrative of legality and citizenship identity to construct a nationality-based identity in the context of Latinidad.

It was precisely this legal identity that allowed even the most vulnerable Puerto Rican barrio residents to articulate citizenship rights and claims over resources by adopting a community-building discourse grounded in a Puerto Rican nationalist rhetoric. A Puerto Rican nationalist discourse and a Latino discourse were alternately deployed to challenge conventional sociological and popular imaginings of Americanization and assimilation. These discourses emphasized that there is no clear path to achieving a desirable social location from which to enact one's rights while retaining the power to produce one's cultural identity in the United States.

LATINIDAD, CITIZENSHIP IDENTITY, AND CLASS

While the negative stereotypes associated with the term *Latinidad* are mostly built upon dominant characterizations of U.S.-born Puerto Ricans and Chicanos, the label also dilutes and homogenizes the national populations it purports to define. For upwardly mobile Puerto Ricans (and perhaps Chicanos), identifying as Latino is sometimes perceived as a way to navigate the U.S. black-white racial polarity. Latinidad allows a flexible and dynamic reconsideration of cultural symbols, social practices, and national markers, and in so doing it often enables the development of political coalitions and mobilization strategies and the formation of social networks. The Latino identification creates spaces for middle-class Puerto Ricans in the United States to straddle a border culture that acknowledges incorporation into certain spaces of U.S. dominant society without necessarily compromising Puerto-Ricanness or drawing the Puerto Rican community's accusation that they are selling out. Hence, a generic Latino identification and its historical and cultural malleability conflate racial acceptability and nationality-based notions of cultural authenticity. The generic Latino also creates commercial market niches for the reification of consumerism through the production of folkloric and artistic goods.[9]

Puerto Rican nationalism among barrio residents was not only expressed in the form of a cultural identity, but also elicited in contact with other Latinos. Many upwardly mobile Puerto Ricans subscribed to the idea that to become integrated into the U.S. mainstream people with ties to Latin America and the Caribbean must unite to achieve the privileges of the white middle class in the United States. In thinking about "the construction of Latino social movements, of Latinidad, it is important to incorporate the idea that they [middle-class Latinos] may also share class backgrounds and status, racial and ethnic prejudices and values that . . . can unite middle-class people beyond their nationalities" (Oboler 1995, 163). These values and attitudes can offset efforts to generate unity across class lines. In the context of the multiple forms of identity formation, to identify as Latino is "more than solely a culturally dictated fact of life. Identifying oneself as Latino or Latina and participating in a Latino social movement is also a *political* decision, one that aims to strengthen *la comunidad* in those terms" (Oboler 1995, 163).

Often middle-class Puerto Ricans and Latinos deployed a dominant U.S. discourse to explain social mobility as individual achievement. Puerto Rican professionals perceived Central American and Mexican migrants' willingness to start at the bottom and move up the ladder as commendable and believed that a work ethic was lacking among poor Puerto Ricans, who were indiscriminately considered to be "welfare-dependent." Without disregarding the tension between Latinos of various nationalities in the public arena of organized politics, it is also critical to recognize that there were multiple spaces in which Latinos—and particularly Mexicans and Puerto Ricans in Chicago—strategically racialized each other and developed alternative means to create collectivity.

Instances of surrealist defamiliarization and humor (De Genova 1999; Urciuoli 1996) and the creation and dissolution of romantic unions (Rúa 2000) serve as a critique of the absurdities of race itself and of how the contradictions of racialization can be negotiated in everyday social practices among Mexicans and Puerto Ricans. The seriousness of racialized difference is deflected by the unpredictable tactics of defamiliarization and irony of the *relajo* among Puerto Ricans and Mexicans.[10] Readings of Mexicanness among Puerto Ricans and social interaction between Mexicans and Puerto Ricans often recurred to the performance of the very racial stereotypes that each group assumed the other had of them. For instance, Puerto Rican men occasionally deflected common Mexican-held stereotypes of Puerto Rican welfare abuse and laziness by joking in the presence of Mexicans about abusing the system or being supported by their wives. In this sense, *relajo* and other forms of humor became strategies to circumvent potentially conflictual situations among Mexicans and Puerto Ricans in everyday social interactions.

In her examination of children of unions between Mexicans and Puerto Ricans, Mérida Rúa (2000) eloquently demonstrates how Mexicanness is Puerto-Ricanized and Puerto-Ricanness is Mexicanized in the construction of "Porto-Mex" and "Mexi-Rican" identities in Chicago. The upwardly mobile bicultural Latinos in Rúa's ethnographic essay point to how romantic liaisons between Mexicans and Puerto Ricans develop at the fringes of social and community sanctions, thus carving spaces of resistance to internal racialization processes among Latinos.

The dissolution of these romantic unions are critical in the tendency toward nationality-based, rather than mixed identification among the children, most of whom claim the nationality of the parent who is more present in their lives. While this tended to be the case in my examination of Puerto Rican Chicago, the impact of neighborhood affiliation was also critical in the identity deployed by children of Mexican and Puerto Rican parents. One young woman, whose mother was Mexican and whose father was half-Mexican and half–Puerto Rican, was racialized as Mexican by other students in the popular education program she attended—most of whom were Puerto Rican. Yet the young woman self-identified as Puerto Rican because she did not have a strong relationship with her parents and because she had grown up in Humboldt Park.

Given the possibilities for circumventing racial tensions in daily social practices and the multiple, often competing, racialization processes at play in the barrio, Frank Rivera questioned the appropriateness of using the Puerto Rican flag as an area marker. Frank's contact with Clemente High School and his role as coach of a boys' basketball team in Humboldt Park had led him to drive by the area where the steel Puerto Rican flags are. I asked him what he thought of the flags on Division Street.

> *Frank*: That's the Puerto Rican community. The community there is Puerto Rican, predominantly. But I've noticed other cultures in there too. I've noticed other Latinos, Guatemalans or Colombians. But, to be honest with you, I really feel that they shouldn't have put the flag there. The reason why, because of the different cultures. You have a diverse number of groups. The Mexican area, the Little Village . . . the entrance says "Bienvenidos a la Villita." But they don't display the flag over there. They just have that "Welcome to the Little Village." There's not a flag being displayed, which means that this is not Mexico. This is Chicago. But when you are putting a *flag* out there, you're almost saying "This belongs to us."
> *Ana Yolanda*: Would it have been different if instead of the flag they had something else . . . a *garita*, a *coquí*, something like that?

Frank: It probably would. Because it would have said that there's an influence of the culture in that sector. It would have less of an effect on people. You see, your initial view, when you see a flag right away . . . that's telling you "This is a country." You're able to go ahead and label that area right away. "This is Puerto Rico."

Like other professionals, Frank suggested that Mexicans showed ethnic pride "respectfully," that is, in accordance with a dominant multiculturalist or ethnic pluralist ideology. To Frank and other white-collar workers in the barrio, expressions of Mexicanness were perceived as complementary—not oppositional—to an identity as American. Puerto-Ricanness and the display of the Puerto Rican flag, by contrast, were perceived as openly oppositional to integration into the U.S. mainstream as Latinos.

Upwardly mobile second-generation Puerto Ricans referred to their college experience as a turning point that allowed them to not only become more aware of their own national identity, but also develop common bonds with other Latinos and minority students on campus. When María Echevarría, a sophomore at the University of Illinois at Urbana-Champaign, came home to Humboldt Park for spring break, she talked to a few local high school students about college. She told a senior at an alternative high school in the barrio: "You talk badly about Mexicans now, but those are the people who'll stand by you when you go to college and everyone else is white."

Because most college courses dealing with Latino issues survey various national groups, these college-educated Puerto Ricans are necessarily exposed to Chicano and other Latino literature. Tony Santiago remarked that he was reading "the books by Mexican authors, Chicano poetry. I was reading anything I could get my hands on. We also brought down speakers like Jaime Escalante, César Chávez, Piri Thomas. We got more radical. I saw the process of my change." Tony perceived Puerto-Ricanness as something that had to be actively learned. His learning process transcended familiarity with the Spanish language and knowledge of Puerto Rican history by including literature by Chicano authors whose realities resonated with Tony's own coming-of-age in Chicago.[11]

While most informants commented on the relation between Mexicans and Puerto Ricans and defined the Puerto Rican community in reference to Mexican neighbors, some residents of slightly more affluent areas of the barrio expressed greater animosity toward other Latinos, especially Cubans, who were indiscriminately assigned classed identities that equated Cubanness with whiteness and the ability to pass. Puerto Ricans saw this assimilationist possibility as a consequence of the group's phenotypical features,

their higher socioeconomic and educational backgrounds even prior to exile, and the political circumstances that contributed to their positive recep-
tion as political exiles by the host society (see Safa 1988; Tienda and Nelson
1985). In unpacking Latinidad, class and race became the prisms through
which nationalities were constructed in the context of U.S. ideological foundations and the migrant experience.[12]

Latino relations become classed and racialized precisely upon the acknowledgment of nationality-based distinctions. In the case of Cubans and
some South American groups, the main discourse of difference and Americanness is grounded not on questions of citizenship or even exile status
alone, but on divisions along racial and class lines. Cubans are invariably
perceived as upper class and thus are higher up in an imagined hierarchy of
Americanness, while Mexicans and other immigrants are constructed as "illegal" and perpetually at the bottom. The connection between Americanness, citizenship, and class, while seriously undertheorized, lies at the
foundation of constructions of Puerto Rican national identity and the performance of popular nationalism in diasporic communities in the United
States. The nationalism performed in Puerto Rican Chicago accentuated the
imagined hierarchies by which some Latinos are constituted as more legal
or culturally closer to the imperialist goals of U.S. citizenship and the enduring Americanization project.

Identifying as Puerto Rican rather than Puerto Rican–American is reflective both of the recognition that Puerto Rico's colonial relation with the
United States makes such hyphenated identification almost redundant and
evidence that Puerto Ricans protect a space of marginality in which nationality and nationalism is performed. These identifications redefine citizenship as community, which is in turn conflated with nationhood. Hence,
citizenship is related not only to nationality and barrio-based mobilization,
but also to an alternative positionality in the mainstream ethnic pluralist discourse.[13]

Residents of Puerto Rican neighborhoods do not inhabit two homogeneous, bounded national cultures, but a continuum in which differences
and similarities coexist in complex and dynamic ways. The Latino label homogenizes the history, migration, and socioeconomic characteristics of the
individual Latino groups (Klor de Alva 1988, 1998; Oboler 1995; Safa 1988;
Sánchez Korrol 1989). U.S. citizenship is perceived as the distinguishing
feature that makes Puerto Ricans different from other Latinos. However,
this citizenship identity is in dynamic interaction with other identities, race
as well as class.

PUERTO RICAN READINGS OF "WHITE CULTURE"
AND "BLACK CULTURE"

In addition to sharing urban spaces with Mexicans and other Latinos, Puerto Ricans in Chicago were encountering an increasing number of white artists in their twenties and African American families moving into the barrio and its outskirts. Puerto Ricans have traditionally exhibited a higher level of residential segregation from both whites and African Americans in Chicago than in any other area of significant Puerto Rican concentration in the United States (Massey and Denton 1989). The relationship between these groups is shaped by the way competing discourses of racial difference and Americanness are contested and appropriated by each group as it negotiates access to electoral, spatial, and economic resources.

Typical of the white population of twenty-somethings in the barrio were the body piercings, tattoos, spiky died hair, and grungy clothes—what Brenda Ramírez, a Puerto Rican in her twenties, wittily described as "the Harley Davidson–meets–Morticia Adams look." The area was advertised as perfect for artists, and indeed, many young, white aspiring artists had moved there. The proliferating cybercafes, art supply and aromatherapy shops, and rock and heavy-metal music clubs were tailored to the white youth.

When Hilda Ayala first opened her bridal shop, most nearby businesses on the commercial strip of Milwaukee Avenue that crosses West Town were owned by Puerto Ricans or other Latinos, mostly Mexicans. These businesses tended to the needs of the largely Puerto Rican population in the area. "We used to sell everything for *quinceañeros,* weddings, and all other occasions Latinos celebrate," Hilda recalled. This is no longer the case, as most Latino businesses have been forced out by higher rents. Hilda's bridal shop was one of the last remnants of a Latino commercial era. Ricardo Ramírez, a worker at a not-for-profit agency in West Town, was looking to purchase a new building in the spring of 1995 so the organization could move closer to the Latino population it serves. Only a small Puerto Rican–owned grocery store and a Mexican *taquerías* remain in the area now promoted in real estate as Wicker Park, souvenirs of Latino commercial efforts of the past.

Studies of whiteness provide an important theoretical framework for examining more than the construction of white identity by whites.[14] A neglected but equally critical aspect of whiteness studies is the question of how whiteness and white culture are conceptualized by those racialized as non-

white Others, especially Latinos (Ramos-Zayas 2001a, 2001b). White culture is considered "invisible" because it is constructed as "normal" (Frankenberg 1993).

Despite their considerable numerical presence in one of Chicago's
largest Latino barrios, whites were perceived as a minority outside the
purview of the social space designated by the Puerto Rican flags, and therefore a rationalization process was promoted in several ways. First, whiteness
was not unproblematically naturalized. While references to white people
abounded in the discursive development of us-them distinctions that aimed
to highlight the power of whiteness, Puerto Ricans in Chicago also recognized that whites living in a mixed neighborhood were forced to grapple
with their identity *as whites*. Puerto Rican barrio residents constructed white
culture as commercial, consumption oriented, and bounded by music,
clothes, demeanor, and other markers. Regardless of Puerto Ricans' recognition of this boundedness of white culture in their everyday life, however,
whiteness was still imagined as cultureless or postcultural in Puerto Rican
nationalist discourse.

Whites deny the importance of the past in the construction of their identity so that whiteness becomes conflated with Americanness and is perceived as lacking a tradition or culture other than those associated with the
state. Whiteness is a present-oriented construction of the self, and past-
oriented values or traditions are considered irrational; individual responsibility and a future orientation of the self become tenets of a postcultural
identity (Clifford and Marcus 1986; Perry 2001).[15] Considering the predominance of history and the invocation of the past and traditions on which
Puerto Rican nationalism was constructed in the barrio, these two populations relied on quite different conceptions of the self and notions of community.

"Whites lack a culture. They don't have an identity, something to be
proud of," commented Carlos, a junior at Clemente High School, echoing
thoughts expressed by most of the barrio residents I interviewed in 1994
and 1995. Yet these same Puerto Ricans who would deculturize whiteness
would also evoke whiteness in discourse as a bounded culture, rather than
naturalizing it as normative or rationalizing it as superior. In discourse
whites and *white people* were almost invariably conflated with *Americans*, but
in daily social practice "white culture" was constructed around local tensions with the white artists who were moving into the neighborhood. From
a Puerto Rican perspective whites didn't have a culture rooted in valued traditions, high morals, hygiene practices, and other elements that were imagined to be embodied in Puerto-Ricanness.

Puerto Ricans bound white culture to the body by reverting to discourses of subjugation through the extreme practice of behavior that was the opposite of what they observed in the dominant culture. One young Puerto Rican high school student echoed what many barrio residents articulated: "Whites never take showers. . . . Have you noticed how they smell funny?" Cleanliness was perceived as inherent to the Puerto Rican culture, while body odor was considered characteristic of white culture. Similarly, barrio residents recognized Western rationalization of self-control, self-sacrifice, repression, and restraint as embodied aspects of white culture. The hierarchy of mind over body that assumes the superiority of these elements was reconfigured through a discourse of emotional inadequacy that took many forms. "Look at those tattoos, the body piercing, the tongue earrings. That's self mutilation!" "If you look around at all the murders that happen, all serial killers are always whites." "They are into this selfish 'finding myself' mode." "They disrespect their parents." Self-mutilation, mass murders, excessive self-indulgence, and disregard for one's family are descriptions that were given by most of the Puerto Ricans I interviewed and with whom I talked informally. The mind became a symbol of the emotional inadequacy paradoxically associated not only with culturelessness, but also with white culture.

Despite these generalizations about white culture, there were instances in which whiteness in the barrio was fragmented by class. "These white kids think that living in poverty is cool," commented Tamika, a young worker at a not-for-profit organization and a part-time social work student. Elisa, one of Tamika's best friends added: "They want to be friends with Latinos to pretend they are homeboys and homegirls themselves." The general feeling was that these gentrifiers were privileged people who mocked the evils of actual poverty by appropriating the discourse of the poor as their own. Moreover, they were able to do this because their imperialist attitudes encouraged these expansive views of the self—that they could go anywhere and have anything. Because most of the young Latino agency workers, elderly people in the area, and grassroots activists themselves grew up in poverty, they were particularly condemning of the romanticized version of the dreadful and still very painful reality of barrio life. They read this as faked poverty, or the poverty look in bodily expressions (e.g., wearing torn clothes, dirty T-shirts).

Most significant, this poverty was perceived as chosen, which points to the social construction of class in the context of interracial relations. The inconsistency of being able to afford an expensive loft while earning coffee house wait-staff wages and continuing to wear grungy clothes, evoked these white artists' relatively privileged past and family background. This was perceived not as a cultural past, but as a past of inadequate parenting or a very sheltered and infantilizing lifestyle.

The oversized, grungy look is the physical expression of sexual personas along the "virgin"/"whore" axis of Latin American sexual discourse (Asencio 1999). When this discourse was projected onto white Generation X youth, the inability to locate white youth sexuality led to a Puerto Rican construction of white culture as simultaneously asexual and promiscuous. The extremely thin bodies and boyish look of young white women, along with the association of white rock music with frigidity and control, were culturalized in opposition to Puerto-Ricanness, which was associated with highly valued rhythm, sensuality, salsa, hyperfemininity and, in turn, hypermasculinity.[16]

The ambiguous sexuality of white youth living in the barrio was also perceived as a desire to have all sexualities. As Hilda Ayala commented when I met her on the street where her bridal shop used to be: "Now these hippies, . . . I don't know if they are gay or what. I don't know because you see the girls and you don't know if they're man or woman." Brenda Ramírez, who had joined our conversation, added: "They want to experience everything. All sexualities. All backgrounds. If you go in there [points to coffee shop across the street] with red nail polish, you are too womanly for them."

Whiteness was culturalized as being associated not only with the image of the white artists, but also with other imagery, such as that of the whites who are "really poor"—especially Appalachians. One of Gina Pérez's (2000) Mexican interviewees called Appalachian whites *jilbilos* (from "hillbillies"), and I heard Puerto Ricans referring to them as "hilly-billies" (Ramos-Zayas 2001a, 2001b). These poor whites were viewed alternately with empathy—as occupying the very bottom of the poverty and marginality barrel—and with the disdain implied in phrases like *white trash* or *trailer trash*. Most barrio residents distinguished between working-class whites, such as the few Italians and Poles still living in the area, and Appalachian whites. Italians and the Polish were perceived as having distinct cultures; food and festivals were mentioned as evidence of these groups' culture.

Puerto Ricans deny, redefine, and bound white culture as they simultaneously characterize African Americans using the prism of a dominant racial discourse that hyperculturalizes blacks. In Chicago intertextual identification between African Americans and Puerto Ricans was discursively limited, despite the physical presence of African Americans in the barrio. Puerto Rican nationalism accommodated blackness as Afro-Caribbean culture or as one element of the foundational triad in which Puerto-Ricanness is constructed as a combination of Spanish, Taíno Indian, and African blood precisely to differentiate Black Puerto Ricans from African Americans. The perceived difficulty of developing alliances between Puerto Ricans and African Americans had to do with elements of the social and physical segregation in Chicago, including territorial gang conflicts among youth and the existence of an affluent African American elite in the Puerto Rican imagination.

Ever since the early days of Puerto Rican settlement in Chicago, parents and residents aiming to distance their children from more powerful African American gangs have moved farther north (Padilla 1987). Carmen Acevedo, a barrio resident who lived on Chicago's South Side before moving to Humboldt Park, admitted that she and her family moved because, as she explains: "The area where we lived was getting worse with blacks moving in. It was customary that when a Puerto Rican moved out of an area, all other Puerto Ricans would continue to move too."

In the Three Wise Men artistic contest, the rejection of blackness was conveyed through the consistent marginalization of Melchor, the king who is characterized for being the darkest of the three. The most important gift—the Puerto Rican flag—was never carried by Melchor, the director of a popular education program mentioned. "Melchor is too close to the black gangs, the enemies," the educator-activist mentioned, and Ricky Perales, a seventeen-year-old student who did not participated in the contest agreed. Even when the artist of the drawing was of obvious African ancestry, or perhaps precisely because of this, the black wise man remained on the sidelines. Melchor was never excluded, but he was never given the prominence of the other two kings.

Puerto Rican residents explained the growing hostility toward incoming African American residents by focusing on the tightening housing market and the diminishing commercial opportunities in the barrio, for which they blamed blacks. For instance, barrio life had represented an uphill struggle for Elda Aponte ever since she arrived in Chicago in the 1980s. Elda was hoping to move into a larger and safer subsidized apartment, but by the time she applied for it the fall of 1994, the waiting list was too long. Many of the residents of the Cabrini-Green housing project, a highly stigmatized housing complex east of Humboldt Park where buildings were slated for demolition, were also competing for the few units that would become available. Elda felt that "there have been houses built since I moved. But the houses that they're building are being given to blacks. I think we Puerto Ricans are more marginalized." Competition over rehabilitated neighborhood housing thus exacerbated racial tensions.

As the influx of African Americans increased in the westernmost section of the Puerto Rican barrio, residents and activists grew uneasy and developed new grassroots efforts to protect the Puerto Rican community. As the unveiling of the flags on Division Street suggests, most efforts evoked nationalist symbols and rhetoric. Some Puerto Rican activists, particularly those involved in recent barrio community development projects, assumed that "blacks won't take as good care of the Puerto Rican area as we would because they don't understand the symbols, the struggles, and they don't experience the cultural pride." Melvin Salgado, the activist who articulated this belief, commented that even Puerto Rican gang members would be better neighbors than African Americans: "They have community pride in the Puerto Rican area. . . . No matter how much gang graffiti there is on building walls, you never see gang signs over Puerto Rican murals." Often I heard Puerto Rican neighbors criticizing "those black men who hang out at corners drinking" or "those black kids who throw garbage into my lawn."

African Americans thus became hypercultural, classed, and capable of co-opting Puerto Rican culture. Yet their political presence in nationalist discourse was selectively acknowledged because nationalist activists did recognize the African American legacy of civil rights activism and the Black Power movement in their own practices. Despite activists' awareness of African American history, black culture as embedded in contemporary social practices was still perceived as selectively discontinuous from that political legacy.

Despite sharing urban spaces with African American residents who harbored similar concerns about housing, street violence, and educational opportunities, Puerto Rican barrio residents categorized blackness as African American culture, a gendered and classed hyperculture capable of co-opting Puerto Rican youth, women, and ultimately, nationalism. Internal racial boundaries and blackness among Puerto Ricans were stretched through dynamic nationalist discourses embodied in the figure of Pedro Albizu Campos and evoked in the racial triad that conflates Spanish, African, and Taíno heritage into the Puerto Rican imagery. By contrast, African American blackness was hyperculturalized through a youth street culture embodied in gangs and in constructions of a threatening black professional elite.

Puerto Rican youths' contact with a mass-marketed popular culture associated with African Americans was perceived as a blackening and denationalization of the Puerto Rican community. Images of gangs as youth culture were alternately criminalized or revered, depending on whether the gang members were African Americans or Puerto Ricans. Similarly, professional solidarities were constructed by barrio residents as gendered, racialized, and conflated through the intermarriage of African American professional men and Puerto Rican professional women. To Puerto Rican barrio residents and activists, the powerful youth gangs and black professional elite represented the dominance of African American blackness over Puerto-Ricanness both in Chicago's mainstream professional settings and in the informal street context.

Just as Mexican–Puerto Rican romantic liaisons were perceived as unstable or unstabilizing in the early years of Puerto Rican settlement in Chicago, so romantic relations between Puerto Ricans and blacks were condemned by many barrio residents and activists. A critical difference between the two situations was in the nature of the perceived threat from Puerto Rican–African American dating. Whenever I noticed public or private condemnation of Puerto Rican–African American romantic relations, the discourse around the couples involved a Puerto Rican professional woman "marrying up." The focus was as much on the co-optation of Puerto Rican culture by a hypercultural blackness as it was on the co-optation of the Puerto Rican community and the presumed "loss of the barrio connection."[17]

Often I heard reference to buppies, black urban professionals, when driving past a number of selective private clubs frequented by middle- and upper-middle-class African Americans. This was even more demarcated in reference to members of the Chicago-based black popular-media elite, such as Oprah Winfrey, Michael Jordan, and Jesse Jackson. Blackness was classed, but not in the same way as whiteness was: in the same system in which whiteness was classed up, blackness was classed down. African Americans were invariably classed through opposite-class discourses that were not just applied to a professional African American male elite that was perceived as powerful and more desirable to Puerto Rican professional women with equivalent levels of education and occupational status. Blackness was also hyperculturalized in the realm of youth culture, located in particular age-peer cultural groups in informal, street contexts, as well as in the media. When applied to youth, black culture became embodied in gang activity and in the markers of this activity: baggy clothes, rap music, sports-team jerseys, gold chains, and so on.

The urban spatial politics around the Puerto Rican flags on Division Street served as a catalyst for discourses of difference and for the insistence on a U.S. citizenship identity among Puerto Ricans. Residents of the Puerto Rican barrio emphasized a U.S. citizenship identity to perform a nationalism that rendered non–Puerto Rican Latinos as "illegal" and thus "less American," while sustaining an anti-assimilationist discourse of Puerto Rican separatism from the United States. In this sense, Puerto Ricans were both not quite American and more American than other Latino migrants. A discourse of racial and national difference straddled the tension between separatism and pluralism by exerting claims to a U.S. citizenship that was insinuated as separate from that of other Latinos and by using this difference as a critical element in the performance of a Puerto Rican popular nationalism.

Puerto Rican nationalism was not only compatible with a U.S. citizenship identity, but also indispensable in the construction of Puerto-Ricanness in relation to other manifestations of Latinidad and in interaction with those racialized as Mexican. The seemingly contradictory conflation of U.S. citizenship identity and anticolonial narratives among Puerto Rican barrio residents in Chicago questioned the racialization of Puerto Ricans in the United States by challenging conditions associated with moral inferiority and by uncovering the invisible whiteness of white barrio residents. Young white artists were represented through negative narratives of sexual mores, hygiene, and social apathy. While the idea prevailed that white people are the "real Americans," there were also instances in which Puerto Ricans insisted that whiteness be problematized by emphasizing that whites are not cultureless and that whiteness looks different depending on class or lifestyle. Likewise, the black culture of African American residents was bounded in ways that stretched the racial spectrum of Puerto Rican blackness while confining Puerto Ricans and African Americans to sharply defined and bounded social spaces.

While admittedly embodying a variety of contested meanings, cultural markers were still grounded in a separatist nationalist discourse of Puerto-Ricanness native to Chicago. Territory was redefined to mean the neighborhood, and the dissolution of the area's physical and social boundaries was perceived as the dissolution of the nation. The weakening of boundaries was met with a resurrection of separatist nationalist imagery that included official symbols of the nation, like the flags. The symbols of the Puerto Rican nation were shaped to become Chicago-specific public icons, which were saturated with a private subtext of conflict and political disagreement.

★ CONCLUSION ★

A *Chicago Sun-Times* cartoon typical of mainstream-media representations of Puerto Rican Chicago speaks volumes about the tense intersection of nationalism, political economy, and colonialist hegemony. Clemente High School, one of the largest community sites in which barrio activists and residents aimed to carve out spaces of resistance and autonomy, is reprovingly portrayed as outside the purview of U.S. boundaries. The high school is portrayed not only as part of Puerto Rico, but also as the property of Puerto Rican nationalists, as evidenced by the sign of "¡Viva P.R. Libre!" that imitates the one on Puerto Rican Cultural Center walls. The cartoonist implicitly configures a dissonance between grassroots interventions to Puerto-Ricanize Clemente and being true to public education in the United States. The subtext speaks to issues that are far more serious than dominant society's xenophobia, however.

The Clemente High School conflict unfolded in the context of so-called welfare reform of the mid-1990s. Under the name of the Personal Responsibility and Work Opportunity Reconciliation Act of 1996, the punitive legislation was passed just a few months into the hostile media and government reaction to the community-driven Clemente High School reform. Initially the state and city governments placed the responsibility for school reform at Clemente High School into the hands of neighborhood parents. However, once parents and community activists became critical of U.S. public education and aimed to recreate the curriculum to address their children's needs—an unintended and "undesirable" politicization that resulted from parents' increased involvement in school and grassroots politics—the

This cartoon of Clemente High School as Puerto Rico and as a landmark that does not belong to the United States suggests the mainstream media's view of Puerto Rican nationalism as incompatible with the creation of a U.S. citizenship identity. (By Jack Higgins, © 1997 Chicago Sun-Times)

state adopted punitive measures. Nationalist activists, many of them parents of Clemente High School students, were criminalized as anti-American terrorists for questioning the role of the public education system as a factory dedicated to produce compliant—and vulnerable, tractable, and inflexible—U.S. citizens.

Under the welfare reform act, welfare recipients were expected either to hold paid employment or to be performing community service within two years of the time they began receiving public assistance (Conte 1999; Jury 1997). Yet Clemente parent volunteers were accused of stealing because they did just that: they received twenty dollars a day of antipoverty discretionary funds allocated to the school as payment for supervising hallways, aiding teachers, and helping around the school. The hostile antiwelfare climate is inseparable from the enduring assumption that students and parents are to blame for the public schools' failure, and ultimately their poverty is viewed as the result of a lack of personal responsibility. This new nativism operates in tandem with the broader ideological climate of the time, in particular the xenophobic reaction to the intervention of people racialized as nonwhites in inherently American—and hence, white—ideological spaces like public high schools. The antimigrant climate is another clear example of this nativism in the United States, and it has been coupled both discursively and in implementation with the dismantling of the social welfare safety net (cf. De Genova and Ramos-Zayas 2000).

The performance of the nation among Puerto Ricans in Chicago was embroiled in the politics of class, race, and space that was variously implicated in everyday social practices. The multiple pedagogical spaces and continuous reconfigurations of the cultural authentic in Puerto Rican Chicago were constantly and repeatedly rehearsed with the awareness that poor people of the barrio were perpetually in the policy and legislative spotlight, under the microscopic of greater ideological locations. Enduring despite the creation of symbolic spaces of resistance, power inequalities regulated decisions over the allocation of funds for improving the lives of Latino children and their families. Son del Barrio, the youth salsa band, as well as other health and education projects organized by nationalist activists, were dismantled shortly after the end of my fieldwork under government claims that Puerto Rican nationalism constituted terrorism and anti-American sentiment. Misperceptions and prescriptive ideas of the mobility routes realistically available to members of marginalized communities were ultimately aided by the government's need to maintain a tight hold at the most fundamental levels of local politics and social reform. This is an underside of the story of Puerto Rican nationalism that the textual critique of many postmodernist studies fails to interrogate. The central problem for cultural analysis is not only to what extent identities are elicited discursively and symbolically, but also how they are deployed strategically in specific settings and at certain historical junctures to convey particular ideological and material conditions.

Grassroots programs, particularly those directed toward youth and education, provide the social context for the reinvigoration of a separatist nationalism at the margins. Modern state-sponsored public education is often explicit in its mission to regulate differences through depoliticized, top-down, and heavily folklorized multiculturalist curricula, thus ensuring social order and national consensus in the supposedly most classless of advanced industrial societies. This is encapsulated in the Department of Education's television-ad-campaign slogan: "Public education: It's how the American dream works."

Yet the new theoretical social Darwinism ardently advanced by Richard Herrnstein and Charles Murray is used to justify fiscal policies that close doors to educational opportunities as they reconfigure the idea of democratic access to mean occupational education rather than critical pedagogy

(Aronowitz 1997; McLaren 1998). The inequality is perpetuated in a hidden curriculum that creates a stratified system of secondary and postsecondary education in which culture is reserved for the few and the cultural capital of the dominant class is protected, as the conflict over the Clemente High School reform clearly illustrates.

Alternative education programs in Puerto Rican Chicago point to the sharp contradictions between the practices, beliefs, and values of the Puerto Rican community and those of U.S. public schooling, which takes place in a system established by a colonizing power. In Chicago popular nationalism was grounded in a critical pedagogy along Freirian lines that focused less on specific educational content than on the relationship between learning and participation—on praxis. These alternative education programs were institutional sites where a grassroots intellectual elite and young program participants contested imposed racialized identities by creating a Puerto Rican nationalism that conflated the cultural and the political in the performance of an anticolonial process.

It is not surprising that many anticolonial writers turn to an examination of their own identity in order to consider the domination of colonialism (Carey-Webb 1998). The emphasis on autobiographical elements in grassroots historiography can be viewed not as a solipsistic exercise but as part of a politicized project of reevaluating dominant colonial culture. The performance of Puerto Rican nationalism in Chicago's barrio was premised on separatist rhetoric, community-building strategies, and historical narratives that discredited the very ideological foundation of the American nation and of the American dream and its postulates of meritocracy, individualism, and equality. Ironically, it is precisely this questioning of the metaphor of the United States as a meritocratic "land of opportunity" that facilitated social mobility among barrio youth. By validating the perception Puerto Rican youths had of themselves as racialized Other and by connecting this racialized identity as Puerto Ricans in the United States to the colonial relationship between Puerto Rico and the United States, grassroots activists facilitated access to mainstream mobility routes often beyond the grasp of these disenfranchised youth.

With regard to the Puerto Rican poor, the allegation of laziness and welfare dependency becomes a disciplining mechanism of the state. Middle-class, working-class, and poor Puerto Ricans are used by the state to discipline each other; they are always at pains to demonstrate to a dominant society that they are hardworking, not lazy, and deserving. The tension between a middle-class elite and the popular classes, which consisted of grass-

roots activists and barrio residents, was mediated by the hegemonic operations of the state in such a way that class stratification and structural obstacles
to mobility remained hidden, while a nationalist discourse took center stage.
This nationalist discourse was in turn criminalized by middle-class state
workers and the media and culturalized by the popular classes. Alternatively
culturalizing and politicizing nationalism became the discursive strategy
through which the popular classes claimed control of community-building
projects and educational institutions, while criminalizing nationalism served
as the discourse that legitimized state funding decisions and explained distinctions between *la gente pobre* and *los profesionales,* or the suburbanites.

State-generated criminalization of nationalist discourses sustains culture-
of-poverty and blame-the-victim arguments by attributing barrio poverty to
cultural deficiencies rather than considering structural elements: those who
remain poor or are downwardly mobile have the wrong political ideology
of nationalism. Blaming political ideologies, particularly separatist Puerto
Rican nationalism, for persistent poverty provide false comfort to those
struggling to maintain the power of the state or a very elusive middle-class
status. Poverty and downward mobility are conditions of "nationalist criminals," but not of law-abiding, hardworking U.S. citizens. Thus, the hegemonic power of the American dream persists, as the idea that mobility can
only occur in an upward direction is upheld in the middle-class collective
imagination, despite evidence pointing to its fallacy. Ample evidence from
fiscal policy and public culture alike suggests that Americans are unlikely to
revise their ideology of individual opportunity, consensus, and the open society or to recognize the limits of the piecemeal approach to reform of which
identity politics is symptomatic.

Even the most separatist elements of Puerto Rican nationalism persist
not in spite of, but largely because of Puerto Ricans' status as U.S. citizens.
This citizenship identity is required for the continuous reinvigoration of
nationalism in light of global processes. A citizenship identity selectively
undermines possible political alliances with other Latinos if such alliances
are perceived as threatening or disadvantageous for Puerto-Ricanness. In
Chicago, where Mexicans constitute a much larger percentage of the Latino
population than Puerto Ricans do, this becomes particularly critical. Despite
its strategic virtues in certain political contexts, Latinidad remains an ahistorical, diluted political identity that underplays the various forms of U.S.
intervention in Latin America and the Caribbean. Some of these interventions have actually led to migration in the first place, while racializing
all peoples of Latin American ancestry as U.S. "minorities." A citizenship

identity sustains nationality-based rather than a Latino identity formation as it is a strategy to navigate Latinidad and black-white racial polarities.

The negotiation of citizenship rights is historically bound to duties, such as serving in the U.S. military, that Puerto Ricans perceive as their payment for the rights to which they are entitled. Puerto Ricans react to the stereotype that they are parasites of the system, often imposed by the dominant culture and other Latinos alike, by emphasizing duties that as citizens they have historically performed for the American nation. This citizenship identity is a defense against racist portraits of Puerto Ricans as lacking the solid work ethic of European white ethnics or even of contemporary immigrants from Latin America and Asia. Finally, this citizenship identity is a strategy for claiming limited resources by engaging in nationality-based, rather than pan-Latino, community-building programs. Its role as a resource-negotiating strategy accommodates the perception of all non–Puerto Rican Latinos as "illegal," a lesser form of U.S. citizens, regardless of actual legal status or rights.

Ironically, it is the Puerto Rican construction of these "illegal" immigrants, particularly Mexicans and Central Americans, as hardworking, in presumed opposition to the native minorities constructed as lazy, that supplies the ideological fuel for the otherwise unsustainable American dream. Puerto Ricans are aware of the stories of Mexican and Central American migrants crossing borders out of their "Third World" countries under terrible conditions and motivated by a fervent belief in the leading U.S. product of transnational exportation: the American dream. The immigrants sustain the dream for those native minorities who have not attained it. The upwardly mobile native minorities deliberately appropriate the migrant success transcripts by selectively deploying a Latino identity that is generally less stigmatized than a Puerto Rican one.

The role of the state remains concealed in its hegemonic project of subordinating labor and rendering the poor more vulnerable and tractable. This project—and the foundational mythologies of the American dream and the land of opportunity—rely on manipulating the desperation of impoverished U.S. citizens and migrants against each other. The migrant worker's tenuous hold on exploitative employment is a predicament readily enlisted by the state into the denigration as unproductive, lazy, and opportunistic of the migrants' most proximate competitors—Puerto Ricans and African Americans. The Puerto Rican and African American native-born deploy other advantages—English fluency, higher levels of formal schooling, and especially a glorified U.S. citizenship.

The underlying script is one of an infinitely fragmented, amorphous culture removed from political economy and history, through which U.S. intervention in Puerto Rico and throughout Latin America remains disguised behind the image of the United States as the land of opportunity. The margins that migrants and native minorities inhabit remain anthropologized, as it is "culture," and the easy leap into the report-card mentality that distinguishes between "model" minorities and "problem" minorities, that enables U.S. hegemonic traditions to endure. These hegemonic traditions are sustained in the face of clear evidence of inequality, colonialism, and power differentials in so-called late capitalism. Ascribing particular cultures to racialized and colonized groups denies not only the generations of economic and ideological interaction with dominant society, but also the strategic emphases and the variations in the choice of strategies within those "cultural groups" (Di Leonardo 1984, 1998).

The representation, historicization, and authentication that shaped Puerto Rican nationalism in Chicago relied on the ability to continuously generate modes of grassroots resistance to the founding myths of the American nation. The hegemonic operations of the American dream endured not only against such modes of resistance, but also partially because of that dream's ability to appropriate them, which in turn forced the dynamic and contingent transformation of Puerto Rican diasporic nationalism. Scholars have shown that the production of a national culture requires the construction of symbolic boundaries and the essentializing of cultural elements that exclude outsiders from the nation. The case of Puerto Ricans in Chicago accentuates ways in which the excluded not only fight for inclusion, but also reshape the very national ideologies and conceptions of the nation in the diaspora.

Nationalist leader Pedro Albizu Campos is a multivalent image throughout Puerto Rican communities in Puerto Rico and the United States. Interestingly, in Puerto Rico his image has been neutralized and has lost virtually all of its criminalized, anti-American terrorist character, except when it is being adopted and praised by U.S. Puerto Rican communities. These communities, otherwise marginalized from Island political discourse, become the surrogate representatives of the "good American citizen" for all Puerto Ricans, on the Island and the Mainland alike, since they get more colonial attention because of their voting capacity and ethnic political machinery.

The image of Albizu Campos is criminalized by the middle class and mainstream media, thus preventing it from being neutralized or relegated to elite pro-independence folklore. The criminalization of the image, while articulated along a discourse of nationalist terrorism, acquired pertinence because those opposing the placement of the Albizu Campos statue had vested real estate interests in the area where it would be placed. Conversely, the nationalist activists who supported the image as a critical component of community building and autonomy engaged the popular classes in debate about the positive value of Albizu Campos, the upwardly mobile Puerto Rican. Among those popular classes Albizu Campos became the representation of Puerto-Ricanness in Chicago, the embodiment of alternative racial classifications, and the interpretative device for the neighborhood's militant history. Most telling, the image of Albizu Campos became the nationalist embodiment of the American dream, the symbol of political presence, and the locus of autonomy.

In Chicago autobiographical documents were published and interpreted as a reminder of the incorporation of Puerto Ricans into the U.S. political economy as unequal colonial subjects, rather than as ethnics or immigrants presumed to be following in the footsteps of European-American populations. This colonial identity became endemic to notions of cultural authenticity generated by Island myth makers, an economic and intellectual Puerto Rican elite, as conspirators with the dominant colonial culture. The Island-nation was selectively glorified by Puerto Ricans in the United States across class and generations. Yet the autobiographical writings and artistic creations of barrio youths challenged stories of paradisiacal bliss narrated by older generations by recognizing the exclusionary quality of Island-generated notions of the authentic.

As many scholars have argued, authenticity and Puerto-Ricanness on the Island are reconfigured on the terrain of culture, for example, speaking "proper" Spanish, having the right cultural capital, and adhering to socially constructed notions of respecting one's elders, rather than on the terrain of the political, for example, fighting for an independent nation-state and seeking political autonomy. On the other hand, popular nationalism best describes the conflation of cultural and political terrains that constituted the social practices and local politics of Puerto Rican Chicago. For Chicago barrio residents the politicization of Puerto Rican culture was a means of securing at least a symbolic collective incorporation into the history of Puerto Rico from which they had been excluded.

The cultural capital that makes it possible for authenticity to be a social act also differentiates those who are operating in already consecrated modes of making Puerto-Ricanness from those who find Puerto-Ricanness in breaking from what was previously agreed upon. The increasing opening up of possibilities for choosing nonconventional ways of producing, representing, interpreting, and communicating Puerto-Ricanness, particularly among U.S. communities and urban youth, is an example of this. As Nestor García-Canclini argues, in the midst of these tensions are constituted the complex and not at all schematic relations between the hegemonic and the subaltern, the included and the excluded. This is one of the causes for which modernity implies processes of segregation—Mainlander and Islander continue to serve as differentiated identities—as well as of hybridization between the various social sectors and the symbolic systems (1992, 39). Mainlanders' cultural nationalism is still defined—and devalued, even by Mainlanders themselves—by always referring to them in terms established by the dominant Islanders, those who supposedly know what true Puerto-Ricanness is.

Puerto Ricans from the Island and from the Mainland share various political and cultural interests. Most recently, struggles over Vieques have created common physical and ideological spaces, if not necessarily enduring coalitions. This is perhaps a space in which the creation of complex transnational networks addresses problems of cultural reproduction for diasporic communities abroad by engaging the politics of nationalism at "home" (Danforth 1995, 81).

In a conversation with me Adela, a barrio activist in Chicago, reflected on three important political events that illuminate the complexity of Puerto Rican nationalism and the newly emergent spaces of authenticity that Mainlanders created in response to exclusionary nation-building practices in Puerto Rico. Adela mentioned the release of the FALN members; the protests against the U.S. military presence in the off-shore municipality of Vieques, Puerto Rico; and the controversy generated in Puerto Rico when the 2000 Puerto Rican National Parade in New York was jointly dedicated to Pedro Albizu Campos and Vieques. Adela commented:

> We are exposing ourselves. Like it or not, the Puerto Ricans on the Island cannot pretend we don't exist or that we don't have a say anymore. It's like the U.S. with Fidel Castro. They may not like him, but they still have to deal with his existence. We are sending delegations to Vieques. The [FALN] prisoners are from Chicago, but they were received as heroes in Puerto Rico. When Island Puerto Ricans want something, they have to ask the Puerto Ricans from here for support. They ask Gutiérrez, Nydia Velásquez, Serrano [members of Congress]. They are the ones who have a voice and a vote. And they are all from here. That bishop that's in Puerto Rico right now, the one who's behind the protests against the U.S. military's occupation [of the municipality of Vieques], he came from here too. Those are the people condemning colonialism . . . and they're all Puerto Ricans from the U.S.

The involvement of the Puerto Rican diaspora in the politically militant spaces on the Island has been received by Island politicians and intellectual elites in various ways, all of which are condescending and paternalistic toward migrant communities. A renowned nationalist activist once mentioned in reference to academics and community building: "I can't think that I'll go back to Puerto Rico to struggle for the Island's independence. The independence movement in Puerto Rico is middle class. A bunch of lawyers and academics that think that it's all about logical arguments."

Rubén Berríos Martínez, one of the most prominent leaders of the independence movement and a candidate for governor from the Puerto Rican Independence Party on the Island, commended the New York Puerto Rican community for dedicating the annual parade to Albizu Campos and to the Island municipality of Vieques. In an editorial commentary that appeared in the Island's main newspaper, Berríos Martínez emphasizes that "as a Puerto Rican from here [Puerto Rico], only during my years studying in the United States . . . do I know, from very far away, the Puerto Rican communities in the United States" (2000). In a misplaced quote from Cervantes's *Don Quixote,* Berríos Martínez nods to the "suffering" Puerto Ricans in the United States who have lived the "tragedy of being deprived from their maternal tongue," but who "refuse to be ashamed" of being Puerto Rican. He even comments that "as a Puerto Rican from [the Island], I have an enormous debt with the Puerto Ricans from [the United States]." What remains conveniently omitted in this understanding of *los de aquí* and *los de allá* is the fact that the linguistic "tragedy" is more of a tragedy for those members of the Puerto Rican intellectual elite who essentialize Puerto-Ricanness as Spanish-speaking. Most significant, the focus on cultural preservation serves as a convenient concealment for the truly tragic material conditions experienced by over 40 percent of all Puerto Ricans—*aquí* and *allá* alike—and reflects a condescending attitude toward grassroots political strategies and Puerto Rican barrio expressions of Puerto-Ricanness. Unfortunately, this attitude is by no means limited to or even found primarily within the pro-independence party, but it crosses political lines among the Island's professional and intellectual elite.

Another space that has to be taken into account involves the production and dissemination of critical reflections around Puerto-Ricanness, which in the case of Chicago barrio activists includes the Internet (and paper-version) production of the *Boricua* newspaper. This newspaper, although produced and disseminated by Chicago barrio activists, incorporates reflections on Puerto-Ricanness by contributors who are scholars and intellectuals from both the Island and the Mainland. Several scholars attending prestigious Chicago universities, many of them born and raised on the Island, have contributed pieces, often based on their own research in the barrio. Most significant is the interaction between these scholars and barrio activists, who are intellectuals in their own right.

"Don't write something that is so high on the academic shelves that my students cannot read it," advised a local activist and high school teacher when he knew about my project and the project of another woman researcher. Similarly, other scholars who engaged in barrio activism were "observers observed"—to use George Stocking's phrase—and evaluated for their community commitment. This level of interest in academic work was also part of an interest in barrio representation and in fostering notions of giving back in a popular ethnographic tradition.

This transnational community centers on a network of museums, galleries, and other cultural institutions, as well as intellectual exchanges between scholars who are based on the Island and in various U.S. universities, mostly in the Northeast (Duany 2000). Often the interaction between Island scholars living in the United States and popular intellectuals requires that symbols, images, and metaphors of preexisting regional and ethnic cultures be politicized, generalized, and reduced to the lowest common denominator. A homogeneous or generic national culture designed to encompass all the specific regional or ethnic cultures that preceded it is evidenced in the common deployment of a symbolic ethnicity (Gans 1979). Eating at local Puerto Rican restaurants, hanging Puerto Rican flags of various textures from rearview mirrors, participating in street festivals, and engaging in occasional volunteer work alongside barrio activists are some of the social practices through which Island scholars display a symbolic solidarity with barrio residents. Through open participation in these processes, Chicago Puerto Ricans contended with Islanders' rejection through the imposition of an alternative we-ness that aimed to break down Island-Mainland boundaries.

Militant political expressions are common among elite intellectuals both from the Island and from the Mainland, and these symbols account for a type of neonationalism that is flexible enough because it relies on a broad common denominator to bring the two groups together. However, in this case, U.S. Puerto Ricans focus on the fact that once Puerto Ricans from the Island have attended U.S. colleges or attained corporate jobs, they tend to keep their distance from the more politicized Mainlanders, including those who claim citizenship rights in the terrain of explicitly militant politics. As one intellectual born and raised on the Island commented: "I can't understand why the Puerto Ricans here adopt a position of subaltern instead of dominant. We have a lot to learn from the Cubans in Miami."

Puerto Rican nationalism is consolidated as a localized—and barrio-based in the case of Chicago—yet decentered identity shaped by political economic conditions and notions of authenticity. Consolidations of the authentic are premised on a subtle appreciation of cultural capital and the reproduction of internal social hierarchies on both sides of the water. These social hierarchies are decontextually created and contested in cultural terms, as levels of Puerto-Ricanness, rather than as differences in resources, status, and privilege. The class dimensions of the various migration flows cannot be concealed under blanket statements about cultural politics or *los de aquí* and *los de allá*. The different migration chains that define the multiple economic tracks of Puerto Rican migrants often remain obscured in discourses that underplay the power struggles behind notions of cultural authenticity.

The increasingly porous boundaries resulting from transnational processes create opportunities for more inclusive forms of national identification previously suppressed in the name of nationalism (Flores 2000; García-Canclini 1992). Nevertheless, the emergence of these hybrid identities also reconfigures a new and perhaps equally hegemonic system for judging the authentic and allows the continued creation of hierarchies of power and exclusion, as the case of Mainlander Puerto Ricans shows. As more members of the Puerto Rican elite enter the migration stream, place of birth will continue to be a symbol of authenticity, while place of residence has been largely disassociated from the determination of real Puerto-Ricanness.

The Island's intellectual elite oftentimes focuses on culture, coded in language, as the criterion for inclusion into the nation that supersedes all others. Intellectuals and scholars often create "the symbolic capital" (Bourdieu 1977b) from which a national culture is formed. They write a national history disseminated through public education, excavate the material culture of national ancestors, enforce a national language, and collect a body of folklore as the symbolic capital that constitutes a national culture and legitimizes the existence of a nation (cf. Chatterjee 1993; Danforth 1995). What resurfaces in my ethnographic fieldwork is the interrogation of the ways in which "diaspora communities are able to maintain their ties to their homelands and to participate in the construction of transnational national communities through 'global cultural flows'" (Appadurai 1990, 11).

Diasporic communities produce and reproduce distinct identities based on pride in hybridity, malleability, and fluidity (Flores 1985), or they redirect the marginalization consequence of that hybridity for artistic production (Acosta-Belén 1992). The geographic frontiers of cultural identity have been blurred by the transnationalization of capital, the expansion of electronic communication technology, and the frequent border crossing of migrants and tourists (García-Canclini 1992). Nevertheless, the flexible deterritorialization of cultural identities cannot be exaggerated, nor can it be assumed that everyday power struggles and material inequalities are solved exclusively on the terrain of the textual or the discursive. Such an approach underplays the social practices and material processes that continually exacerbate internal boundaries and unequal power dynamics, and how these dynamics consequently reflect increasing global inequality and economic polarization. The processes of global flows—cultural or otherwise—are not autonomous from the social and material tensions embedded in conceptualizations of the culturally authentic.

An ethnographic research that combines cultural and political economic critique shows that it is possible to reject essentialist and primordialist approaches to nationalism without abandoning the search for understanding of the lived experiences of people whose subjective and material relations shape particular forms of collective identification. Rethinking diasporic nationalism entails approaching the nation as a collection of dispersed yet tangible tensions of social practices and political economy, state power and cultural resistance. Postmodernist studies rightly emphasize that easy dichotomies between here and there, national and migrant, Island and Mainland, identity and alterity are no longer possible, if they ever were. However, some postmodernist examinations fail to account for the local politics and state power upon which nationalism is based, or for the reformulations of nationalism in the diaspora. It is at best questionable that deploying identity politics will address the economic marginality of Doña Luz and Marisol, or any of the other barrio residents whose voices have surfaced throughout this volume, or will nudge the conscience of state power, let alone influence its fiscal policy.

This ethnography has insisted on the importance of viewing Puerto Rican nationalism as a dimension of Latino identity formation, as a dynamic performance that must be understood contextually as a vocabulary for denouncing inequality and marginality, and in some instances even as proxy for complex experiences of race and class in the everyday ideological context of white supremacy in the United States.

★ NOTES ★

Introduction

1. The names used throughout the text are pseudonyms that have been changed from those used in previous manuscripts and publications to further protect people's identities. Only when the name of a person or place has already appeared in local publications or in the media is the real name used.

2. Spanglish is a hybrid language that combines elements from the Spanish and English languages but has its own grammatical codes that are independent of Spanish and English. Code switching is the use of words from the Spanish and English languages while following the grammatical codes of one of the two languages. For a rigorous treatment of the role of language—and of Spanglish and code switching—see Zentella 1995, 1997a, 1997b, 2000.

3. For a thorough discussion of the concept of the "native anthropologist" in reference to Puerto Rican scholars, see LaSalle and Pérez 1997.

4. Throughout the text I distinguish between grassroots activists and not-for-profit-sector workers. Grassroots activists were barrio residents, including the nationalist activists, who were involved in a politics "from below." Unlike the workers in the not-for-profit sector, whose activism is funded by government or private agencies, grassroots activists depended on local fundraising and barrio support. Hence, grassroots activists' access to government funding agencies was more limited than that of not-for-profit workers. The not-for-profit workers I interviewed worked for local branches of nationally renowned not-for-profit agencies. The grassroots activists created groups that specifically aimed to address the needs of Humboldt Park, Logan Square, and West Town residents.

5. When used to designate Latinos, the term *elite* describes people who consider themselves and are considered by others to be middle-class, white-collar professionals. Given that most Latinos are working class or poor and are exploited in low-paying manufacturing or service-sector work, middle-class and white-collar Latinos are an elite. Thus, the term *elite* suggests both upward mobility and the group's small size relative to the total number of people racialized as Latinos in the United States.

Chapter 1

1. Cultural nationalism is disassociated from demands for an autonomous state and involves an incursion into identity politics. In this sense, cultural nationalism has provided an anticolonial discourse and historiography in India under British domination (e.g., Chatterjee 1993; Spivak 1988); has served as an instrument of political mobilization around linguistic

rights among the most marginalized sectors of an independent nation-state, as in the case of the Guatemalan Maya population (Warren 1995); and has supported claims to ethnic agency in struggles against civil rights violations, as in the cases of the Chicano and Nation of Islam movements in the United States (Klor de Alva 1998). Chatterjee (1993) draws a distinction between British imperial nationalism and Indian anticolonial nationalism, emphasizing that the latter developed in the context of an inner "spiritual domain" even before it developed in the political, material context. In this sense, the British are associated with the modern and the material. Carving out a local "domain of sovereignty" associated with moral and spiritual spheres that are independent of the domain controlled by the colonial power allows the Indian elites and government to exert a degree of power and autonomy in the midst of colonial control. Cultural nationalists have examined certain domains of sovereignty as potential spaces of popular resistance and agency. By perceiving the nation as fragmented into various domains of sovereignty, some of which can flourish separately from the existence of an autonomous nation-state, cultural nationalists can limit colonial power and create spaces of subaltern agency, particularly in the power of the local elites (Chatterjee 1993).

2. Scarano has challenged the labor historians who have interpreted the era of Americanization in Puerto Rico as one of total unity and cooperation across racial divides (Guerra 1998). As Lillian Guerra (1998) notices, these historians have argued that unionization stretched or blurred the boundaries of racial acceptability by making class, not race, the key component of popular culture. Guerra agrees with Scarano's argument that the opposite seems to have been the case. The ways in which racial acceptability were stretched may have reinforced the importance of whitening in the development of a popular-class sense of identity. In fact, in Puerto Rico North American colonizers actively tried to prevent the development of racial consciousness in the nineteenth century while the Jim Crow laws were being enacted in the American South (Guerra 1998, 227).

3. The classic text most emblematic of the Generation of the 1930 is Antonio S. Pedreira's *Insularismo*, in which the author poses the key question: "What are we? Or how are we Puerto Ricans globally considered?" (1934, 21 in Duany 2000, 7). As Duany and others (e.g., Flores 1993) have pointed out, Pedreira answers this question by emphasizing that culturally Puerto Rico is a Hispanic colony, racially it is a mixed and confused population, and geographically it is an island characterized by territorial and political isolation. As the title suggests, Pedreira believes that territorial isolation creates a dependent and passive population with an intense inferiority complex that leads them to rely on more powerful countries, like Spain and the United States. Pedreira's ideological tone is characteristic of existentialist trends of the time, but this book remains a required text in public schools on the Island, and, as some scholars have argued (e.g., Duany 2000; Pabón 1995), dominant intellectual discussions on national identity in Puerto Rico are still framed largely in Pedreira's terms.

4. Electoral support is not the only indicator of nationalist sentiment. Nevertheless, in a country of such high electoral participation in which each of the three political parties explicitly advocates a particular political status for the Island, electoral outcomes are fairly reliable predictors of the general population's preference for commonwealth, statehood, or independence (Barreto and Eagles 2000).

5. See, for example, *Labor Migration under Capitalism* (History Task Force 1979), published by the Centro de Estudios Puertorriqueños, Hunter College, City University of New York.

6. Even at the time of massive migration, migrants were excluded from political speeches, literary texts, and local newspapers on the Island. In the 1950s some Island-based Puerto Rican authors began to write about the experiences of the hundreds of thousands of Puerto Rican migrants to New York City and, to a much lesser extent, to other eastern-seaboard states. As Flores (1993) has argued, such writers did not capture the complex and dynamic nature of the bilingual and bicultural Puerto Rican communities, but generally emphasized issues of cultural assimilation or painted portraits of the migrants' nostalgic longing for the Island.

7. Also *cadenados*, which means chains, because migrants from the Dominican Republic are presumed to wear heavy gold chains as jewelry (Pessar 1995). Janet Crespo, a U.S.-born Dominican student in one of my classes at Rutgers, commented that another popular name for re-

turnees to the Dominican Republic is *yos,* suggesting that they use the stereotypically urban way of calling someone or getting someone's attention (as in "yo, come here").

8. The spatial extension of household and kinship networks across national boundaries implies the creation of transnational identities and the development of what Anderson (1992) calls long-distance nationalism. Schiller, Basch, and Blanc-Szanton (1992) define *transnationalism* as the process whereby migrants establish and maintain sociocultural connections across geopolitical borders. The migrants' kinship networks, economic resources, and political involvement span at least two nations and are sustained by back-and-forth migration. Hence, migrants hold multiple identities that interact in complex ways with ethnicity, race, class, gender, and other variables. This valuable work on transnational identities, however, does not preclude popular images of migration as a form of cultural stripping away and complete absorption into the host society (e.g., García-Canclini 1992; Rosaldo 1989). See also Jorge Duany's (1993) study of Dominicans in New York City. Duany illustrates how border crossing becomes an apt image not just for the physical act of moving to another country, but also for the crossover between cultures, languages, and nation-states in which transnational migrants participate (Duany 1993, 17).

9. Ironically, this criterion includes, by definition, second-generation immigrants from Cuba and the Dominican Republic, but excludes second-generation, U.S.-born Puerto Ricans.

10. The migration of many Puerto Ricans is best characterized by the "circular," or "revolving-door," model, according to which migrants remain for short periods of time in the receiving society and travel back and forth frequently (Hernández Cruz 1985; Vargas-Ramos 2000). This bilateral movement of people creates a porous border zone that migrants continually cross, sometimes several times a year (Duany 2000). Estimates of the volume of circular migration between the Island and the Mainland range from 10 to 45 percent of the total flow, depending on various definitions, sources, samples, and methods (see Duany 2000). In the 1980s 130,000 people commuted back and forth between the Island and the Mainland (Rivera-Batiz and Santiago 1996). As Duany eloquently explains: "these transnational flows preceded by several decades the current trend toward the globalization of financial and labor markets. . . . But more than simply returning to their homeland (like many other migrants have done before), Puerto Ricans have traced a complex circuit, often involving frequent moves in multiple directions, not necessarily beginning or ending at the same point" (2000, 15). In an exhaustive study of return migrants in the municipality of Aguadillas, Puerto Rico, Vargas-Ramos found that 44 percent of those who have resided outside Puerto Rico fall into the circular migrant category (2000, 48). One challenge to nationalist projects, then, is the malleability of geopolitical boundaries resulting from the globalization of the capitalist world economy; increased labor migration; and, in the case of Puerto Ricans, the colonial relationship between Island and metropolitan governments.

11. Here I am using the term *elite* to describe a group of upper- and upper-middle-class Puerto Ricans who are responsible for the documentation, production, and reproduction of the "authentic" national culture. By controlling political and educational institutions—like the Instituto de Cultura Puertorriqueño [Institute for Puerto Rican Culture] as well as exclusive secondary education institutions and informal social networks—members of this elite consider themselves to be responsible for preserving cultural purity and national identity.

12. I recognize the problem of using *Islander* and *Mainlander* as designators of a difference that is not rooted exclusively or even primarily on geographical location. The terms are also problematic because the distinction between Puerto Rican Islanders and Mainlanders ignores the very political, economic, and social factors that govern back-and-forth migration—in particular, Puerto Rico's status as a U.S. colonial territory. Notwithstanding these limitations, I have chosen to use the terms *Mainlander* and *Islander* as proxy designators for the arguments advanced in chapter 5.

13. Through the cultural and literary achievements of Puerto Ricans artists in New York, reflected in the trendy Nuyorican Poets Cafe and numerous poetry anthologies, the term *Nuyorican* was adopted by younger Puerto Ricans to signify a new identity consciousness and cultural syncretism (Flores 1993; Acosta-Belén 1992). The term also designates a growing literary canon illustrative of their unique migration and barrio-life experiences and thus has been con-

ceived primarily as a classification for the literature produced in the emerging Puerto Rican enclaves of New York (Acosta-Belén 1992, 980).

14. Some historical events have triggered the revival of white ethnicity. The civil rights and
Black Power movements are instances in which white ethnics appropriated the discourses of
racial and ethnic pride. See Novak's *The Rise of the Unmeltable Ethnics* (1972).

Chapter 2

1. Most studies of Puerto Rican migration to the United States have focused on communities in New York City (e.g., Sánchez Korrol 1980, 1989; Sullivan 1992) and, to a lesser extent,
other northeastern Puerto Rican areas (e.g., Rogler 1972; Hardy-Fanta 1993). However, ever
since the U.S. occupancy of Puerto Rico began in the late-nineteenth century, Puerto Ricans
have migrated to all regions of the United States. They were transported to Hawaii to work in
the sugar cane fields in the early 1900s; to Arizona to cultivate and pick cotton after a tightening of immigration laws created a shortage of Mexican labor in the 1920s; and to Maryland,
Louisiana, and Ohio during World War II, when unskilled workers were hired to work on rail-
road construction projects, in food processing plants, and in copper mines (Maldonado 1979).
Noteworthy progress in the direction of expanding scholarship on Puerto Ricans in Chicago
has been made by Marixa Alicea's (1997) research on substance abuse, Nilda Flores-González's
(1999) study on the formation of student identities in a public high school in West Town, Irma
Olmedo's (1997) oral history project with elderly Puerto Rican women, and Gina Pérez's
(2000) and Maura Toro-Morn's (1995) studies on Puerto Rican women and migration to
Chicago. Likewise, the theme of the Fall 2001 issue of the *Centro Journal* (vol. 13, no. 2) was devoted to Puerto Rican Chicago. Produced by the Center for Puerto Rican Studies and edited by
Gina Pérez and Xavier Totti, the issue foregrounds contemporary research on Puerto Rican
Chicago.

2. It was not until the mid-1940s that Puerto Rican contract laborers started arriving en
masse in Chicago, recruited by Castle, Barton, and Associates. This Chicago-based private employment agency had opened offices in various cities throughout the United States and Puerto
Rico (Martínez 1989, 93; Chicago Welfare Council and Office of the Department of Labor
1957). In agreement with Puerto Rico's Department of Labor, the agency recruited Puerto Rican
men and women and placed the women as domestics in general household service and the
men in foundry work at the Chicago Hardware Foundry Company. Thereafter, laborers were
brought north to work on Midwestern farms as well (Padilla et al. 1946; 1957, 16).

3. Sexual harassment of Puerto Rican women working as domestic employees in private
households was so common that a commission was designated to handle the cases. Government reports indicate that about 60 percent of workers did not complete their contracts, and
only about 15 percent of contract laborers returned to Puerto Rico (War Manpower Commission
on Contract Labor, 1957 report, Chicago Historical Society welfare office files, 6–7; see also
Maldonado 1979, 111).

4. War Manpower Commission on Contract Labor, 1957 report.

5. A combination of factors, including the Island's supposed overpopulation, the labor
needs of the United States, and Puerto Rico's strategic location during the Cold War, have been
cited as reasons for the Operation Bootstraps project. For a detailed account of the project and
of industrialization in Puerto Rico, see *Labor Migration under Capitalism: The Puerto Rican Experience* (History Task Force 1979) and *The Puerto Ricans: A Documentary History* (Wagenheim
and de Wagenheim 1996).

6. The careless recruitment and deplorable working conditions of contracted workers in
Chicago became a source of widely publicized controversy. A 1946 study by Elena Padilla,
Muna Muñoz, and others (Padilla et al. 1946) indicates that the Department of Labor did not require proof of age or medical certificates from any of the workers, so extremely young and often
physically ill Puerto Ricans were hired to perform strenuous work (Padilla et al. 1957). Charges
regarding the mistreatment of Chicago's Puerto Rican workers—including fifteen-hour work-
days, wages substantially lower than those of other Chicago workers, and unannounced transferring of domestic workers between work sites—triggered a storm of controversy that

occupied the front pages of Island newspapers (see multiple issues of *El Mundo* [San Juan], December 19, 1946–February 9, 1947; Maldonado 1979, 114). As Maldonado (1979), Senior and Watkins (1966), and Jones (1955) have noted, the seasonal farm labor system both augmented already existing Puerto Rican communities and prompted the creation of new ones.

Some agricultural workers stayed beyond the determined employment season and sought work at better-paid industrial jobs. This was the case for many early Puerto Rican agricultural workers in Wisconsin, Michigan, Indiana, and Illinois who were hired as seasonal contract laborers to harvest crops and found employment in foundry work thereafter (Maldonado 1979, 117). The shortage of steel mill workers after World War II provided fertile terrain for new Puerto Rican communities to develop and existing Puerto Rican areas to flourish during the early stages of Puerto Rican migration to Chicago. In 1946 and 1947 about two thousand Puerto Ricans were recruited through private employment agencies, and about fifteen thousand others were hired as seasonal farm workers (Padilla et al. 1957, 17).

7. Minutes of the Welfare Council of Metropolitan Chicago, April 9, 1954, Chicago community archives, Chicago Historical Society.

8. Notable exceptions are the pioneer works of Elena Padilla (1947) and Felix Padilla (1985, 1987), as well as the contributions of several more contemporary scholars: Marixa Alicea's study on substance abuse; Gina Pérez's (2000) and Maura Toro-Morn's (1995) studies on migration and gender; Nilda Flores-González's (1999) research on education; and Mérida Rúa's (2000) research on Puerto Rican identity and Latinidad.

9. Official letter from Waitstill H. Sharp, Director of Chicago Council against Racial and Religious Discrimination, to Hagel Holm of Maryville College, Tennessee, in reference to Anthony Vega's policy of integrating Puerto Ricans, January 25, 1951 (Welfare Council folder, Chicago community archives, Chicago Historical Society).

10. Minutes of the Welfare Council of Metropolitan Chicago, April 9, 1954.

11. In fact, in 1953, the Chicago Housing Authority endorsed a study on Puerto Ricans in Chicago claiming that "it will be of great help to know the number and makeup and other relevant data on Puerto Rican families residing in areas which the [Chicago Housing Authority] may clear for the construction of a project" (Chicago Housing Authority, interoffice memo, September 22, 1953, Chicago Historical Society).

12. This was not the only riot in the Chicago Puerto Rican barrio. In a term paper written for her English class at a local alternative high school, Diana Sánchez, a sixteen-year-old Puerto Rican woman, interviewed one of the spectators of the riot of 1977. In her high school's 1995 yearbook Diana published her interview with Viola Salgado, a community activist who directed a grassroots AIDS education clinic in Humboldt Park. Diana recorded Viola's description of the riots:

In 1977, when Rafael Cruz and Julio Osorio were killed by the police in Humboldt Park, I was 30 years old, the same age as Rafael's sisters, María, Milagros, and Mercedes. On Saturday, June 4th, after the Puerto Rican Parade, I was at a fund-raiser at Northwest Hall on North Avenue and Western. It was getting dark when I heard about the police killings. An hour or so later, some friends and I headed towards Division Street and California [Avenue]. The police had closed off these streets and people were running to avoid contact with them. Many people were afraid because there was a building on fire and the Fire Department was refusing to respond, because the Puerto Rican community was rioting. If the fire department had responded, a person would not have died in the fire. Although many Puerto Ricans were angry, defiant, and burned police cars, there was an army of police officers in military formation up and down Division Street. They were definitely a show of force to intimidate, not to serve and protect. This scene was unforgettable.

Following Viola's description, Diana added, "While the police riot in Humboldt Park was a tragedy for our community, many other incidents of police brutality were also experienced in the black and Mexican communities during the summer of 1977."

13. The civic organizations of the early 1960s, particularly the hometown clubs, whose

members came from the same town in Puerto Rico, had mostly focused on providing recreational activities and social structure for recently arrived Puerto Rican families. After the riots of 1966 and the implementation of community action programs—including Saul Alinsky-style community development projects characteristic of Chicago neighborhoods in the 1970s (Cruz 1987)—other grassroots militant efforts emerged.

14. Many Chicago activists have pointed out that the Young Lords originated in Chicago, but most people mistakenly think they began in New York. In fact, the Chicago Young Lords and their New York counterparts attempted to develop parallel strategies to address problems common to all U.S. Puerto Ricans, but the partnership between the two groups was short-lived due to differences in the class and educational backgrounds of the members. The New York Young Lords organization, which later called itself the Young Lords Party, implying a political shift toward the mainstream, had emerged out of philosophical traditions as they were understood by college-educated Puerto Rican youth. While the New York Young Lords included members of a variety of Latino nationalities and class alliances in their constituency, the Chicago Young Lords were decidedly Puerto Rican and barrio poor. High school dropouts, they were more interested in immediate barrio needs than were their New York counterparts. As one Chicago Young Lord commented,

> Here in Chicago we're more concerned with the immediate needs of the people, but we still understand that the real struggle is not a local one. . . . That's why we entered the coalition with the Panthers and the Young Patriots at a national and international level. Yet if we talk of being the vanguard, we need to be up ahead and still have something behind us too. We're better able to analyze when we're out on the streets talking with the people. Ideas must come after actions, not just from reading Marx, Lenin, or Mao. (Browning 1973, 25)

15. Prior to the U.S. occupation of the Island in 1898, political protest and insurgency was directed against Spain, reaching its pinnacle in 1868 with El Grito de Lares, a rebellion in the town of Lares, where the Free Republic of Puerto Rico was proclaimed for two days before the Spanish army quelled the insurgency and reinstituted colonial domination. El Grito de Lares, the Lares flag, and the revolutionaries who partook in the anti-Spanish rebellion are revered icons of contemporary Puerto Rican militant groups, including nationalist activists in the United States. See, for instance, Seijo-Bruno's *La insurrección nacionalista en Puerto Rico, 1950* (1989) and Ferrao's *Pedro Albizu Campos y el nacionalismo puertorriqueño* (1990).

16. The individual and collective motifs that guided these prisoners to organize the FALN and take upon themselves the independence of Puerto Rico, although important questions that merit research, are beyond the scope of this book. Because I am focusing mostly on the nature of current Puerto Rican activism in Chicago, I consider the prisoners to the extent that they and their images affected collective memory, understandings of history in everyday life, contemporary philosophical debates among the prisoners' advocates, and social reform efforts in Chicago's Puerto Rican community. Other researchers have examined the motivating historical and even psychological factors behind the political prisoners' commitment to Puerto Rican independence "by any means necessary." For instance, Ronald Fernández thoroughly analyzes the particularities of the arrests, trials, and convictions of FALN members in the context of the Puerto Rican anticolonial struggle in his book *Prisoners of Colonialism: The Struggle for Justice in Puerto Rico* (1994). From a psychological perspective, Gilda Zwerman examines the gender dimensions of post–New Left militant organizations in her articles "The Identity Vulnerable Activist and the Emergence of Post–New Left Armed, Underground Organizations in the United States" (1995) and "Mothering on the Lam: Politics, Gender Fantasies, and Maternal Thinking in Women Associated with Armed, Clandestine Organizations in the United States" (1994).

17. The conditions of their release generated conflict and were debated at each step of the way, and the issue appeared on the front page of most national U.S. newspapers. Most Puerto Ricans in the United States and on the Island supported the release of the prisoners on humanitarian, rather than political or ideological, grounds. Supporters claimed that the prisoners had been given sentences disproportionate to the crimes for which they had been convicted.

Mainstream public opinion in the United States could not get past the theory that President Clinton had released the prisoners to attract Puerto Rican voters for his wife's Senate campaign in New York. Families of a white ethnic police officer who had been hurt in a bombing in New York City's Franklyn Tavern attributed to the FALN came forward and condemned the Clinton administration for siding with the "Puerto Rican terrorists." Most of the released prisoners decided to relocate in Puerto Rico rather than come back to their neighborhood in Chicago because they feared retaliation by the Daley administration and local surveillance agents. In Chicago nationalist activists recognized the prisoners' release as a bittersweet victory after fifteen years of amnesty campaigns. The victory was bittersweet both because the release was conditional (those who were released were required to admit regret for past actions) and because two of the most revered prisoners were not considered for clemency. The two prisoners who remained in prison, considered the masterminds of the FALN, were the brother of a renowned Chicago activist and the son of a minister of a local church.

18. *Claridad* is the only pro-independence newspaper and is read by a small elite of university professors, students, and other intellectuals. Ironically, it has historically published more articles on Puerto Ricans in the United States than any other Puerto Rican newspaper; in particular, *Claridad* has published several articles on the Chicago political prisoners and the Chicago monuments to the Puerto Rican flag.

19. Later Seijo-Bruno told me that her experiences in Chicago confirmed her belief that members of the most militant nationalist sectors are from the working class (see Seijo-Bruno 1989).

20. Miñi Seijo-Bruno interviewed Oscar and José López's mother, Andrea Rivera Méndez. Andrea was born in Isabela, Puerto Rico, in 1917 and emigrated to Chicago in the 1950s with her six children. Once they were in Chicago, her husband left her and her children, so Andrea and her older son worked day and night doing laundry and child care to support the family. She was able to put all of the children through school until they started to contribute to the household themselves by selling newspapers and working in drug stores and at other part-time jobs.

When Seijo-Bruno asked her why she thought her sons were in the pro-independence struggle if they were raised in Chicago, why hadn't they "assimilated," Andrea replied: "I'd NEVER allow my children to be Americans! I've never spoken a word of English to them and I never let them speak a word of English to me. They have to speak Spanish first, and my grandchildren too. I'm very proud of my Puerto Rican blood." Moreover, when Seijo-Bruno asked her, "Are you going to tell your sons to quit the struggle?" Andrea answered emphatically: "No, no, no! Let them continue! A mother should never coerce her children's ideals. If they have chosen the struggle, they have a reason. They know what's going on. It's going to be five years since I last heard from my son [Oscar] and I know I cannot die until I see him. I never lose that hope." Both Josefina, the mother of two of the women prisoners, and Andrea, the mother of a prisoner and of one of the leading community activists in the Puerto Rican barrio of Chicago, remained active in the community after their children's arrests. Josefina, an active and young-looking woman in her sixties, was a core member of the Puerto Rican Cultural Center and worked at the center's bakery during the early stages of my fieldwork; toward the end of my work she was in charge of various aspects of the Boricua Festival (Seijo-Bruno 1981).

21. Prior to their arrests, the prisoners were involved in a variety of community activities: developing Latino recruitment and support services at local colleges, establishing community programs to offer jobs and recreation opportunities to young people, assisting in workers' rights programs, cofounding grassroots popular education programs, actively participating as members of the First Congregational Church, receiving high academic and leadership honors in their high school and college classes, and teaching at the local public high school and criticizing its curriculum. One of them was a decorated Vietnam veteran who worked to address community issues related to housing, unemployment, and health, including infant mortality.

22. In the mid-1950s, at the height of Puerto Rican migration to Chicago, four Puerto Rican men led by a Puerto Rican woman—the "Five Nationalists"—opened fire at the U.S. Congress, wounding five congressmen and drawing international attention to the cause of Puerto Rican independence. After their attack on Congress, the Five Nationalists—Rafael Cancel Miranda, Andrés Figueroa Cordero, Irvin Flores, Oscar Collazo, and Lolita Lebrón—were given life sen-

tences, and became heroes to many pro-independence sympathizers, including the founders
and members of the Chicago Cultural Center. Some Cultural Center members engaged in an
intensive amnesty campaign on their behalf; many of them followed their example. In 1979,
the intensive amnesty campaign in Puerto Rico and among Puerto Ricans in the United States,
particularly in Chicago, paid off, and President Jimmy Carter granted the Nationalists amnesty.
This was part of two major coordinated events by Albizuist nationalists drew international attention to Puerto Rico: two Puerto Ricans attacked the Blair House and a historical anti-U.S. rebellion unraveled in the mountain town of Jayuya, Puerto Rico. When the Five Nationalists
were released, they were received as heroes in Puerto Rico and other U.S. Puerto Rican communities. In Chicago, "the Nationalists came to the First Congregational Church. The Church
was packed. That was one of their first stops after they were released. They were received like
heroes and patriots," commented a local activist.

23. As I conducted my many formal and informal interviews in Chicago with both antinationalists and militant nationalists, I was astonished by how many Puerto Ricans in Chicago
have had some type of contact with the FBI. The bureau is not something from the past in the
community. Agents have continued to raid community agencies with unusual frequency. During the time of my fieldwork about fifty FBI agents wearing riot gear entered the offices of the
Humboldt Park Infant Mortality Reduction Initiative (HIMRI). Claiming that the agency had
been accused of fraud, the agents searched and appropriated records, personal agenda books,
and calendars and scared many HIMRI employees. The agency had provided the first employment opportunity for many of its employees, because many of them had been on welfare, were
on probation, or had some type of criminal record. "HIMRI is an agency that believes in community self-actualization. We believe in giving jobs to Puerto Ricans who would otherwise be
unemployed," commented Jaime Delgado, HIMRI director and a close friend of cultural center
activists.

24. Profiles of General Demographic Characteristics for Chicago City and Cook County, Illinois, 2000 Census.

Chapter 3

1. In addition to the cultural center's main building, where Pedro Albizu Campos High
School (PACHS) and other alternative educational programs are located, the center owns other
buildings in the area, most of which have been purchased through the center's cooperative
housing project, BOHIO. A bakery, a museum, offices of the National Committee for the Liberation of Puerto Rican Political Prisoners, and a Vida SIDA (HIV and sexually transmitted diseases information and prevention) clinic are housed in buildings in the general Division Street
area. People who worked with the cultural center often relocated to other buildings as needed.
For instance, when the bread machine at the bakery broke down, people from the high school,
the child care center, and Vida SIDA clinic volunteered extra hours to take turns baking bread
in a smaller oven.

2. Ana Mendieta, in *¡Exito!* September 26, 1996, 28.

3. Ibid.

4. Many cultural center participants were bound not only by their common interest in free-
ing the political prisoners, but also by complicated kinship ties and work relations. The center
provided employment and services to the prisoners' families, and this common connection to
the cultural center and the prisoners created other personal and job-related liaisons among the
prisoners' relatives. For instance, the son of prisoner Carmen Valentín and the daughter of in-
mate Oscar López met through their amnesty work and eventually had a child together.
Miguelina Cortés, a prisoner's sister, taught at PACHS. Several of the prisoners' children graduated from PACHS and were later offered employment on various cultural center projects. Romantic relationships between prisoners and their advocates who worked at the center, many of
whom were relatives of other prisoners, were common. The personal networks and financial
livelihood of many of the prisoners' relatives were strongly connected to the center. Hence,
when disagreements about the prisoners occurred, the ramifications were far-reaching.

5. Raquel Rivera (1997) challenges theories of cultural imperialism by showing how "rap

culture and music in Puerto Rico give voice to urban, black, and poor youth against state and nationalist discourses that tend to negate or criminalize them. In this sense, rap culture also re-aligns solidarities beyond the colonial/national discursive dichotomy by recognizing class and race as important elements in the building of solidarities" (Rivera 1997, 248). Rap brings racism into the public discourse, as opposed to maintaining the myth of a racial democracy as embodied in the Spanish/African/Indian triad that has been evoked as the racial makeup of all Puerto Ricans regardless of color. Edwin takes this a step further by problematizing racialization as an inherently classed process subjected to totalizing capitalist notions of "the culturally authentic." See also Raquel Rivera's (1997) and Juan Flores's (1993) discussions on rap music in Puerto Rico and among Puerto Ricans in the United States.

6. The term *machista* (a derivative of *macho*) has been widely disseminated both by scholarly works (e.g., Gutmann 1996; Lancaster 1992) and in popular discourse. In this instance I use it to refer to the appreciation and even reverence for all things and characteristics typically associated with "being a man" or a "cult of manhood," and likewise the demotion of characteristics socially constructed as typically female. The term *machista*, when used as an adjective, can describe any individual—man or woman—who believes in the superiority of an individual on the basis of gender.

7. The incident echoes the situation described by Sara Evans (1979), who discusses the position of white women in a black-led civil rights group of the 1960s. Referring to the "non-interventionism" expected of white female volunteers, Evans remarks: "As white women they were in an increasingly ambiguous position in a black-led movement. Compared to the black women's growing power, whites were losing ground. . . . Their roles in many ways had to be supportive, the movement must be led by blacks. Yet they wanted to be taken seriously and to be appreciated for the contributions they made" (1979, 85). Eventually, the Black Power movements solidified racial identity as the leading principle of group cohesiveness, weakening internal coalitions along gender lines.

8. Arlie Hochschild (1979) presents an interactive account of emotion that draws from Goffman's dramaturgical and Freud's psychoanalytical approaches. Unlike these earlier approaches, however, Hochschild allows a closer inspection of the reaction in emotive experience, emotion management, feeling rules, and ideology.

9. In her study of women in underground organizations, Gilda Zwerman (1995) noticed the "impression management" demanded of women in such clandestine groups. In particular, Zwerman discovered that the infidelity and deceptions experienced while living underground surfaced throughout the time of legal proceedings and incarceration. She explains: "Within the underground, the requisites of security took precedence over all other realms of activity as well as all ethical considerations. To this end, hiding, misrepresentation and deception were integrated into the organizational and personal lives of the insurgents, creating extraordinary conditions for impression management both within the group and in the external world" (1995, 20). Intragroup deception erodes friendships and romantic liaisons. Stories of men betraying wives, lovers, and partners by being unfaithful with other female comrades are not uncommon even among less invested nationalists.

10. Members of the *nueva trova* music group Haciendo Punto, for instance, describe this New Woman when they describe the subject of their song "María del Carmen" as a twenty-something woman, who is "clean from being a virgin and free of prejudices." Her devotion (to the political work) is absolute, and she makes every head turn when she walks by. As the singer says, if he ever found a revolutionary woman like the imagined María del Carmen, he would have "to love her and love her." The eclectic mixture of traditional and leftist imagery in the song articulates a sexual politics of solidarity. The song highlights the "female virtues" valued among male, and even female, political activists: María del Carmen is young and sexualized ("people turn to look at her"), is apparently rebellious against Puerto Rican mores ("clean from being a virgin"), and views traditional femininity as an embodiment of materialism ("old dolls, clothes, ribbons"). And while the male singer would like to love such a woman, she is unattainable because her only love is the *patria* and she has no time for "boyfriends." She remains a dream with no demands attached.

11. An example is Martín Espada's "The Lover of a Subversive Is Also a Subversive" (1993, 21). In this poem, the woman exists through her romantic attachment to a convicted revolutionary. Her martyrdom renders her "subversive." In the images the woman paints she emphasizes her lover's traditionally feminine qualities ("long black twisted hair"), while appropriating the revolutionary elements ("wearing a mask") for herself. However, even when she wears the mask, her revolutionary role remains marginal. She "has no mouth."

12. In her analysis, Zwerman coined the phrase *identity vulnerable activist* to describe women who have participated in armed struggle to conceal a more vulnerable female identity by embracing a revolutionary cause. Among Puerto Rican male and female activists, cultural authenticity and personal autonomy are pursued through community-building efforts grounded in a nationalist ideology with a rigid set of feeling rules. In this respect the quest for authenticity is not unique to the women in the group.

13. For instance, in "Third World" nationalisms male nationalists determined which female customs must be sacrificed to achieve an appearance of modernity in tune with national aspirations and which ones, particularly relating to women's spousal and maternal duties, must be preserved to embody national distinctiveness and worth (Di Leonardo 1998, 133).

Chapter 4

1. I follow Bourdieu's (1977a, 1979) theoretical examination of class as a conflation of economic and cultural locations defined within objective social realities. This theoretical approach recognizes that the term *class* describes the economic dimensions of social stratification, inequality, and privilege while also designating an identity. In fact, as Sherry Ortner argues, "class is the only American identity term that is organized primarily around an economic axis" (1998, 8). However, rather than embracing an exclusively discursive analysis of class, it is critical to understand the actual lives and social relations—the political economy—upon which class identities and power structures are constructed (Di Leonardo 1984, 1998).

2. The activists implicated in the media-generated scandal responded by convening a community hearing, in which a group of reputable education experts explained and deconstructed the charges of terrorism launched at those people involved in the Clemente school reform by providing academic, scholarly evidence in support of Clemente's reformed pedagogical strategies. The publication that came out of these hearings is entitled "Community Hearings: Determining the Truth behind the Clemente Story" (Ad-Hoc Committee for Clemente Community Hearings 1998).

3. See Pedro Cabán's (1999) analysis of the Americanization process and the public education system in Puerto Rico during the early decades of U.S. occupation.

4. As Ortner (1998) argues, to be middle class is almost always to be really something else. *Middle class* is a modest self-label for the upper-middle class or a covering label for the lower-middle class. The middle class is everybody except the very rich and the very poor. In many usages it means simply: "all those Americans who have signed up for the American dream, who believe in a kind of decent life of work and family, in the worth of the 'individual' and the importance of 'freedom,' and who strive for a moderate amount of material success" (Ortner 1998, 8).

5. While U.S.-born Puerto Ricans who move to the suburbs are slightly better off than their barrio counterparts (Enchautegui 1992), the Chicago suburbs also attract high-paid corporate professionals from Puerto Rico itself. As some barrio informants commented, national corporations, including Kraft, IBM, and General Electric, recruit Puerto Rican professionals directly from Puerto Rico. Class divisions are then complicated by an Island-generated cultural capital that renders some Puerto Ricans more "real" than others. Class and national identities are articulated in the context of distinctions between Puerto Rican professionals from the Island and from the Mainland, and these distinctions are constructed around notions of cultural authenticity. In contrast to Island professionals, who never lived in a Puerto Rican area of the United States, most Puerto Ricans who move to the Chicago suburbs have lived in Puerto Rican enclaves of United States at some point in their lives. Many of them have relatives and friends who still live in the Division Street area.

6. As Newman (1988) points out, downward mobility is an ever-increasing phenomenon among white Americans who find themselves unemployed and in rapid economic decline due to unanticipated structural changes and widespread layoffs after years of steady employment. While most of these white Americans never thought they would end up unemployed, many Puerto Ricans who make it are perfectly aware of the shaky ground on which they walk. They are reminded of the proximity of poverty—not just working-class status, but sheer poverty—when they look at neighbors, long-time friends, and members of their own extended families.

7. Ana Mendieta in *¡Exito!* September 26, 1996, p. 27.

8. Beliefs about Puerto Rican identities deployed along political party lines in Puerto Rico have been undermined in studies of cultural nationalism on the Island. Yet in Chicago these affiliations are critical references to a political culture that is promoted even among Puerto Ricans who distance themselves from Puerto Rico's electoral politics. Puerto Rico's party politics become conceptual elements of nationalist identity formation. Associating a pro-statehood stance with upper-class status and assimilation has many different problems, because this categorization does not necessarily reflect the actual divisions, even though making such associations is a social practice in the barrio.

9. Ana Mendieta in *¡Exito!* September 26, 1996.

Chapter 5

1. Inspired by Pierre Bourdieu's work (1977a, 1977b), I understand cultural capital as the knowledge, meanings, and symbolic markers that are considered legitimate in a given society and that contribute to the reproduction of dominance and privilege in that society.

2. Literally *guagua aerea* means "air bus." Metaphorically it refers to the back-and-forth nature of Puerto Rican migration between the Island of Puerto Rico and the U.S. Mainland.

3. For instance, in the movie *La guagua aerea*, Island-based cinematographer Luis Molina satirizes a 1940s journey of Puerto Rican migrants, who carry live crabs that break loose through the airplane floor, to the North American flight attendant's dismay; pull out *fiambreras* (lunch pails) of rice and beans when the airplane food is unsavory, unseasoned, or simply unrecognized; and clap as the airplane lands successfully. Flashes of the passengers' past lives, the ones they were now leaving behind in their towns in Puerto Rico, and visions of a future in the United States provide the bitter sweetness and intensely emotional dimensions of this otherwise comic movie. Similarly, a protest song, Roy Brown's "Boricua en la Luna," narrates the story of a migrant who dies on the streets of the United States.

4. For instance, the local alderman, born and raised in Chicago, conducted a successful electoral campaign in the barrio by wearing a straw hat and emphasizing his *jíbaro* background. In Puerto Rico the image of the *jíbaro*, when deployed in the context the electoral politics, is the symbol of the Partido Popular Democrático, the pro-commonwealth party. In many diasporic Puerto Rican communities the *jíbaro* is a general symbol of authenticity and is considered a lowest common denominator useful in political campaigning. Hence, in Chicago the *jíbaro* was not associated with a specific political party, but was common in the strategies of urban ethnic politics.

5. As Mayra Santos (1996) remarks, if before the *cocolos* were the ones regarded as the biggest delinquents in Puerto Rico and the ones who deployed discourses of "Latinidad" and "blackness" on the Island, now it is the rappers who create a new identity designated with the epithet *la raza* [the race] (see also Rivera 1997). In personal correspondence with me, Jorge Duany commented that the distinction in the 1990s youth culture scene was between rock fans and rappers, rather than between rock fans and salsa lovers. This may be due to the way salsa has become a popular genre among the Island middle classes. Studies of salsa music suggest that it has become more middle class in its lyrics. Hence, it is not unlikely that Chicago Islanders would listen to "upper-class" salsa, such as that of Gilberto Santa Rosa or more mainstream singers like Marc Anthony. Given this tendency, the term for salsa lover, *cocolo*, has lost its significance as a mark for distinguishing among social classes. That role is now played by the term *rapero*, because rap music remains associated with Mainlanders who return to the Island. For an extensive analysis of the role of salsa, hip hop, and Latin rap in Puerto Rico and the

United States, see Aparicio 1997; Glasser 1995; Quintero Rivera 1991; and Flores 2000. Also see Mayra Santos's (1996) discussion on Boricua rap. I would add to Santos's observations by arguing that rappers are not only "young men, blacks and mulattos, between the ages of 14 and 25 from the 'lower' classes of the unemployed and underemployed"; they are also assumed to have been born in New York and by popular definition are Nuyorican Others. The fact that rap forms part of an entire well-articulated cultural system that includes fashion, social groups (posses), linguistic expression, a discourse of identities, and an economics of violence further accentuates the association of Nuyorican Otherness with Island elite ideas of cultural capital. Knowledge of the streets is the implicit social knowledge valued by Mainland youth, and it is this same knowledge that renders Mainlanders violent outsiders in the eyes of the Islander elite in Carolina, Farjardo, Chicago, or New York.

6. In contrast to Puerto Rico, where the best-quality higher education is provided by the state, interviewee Juan Cruz perceived quality education for Puerto Ricans in the United States as available only to those few students who adapted or assimilated to the system by giving up their Puerto-Ricanness. Nevertheless, while cultural adaptation was subjectively perceived as the requirement for mobility, such an understanding of mobility underscores the fact that Puerto Ricans both in the United States and on the Island have been dependent on U.S. government initiatives—like affirmative action, IRS Section 936, and public aid—to barely remain afloat.

7. The same shame that pushes people to stay in the United States is reported by Sarah Mahler (1995) in her study of Central and South American immigrants on Long Island.

8. As Micaela Di Leonardo (1984) effectively demonstrates, ethnic labels often become confused with class affiliations, since racial and ethnic divisions coincide closely with occupational and residential segregation and economic stratification. When upwardly mobile ethnics do not conform with the behavior stereotypically expected from their "culture," they are perceived as inauthentic or atypical. Thus, for instance, the Italian families of TV pasta commercials become the cultural rule against which Italians themselves measure their Italianness and according to which they understand what the real Italian family is, even when such a media image has little resemblance to their own or their relatives' life experiences. In this sense, class identities are inherently racialized, and racial identities are decidedly classed (Di Leonardo 1984, 1998; Ortner 1992).

9. As Mayra Santos (1996) eloquently argues, in Puerto Rico the discourses through which rap identity is articulated are inextricable from constructions of masculinity. The laying of the foundations of masculinity is connected to the urban primitive, that is, to violence (see also Rivera 1997). The figure of the gangsta, of the rapper with a beeper, a cellular phone, heavy gold chains, a hooked-up BMW, a mansion, and so on is part of the rapper iconography that becomes the rhetorically established violence and competitive superiority on which masculine identity is grounded.

10. Literally dozens of regular publications, like *Qué Ondée Sola*, published by students at Northeastern Illinois University, were distributed at the local bakery, school student lounges, corner stores, neighborhood festivals, health clinics, and not-for-profit organizations. Popular education programs encouraged their participants to write about their lives while becoming more aware of neighborhood political and social conflicts. For instance, a publication titled *Aquí en mi barrio . . . es donde vivo, lucho y triunfo* [Here in my barrio . . . is where I live, struggle, and triumph] is a journal containing writings by adults in the High School without Walls, a continuing education program grounded in cultural nationalist ideologies. Students of this program were parents of Clemente High School students who had decided to attend the High School without Walls as an alternative to formalized GED and Adult Basic Education programs—students could prepare for the GED there, but the program was not focused only on passing the GED examination. The journal published participants' stories about childhood and migration; about their experience of pursuing education later in life; and about their families, parenting, day-to-day concerns, and aspirations. It also integrated the variety of life stories with the broader conflicts surrounding Clemente High School, gentrification, and the barrio. In a section titled "¡Clemente es Nuestra!" [Clemente is ours], participants wrote about their

involvement in parenting programs sponsored by Clemente in collaboration with other neighborhood-based organizations. Students who wrote for the journal praised Clemente High School for its attempts to include parents, challenge media and city officials' accusations, and promote barrio youths' involvement in the community.

11. The activists with whom I worked believed that the Puerto Rican authors who had visited the Chicago barrio had been impacted by the history of militancy and grassroots community projects. Elena Colón, a staff and administrator of an adult literacy program, commented that in the 1970s, when Piri Thomas had visited the Chicago barrio for the first time, the visit had changed his political visions and social commitments. "He became more political and took more definite political views," Elena mentioned, and proudly added: "It was the contact with the students and the work we do in the community that did that." By the time of graduation, students in the popular education programs, like many other Latino youth across the United States, had read Piri Thomas's book—or the works by Martin Espada, Sandra Maria Esteves, and other Latino writers—at least once. Students and teachers had seen Piri Thomas improvising poetry impromptu in the oddest circumstances, like a small classroom or school hallways in front of a handful of people. The impact of these published writers on definitions of Puerto-Ricanness, particularly among younger-generation readers, cannot be denied. These writers served as points of reference for narratives published locally through popular education programs.

12. Wanda's poem and the other writings that appear throughout this chapter were submitted as class assignments or journal entries either to me or to other teachers at various popular education programs. Frequently these assignments were published and distributed in local publications. Danny's brother kindly loaned me Danny's journal and its published version, excerpts of which appear later in the chapter.

13. *Qué Ondée Sola* 18, no. 27 (December 1995). Quotes from Danny's journal are from this issue of the magazine.

14. In their study of the role of literature in Central American revolutionary settings, John Beverly and Marc Zimmerman distinguish between the autobiography and *testimonio* genres, arguing that

> Testimonio cannot affirm a self-identity that is separate from a group or class situation marked by marginalization, oppression, and struggle. Testimonio always signifies the need for a general social change in which the stability and complacency of the reader's world must be brought into question. . . . In testimonio the distinction between public and private spheres of life has been transgressed. The narrator in testimonio is a real person who continues living and acting in a real social history that also continues. (1990, 177–78)

Autobiographical and testimonial narratives become public ideological domain. The *testimonio* is a "basic form of ideology since it serves to organize the randomness of lived experiences into a meaningful sequence that appears to have the character of necessity or fate" (Beverly and Zimmerman 1990, 177). Authors produce autobiographical writings, and activists interpret these writings as testimonials that collectively constitute a grassroots historiography. As Beverly and Zimmerman argue,

> Testimonio is not so much concerned with the life of a "problematic hero" . . . as with a problematic collective social situation that the narrator lives with or alongside others. The situation of the narrator in testimonio has to be representative of a social class or group. . . . The narrator in the testimonio speaks for or in the name of a community or group, approximating in this way the symbolic function of the epic hero, without at the same time assuming his hierarchical and patriarchal status. (1990, 174)

Chapter 6

1. Exhaustive research on Albizu Campos has focused on the historical trajectory of his leadership of the Puerto Rican nationalist movement (Tirado 1993); the political and economic projects of Albizuist nationalism in Puerto Rico and Latin America (Alvarez Curbelo 1993); the

impact of socialist Christianity on Albizuist thought (Sánchez Huertas 1993); the imagery, narrative, and mythology around Albizu (Santos Febres 1993b; Sotomayor 1993); and many other themes. While most of the studies tend to preserve the leader's mythological qualities by exalting his contribution to the formation of the Puerto Rican nation, some others offer a more critical appraisal of him. The latter studies emphasize the dissonance between Albizu Campos's economic interests as an *hacendado* [a member of the landowning class], his Hispanophile identity, and his advocacy for the peasant poor in Puerto Rico (Ferrao 1990). These studies have centered on the impact of Albizuist imagery on contemporary social practices that emphasize Albizu Campos as a multivalent symbol of resistance. As Santos Febres cleverly explains: "Pedro becomes a metaphor for quotidian resistance, a representation of the small wars won on the battlefields of the bed, the stores, the mirrors, the payment lines. Pedro Albizu Campos becomes not so much the almighty Father as a partner in sexual enjoyment, an ingredient for home remedies, a political object" (1993b, 244–45, author's translation).

2. A cartoon of the statue of Pedro Albizu Campos comparing the nationalist hero to Lee Harvey Oswald appeared in the *Chicago Sun-Times*. It is one of numerous images that implicate Albizu as anti-American.

3. See *El Nuevo Dia*, March 21–April 10, 2000.

4. This quote is from one of Pedro Albizu Campos's speeches, in which the nationalist leader stated that "La patria es valor y sacrificio" [The fatherland is valor and sacrifice]. The quote appeared on a framed poster of Albizu Campos at PACHS.

5. In 1950 two major events coordinated by Albizuist nationalists drew international attention to Puerto Rico: Oscar Collazo and another Puerto Rican man attacked Blair House in Washington, D.C., and attempted to assassinate President Truman, and a historic anti-U.S. rebellion was staged in the mountain town of Jayuya, Puerto Rico. In 1954, at the height of Puerto Rican migration to Chicago, three Puerto Rican men, Rafael Cancel Miranda, Andrés Figueroa Cordero, and Irvin Flores, led by a Puerto Rican woman, Lolita Lebrón, opened fire at the U.S. Congress, wounding five congressmen and drawing international attention to the cause of Puerto Rican independence. They were given life sentences. The Five Nationalists—Oscar Collazo and the four who staged the attack on Congress, became heroes to many independence sympathizers, including the founders of the Chicago Cultural Center.

6. One of the main discussions during the time of my research involved one of the FALN prisoners' decision to seek release through parole instead of amnesty. The political prisoners sometimes saw parole as a violation of the noncollaboration code they had adopted. This caused much commotion, anger, pain, and confusion at the cultural center. Jaime's decision as expressed in several letters to the other political prisoners challenged emotionally charged aspects of militant nationalism and the community role of the cultural center. A high school teacher and a Vida SIDA worker abandoned their jobs and distanced themselves from the cultural center in support of Jaime. Similarly, Jaime's own daughter, a bright and upbeat junior at PACHS, decided to graduate a year early so she wouldn't have to be at the cultural center throughout the ordeal of the center's reactions to her father's plea. Jaime was not the first of the prisoners to seek release through parole; however, as the center and the other thirteen prisoners saw it, Jaime was the first one to admit that his actions against the U.S. government and as part of the FALN had been wrong. The cultural center and most of the other political prisoners, on the basis of their principle of noncollaboration, considered Jaime's action unacceptable and weak. Jaime's letters to the parole board and his open letter to the other prisoners questioned the historical validity for the present case of the designation Prisoner of War (POW), which the FALN prisoners embraced during their trials in the 1980s. He wrote: "I recognize the Albizuista roots of the POW position. But that position must be tested constantly by the real world. I feel that we the POWs have failed in that. We have allowed the position to become larger than life, larger than the very humans who sit in prison cells upholding it. It has genuinely become a fetish." Moreover, in reference to the cultural center's community-building projects, Jaime accuses the center being "advocate of small businesses and then turn around and demand of us [the political prisoners] the maximum sacrifice?" This situation shows tension between two perspectives: one that aimed to bring back the political prisoners' actions to

the grounds of militant Puerto Rican history, and another that attempted to update the prisoners' actions in light of present conditions. Replies to Jaime's letter reflect conflict around the contemporaneousness of the POW position. One prisoner replied that Jaime's parole statement "sets a precedent whereby to merit parole, and perhaps even general amnesty, we would all have to follow suit and condemn our politics, spit on the legacy of the Albizus, Corretjers, Canales, Lebróns and all who have confronted the enemy without dropping to their knees and denouncing the right of a colonized nation to wage war while at the same time applauding the apparatus which perpetuates colonialism" (from letters circulated at the cultural center).

7. Furthermore, cultural center activists and supporters of the political prisoners emphasized that like the Chicago prisoners, Albizu Campos had been imprisoned for advocating independence for Puerto Rico. As an interviewee explained, Albizu "was imprisoned in 1937 after being accused twice (under the 'Gag Law') in two separate courts of law for the same 'crime,' of advocating the independence of his homeland." Hence, activists and some barrio residents drew similarities between the Chicago prisoners and Albizu Campos, contending that they were all given lengthy prison sentences for controversial political ideals about Puerto Rican independence. Finally, Albizu's renowned quote—"la patria es valor y sacrificio" [the fatherland is valor and sacrifice]—was considered to be illustrated by the leader's own martyrdom. As explained in a Humboldt Park flyer, Albizu "was subjected to a slow death by way of radiation in prison." A Puerto Rican political analyst and educator who visited Chicago noticed these historical connections. He commented:

> The Puerto Rican men and women who are currently incarcerated in North American prisons are continuing the Albizuist tradition of struggle. . . . They are the ones who have confronted the empire with a grave colonial crisis. They are the ones who do not hesitate to seek a resolution to Puerto Rico's colonial tragedy. They are the ones who project ahead in time the wish to be free. They can be confused with the martyrs of Lares and nationalism. Without a doubt, Don Pedro lives in each one of the incarcerated patriots, in each Puerto Rican political exile, in each person in clandestiny who advances the struggle for independence. (from a flyer titled "Albizu" that was distributed in the community, author's personal files)

The quasi-spiritual presence of Don Pedro as he "lives in each one of the incarcerated patriots," who were in turn compared to the "martyrs of Lares," points to the implicit parallels between the political and the messianic.

8. It is telling that there is evidence that Albizu Campos rejected any affiliation with African Americans during his years in the United States even though he was considered black. In her autobiography Belmira Nunes Lopes, a Cape Verdean–American Harvard student and one of Albizu's girlfriends during his days at Harvard, candidly mentions Albizu's posture on racial alliances. During the time she was a teacher in Puerto Rico in the mid-1940s, she lived on the same street as Albizu Campos. She recalls: "The last time I saw him in San Juan, I believe it was in 1945, he said to me: 'When you go back to the United States, don't identify with the American blacks.' I don't know why, but he never wanted to be identified as an American black" (Lopes 1982).

9. Some scholars have contended that Puerto Rico's racial order may currently be undergoing profound ideological re-elaborations that reflect increasing commonalities with dominant U.S. racial polarity rather than the fluidity and ambiguity presupposed by Latin American racial taxonomies (Dinzey 2000). Similarly, Santos Febres recognizes that spaces of African and Afro-centric pride have surged in Puerto Rico, as suggested by the growth of Rastafarianism and the celebration of Kwanzaa (Santos Febres 1993a).

10. *Negro* is a peculiar term of endearment because calling someone a negro is a way of asserting that a relationship is so close and so strong that people can use otherwise potentially offensive terms without causing offense (see Wade 1993).

11. Interestingly, in Puerto Rico, blackness is displaced onto specific marginal populations, like Dominicans or Puerto Rican return migrants, rather than deployed as inherent to Puerto-Ricanness. The contemporary racialization of Dominican immigrants in Puerto Rico associ-

ates them closely with black Puerto Ricans, who remain on the fringes of the nationalist imaginary. As Jorge Duany (2000) argues, the popular conflation of the term *negro* [black] with *dominicano* [Dominican] is a sign of increasing concern to those interested in promoting cultural diversity in Puerto Rico because it represents the growing ethnicization of racial stigmas on the Island. This accentuates the continuing perception that being black is somehow alien to national identity.

12. In Puerto Rico, as in Brazil, other parts of the Caribbean, and to some degree U.S. Latino communities, racial identity has less to do with ethnicity than with the subtle way in which stereotyped characteristics of that ethnicity are physically expressed. This problematizes the U.S. idea that "black blood" dilutes "white blood" and the Puerto Rican idea of *mejorando la raza* [improving the race], which implies that white blood dilutes black blood. The argument that racial identity is connected to phenotype fails to recognize that race is directly related to social hierarchies of power and domination, rather than to phenotypical characteristics. The racialization of Irish, Italian, and Jewish immigrants, who were initially identified as non-white Others, was not based on the one-drop rule, but was directly related to reconfigurations of power and domination on both sides of the Atlantic (Rodríguez-Morazzani 1998, 154). Charles Wagley (1952) uses the term *social races* to name the system of individual classification persistent in Puerto Rico, by which race is determined by physical appearance, ancestry, and sociocultural background.

13. From a flyer entitled "FACTS about Pedro Albizu Campos," Puerto Rican Cultural Center archives.

14. In this context *personalismo* can be understood as the social arrangement in which personal relationships, rather than more "objective" criteria like professional competence, credentials, and experience, determine an individual's access to power, services, goods, or political backing.

Chapter 7

1. I am using the terms *racial readings, racialization,* and *racial formation* to indicate the ways in which people attribute all their difference to race, and race becomes the leading lens through which all else is filtered. Important literature has been published on the subject of race and class relations in the context of gentrification (Anderson 1990), urban renewal and homesteading (Hassell 1996), and community dissolution as a consequence of residential desegregation (Molotch 1972). The impact of these processes on the lives and identity of residents, who view displacement as undesirable, fuels suspicion of incoming whites.

2. See Teresita Martinez's *Shaping the Discourse of Space* (1999) for a discussion of how community members have gained access to services and rights to urban spaces. Martinez argues that women have accomplished this by writing letters to benefactors, and blacks have used the courts and local newspapers to gain power and access to local resources.

3. A newspaper article titled "Exodo Boricua de Humboldt Park" [Humboldt Park's Puerto Rican exodus] discusses the "efforts undertaken in the past two years to stop the Puerto Rican exodus," including the urban development project known as Paseo Boricua. The article quotes the director of the Federal Affairs Administration of Puerto Rico in Chicago, who said that "in the first couple of weeks of August alone, we have received approximately a dozen phone calls from people who ask us to change their mailing address because they have decided to move out of Humboldt Park given the uncertainty and insecurity of the area" (Boscán 1995). While it is impossible to determine how effective community development projects were for retaining residents, they had become the leading strategy of many residents and most community activists and politicians of Humboldt Park.

4. Nationalist activists encourage barrio residents to play an active role in promoting the neighborhood's economic progress by sponsoring local Puerto Rican businesses and investing in Humboldt Park: "Buy your house here, in this barrio! Invest what you have here in this community! Puerto Rican house owners, rent to a Boricua. Boricuas, rent property inside the barrio! Boricua small business owners disappear while others get richer. The Puerto Rican bodegas in our barrio are disappearing and all the Puerto Rican businesses are disappearing

while our people buy more and more. Boricua, purchase from another Boricua! Support Puerto Rican businesses and enterprises!" (flyer posted in Humboldt Park, author's collection). Because the cultural center is one of the organizations most invested in the community-building process, its activists have recently earned the appreciation of small business owners and residents who would otherwise reject the center on the basis of its militant political stands.

5. As Nicholas De Genova (1998) argues, Mexican migrants in Chicago cannot be enclosed within a homogeneous space of cultural isolation—not even in the several neighborhoods, like Pilsen or La Villita, that are almost exclusively Mexican. Instead, "Chicago as an urban space is itself contiguously *produced* and *reproduced* through the contradictions of struggles in which Mexican migrants are centrally implicated—struggles over the city, for and against the city, with the city much more than struggles *in* the city—where Mexican communities themselves can be constituted not in isolation but indeed only in the midst of social conflict" (De Genova 1998, 97, emphasis in original). Chicago's Mexican population increased by nearly 40 percent in the 1980s alone, and it is the second-largest concentration of Mexican/Chicano settlement in the United States numbering well over half a million in the metropolitan area and over 15 percent of the population within the city limits (De Genova 1998, 100).

6. *La Raza* (June 8–14, 1995); *¡Exito!* (June 1, 1995).

7. Felix Padilla (1985) argues that among Puerto Ricans and Mexicans in Chicago, a "situational Latino ethnic identity" coexists with the national group identities. This Latino identity serves as a mobilization tool for Puerto Rican and Mexican leaders in instances when they believe that a panethnic coalition will attain common goals more effectively than nationality-based alliances. Franco, Yúdice, and Flores (1992) embrace a "new social movement" approach to Latinidad that addresses forms of social stratification that cannot be fully explained by class analysis, and that launches political struggles in the realm of the body, sexuality, language, music, and other terrains considered to be of the private or cultural sphere. A limitation of this study is that it does not unpack the tensions upon which Latinidad as a fragmented, conflictual, and largely contested identity is constructed. Suzanne Oboler's (1995) examination of panethnic identification among Latinos of various nationalities in New York City addresses some of the lacunae in the current debates about Latinidad. She found that middle-class Latinos perceive the term *Hispanic* as discriminatory and identify it as a term that segregates all people of Latin American and Caribbean descent from mainstream U.S. society. Nevertheless, members of this Latino middle class continue to use the term to identify themselves within the U.S. context, thus accepting dominant racial and ethnic categories. Conversely, working-class respondents sought to distance themselves from the label of *Hispanic*, emphasizing a national rather than a panethnic identity. For these working-class Latinos the label's negative connotation has direct personal implications (Oboler 1995, 141). In conversation with Bonnie Urciouli, Oboler also mentioned the critical role of mainstream institutions like colleges in the promotion of a Latino identity. See also Klor de Alva 1988, 1998, and Sánchez Korrol 1989.

8. I would argue that the status of "illegal" and a history of border crossing serve as powerful historical and symbolic bonds among people who lack U.S. citizenship rights, while also rendering Puerto Ricans, Chicanos, and other U.S.-born Latinos occupying various positions as inauthentic hybrids. Hence, at times, Puerto Ricans are excluded from discourses and practices of Latinidad because of their status as U.S. citizens, even though they are not considered quite American—a designation nearly always reserved for whites.

9. In Puerto Rico although commercial sponsors are perceived as a threat to the authenticity of the nation, they nevertheless add to the national dialogue over what constitutes real Puerto-Ricanness and authentic Puerto Rican culture. Festivals are deemed cultural or commercial on the basis of whether they reflect official notions of Puerto Rican culture. In the case of Chicago, the distinction between commercial and cultural activity was conditioned by what segment of the Puerto Rican community sought the activity's sponsors' support. Even though "consumerism and materialism have become constructed as major threats to Puerto Rican culture" (Dávila 1997, 218), in Chicago not all consumerism was regarded the same way. In sharp contrast to advertising campaigns developed in Puerto Rico, which deliberately try to represent Puerto Rican culture, corporate sponsors in Chicago were careful not to imply a reference any

one Latino group, but strove to create a generic Latino. Representations of Puerto Rican culture outside the context of official events, like the Downtown Parade described below, were avoided so as not to alienate potential Cuban, Mexican, Guatemalan, or other Latino consumers. The hyperstandardized Spanish, purposely ambiguous phenotypical characteristics, and the generic event or setting surrounding the presentation of the marketed product paradoxically included everyone and represented no one at all. The commercialization of culture and the contestation of that commercialization took on different forms in Chicago from those observed in Puerto Rico. First, the commercialization was accepted or contested depending on who was doing the commercializing. Local working-class merchants and ambulatory vendors sold these cultural markers. Culture was commercialized so that it promoted community-based entrepreneurship. Because these images were associated with the local activists, who in turn sought validation and support from other barrio residents, the objectification of the Puerto Rican flag or of nationalist leaders was perceived as evidence of the far-reaching impact of the activists' nationalist discourse and community-building strategies.

By contrast, the involvement of corporate sponsors, so widely accepted in Puerto Rico (Dávila 1997) was associated with events organized by middle-class factions, and was therefore contested by the barrio activists. While there were several annual festivals organized by barrio activists, there was only one major community-wide event organized primarily by the elite: the Puerto Rican Downtown Parade. As the "Downtown" specification suggests, there was a second Puerto Rican parade, and it took place right after the Downtown Parade was over. Known as the People's Parade, this second parade, which was founded almost two decades ago by grassroots activists and barrio residents, took place in the barrio. There were several distinctions between the two celebrations, besides their location and the class background of their organizers. Like the Three Wise Men Celebration, the People's Parade purposely rejected the participation of corporate sponsors. In fact, many of its organizers explained that the People's Parade exists in denunciation of the increasing corporate sponsorship noticed in the Downtown Parade. "That parade downtown is all about Coca-Cola and beer ads, very commercial, not about Puerto Rican culture," commented one of the organizers of the People's Parade.

10. Nicholas De Genova (1999) contemplates the possibility of operationalizing concepts such as *relajo* to examine the ironic workings of performative genres in the re-racialization processes of Mexican immigrants in Chicago that go unrecognized by the anthropologist and unrecorded as straight data. *Relajo*, including racialized joking and teasing in contexts of differently attributed social power, reinforces racist stereotypes—which are invariably gendered and classed—by mobilizing playful ambiguity to obfuscate intent (Urciuoli 1996, 151–55; De Genova 1999). The reinforced stereotypes are appropriated and selectively deployed as essentialist self-representations and instruments for manipulating the essentialization of those considered Other.

11. Suzanne Oboler notices that "instead of recognizing diversity, [upwardly mobile Latino college students] opt to emphasize a nebulous definition of Latino group identity—creating, for example, the 'ideal Latina' or 'Latino,' the stereotyped version of a homogenized Latino or Latina self" (1995, 172). These upwardly mobile or college identities invariably rely on the creation of a bounded Latino culture grounded in multiple subjectivities of the authentic Latino. In this sense, people in the dominant sector of society enjoy the privilege of individuality, but people at the margins tend to be construed as representative specimens (cf. Hernández and Torres-Saillant 1992).

12. These readings of Cubanness are similar to those noticed between Puerto Ricans and Cubans on the Island (see Duany 2000). The public image of Cubans in Puerto Rico is highly ambivalent. On the one hand, Puerto Ricans consider Cubans to be hardworking, independent, and united; on the other hand, they consider them dishonest, selfish, and materialistic. Negative stereotypes about Cubans abound, particularly among nationalist intellectuals who reject Cuban immigrants primarily for ideological reasons. Cubans have also been shunned because of their association with the white elite of San Juan. Nevertheless, Cubans still experience a lesser marginalization than Dominican immigrants on the Island. Television and radio programs and journalistic and literary texts reify perceptions of Dominicans as undesirable aliens

who occupy a marginal and clandestine status. Anti-Dominican discourse includes the immigrants' condition as undocumented, the group's lower-class socioeconomic composition, the predominance of female migrants and their sexualization as prostitutes or "easy" women, and the racial perception of Dominicans as black. These representations emphasize the Dominicans' peasant origins, poor background, low educational levels, and supposedly limited intellectual capacity (Duany, Hernández Angueira, and Rey 1993; Duany 2000). As Puerto Rico has become more ethnically diverse over the last several decades, the nationalist discourse has excluded Cuban and Dominican immigrants from official and popular definitions of the nation.

13. In her study of Koreans and Puerto Ricans in Philadelphia, Judith Goode (1999) found that the intimacy and trust between women and children in the neighborhood did not undermine the conflict that arose in relation to differences in class background and position. As long as race is the prism through which we see a group's members' position as victims, economic power differences are masked. Goode's two groups, successful Koreans and impoverished Puerto Ricans, are at opposite ends of the minority discourse. Dominant discourses of difference and the way in which these discourses are deployed by marginal groups themselves point to how groups are differently located in terms of economic and political power. While both Koreans and Puerto Ricans are racial minorities, the American racial formation is grounded in the historical experience of African Americans. Goode recognizes the significance of the local context, pointing out that middle-class Puerto Ricans and Koreans become equal parts of a mosaic of proud cultures in a middle-class neighborhood, while these same Puerto Ricans define themselves as victims seeking rights when they are in the barrio. In the barrio context they deploy the civil rights and postcolonial discourses of race, while in the middle-class-neighborhood context they adopt an ethnic pluralist discourse.

14. As these studies show, whiteness relies on a dualistic sense of whites versus bounded, or clearly named and defined, nonwhite Others. Moreover, white culture is not merely absent, but it is predicated on the subordination of those who "have culture"; thus whiteness becomes "anti-culture" (Perry 2001; Roediger 1994). Cultural invisibility becomes a characteristic of those who hold full citizenship and institutional power in the nation-state and who are "post-cultural" (Rosaldo 1989). White culture has historically been molded by the tenets of Western rationalism, which unconditionally benefits whites by constructing them as the most "culture-less" of all people (Goldberg 1993). In this sense, in contexts in which naturalization processes are weak (where whites are a numerical and cultural minority), rationalization comes to the foreground (cf. Perry 2001).

15. As Perry claims, the denial of the past is not only a defense mechanism whites adopt to undermine legacies of slavery and discrimination against colonized Others, but also evidence that a past orientation simply does not make sense to many whites from their cultural perspective (Perry 2001).

16. Ironically, these processes of crafting a racialized sexuality are not entirely different from the ways in which Puerto Ricans and Mexicans sexualize each other (De Genova and Ramos-Zayas, forthcoming). Puerto Rican women are sexualized between racist stereotypes of the barefoot-and-pregnant Mexican and the African American emasculating welfare queen. Puerto Rican women themselves appropriate the stereotype placed upon them by Mexican women, and even Puerto Rican men, to negotiate piecemeal personal liberties, rather than attaining any enduring power or subverting fundamental gender ideologies. Stereotyped as being more *fiesteras* (party goers) and *andariegas* (less homebound) than the relative *de su casa* (homebound) and self-sacrificing Mexican women, Puerto Rican women often comment on the benefits of performing such stereotypes. Both Mexican and Puerto Rican women are subjected to patriarchal gender ideologies that regard women's subjugation as authentic ethnic behavior. Gina Pérez (2000) shows how Mexican women consider Puerto Rican women to be *rencorosas* (tending to hold grudges), whereas Puerto Rican women consider Mexican women to be *sufridas* (self-sacrificing). Yet in practice these gender identities are at odds with the social practices Pérez observed in which the self-proclaimed aggressive Puerto Rican women buy into the traditional gender roles they associate with Mexican women.

17. At a national level out-of-group marriage is higher among Puerto Ricans than among

other Latinos. Among Puerto Ricans the rate of exogamous marriages is 30 percent, followed by Central and South Americans (23 percent), Cubans (22 percent), and Mexicans (15.5 percent). Popular claims about Puerto Rican women in Chicago marrying non–Puerto Ricans of equivalent or higher educational levels than themselves seems unfounded according national Puerto Rican statistics. A June 1994 Institute for Puerto Rican Policy study shows that Puerto Rican men have a slightly higher out-of-group-marriage rate (30.7 percent) than Puerto Rican women (29.3 percent). However, these are national, not Chicago-based, percentages, so they may not be accurate indicators of the rate of Puerto Rican out-of-group marriage in the Windy City (Institute for Puerto Rican Policy 1994). Nevertheless, given these statistics, the perception of a high rate of exogamy among Puerto Rican women is particularly interesting and points to the social construction of national loyalties in the realm of feelings and emotions.

★ REFERENCES ★

Abu-Lughod, Lila. 1986. *Veiled Sentiments: Honor and Poetry in a Bedouin Society*. Berkeley: University of California Press.

Acosta-Belén, Edna. 1992. "Beyond Island Boundaries: Ethnicity, Gender, and Cultural Revitalization in Nuyorican Literature." *Callaloo* 15:979–98.

Acosta-Belén, Edna, and Carlos E. Santiago. 1998. "Merging Borders: The Remapping of America." Pp. 29–42 in *The Latino Studies Reader: Culture, Economy and Society*, ed. Antonia Darder and Rodolfo Torres. Malden, Mass.: Blackwell.

Ad-Hoc Committee for Clemente Community Hearings. 1998. "Community Hearings: Determining the Truth behind the Clemente Story." Panel held at Malcolm X College, September.

Alicea, Marixa. 1997. "'A Chambered Nautilus': The Contradictory Nature of Puerto Rican Women's Role in the Social Construction of a Transnational Community." *Gender and Society* 2, no. 5: 597–626.

Alvarez, Sonia, Evelina Dagnino, and Arturo Escobar, eds. 1998. *Cultures of Politics, Politics of Cultures: Re-Visioning Latin American Social Movements*. Boulder, Colo.: Westview.

Alvarez Curbelo, Silvia. 1993. "La patria desde la tierra: Pedro Albizu Campos y el nacionalismo económico antillano." Pp. 83–95 in *La nación puertorriqueña: Ensayos en torno a Pedro Albizu Campos*, ed. Juan Manuel Carrión, Teresa Gracía Ruiz, and Carlos Rodríguez Fraticceli. Río Piedras, P.R.: Editorial de la Universidad de Puerto Rico.

Anderson, Alan B., and George W. Pickering. 1986. *Confronting the Color Line: The Broken Promise of the Civil Rights Movement in Chicago*. Athens: University of Georgia Press.

Anderson, Benedict. 1983. *Imagined Communities: Reflections on the Origins and Spread of Nationalism*. London: Verso.

———. 1992. *Long-Distance Nationalism: World Capitalism and the Rise of Identity Politics*. Berkeley: Center for German and European Studies, University of California.

Anderson, Elijah. 1990. *Streetwise: Race, Class, and Change in an Urban Community*. Chicago: University of Chicago Press.

Aparicio, Frances. 1997. *Listening to Salsa: Gender, Latin Popular Music, and Puerto Rican Culture*. Middletown, Conn.: Wesleyan University Press.

Aponte-Parés, Luis. 1998. "What's Yellow and White and Has Land All Around It? Appropriating Place in Puerto Rican Barrios." Pp. 271–80 in *The Latino Studies Reader: Culture, Economy, and Society*, ed. Antonia Darder and Rodolfo Torres. Malden, Mass.: Blackwell.

Appadurai, Arjun. 1983. "The Past as a Scarce Resource." *Man* 16:201–19.

———. 1990. "Disjuncture and Difference in the Global Cultural Economy." *Public Culture* 2, no. 2: 1–24.

Arocho, Eduardo. 1993. "El Maestro of the Hurricane." *Qué Ondée Sola* 27, no. 6: 6–7.

———. 1994. "Tres Reyes Magos." *Qué Ondée Sola* 27, no. 1: 6.

———. 1995. Editor's Note. *Qué Ondée Sola* 28, no. 27: 2.

Aronowitz, Stanley. 1992. *The Politics of Identity: Class, Culture, Social Movements*. New York: Routledge.

———. 1997. "Between Nationality and Class." *Harvard Educational Review* 67, no. 2: 188–207.

Asencio, Marisol. 1999. "Machos and Sluts: Gender, Sexuality, and Violence among a Cohort of Puerto Rican Adolescents." *Medical Anthropology Quarterly* 13, no. 1: 107–26.

Attinasi, John J. 1990. "Chicago Options Schools: An Alternative for Latinos?" *Latino Studies Journal* (January): 70–94.

Barradas, Efraín. 1980. "Puerto Rico acá, Puerto Rico allá." *Revista Chicano-Riqueña* 8, no. 2: 43–49.

Barrera, Mario. 1979. *Race and Class in the Southwest: A Theory of Racial Inequality*. Notre Dame, Ind.: University of Notre Dame Press.

Barreto, Amílcar. 1998. *Language, Elites, and the State: Nationalism in Puerto Rico and Quebec*. Westport, Conn.: Praeger.

———. 2001. *The Politics of Language in Puerto Rico*. Gainesville: University Press of Florida.

Barreto, Amilcar, and D. Munroe Eagles. 2000. "Modelos ecologicos de apoyo partidista en Puerto Rico, 1980–1992." *Revista de Ciencias Sociales* 9:135–65.

Barth, Fredrik. 1969. *Ethnic Groups and Boundaries: The Social Organization of Cultural Differences*. London: George Allen and Unwin.

Bean, Frank. 1987. *The Hispanic Population of the United States*. New York: Russell Sage Foundation.

Berríos Martínez, Rubén. 2000. "Perspectiva." *El Nuevo Día*, March 27.

Beverly, John, and Marc Zimmerman. 1990. *Literature and Politics in Central American Revolutions*. Austin: University of Texas Press.

Bhabha, Homi, ed. 1990. *Nation and Narration*. London and New York: Routledge.

Bigler, Ellen. 1999. *American Conversations: Puerto Ricans, White Ethnics, and Multicultural Education*. Philadelphia: Temple University Press.

Blanchard, Elizabeth. 1988. "Three Teachers Talking." *The Reader*, January 22.

Boscán, Saúl. 1995. "Exodo Boricua de Humboldt Park" [Humboldt Park's Puerto Rican exodus]. *La Raza*, August 10–16.

Bourdieu, Pierre. 1977a. *Outline of a Theory of Practice*. Translated by Richard Nice. Cambridge: Cambridge University Press.

———. 1977b. "Cultural Reproduction and Social Reproduction." Pp. 484–95 in *Power and Ideology in Education*, ed. A. H. Halsey and J. Karabel. New York: Oxford University Press.

———. 1979. *Distinction: A Social Critique of the Judgment of Taste*. Cambridge, Mass.: Harvard University Press.

Bourdieu, Pierre, and Jean-Claude Passeron. 1971. *Reproduction in Education, Society, and Culture*. Beverly Hills, Calif.: Sage.

Browning, Frank. 1973. "From Rumble to Revolution: The Young Lords." Pp. 231–43 in *The Puerto Rican Experience: A Sociological Sourcebook*, ed. Francesco Cordasco and Eugene Bucchioni. Totowa, N.J.: Rowman and Littlefield.

Cabán, Pedro. 1999. *Constructing a Colonial People: Puerto Rico and the United States, 1898–1932*. New York: Westview.

Campos, Ricardo, and Juan Flores. 1979. "Migración y cultura nacional puertorriqueñas: Perspectivas proletarias." Pp. 81–146 in *Puerto Rico, identidad nacional y clases sociales: coloquio de Princeton*, ed. A. Quintero Rivera, Jose Luis Gonzalez, Ricardo Campos, and Juan Flores. Río Piedras, P.R.: Ediciones Huracán.

Carey-Webb, Allen. 1998. *Making Subject(s): Literature and the emergence of National Identity.* New York: Garland.

Chapman, Malcolm, Maryon McDonald, and Elizabeth Tonkin. 1989. Introduction to *History and Ethnicity.* Association of Social Anthropologists Monographs, vol. 27, ed. E. Tonkin, M. McDonald, and M. Chapman. London: Routledge.

Chatterjee, Partha. 1993. *The Nation and Its Fragments: Colonial and Postcolonial Histories.* Princeton, N.J.: Princeton University Press.

Chicago Welfare Council and Office of the Department of Labor. 1957. *Report on Puerto Rican Americans in Chicago,* February 12, 1954. Chicago: Chicago Welfare Council and Office of the Department of Labor.

Clifford, James, and George Marcus, eds. 1986. *Writing Culture: The Poetics and Politics of Ethnography.* Berkeley: University of California Press.

Conte, Christopher. 1999. "Welfare, Work, and the States." Pp. 79–97 in *Issues for Debate in American Public Policy: Selections from the CQ Researcher,* ed. S. L. Stencel. Washington, D.C.: CQ Press.

Cruz, Wilfredo. 1987. "The Nature of Alinsky-Style Community Organizing in the Mexican American Community of Chicago." Ph.D. diss., University of Chicago.

———. 1995. "Witch Hunt at Clemente High: Puerto Rican Nationalism and Chicago Politics." *Crítica: A Journal of Puerto Rican Policy and Politics* (March–April): 1, 8–9.

Cruz-Malavé, Arnaldo. 1988. "Teaching Puerto Rican Authors: Identity and Modernization in Nuyorican Texts." *ADE Bulletin* (winter): 45–51.

Danforth, Loring. 1995. *The Macedonian Conflict: Ethnic Nationalism in a Transnational World.* Princeton, N.J.: Princeton University Press.

Dávila, Arlene. 1997. *Sponsored Identities: Cultural Politics in Puerto Rico.* Philadelphia: Temple University Press.

De Genova, Nicholas. 1998. "Race, Space, and the Reinvention of Latin America in Mexican Chicago." *Latin American Perspectives* 25, no. 5: 87–116.

———. 1999. "Working the Boundaries, Making the Difference: Race and Space in Mexican Chicago." Ph.D. diss., University of Chicago.

De Genova, Nicholas, and Ana Y. Ramos-Zayas. 2000. "Racialization and the Politics of Citizenship among Mexicans and Puerto Ricans in Chicago." Paper presented at the American Anthropological Association, San Francisco, November.

———. Forthcoming. *Latino Optics: Racialization and the Politics of Citizenship among Mexicans and Puerto Ricans in Chicago.* New York: Routledge.

Delpit, L. 1995. *Other People's Children: Cultural Conflict in the Classroom.* New York: New Press.

Díaz-Quiñones, Arcadio. 1993. *La memoria rota.* Río Piedras, P.R.: Ediciones Huracán.

Di Leonardo, Micaela. 1984. *The Varieties of Ethnic Experience: Kinship, Class, and Gender among California Italian-Americans.* Ithaca, N.Y.: Cornell University Press.

———. 1998. *Exotics at Home: Anthropologies, Others, American Modernity.* Chicago: University of Chicago Press.

Dinzey, Zaire. 2000. "Slicing the Fantasy of the Racial Continuum into Two: Writing Blacks into the Puerto Rican Nation." Paper presented at the Puerto Rican Studies Association, Amherst, Mass., November.

Duany, Jorge. 1993. "Quisquella on the Hudson: The Dominican Community of Washington Heights." Draft report submitted to the Institute for Dominican Studies at the City University of New York.

———. 2000. "Nation on the Move: The Construction of Cultural Identities in Puerto Rico and the Diaspora." *American Ethnologist* 27, no. 1: 1–26.

Duany, Jorge, Luisa Hernández Angueira, and César A. Rey. 1993. *El Barrio Gandul: Economía subterránea y migración indocumentada.* Unpublished manuscript.

Enchautegui, María. 1992. "Geographical Differentials in the Socioeconomic Status of Puerto Ricans: Human Capital Variations and Labor Market Characteristics." *International Migration Review* 26:1267–90.

Eriksen, Thomas H. 1993. *Ethnicity and Nationalism: Anthropological Perspectives.* Boulder, Colo.: Pluto Press.

Espada, Martín. 1993. *City of Coughing and Dead Radiators.* New York: Norton.

Evans, Sara. 1979. *Personal Politics: The Roots of Women's Liberation in the Civil Rights Movement and the New Left.* New York: Random House.

Fernández, Ronald. 1994. *Prisoners of Colonialism: The Struggle for Justice in Puerto Rico.* Monroe, Maine: Common Courage Press.

Ferrao, Luis Angel. 1990. *Pedro Albizu Campos y el nacionalismo puertorriqueño.* Río Piedras, P.R.: Ediciones Cultural.

Fischer, Michael M. J. 1986. "Ethnicity and the Post-Modern Arts of Memory." Pp. 194–233 in *Writing Culture: The Poetics and Politics of Ethnography,* ed. James Clifford and George Marcus. Berkeley: University of California Press.

Flores, Juan. 1985. "'Que Assimilated, Brother, Yo Soy Asimilao': The Structuring of a Puerto Rican Identity in the United States." *Journal of Ethnic Studies* 8 (fall): 1–16.

———. 1993. *Divided Borders: Essays on Puerto Rican Identity.* Houston, Tex.: Arte Público Press.

———. 2000. *From Bomba to Hip-Hop: Puerto Rican Culture and Latino Identity.* New York: Columbia University Press.

Flores-González, Nilda. 1999. "Puerto Rican High Achievers: An Example of Ethnic and Academic Identity Compatibility." *Anthropology & Education Quarterly* 30, no. 3: 343–62.

Fox, Richard G. 1990. Introduction to *Nationalist Ideologies and the Production of National Cultures.* Pp. 1–14. American Ethnological Society Monograph Series, vol. 2. Washington, D.C.: American Anthropological Association.

Franco, Jean, George Yúdice, and Juan Flores, eds. 1992. *On Edge: The Crisis of Contemporary Latin American Culture.* Minneapolis: University of Minnesota Press.

Frankenberg, Ruth. 1993. *White Women, Race Matters: The Social Construction of Whiteness.* Minneapolis: University of Minnesota Press.

Freire, Paulo. 1993. *Pedagogy of the City.* Translated by Donaldo Macedo. New York: Continuum.

———. 1998. *Teachers as Cultural Workers: Letters to Those Who Dare Teach.* New York: Westview.

Friedman, Jonathan. 1992. "Myth, History, and Political Identity." *Cultural Anthropology* 7:194–210.

———. 1994. *Cultural Identity and Global Process.* Thousand Oaks, Calif.: Sage.

Gándara, Patricia. 1995. *Over the Ivy Walls: The Educational Mobility of Low-Income Chicanos.* New York: SUNY Press.

Gans, Herbert J. 1979. "Symbolic Ethnicity: The Future of Ethnic Groups and Cultures in America." *Ethnic and Racial Studies* 2, no. 1: 1–20.

García, Ana María. 1982. *La Operación.* Latin American Film Productions.

García-Canclini, Nestor. 1992. "Cultural Reconversion." Pp. 29–44 in *On Edge: The Crisis of Contemporary Latin American Culture,* ed. Jean Franco, George Yúdice, and Juan Flores. Minneapolis: University of Minnesota Press.

Gellner, Ernest. 1983. *Nations and Nationalism.* Ithaca, N.Y.: Cornell University Press.

———. 1994. *Encounters with Nationalism.* Cambridge, Mass.: Blackwell.

Gelpí, Juan. 1993. *Literatura y paternalismo en Puerto Rico.* Río Piedras, P.R.: Editorial de la Universidad de Puerto Rico.

Giroux, Henry. 1983. "Theories of Reproduction and Resistance in the New Sociology of Education: A Critical Analysis." *Harvard Educational Review* 53, no. 3: 257–93.

Glasser, Ruth. 1995. *My Music Is My Flag: Puerto Rican Musicians and Their New York Communities, 1917–1940.* Berkeley: University of California Press.

Glazer, Nathan, and Daniel Moynihan. 1970. *Beyond the Melting Pot: The Negroes, Puerto Ricans, Jews, Italians, and Irish of New York City.* Rev. ed. Cambridge, Mass.: MIT Press.

Goldberg, David Theo. 1993. *Racist Culture: Philosophy and the Politics of Meaning.* Cambridge: Cambridge University Press.

Gomes da Cunha, Olivia María. 1998. "Black Movements and the 'Politics of Identity' in Brazil." Pp. 220–51 in *Cultures of Politics, Politics of Cultures: Re-Visioning Latin American*

Social Movements, ed. Sonia E. Alvarez, Evelina Dagnino, and Arturo Escobar. Boulder, Colo.: Westview.

Gómez-Quiñones, Juan. 1982. "Critique on the National Question, Self-Determination, and Nationalism." *Latin American Perspectives* 9:62–83.

González, José Luis. 1987. *El país de cuatro pisos y otros ensayos.* Río Piedras, P.R.: Ediciones Huracán.

González, Nacho. 1989. "Latino Politics in Chicago." *Centro: Journal of the Center for Puerto Rican Studies* 2, no. 5: 46–57.

Goode, Judith. 1999. *Koreans and Puerto Ricans in Philadelphia: How Interethnic Relations Are Shaped by Local Situations and Racialist Discourse.* Philadelphia: Balch Institute for Ethnic Studies.

Gordon, Milton. 1964. *Assimilation in American Life: The Role of Race, Religion, and National Origin.* New York: Oxford University Press.

Greer, Colin. 1972. *The Great School Legend.* New York: Basic Books.

Grosfóguel, Ramón. 1997. "The Divorce of Nationalist Discourses from the Puerto Rican People." Pp. 57–76 in *Puerto Rican Jam: Rethinking Colonialism and Nationalism,* ed. Frances Negrón-Muntaner and Ramón Grosfóguel. Minneapolis: University of Minnesota Press.

———. 1999. "Puerto Ricans in the USA: A Comparative Approach." *Journal of Ethnic and Migration Studies* 25, no. 2: 233–49.

Guerra, Lillian. 1998. *Popular Expression and National Identity in Puerto Rico: The Struggle for Self, Community, and Nation.* Gainesville: University Press of Florida.

Guss, David. 1993. "Selling of San Juan: The Performance of History in an Afro-Venezuelan Community." *American Ethnologist* 20, no. 3: 451–73.

Gutmann, Matthew C. 1996. *The Meanings of Macho: Being a Man in Mexico City.* Berkeley: University of California Press.

Guzmán, Manuel. 1997. "'Pa' La Escuelita con Mucho Cuida'o y por la Orillita': A Journey through the Contested Terrains of the Nation and Sexual Orientation." Pp. 209–28 in *Puerto Rican Jam: Rethinking Colonialism and Nationalism,* ed. Frances Negrón-Muntaner and Ramón Grosfóguel. Minneapolis: University of Minnesota Press.

Hall, Stuart. 1990. "Cultural Identity and Diaspora." Pp. 392–403 in *Identity, Community, Culture, Difference,* ed. J. Rutherford. London: Lawrence and Wishart.

Halle, David. 1984. *America's Working Man.* Chicago: University of Chicago Press.

Handler, Richard. 1988. *Nationalism and the Politics of Culture in Quebec.* Madison: University of Wisconsin Press.

Hardy-Fanta, Carol. 1993. *Latina Politics, Latino Politics: Gender, Culture, and Political Participation in Boston.* Philadelphia: Temple University Press.

Hassell, Malve Von. 1996. *Homesteading in New York City, 1978–1993: The Divided Heart of Loisaida.* Westport, Conn.: Bergin & Garvey.

Hernández, Carmen Dolores. 1997. *Puerto Rican Voices in English: Interviews with Writers.* Westport, Conn.: Praeger.

Hernández, Ramona, and Silvio Torres-Saillant, eds. 1992. "Minorities, Education, Empowerment." *Punto 7 Review: A Journal of Marginal Discourse* 2, no. 2.

Hernández Cruz, Juan E. 1985. "Migración de retorno o circulacion de obreros boricuas?" *Revista de Ciencias Sociales* 24, nos. 1–2: 81–110.

Herzfeld, Michael. 1991. *A Place in History: Social and Monumental Time in a Cretan Town.* Princeton, N.J.: Princeton University Press.

———. 1997. *Cultural Intimacy: Social Poetics of the Nation-State.* New York: Routledge.

History Task Force. 1979. *Labor Migration under Capitalism: The Puerto Rican Experience.* New York: Centro de Estudios Puertorriqueños.

Hobbs, Dick, and Tim May. 1993. *Interpreting the Field: Accounts of Ethnography.* Oxford: Clarendon Press.

Hobsbawm, Eric, and Terence Ranger, eds. 1983. *The Invention of Tradition.* Cambridge: Cambridge University Press.

Hochschild, Arlie. 1979. "Emotion Work, Feeling Rules, and Social Structure." *American Journal of Sociology* 85, no. 3: 551–75.

Hochschild, Jennifer. 1995. *Facing Up to the American Dream: Race, Class, and the Soul of the Nation.* Princeton, N.J.: Princeton University Press.

hooks, bell. 2000. *Where We Stand: Class Matters.* New York: Routledge

Horowitz, Ruth. 1983. *Honor and the American Dream: Culture and Identity in a Chicano Community.* New Brunswick, N.J.: Rutgers University Press.

Hutchinson, John. 1992. "Moral Innovators and the Politics of Regeneration: The Distinctive Role of Cultural Nationalists in Nation-Building." *International Journal of Comparative Sociology* 33, nos. 1–2: 102–17.

Ignatiev, Noel. 1995. *How the Irish Became White.* New York: Routledge.

Institute for Puerto Rican Policy. 1994. Data Note no. 16, June/July. New York: Institute for Puerto Rican Policy.

Jankowski, Martín Sánchez. 1991. *Islands in the Street: Gangs and American Urban Society.* Berkeley: University of California Press.

Jennings, James, and Monte Rivera, eds. 1984. *Puerto Rican Politics in Urban America.* Westport, Conn.: Greenwood.

Jones, Isham. 1955. *The Puerto Rican in New Jersey: His Present Status.* Trenton, N.J.: State Department of Education, Division against Discrimination.

Jury, Mary. 1997. "Out of Work and into the Community: The Place of Local Narratives in Rethinking School-to-Work and Work-to-Work Transitions." Paper presented at the Spencer Foundation Dissertation Fellows Winter Forum, Los Angeles, February.

Kincheloe, Joe, and Shirley Steinberg. 1997. *Changing Multiculturalism.* Buckingham: Open University Press.

Klor de Alva, Jorge. 1988. "Latino Sociocultural Diversity in the United States." In *The Hispanic Experience in the United States: Contemporary Issues and Perspectives,* ed. Edna Acosta-Belén and Barbara R. Sjostrom. New York: Praeger.

———. 1998. "Borinquen, Aztlán, and Latino Cultural Nationalism." Pp. 63–82 in *The Latino Studies Reader: Culture, Economy, and Society,* ed. Antonia Darder and Rodolfo Torres. Malden, Mass.: Blackwell.

Kohn, H. 1946. *The Idea of Nationalism.* New York: Macmillan.

La Fountain-Stokes, Lawrence. 1999a. "Culture, Representation, and the Puerto Rican Queer Diaspora." Ph.D. diss., Columbia University.

———. 1999b. "1898 and the History of a Queer Puerto Rican Century: Imperialism, Diaspora and Social Transformation." *Centro: Journal of the Center for Puerto Rican Studies* 11, no. 1: 91–110.

———. 2002. "Dancing La Vida Loca: The Queer Nuyorican Performances of Arthur Avilés and Elizabeth Marrero." Pp. 162–75 in *Queer Globalizations: Citizenship and the Afterlife of Colonialism,* ed. Arnaldo Cruz and Martin F. Manalansan. New York: New York University Press.

Lamont, M., and A. Lareau. 1988. "Cultural Capital: Allusions, Gaps and Glissandos in Recent Theoretical Developments." *Sociological Theory* 6:153–68.

Lancaster, Roger. 1988. *Thanks to God and the Revolution: Popular Religion and Class Consciousness in the New Nicaragua.* New York: Columbia University Press.

———. 1992. *Life Is Hard: Machismo, Danger, and the Intimacy of Power in Nicaragua.* Berkeley: University of California Press.

LaSalle, Yvonne, and Marvette Pérez. 1997. "'Virtually' Puerto Rican: 'Dis'-Locating Puerto Rican-ness and Its Privileged Sites of Production." *Radical History Review* 68:54–78.

Laviera, Tato. 1981. *La Carreta Made a U-Turn.* Houston, Tex.: Arte Público Press.

Levin, M. 1998. *Teach Me! Kids Will Learn When Oppression Is the Lesson.* New York: Monthly Review Press.

Levitt, Peggy. 2001. *Transnational Villagers.* Berkeley: University of California Press.

Lewis, Oscar. 1965. *La Vida: A Puerto Rican Family in the Culture of Poverty—San Juan and New York.* New York: Random House.

———. 1966. "The Culture of Poverty." *Scientific American* 215, no. 4: 19–25.

Lopes, Belmira Nunes. 1982. *A Portuguese Colonial in America, Belmira Nunes Lopes: The Auto-biography of a Cape Verdean American.* Pittsburgh: Latin American Literary Review Press.

López, Ramón. 1995. "Paseo entre dos banderas." *Claridad,* January, 20–23.

Lucas, Isidro. 1980. "Puerto Rican Dropouts in Chicago: Numbers and Motivations." Pp. 105–18 in *Regional Perspectives on the Puerto Rican Experience,* ed. Carlos E. Cortes. New York: Arno.

———. 1984. "Puerto Rican Politics in Chicago." Pp. 92–120 in *Puerto Rican Politics in Urban America,* ed. James Jennings and Monte Rivera. Westport, Conn.: Greenwood.

Luna, L. 1993. "Movimientos de mujeres y participación política en América Latina." Paper prepared for the Seminario Internacional Presente y Futuro de los Estudios de Genero en America Latina, Cali, Colombia, November.

Mahler, Sarah. 1995. *American Dreaming: Immigrant Life on the Margins.* Princeton, N.J.: Princeton University Press.

Maldonado, Edwin. 1979. "Contract Labor and the Origins of Puerto Rican Communities in the United States." *International Migration Review* 13, no. 1: 103–21.

Malkki, Liisa. 1990. "Context and Consciousness: Local Conditions for the Production of Historical and National Thought among Hutu Refugees in Tanzania." Pp. 32–62 in *Nationalist Ideologies and the Production of National Cultures,* ed. Richard G. Fox. American Ethnological Societies Monograph Series, vol. 2. Washington, D.C.: American Anthropological Association.

Martínez, Manuel. 1989. *Chicago: Historia de nuestra comunidad puertorriqueña.* Unpublished manuscript.

Martínez, Teresita. 1999. *Shaping the Discourse of Space: Charity and Its Wards in Nineteenth-Century San Juan, Puerto Rico.* Austin: University of Texas Press.

Massey, Douglas, and Brooks Bitterman. 1985. "Explaining the Paradox of Puerto Rican Segregation." *Social Forces* 64, no. 2: 306–31.

Massey, Douglas, and Nancy Denton. 1989. "Residential Segregation of Mexicans, Puerto Ricans, and Cubans in Selected U. S. Metropolitan Areas." *Sociology and Social Research* 73, no. 2: 73–83.

McLaren, Peter. 1995. *Critical Pedagogy and Predatory Culture.* London and New York: Routledge.

———. 1997. *Life in Schools: An Introduction to Critical Pedagogy in the Foundations of Education.* New York: Longman.

———. 1998. "The Pedagogy of Ché Guevara: Critical Pedagogy and Globalization Thirty Years after Ché." *Cultural Circles* 3:28–104.

Molotch, Harvey. 1972. *Managed Integration: Dilemmas of Doing Good in the City.* Berkeley: University of California Press.

Moore, Joan, and Raquel Pinderhughes, eds. 1993. *In the Barrios: Latinos and the Underclass Debate.* New York: Russell Sage Foundation.

Morales, Iris. 1996. *¡Pa'lante Siempre Pa'lante! The Young Lords.* New York: Latino Education Network Service. Film.

Morris, Nancy. 1995. *Puerto Rico: Culture, Politics, and Identity.* Westport, Conn.: Praeger.

Negrón-Muntaner, Frances. 1994. *Brincando el charco.* Film distributed by Women Make Movies.

Negrón-Muntaner, Frances, and Ramón Grosfóguel, eds. 1997. *Puerto Rican Jam: Rethinking Colonialism and Nationalism.* Minneapolis: University of Minnesota Press.

Newman, Katherine. 1988. *Falling from Grace: The Experience of Downward Mobility in the American Middle Class.* New York: Vintage.

———. 1999. *No Shame in My Game: The Working Poor in the Inner City.* New York: Knopf and Russell Sage Foundation.

Novak, Michael. 1972. *The Rise of the Unmeltable Ethnics: Politics and Culture in the Seventies.* New York: Macmillan.

Oboler, Suzanne. 1995. *Ethnic Labels, Latino Lives: Identity and the Politics of (Re) Presentation in the United States.* Minneapolis: University of Minnesota Press.

O'Brien, R. 1954. *A Survey of the Puerto Ricans in Lorain, Ohio.* Lorain, Ohio: Neighborhood House Association of Lorain.

Oclander, Jorge. 1995. "Public School's 'Pathetic' Use of Poverty Funds." *Chicago Sun-Times,* June 15.

Ogbu, John. 1985. "Research Currents: Influences on Minority School Learning." *Language Arts* 62, no. 8: 860–69.

Olmedo, Irma. 1997. "Voices of Our Past: Using Oral History to Explore Funds of Knowledge within a Puerto Rican Family." *Anthropology and Education Quarterly* 28, no. 4: 550–73.

Omi, Michael, and Howard Winant. 1986. *Racial Formation in the United States: From the 1960s to the 1980s.* New York: Routledge.

Ortner, Sherry. 1992. "Reading America: Preliminary Notes on Class and Culture." Pp. 163–90 in *Recapturing Anthropology: Working in the Present,* ed. R. G. Fox. Santa Fe, N.M.: School of American Research Press.

———. 1998. "Identities: The Hidden Life of Class." *Journal of Anthropological Research* 54, no. 1: 1–17.

Ostolaza-Bey, Margarita. 1987. *Política sexual y socialización política de la mujer puertorriqueña en la consolidación del bloque histórico colonial de Puerto Rico.* Río Piedras, P.R.: Ediciones Huracán.

Pabón, Carlos. 1995. "De Albizu a Madonna: para armar y desarmar la nacionalidad." *Bordes* 1:22–40.

Padilla, Elena. 1947. "Puerto Rican Immigrants in New York and Chicago: A Study in Comparative Assimilation." M.A. thesis, Department of Anthropology, University of Chicago.

———. 1957. "Puerto Ricans in Eastville." Ph.D. diss., Department of Anthropology, Columbia University.

Padilla, Elena, et al. 1946. "Preliminary Report on Puerto Rican Workers in Chicago." November 25. Chicago: Chicago Historical Society Archives.

———. 1957. *Puerto Rican Americans in Chicago.* Chicago: Chicago Historical Society Archives.

Padilla, Felix M. 1985. *Latino Ethnic Consciousness: The Case of Mexican Americans and Puerto Ricans in Chicago.* Notre Dame, Ind.: University of Notre Dame Press.

———. 1987. *Puerto Rican Chicago.* Notre Dame, Ind.: University of Notre Dame Press.

Pantojas-García, Emilio. 1990. *Development Strategies as Ideology: Puerto Rico's Export-Led Industrialization Experience.* Boulder, Colo.: Lynne Rienner.

Pedreira, Antonio S. [1934] 1973. *Insularismo.* Río Piedras, P.R.: Editorial Edil.

Pérez, Gina. 2000. "Puertorriqueñas sufridas y mexicanas rencorosas: Constructions of Self and Other in a Chicago Latino community." Paper presented at the American Anthropological Association, San Francisco, November.

Perry, Pamela. 2001. *Shades of White: White Kids and Racial Identities in High School.* Durham, N.C.: Duke University Press.

Pessar, Patricia. 1995. *A Visa for a Dream: Dominicans in the United States.* New Immigrants Series, edited by Nancy Foner. Boston: Allyn and Bacon.

Pope, Richard. 1985. "North American Indian Nationalism and the Decline of Sacred Authenticity." *Canadian Journal of Native Studies* 2:253–59.

Popper, Karl. 1951. *The Open Society and Its Enemies.* London: Routledge and Kegan Paul.

Quintero Rivera, Angel. 1991. "Culture-Oriented Social Movements: Ethnicity and Symbolic Action in Latin America and the Caribbean." *Centro: Journal of the Center for Puerto Rican Studies* 3, no. 2: 97–104.

Quintero Rivera, Angel, Jose Luis González, Ricardo Campos, and Juan Flores. 1979. *Puerto Rico: Identidad nacional y clases sociales.* Coloquio de Princeton. Río Piedras, P.R.: Ediciones Huracán.

Radcliffe, Sarah, and Sallie Westwood. 1996. *Remaking of the Nation: Place, Identity and Politics in Latin America.* London: Routledge.

Ramírez, Rafael L. 1973. "Political Rituals in Puerto Rico." *Revista de Ciencias Sociales* 17, no. 3: 309–23.

Ramírez de Arellano, Annette, and Conrad Scheipp. 1983. *Colonialism, Catholicism, and Contraception: A History of Birth Control in Puerto Rico*. Chapel Hill: University of North Carolina Press.

Ramos-Zayas, Ana Y. 1998. "Nationalist Ideologies, Neighborhood-Based Activism, and Educational Spaces in Puerto Rican Chicago." *Harvard Educational Review* 68, no. 2: 164–92.

———. 2001a. "'All this is turning white now': Latino Constructions of 'White Culture' and Whiteness in Chicago." *Centro: Journal of the Center for Puerto Rican Studies* 13, no. 2: 72–95.

———. 2001b. "Racializing the 'Invisible' Race: Latino Constructions of 'White Culture' and Whiteness in Chicago." *Urban Anthropology* 30, no. 4: 341–80.

Renan, Ernest. 1990. "What Is a Nation?" Pp. 8–22 in *Nation and Narration*, ed. Homi Bhabha. London and New York: Routledge.

Rivera, Raquel. 1997. "Rapping Two Versions of the Same Requiem." Pp. 243–56 in *Puerto Rican Jam: Rethinking Colonialism and Nationalism*, ed. Frances Negrón-Muntaner and Ramón Grosfóguel. Minneapolis: University of Minnesota Press.

Rivera-Batiz, Francisco, and Carlos E. Santiago. 1996. *Island Paradox: Puerto Rico in the 1990s*. New York: Russell Sage Foundation.

Rodríguez, Clara. 1990. "Racial Classification among Puerto Rican Men and Women in New York." *Hispanic Journal of Behavioral Sciences* 12, no. 4: 366–79.

Rodríguez Fraticelli, Carlos. 1992. "Pedro Albizu Campos: Strategies of Struggle and Strategic Struggles." *ECNTRO Bulletin* (Center for Puerto Rican Studies, Hunter College, New York) 4, no. 1: 24–33.

Rodríguez-Morazzani, Roberto. 1998. "Beyond the Rainbow: Mapping the Discourse on Puerto Ricans and 'Race.'" Pp. 143–62 in *The Latino Studies Reader: Culture, Economy, and Society*, ed. Antonia Darder and Rodolfo Torres. Malden, Mass.: Blackwell.

Roediger, David. 1994. *Towards the Abolition of Whiteness: Essays on Race, Politics, and Working Class History*. New York: Verso Press.

Rogler, Lloyd. 1972. *Migrant in the City: The Life of a Puerto Rican Action Group*. Maplewood, N.J.: Waterfront Press.

Rosaldo, Renato. 1989. *Culture and Truth: The Remaking of Social Analysis*. Boston: Beacon.

Rúa, Mérida. 2000. "Colao Subjectivities: Puerto-Mex and Mexi-Rican Perspectives on Language and Identity." Unpublished paper submitted to the University of Michigan, Ann Arbor.

Safa, Helen. 1988. "Migration and Identity: A Comparison of Puerto Rican and Cuban Migrants in the United States." In *The Hispanic Experience in the United States: Contemporary Issues and Perspectives*, ed. Edna Acosta-Belén and Barbara R. Sjostrom. New York: Praeger.

Sánchez, Luis Rafael. 1994. *La guagua aerea*. Río Piedras, P.R.: Editorial Cultural.

Sánchez Huertas, Ernesto. 1993. "Algunas ideas tentativas del pensamiento social cristiano en Albizu Campos." Pp. 139–60 in *La nación puertorriqueña: Ensayos en torno a Pedro Albizu Campos*, ed. Juan Manuel Carrión, Teresa Gracía Ruiz, and Carlos Rodríguez Fraticceli. Río Piedras, P.R.: Editorial de la Universidad de Puerto Rico.

Sánchez Korrol, Virginia. 1980. "Survival of Puerto Rican Women in New York before World War II." Pp. 47–57 in *The Puerto Rican Struggle: Essays on Survival in the U.S.*, ed. Clara E. Rodríguez, Virginia Sánchez Korrol, and José Oscar Alers. Maplewood, N.J.: Waterfront Press.

———. 1989. "Latinismo among Early Puerto Rican Migrants in New York City: A Sociohistoric Interpretation." Pp. 151–61 in *The Hispanic Experience in the United States: Contemporary Issues and Perspectives*, ed. Edna Acosta-Belén and Barbara R. Sjostrom. New York: Praeger.

Sandison, David. 1997. *Ché Guevara*. New York: St. Martin's Griffin.

Sandoval-Sánchez, Alberto. 1997. "Puerto Rican Identity Up in the Air: Air Migration, Its Cultural Representations, and Me 'Cruzando el Charco.'" Pp. 189–208 in *Puerto Rican Jam: Rethinking Colonialism and Nationalism*, ed. Frances Negrón-Muntaner and Ramón Grosfóguel. Minneapolis: University of Minnesota Press.

Santos, Mayra. 1996. "Puerto Rican Underground." *Centro: Journal of the Center for Puerto Rican Studies* 8, nos. 1–2.

Santos Febres, Mayra. 1993a. "A veces miro mi vida." *Diálogo* (October): 42.

———. 1993b. "Albizu." Pp. 241–49 in *La nación puertorriqueña: Ensayos en torno a Pedro Albizu Campos*, ed. Juan Manuel Carrión, Teresa Gracía Ruiz, and Carlos Rodríguez Fraticceli. Río Piedras, P.R.: Editorial de la Universidad de Puerto Rico.

Sassen, Saskia. 1998. *Globalization and Its Discontents*. New York: Columbia University Press.

Schiller, Nina Glick, Linda Basch, and Cristina Blanc-Szanton, eds. 1992. *Towards a Transnational Perspective on Migration: Race, Class, Ethnicity, and Nationalism Reconsidered*. New York: New York Academy of Sciences.

Schiller, Nina Glick, and Georges Eugene Fouron. 2001. *Georges Woke Up Laughing: Long-Distance Nationalism and the Search for Home*. Durham, N.C.: Duke University Press.

Schneider, J. A. 1990. "Defining Boundaries, Creating Contacts: Puerto Rican and Polish Presentation of Group Identity through Ethnic Parades." *Journal of Ethnic Studies* 18, no. 1: 33–57.

Scott, James C. 1985. *Weapons of the Weak: Everyday Forms of Peasant Resistance*. New Haven, Conn.: Yale University Press.

Scott, Joan. 1988. "On Language, Gender, and Working-Class History." Pp. 1–36 in *Gender and the Politics of History*, ed. J. Scott. New York: Columbia University Press.

Seijo-Bruno, Miñi. 1981. "Los once prisioneros de guerra 'Son pobres y puertorriqueños.'" *Claridad*, February 27–March 5, "En Rojo" section.

———. 1989. *La insurrección nacionalista en Puerto Rico, 1950*. Río Piedras, P.R.: Editorial Edil.

Senior, Clarence, and Donald Watkins. 1966. "Towards a Balance Sheet of Puerto Rican Migration." Pp. 715–16 in *Status of Puerto Rico: Selected Background Studies for the United States–Puerto Rico Commission on the Status of Puerto Rico*. Washington, D.C.: U.S. Government Printing Office.

Siegel, Arthur, Harold Orlans, and Loyal Greer. 1954. *Puerto Ricans in Philadelphia: A Study of Their Demographic Characteristics, Problems, and Attitudes*. Philadelphia: Commission on Human Relations.

Smith, Anthony D. 1984. "Ethnic Myths and Ethnic Revivals." *European Journal of Sociology* 25:283–305.

Sotomayor, Aurea María. 1993. "La imaginería nacionalista: De la historia al relato." Pp. 251–76 in *La nación puertorriqueña: Ensayos en torno a Pedro Albizu Campos*, ed. Juan Manuel Carrión, Teresa Gracía Ruiz, and Carlos Rodríguez Fraticceli. Río Piedras, P.R.: Editorial de la Universidad de Puerto Rico.

Spivak, Gayatri. 1988. *In Other Worlds: Essays in Cultural Politics*. New York: Routledge.

Stanton-Salazar, Ricardo. 1997. "A Social Capital Framework for Understanding the Socialization of Racial Minority Children and Youths." *Harvard Educational Review* 67, no. 1: 1–40.

Sullivan, Mercer L. 1992. "Puerto Ricans in Sunset Park, Brooklyn: Poverty amidst Ethnic and Economic Diversity." Pp. 1–25 in *In the Barrios: Latinos and the Underclass Debate*, ed. Joan Moore and Raquel Pinderhughes. New York: Russell Sage Foundation.

Thomas, Piri. 1967. *Down These Mean Streets*. New York: Knopf.

Tienda, Marta, and Candace Nelson. 1985. "The Structuring of Hispanic Ethnicity." *Ethnic and Racial Studies* 8, no. 1: 49–74.

Tirado, Amílcar. 1993. "La forja de un lider." Pp. 65–81 in *La nación puertorriqueña: Ensayos en torno a Pedro Albizu Campos*, ed. Juan Manuel Carrión, Teresa Gracía Ruiz, and Carlos Rodríguez Fraticceli. Río Piedras, P.R.: Editorial de la Universidad de Puerto Rico.

Toro-Morn, Maura. 1995. "The Family and Work Experiences of Puerto Rican Women Migrants in Chicago." Pp. 277–94 in *Resiliency in Ethnic Minority Families*. Vol. 1, *Native and Immigrant American Families*, ed. H. I. McCubbin, E. A. Thompson, and J. E. Fromer. Madison: University of Wisconsin System, Center for Excellence in Family Studies.

Torre, Carlos Antonio, Hugo Rodríguez-Vecchini, and William Burgos, eds. 1994. *The Commuter Nation: Perspectives on Puerto Rican Migration*. Río Piedras, P.R.: Universidad de Puerto Rico.

Torre, Carlos Antonio, and José E. Velázquez, eds. 1998. *The Puerto Rican Movement: Voices from the Diaspora*. Philadelphia: Temple University Press.

Torres, Arlene. 1998. "La Gran Familia Puertorriqueña: 'Ej prieta de belda.'" Pp. 285–306 in *Blackness in Latin America and the Caribbean: Social Dynamics and Cultural Transformations*, ed. Arlene Torres and Norman E. Whitten. Bloomington: Indiana University Press.

Unger, Monte C. 1966. "The Puerto Rican Who Didn't Riot." *Viewpoint* (summer): 1–3.

Urciuoli, Bonnie. 1993. "Representing Class: Who Decides?" *Anthropological Quarterly* 66, no. 4: 203–10.

———. 1996. *Exposing Prejudice: Puerto Rican Experiences of Language, Race, and Class*. Boulder, Colo.: Westview.

Vargas-Ramos, Carlos. 2000. "The Effects of Return Migration on Political Participation in Puerto Rico." Ph.D. diss., Columbia University.

Vega, Ana Lydia, ed. 1989. *El tramo ancla: Ensayos puertorriqueños de hoy*. Río Piedras, P.R.: Editorial de la Universidad de Puerto Rico.

Verdery, Katherine. 1991. *National Ideology under Socialism*. Berkeley: University of California Press.

Vivas, J. 1951. "The Puerto Ricans of Cleveland: A Challenge to Community Organization." M.A. thesis, Case Western Reserve University.

Wade, Peter. 1993. *Blackness and Racial Mixture: The Dynamics of Racial Identity in Colombia*. Baltimore: Johns Hopkins University Press.

Wagenheim, Kal, and Olga Jiménez de Wagenheim, eds. 1996. *The Puerto Ricans: A Documentary History*. Princeton, N.J.: Markus Wiener Publishers.

Wagley, Charles. 1952. *Race and Class in Rural Brazil*. Paris: UNESCO.

Wagner, Carl. 1995. "Urban Gateway." *Chicago Tribune*, June 4.

Warren, Kay B. 1995. "Reading History as Resistance: Mayan Public Intellectuals in Guatemala." Pp. 121–45 in *Mayan Cultural Activism in Guatemala*, ed. Edward Fischer and McKenna Brown. Austin: University of Texas Press.

———. 1998. "Pan-Mayanists, Upward Mobility, and Different Ways of Being 'Middle Class.'" Pp. 180–95 in *Cultures of Politics, Politics of Cultures: Re-Visioning Latin American Social Movements*, ed. Sonia E. Alvarez, Evelina Dagnino, and Arturo Escobar. Boulder, Colo.: Westview.

Waters, Mary C. 1990. *Ethnic Options: Choosing Identities in America*. Berkeley: University of California Press.

Whitten, Norman, and Arlene Torres, eds. 1992. "Blackness in the Americas." *NACLA* 15, no. 4.

Williams, C., and Smith, A. 1983. "The National Construction of Social Space." *Progress in Human Geography* 7:502–18.

Williams, Raymond. 1977. *Marxism and Literature*. Oxford: Oxford University Press.

Willis, Paul. 1977. *Learning to Labor: How Working Class Kids Get Working Class Jobs*. New York: Columbia University Press.

Wilson, H. T. 1977. *The American Ideology*. London: Routledge and Kegan Paul.

Wilson, William Julius. 1987. *The Truly Disadvantaged: The Inner City, the Underclass, and Public Policy*. Chicago: University of Chicago Press.

Zentella, Ana Celia. 1990. "Returned Migration, Language, and Identity: Puerto Rican Bilinguals in Dos Worlds / Two Mundos." *International Journal of the Sociology of Language* 84:81–100.

———. 1995. "The 'Chiquita-fication' of U.S. Latinos and Their Languages, or Why We Need an Anthro-Political Linguistics." *SALSA III: The Proceedings of the Symposium about Language and Society at Austin*. Austin: Department of Linguistics, University of Texas.

———. 1997a. "Spanish in New York City." In *The Multilingual Apple: Languages in New York City*, ed. Ofelia García and Joshua Fishman. Berlin: Mouton de Gruyter.

———. 1997b. *Growing Up Bilingual: Puerto Rican Children in New York*. New York: Blackwell.

———. 2000. "Puerto Ricans in the U.S.: Confronting the Linguistic Repercussions of Colonialism." Pp. 137–64 in *New Immigrants in the United States: Background for Second Language Educators*, ed. Sandra Lee McKay and Sau-ling Cynthia Wong. New York: Cambridge University Press.

Zwerman, Gilda. 1994. "Mothering on the Lam: Politics, Gender Fantasies, and Maternal Thinking in Women Associated with Armed, Clandestine Organizations in the United States." *Feminist Review*, no. 47 (summer): 462–82.

———. 1995. "The Identity Vulnerable Activist and the Emergence of Post–New Left Armed, Underground Organizations in the United States." The Working Paper Series, Working Paper no. 218. New York: Center for Studies of Social Change, New School for Social Research.

★ INDEX ★

Acosta-Belén, Edna, 33

African Americans: attitude toward Puerto Rican-black romantic liaisons, 231; barrio residents' fear of a cooption of Puerto Rican culture by blacks, 123; *cimarrones* in Puerto Rican racial triad, 199; class-based racial tension between Puerto Ricans and, 229–30; Puerto Ricans' characterization of, 228–29; Puerto Ricans' racialization as black, 36. *See also* race

Albizu Campos, Pedro: appropriation as a hero, 187, 196, 261n7; association with intellectual elite, 56; militancy of, 25–26, 185–86; multivalent image of, 239–40; Nationalist Party and, 25; personal accomplishments, 171–72, 188–89, 202–3; presented as a challenge to Puerto Ricans' racialization as blacks, 36; religious depictions by nationalists, 173, 174, 175–76, 205; statue controversy (*see* Albizu Campos statue); writings on, 259–60n1

Albizu Campos statue: barrio residents' reaction to the criminalization by the state, 183, 195; black-white racial taxonomy resulting from controversy, 196; centennial celebration in Chicago, 169; commercialization of image related to community development, 177, 180–81; emergence as a representation of Puerto-Ricanness in Chicago, 173, 202; identified as black as a denunciation of racial attitudes, 189, 198–99, 201–2; internal racialization among Puerto Ricans illuminated by,

187–88, 173, 177; media coverage, 173, 180–81; multivalent meanings generated by the conflict, 204–5, 169–71; Park District's opposition to, 169; placement in casita garden, 172–73, 201; popular education processes resulting from debate, 179–80, 195; *los profesionales'* positions on, 187, 194–95, 202; results of extensive dialogue over statue, 178–79, 181–83, 189–91, 204; significance of community's discourse of history, 171–72, 183–89, 202–3

Alicea, Marixa, 250n1

Alvarez, Daniel, 190

American dream: contradiction between belief in the myth and individual experiences, 38–39, 41, 51; displacement of overt class discourse with emphasis on social differences, 41–42; as main ideological export of the U.S., 38; persistence of, 237, 239; Puerto Rican nationalism and, 8, 9, 37–38, 51, 236, 239; whiteness seen as the criteria for inclusion in, 39–40

Anderson, Benedict, 165, 249n8

Aronowitz, Stanley, 35

autobiographies. *See* grassroots historiography

Aztlán, 34

Barreto, Amílcar, 26

barrio residents and activists: Albizu Campos statue controversy and (*see* Albizu